VOTERS ON THE MOVE OR ON THE RUN?

Voters on the Move or on the Run?

Edited by
BERNHARD WEßELS, HANS RATTINGER,
SIGRID ROßTEUTSCHER, AND
RÜDIGER SCHMITT-BECK

UNIVERSITY PRESS

Great Clarendon Street, Oxford, OX2 6DP,
United Kingdom

Oxford University Press is a department of the University of Oxford.
It furthers the University's objective of excellence in research, scholarship,
and education by publishing worldwide. Oxford is a registered trade mark of
Oxford University Press in the UK and in certain other countries

© The several contributors 2014

The moral rights of the authors have been asserted

First Edition published in 2014

Impression: 1

All rights reserved. No part of this publication may be reproduced, stored in
a retrieval system, or transmitted, in any form or by any means, without the
prior permission in writing of Oxford University Press, or as expressly permitted
by law, by licence or under terms agreed with the appropriate reprographics
rights organization. Enquiries concerning reproduction outside the scope of the
above should be sent to the Rights Department, Oxford University Press, at the
address above

You must not circulate this work in any other form
and you must impose this same condition on any acquirer

Published in the United States of America by Oxford University Press
198 Madison Avenue, New York, NY 10016, United States of America

British Library Cataloguing in Publication Data

Data available

Library of Congress Control Number: 2014936667

ISBN 978–0–19–966263–0

Printed and bound by
CPI Group (UK) Ltd, Croydon, CR0 4YY

Links to third party websites are provided by Oxford in good faith and
for information only. Oxford disclaims any responsibility for the materials
contained in any third party website referenced in this work.

Preface and Acknowledgements

This book is about electoral change and the challenges of electoral research. It is the product of a group of researchers engaged in the German Longitudinal Election Study (GLES). The project itself has a history resulting from the insight that research on electoral behavior needs an integrated and encompassing design in order to come to grips with the challenges of increasing heterogeneity and complexity of voting and to contribute to the understanding of election outcomes. The German Longitudinal Election Study is a research program long-term funded by the German Science Foundation. It is located at four different institutions, the University of Frankfurt, the University of Mannheim, the GESIS Leibniz Institute for the Social Sciences at Mannheim, and the WZB Berlin Social Science Center. In addition, there is a close cooperation between the project and the German Society of Electoral Research (Deutsche Gesellschaft für Wahlforschung, DGfW). Without the support of the members of this society and of the scientific community of electoral researchers, the project would probably never have seen the light of day.

The study design includes cross-section surveys, long-term and short-term panels, rolling cross-section data, online tracking surveys, a candidate survey, media-content analysis, and a module specifically addressing TV debates of the leading candidates. The idea was born from the perception that only an integrative design allowing for in-depth cross-sectional as well as dynamic, comparative, and multilevel analyses can provide insights needed for understanding electoral behavior, electoral outcomes, and the contribution of elections to the working of democracy.

The chapters in this volume have all been contributed by project team members. The contributions result from an intense discussion within the group about the core topics and core problems of electoral research. The book is thus a fully cooperative endeavor. It provides an integrative way of coping with the complexities of voting behavior in Germany and in comparative perspective. Inspired by the international debate and putting the research questions into this context, the findings are of general theoretical relevance and provide new insights into the conditions of voting and its heterogeneity in an increasingly complex environment of elections.

Such a book needs support and helping hands. In Dominic Byatt of Oxford University Press we found an understanding and helpful editor. The numerous international and national reviewers of the chapter drafts shall stay anonymous to the authors and are thus not mentioned by name here. But we want to express our gratitude to all of them. Their critique and advice significantly helped to strengthen arguments, improve analyses, and delete flaws. Special thanks go to Katarina Pollner, WZB Berlin Social Science Center, who managed to handle the manuscripts, tables and figures, the bibliography, and many other complex technicalities necessary. Without her extraordinary engagement, everything would have taken much longer.

Bernhard Weßels
Hans Rattinger
Sigrid Roßteutscher
Rüdiger Schmitt-Beck

Berlin/Mannheim/Frankfurt am Main, August 2013

Contents

List of Contributors   ix

Part I   Introduction

1. The Changing Context and Outlook of Voting   3
   Bernhard Weßels, Hans Rattinger, Sigrid Roßteutscher, and Rüdiger Schmitt-Beck

Part II   Increasing Heterogeneity of Voting

2. Voter Fragmentation and the Differentiation of Vote Functions   17
   Jan Eric Blumenstiel

3. Party-Specific Vote Functions   40
   Aiko Wagner

4. Coalitions and Voting Behavior in a Differentiating Multiparty System   65
   Sascha Huber

5. Voting Complexity in a Multilayered System. Or: How Voting Choices in Second-order Elections Impact the Stability of Party Identification   88
   Sigrid Roßteutscher, Ina Bieber, and Philipp Scherer

6. Contextualizing Turnout and Party Choice: Electoral Behavior on Different Political Levels   115
   Heiko Giebler

7. Does Personal Campaigning Make a Difference?   139
   Heiko Giebler, Bernhard Weßels, and Andreas M. Wüst

Part III   Increasing Complexity and Voting

8. Network Politicization and Political Integration: From Grand Cleavages to Private Network Structures   167
   Sigrid Roßteutscher and Daniel Stegmueller

9. Political Information Flows and Consistent Voting: Personal Conversations, Mass Media, Party Campaigns, and the Quality of Voting Decisions at the 2009 German Federal Election   193
   Rüdiger Schmitt-Beck and Patrick Kraft

10. Activation of Fundamentals in German Campaigns *Richard Johnston, Julia Partheymüller, and Rüdiger Schmitt-Beck*	217
11. Voters' Motivations: How and Why Short-Term Factors Grow in Importance *Bernhard Weßels*	238
12. Are Alienation and Indifference the New Features of Elections? *Markus Steinbrecher*	263
13. Volatility on the Rise? Attitudinal Stability, Attitudinal Change, and Voter Volatility *Hans Rattinger and Elena Wiegand*	287

Part IV Conclusion

14. Voters on the Move or on the Run? *Bernhard Weßels, Hans Rattinger, Sigrid Roßteutscher, and Rüdiger Schmitt-Beck*	311
Appendix: Study Description and Data Sources	319
References	321
Index	355

List of Contributors

Ina Bieber, Goethe-University Frankfurt am Main, Institute for Social and Political Research, Department of Social Sciences, Germany.

Jan Eric Blumenstiel, University of Mannheim, MZES, Germany.

Heiko Giebler, WZB Berlin Social Science Center, Research Unit "Democracy and Democratization," Germany.

Sascha Huber, University of Mannheim, Faculty of Social Sciences, Chair of Political Science I, Germany.

Richard Johnston, University of British Columbia, Department of Political Science, Vancouver, Canada.

Patrick Kraft, Stony Brook University, Stony Brook, New York, USA.

Julia Partheymüller, University of Mannheim, MZES, Germany.

Hans Rattinger, University of Mannheim, Chair of Comparative Political Behavior, Germany.

Sigrid Roßteutscher, Goethe-University Frankfurt am Main, Institute for Social and Political Research, Department of Social Sciences, Germany.

Philipp Scherer, Goethe-University Frankfurt am Main, Institute for Social and Political Research, Department of Social Sciences, Germany.

Rüdiger Schmitt-Beck, University of Mannheim, Faculty of Social Sciences, Chair of Political Science I, Germany.

Daniel Stegmueller, University of Essex, Department of Government, Colchester, United Kingdom.

Markus Steinbrecher, University of Mannheim, Chair of Comparative Political Behavior, Germany.

Aiko Wagner, WZB Berlin Social Science Center, Research Unit "Democracy and Democratization," Germany.

Bernhard Weßels, WZB Berlin Social Science Center, Research Unit "Democracy and Democratization," Germany.

Elena Wiegand, University of Mannheim, Chair of Comparative Political Behavior, Germany.

Andreas M. Wüst, University of Mannheim, MZES, Germany.

Part I

Introduction

1

The Changing Context and Outlook of Voting

Bernhard Weßels, Hans Rattinger, Sigrid Roßteutscher, and Rüdiger Schmitt-Beck

1.1 THE CHALLENGE OF ELECTORAL RESEARCH

If one wants to summarize the findings of voting research over the last decades in one word, the appropriate term is change. The close observation of voting behavior indicates tremendous shifts during the last decades in almost all characteristics of voting. Recent elections show that this process has been accelerating during the last ten to fifteen years. The contribution of the studies on voting behavior to the explanation of what is changing and why seems unsatisfying, at least to some scholars in the field. Bartels concluded that "contemporary voting research has become increasingly eclectic and opportunistic" (2010: 251, 252). Indeed, electoral research has become a highly diversified and specialized field. Methodological and statistical sophistication contribute a lot to this development as well as the diversification in voting behavior. Recent developments include decreasing turnout, decreasing party identification and political loyalties, higher volatility and vote switching, and less cleavage voting. It has become more difficult to understand and explain the way in which voters arrive at their vote choices.

Patterns of relations between voters, parties, media, and their ways of communication have become more complex just as have the voters' ways of processing information. The debate about decreasing stability in determinants and patterns of voting behavior started in the 1970s at the latest. Parsons (1977: 190, 331–4), from a sociological perspective, and Allardt (1968: 72–3), from a political-science perspective, highlighted the role of the so-called educational revolution for changing patterns of behavior and possible changes in Western party systems. Shively (1979: 1050) noted an alteration in the "decisional function" of voting due to the systematic change in levels of education, implying a greater capacity for handling information and a resulting decline in information costs. Dalton (1984) observed substantial change in the characteristics of mass publics: The expansion of education and sophistication has made voters more independent of party cues and, at the same time, changed the structure of interest in societies toward postmaterialist values. He foresaw a long-term trend toward partisan dealignment in advanced industrial societies. In general, partisan effects seem to decrease due to a process of individualization, replacing social-group concerns with more individualistic policy concerns. Social milieus have lost their cohesiveness regarding political behavior and choices (Beck 1992; Beck and Beck-Gernsheim 2002). Findings of Andersen, Yang, and Heath (2006) suggest that individualization occurs at a similar rate in all social classes. In line with Weakliem (1991), they regard these trends as a general shift in attitudes. One consequence of these societal changes might be increased voter rationality that finds its expression in a rise of issue voting (Dalton 1984: 282; Dalton, Flanagan, and Beck 1984; Schulman and Pomper 1975; Franklin, Mackie, and Valen 1992) and more performance-dependent choices (Tufte 1978; Kinder and Kieweit 1981; Anderson 1995; Miller and Wattenberg 1985). These developments point to the fact that the demand side of politics has changed dramatically over the last decades.

Much the same can be said about the supply side of politics. Shifts have taken place beyond the micro level at the meso and macro levels (Dalton and Wattenberg 2000c). For the meso level, Wattenberg has pointed to the rise of candidate-centred politics (Wattenberg 1991). The so-called personalization of politics does not only affect leading candidates. There is an increasing tendency toward personalized local campaigning in any type of electoral system regardless of the provision of a nominal vote (Denver, Hands, and MacAllister 2004; Pattie, Johnston, and Fieldhouse 1995; Shugart, Valdini, and Suominen 2005; Karp 2009; Gschwend and Zittel 2012; Zittel and Gschwend 2008). Research demonstrates that local campaigning matters and does so increasingly because "voters may now be more in tune with the messages of the parties than they were in the past" (Andersen, Yang, and Heath 2006: 223). Mass media and TV in particular have not only changed the accessibility of information. They have also influenced the attitudes of politicians and parties and the way that they are presenting themselves. Television debates of leading candidates have become an international success story after their first application in the United States in 1960, which demonstrated a high impact on voting behavior (Middleton 1962). Although it is contested that personalization of politics has been increased by TV (Hayes 2009), the effects of TV debates of leading candidates have been demonstrated beyond the United States. In Germany, for example, their impact on vote choice is a sustaining feature over time (Schrott 1990). They have changed the public presentation of political parties and their personnel. Parties' organizations and campaigning, including the use of electronic media, have been professionalized (Katz and Mair 1995;

Scarrow 1996). Furthermore, in many modern democratic societies, party systems have become bigger in terms of the number of parties running at each election and in parliament.

Looking at the answers electoral research has provided regarding the explanation and consequences of these developments, a quite obscure picture emerges, characterized by scattered and contradictory findings.

In this regard, prior research points to several aspects: Any focus—on the rise of issue voting, the rise of candidate-centred politics, the decisiveness of TV debates, the role of new media, or other aspects—claims to be dealing with the most crucial change in the electoral process and, in fact, there may be good reasons for this in each single case. The pessimistic conclusion that the search for *the* causal mechanisms in voting behavior "seems to have reached an unhappy end" is certainly too far-reaching (Bartels 2010: 251). This type of skepticism has been around as long as advanced electoral research has existed. Already in 1961, V.O. Key came to the conclusion that for the large body of research findings since the 1940s the "relevance for the workings of the governmental system is not always apparent" (Key 1961: vii). But even Bartels acknowledges with reference to the work of Erikson, MacKuen, and Stimson (2002) that research has demonstrated that elections and electoral behavior matter for politics and policies (Bartels 2010: 256). He concludes that electoral research should not be abandoned, despite his disappointment with it. He argues: "If the course of public policy is powerfully shaped by 'volatile' and 'unaccounted-for causes' of election outcomes," any integrative analysis "will have to build upon a more detailed understanding of electoral behaviour" (Bartels 2010: 257).

1.2 HETEROGENEITY AND COMPLEXITY

Electoral research has to come to grips with the increasing flexibility of voters' behavior and choices as well as the apparent entropy of all party alignments (Carmines, McIver, and Stimson 1987: 380). The tremendous changes electoral behavior has been undergoing can be easily summarized in two big trends. Increase in volatility—even if measured in the aggregate and thus underestimated in its real extent—is enormous across developed democracies. This macroscopic perspective is only the tip of the iceberg of complex developments in individual behavior and the calculus of voting, such as increasing issue voting, performance-based choices, vote-switching, tactical voting, and late deciding.

Looking at eighteen West European democracies for the long-term trend in voters' movements, figures show that aggregate volatility has been increasing more or less steadily in the post-World War II period. Until the mid-1960s, the

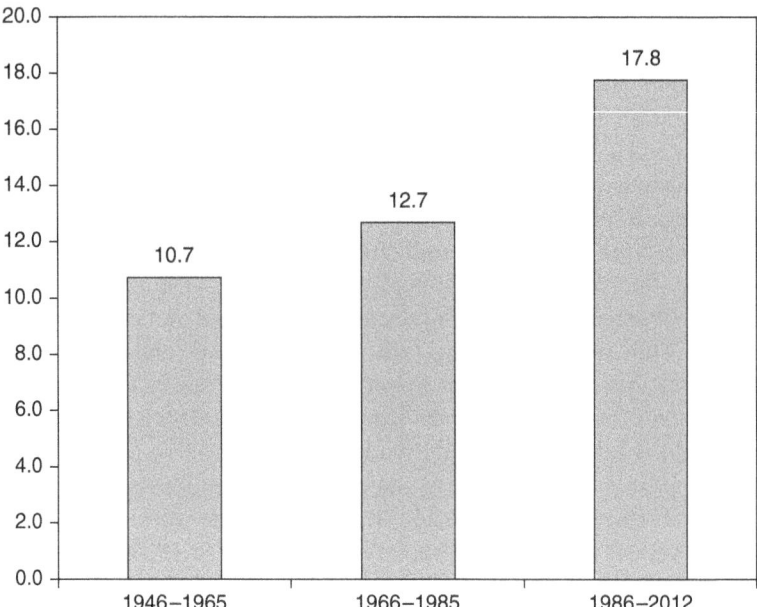

Figure 1.1 Aggregate volatility in eighteen West European democracies in three periods

Countries: Austria, Belgium, Denmark, Finland, France, Germany, Great Britain, Greece, Iceland, Ireland, Italy, Luxembourg, the Netherlands, Norway, Portugal, Spain, Sweden, Switzerland.

Source: Data bank "Elections and Governments" of the research unit "Democracy and Democratization," WZB Berlin Social Science Center.

overall changes in party shares amounted to about 11%; the period between the mid-1960s and mid-1980s showed a slight increase to almost 13% on average; and from the mid-1980s to 2012 average volatility rose to about 18% (Figure 1.1). These figures were aggregated across time periods and countries, and they are statistically reliable. Cluster-corrected regression analysis reveals a significant effect of time on volatility, with a significant coefficient for "year," amounting to an average increase of volatility of about 1.8 percentage points every ten years. Whereas the difference in volatility between the earliest and the second period is statistically not significant, differences between the earliest and the most recent period have shown to be (Bonferoni test).

These figures indicate the movement and flexibility on the demand side. The second big trend is the change on the supply side. Party systems have become bigger with more parties on offer. The effective number of electoral parties has increased from an average of 3.7 parties across countries in the period from 1946 to 1964 to 4.3 effective parties on offer for the latest period from the mid-1980s until today (Figure 1.2). Regression analysis again supports statistical significance for cluster-corrected estimates for "year" with an

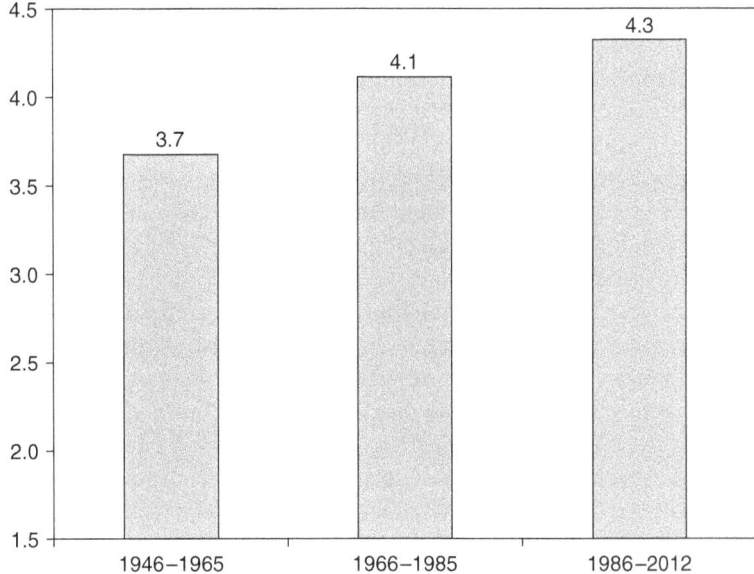

Figure 1.2 Effective number of electoral parties in eighteen West European democracies in three periods

Countries: Austria, Belgium, Denmark, Finland, France, Germany, Great Britain, Greece, Iceland, Ireland, Italy, Luxembourg, the Netherlands, Norway, Portugal, Spain, Sweden, Switzerland.

Source: Data bank "Elections and Governments" of the research unit "Democracy and Democratization," WZB Berlin Social Science Center.

estimated average increase of the size of party systems of about one seventh party per decade. The Bonferoni test shows the statistical significance of mean differences between the earliest period and the two more recent ones. The significant shift in party-system differentiation thus took place between the mid-1960s and the mid-1980s.

These two macroscopic developments indicate that changes have taken place in two dimensions: Voters' heterogeneity has increased and complexity of political supply has shifted. These trends are certainly not independent. It is hard to tell which drives which. However, it seems to be a quite safe assumption that it is not only voters who are causing change. Increasing opportunities to choose certainly contribute to change as well.

These two dimensions define the analytical anchors applied in this book in order to find answers to the increasing challenge of explaining voters' behavior and choices. From a theoretical perspective, complexity of political supply could be a cause of increasing heterogeneity of demand, and heterogeneity in voting behavior could be a reaction to a differentiation of supply. Regarding partisan alignments, the consequences would be similar. New offers and new issues are a "natural threat" to alignments. Stability of supply has a direct positive relationship to the stability of alignments (Carmines, McIver, and Stimson 1987: 380). Supply and demand are communicating vessels—at least in political competition. Change in the one dimension produces change in the other. On the one hand, this poses a chicken-and-egg problem. On the other hand, this is obviously a reinforcing cycle for which one can hardly answer where it begins. Thus, we will not attempt to do so in this book. We will rather systematically investigate both dimensions: the seemingly increasing heterogeneity of the demand side and the increasing complexity of the supply side, as intertwined as they are.

Heterogeneity in voting behavior has several aspects. The traditional perspective is on social change resulting in dissolving groups and milieus as well as partisan dealignment. In conjunction with this angle is the temporal aspect. It highlights that the calculus of voting may change in the course of social change. Examples are the increase in issue voting or the rise of candidate-centered politics. A third aspect of heterogeneity relates to the objects and the criteria of choice. It challenges the assumption of homogeneity of classic approaches like the Michigan model and its funnel of causality (Campbell et al. 1960b). Vote functions of voters have become so diverse that the assumption of one common model and one causal order may no longer be appropriate.

Complexity can be defined along the same lines. The dominant parties in politics may change, as indicated by the debate about the presidentialization of politics (Poguntke and Webb 2005). The temporal aspect relates to the fact that change in political supply is becoming more differentiated, as shown in Figure 1.2. Complexity also increases with the amount of available information. The easier information can be accessed, the less costly it is for voters to consider it. The more they consider it, the more information they have to process.

1.3 APPROACHING HETEROGENEITY AND COMPLEXITY

This brief review and the considerations regarding heterogeneity and complexity suggest that both the motivations and the processes leading to voter decisions have changed. Today, more than ever before in the history of modern democracies, voters rather seem to decide according to short- and medium-term evaluative criteria than according to loyalties and long-standing experience. This seems to indicate communalities at a general level, but not concerning the specific criteria that are applied: Here, fragmentation and heterogeneity are growing. Despite this increasing diversity of criteria for evaluation and choice, short-term factors and information gathered during the campaign become more important for voters' motivations. At the same time, parties and candidates have modified the informational environment of voters by changing the way they campaign, either as a reaction to the more evaluation-oriented perspective of voters or as a trigger for this process. "Americanization," "modernization," and "globalization" of campaign forms are the catchwords for a process leading to so-called postmodern campaigning. This includes changing strategies and means to address voters, as well as different kinds of information and communication. Localized campaigning that had been regarded as extinct in modern media societies has received new attention by political actors, supported by new forms of electronic communication like text messaging and the internet. Media campaign strategies have changed as a result of the professionalization of marketing practices in politics.

Voters are not only confronted with more information but also with different kinds of information about all factors relevant for the evaluation of political supply. The classic triad of issues, parties, and candidates as the objects of evaluation becomes more complex owing to the increase of information, its complexity, and the different criteria they have to apply. Voters can no longer simply rely on retrospection and prospection. Voting today may require considering this triad of issues, parties, and candidates, not only in its classical definition. Media performance, personality traits, performance of local candidates, evaluation of communication with parties and candidates and of responsiveness during the campaign, discounting preferences by realistic possibilities, etc. may all be criteria to be additionally considered. A general question—in analogy to the development of electoral research—is whether voting behavior has become more fragmented or the calculus has just changed. Voters are not alike; it seems that they become less alike all the time.

The insight that voters are heterogeneous regarding the criteria they apply to decide about political offers, the emphasis they put on different issues, and the way that they process information is not new. Already in 1971, RePass noted the effect of differences between voters regarding the salience of issues and the vote (RePass 1971). Bartle more generally pointed to the fact that "voters place different weights on considerations ('type one heterogeneity') and/or that they think about politics in different ways ('type two heterogeneity')" (2005: 654). But what can be gained by taking heterogeneity into consideration? In voting research and respective models it is common to assume that voters share the same decision rules. Rivers concluded that "such procedures might be justified if one's goal was to explain election outcomes …". They remain unsatisfactory, however, "if one's goal is to characterize voter decision processes" (Rivers 1988: 737). The developments in voting behavior over the last decades suggest that a more refined understanding of the decision process is necessary in order to rebuild the connection between voting, elections, and politics.

You cannot just choose any route to address this research problem. Results would then contribute to even more scattered findings. Rather, a conceptual orientation has to be applied. The most encompassing frame theory of electoral behavior provided is still the "funnel of causality" developed by the "Michigan school" and lately re-analysed (Campbell et al. 1960; Miller and Shanks 1996). The funnel as such is not bound to any particular approach. It provides the core elements of preconditions, determinants, political objects, and context to which different traditions of electoral research can be applied—from macro-sociological cleavage theory to rational choice. Different approaches seem to put different emphasis on particular parts of the funnel of causality (Figure 1.3).

Thus, the external and internal elements of the funnel of causality have to be considered and combined with the findings on heterogeneity and complexity. From a theoretical perspective, this implies investigating the conditions under which causal reasoning persists and needs modification or contextualization. Any attempt to tackle the considerable challenge of change in voting behavior demands a closer look at its conditions. Heterogeneity must not imply unstructured fragmentation. If we can identify the conditions of heterogeneity we may have the key to "unaccounted-for causes" (Bartels 2010). Thus, the logic of such a search for explanation takes up the causal elements of the funnel of causality and puts them into context or under condition. If heterogeneity and the consequences of complexity can be explained taking this route, so

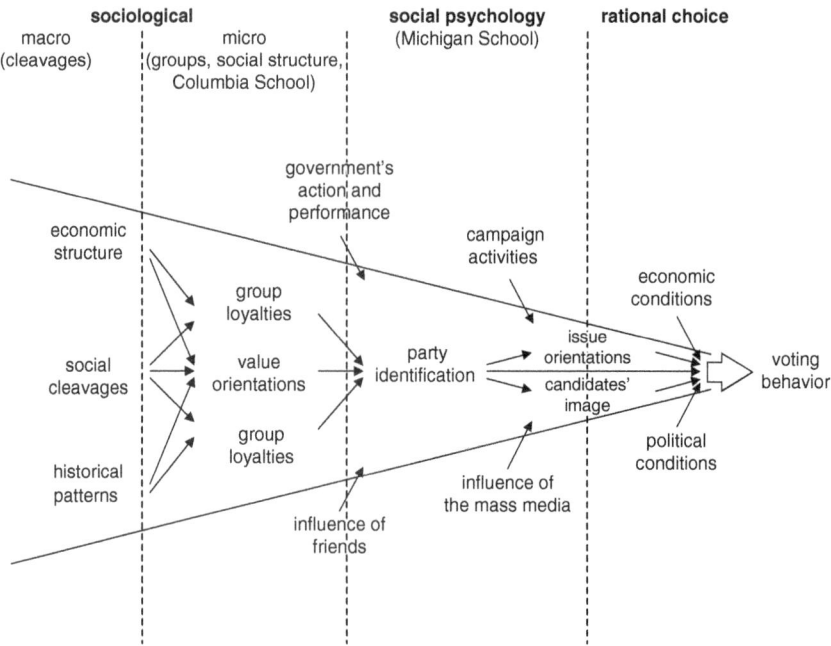

Figure 1.3 The funnel of causality of voting behavior

far unidentified structures may become discernable in the apparently increasingly unstructured voting patterns.

The application of a micro perspective to the funnel of causality approach implies a prioritization of *voters' attributes*. The weight put on different criteria in judging political objects may vary with the individual characteristics of voters. Characteristics like demographics, cognitive capacity, and attitudinal or belief structure should be taken adequately into account, alongside an emphasis on the different choice criteria.

A second perspective on the conditioning of voters' calculi is on the differences between *political objects* themselves. Political parties certainly are among the core political objects. So far, electoral research has obviously dealt with parties under the assumption that they are all assessed by the same criteria. This seems to be true for long-term factors like party identification and short-term factors like spatial utility. That the weight of different evaluations can vary depending on the role a party takes in the governmental system or on issue ownership seems evident. It can be assumed that the performance evaluation of a party in opposition must play a different role than that of a party in government. Just as reasonably, it can be supposed that parties with different issue ownership are not judged equally according to all issues. Another case in point is government as an object. Multiparty systems do not only provide more choices than two-party systems; government alternatives are quite often coalitions. If some voters show coalition preferences while others do not, this should point to different sets of considerations in the two groups.

A third factor producing heterogeneity is of *institutional* nature. The political systems of the European Union and, in addition, federal states, experience elections at different political levels. The meaning and meaningfulness of these elections may differ. The so-called "second-order election" approach (Reif and Schmitt 1980) evaluates elections that are not at the national level. So-called second-order elections—according to common wisdom—offer alternatives for voting behavior at low cost, whereby voters abstain, punish a party they support at the national level, or "vote with the heart," otherwise known as sincere voting (Weber 2011). The consequences for the individual vote function can be manifold. Due to voting experience and voting practice, the weight attached to specific aspects of voters's considerations or partisan ties may change or be applied differently at different levels of voting.

Furthermore, certain features of campaigns that increase their complexity or diversification may lead to higher heterogeneity. One aspect of campaigns is their temporal dynamic. A second aspect is the "localization" of campaigning. International trends suggest that the relevance of local campaigning and, in particular, local personal campaigning is growing—even in non-plurality systems. This implies that the consideration set of voters becomes more complex by additional elements that make the calculus of voting, depending on the particular context, more or less heterogeneous.

Thus, in order to cope with heterogeneity, the following aspects seem to be of relevance: (1) voters' characteristics, (2) characteristics of political objects, (3) institutional aspects, and (4) campaign features.

Complexity is the second dimension that contributes to changes in voting behavior. No doubt, heterogeneity and complexity influence each other. It is doubtful if we will ever be able to identify the exact temporal order of effects in the funnel of causality. In order to identify whether, and under which circumstances, complexity conditions the vote function, several aspects need to be taken into account.

One such aspect is *social structure*, not only meant as a characteristic of individuals but also as a context of individuals. If individualization processes are under way, social structures in the broad understanding of Blau (1977a, 1977b) become more complex; the contexts and networks of individual voters more differentiated. Macro-social group characteristics certainly lose relevance, as indicated by the decline in class voting. This does not necessarily imply that micro-social characteristics will become completely individualized. It may just compensate for higher complexity of higher social differentiation.

The *information environment* is also adding to complexity. However, this development has two sides. On one hand, the expansion of media systems into electronic media adds to complexity by providing an amount of information previously unknown. On the other hand, the large quantities of information offered by electronic media could be used to understand the increasing political complexity.

Thirdly, the shape and scope of *political agendas and issues* have shifted with the rise of new politics, postmaterialism, and parties' responses. How do voters deal with this, and do campaigns help them to navigate this new environment? Campaigns serve several purposes, including general mobilization and distinguishing oneself from the competition. Thus, campaigns are a particular means of providing information. They may increase complexity or reduce it. As the core instrument of politicians and political parties in competing for votes, campaigns are an indispensable tool to inform the voter. But even if they succeed in reducing complexity, difficulties remain over the degree to which voters will follow them. The trend in the calculus of voting is towards an increase in issue voting, which implies increasing complexity. Because cues and loyalties seem not to work as they did before, voters may have to give greater consideration to the issues at stake than they did in the past.

The *decline of norms and loyalties* also increases voting complexity, and this may have two different consequences. The first is that voters' choices will become more difficult as more information will have to be retrieved and evaluated in order to draw conclusions. A second consequence may be that what is on offer will be viewed more critically if the straitjacket of norms and loyalties no longer produces consistent judgments. The consequences of this loss of complexity-reducing factors like norms and loyalties could be less positive orientations towards, and evaluations of, political supply, as well as rather instable political behavior and choices.

In this view, voting complexity at least involves consideration of (1) characteristics of social structure, (2) political information flows, (3) agendas and issues, and (4) the declining role of norms and loyalties.

This sketch of aspects of heterogeneity and complexity makes clear that the two can only be analytically disentangled. Heterogeneity implies that the general vote function is conditioned by particular aspects. Complexity implies that the conditions of voting have changed. Changing conditions quite likely translate into greater heterogeneity of the vote function across voters.

Taking into account heterogeneity and complexity as the two main dimensions of changing electorates implies that the explanation of voting behavior needs to be addressed in a specific way in order to understand the changing mechanisms of decision-making. The key to regaining the link between micro-politics and the working of the governmental system lies in our understanding of these mechanisms. Such an approach most certainly contributes to complexity. The idea, however, is that integrated complexity contributes to understanding rather than to further fragmentation of the already quite fragmented body of voting research.

1.4 PLAN OF THE BOOK

This book attempts to shed light on the increasing difficulty of understanding voting behavior. This difficulty has apparently weakened the link between electoral research and the elaboration of the consequences of voting and elections, i.e., the clarification of the relationship between voting and the working of the governmental system. The solution for reviving the link lies in a better understanding of voting behavior. The discussion above shows that the traditional way of applying one universal model to all voters has reached its limit and is unlikely to reduce the gap between the extensive research literature on the one hand and its minimal relevance for the bigger questions on the working of democracies on the other hand.

The contributions are a product of a common endeavor of researchers of the team of the German Longitudinal Election Study (GLES). Thus, the book heavily draws on the huge amount of data GLES has produced. One reason for relying on the German data is that, with the support of the German National Science Foundation (Deutsche Forschungsgemeinschaft, DFG), it was possible to accomplish a complex data and research design that goes beyond what election studies normally can do, perhaps with the exception of the American National Election Study (ANES). The integrated multicomponent design with large cross-section surveys, long-term panel surveys, a rolling cross-section survey, candidate survey, media-content analysis, and online tracking surveys enabled us to answer questions that normally cannot be addressed (see the appendix for details of the study design). The questions that are the subject of this book not only refer to German voters but are of general theoretical relevance for voting and election research. The answers given in the book can be theoretically generalized. Moreover, it is not only German data that is used in this book. Wherever the research question and available data could be matched, comparative data of the Comparative Study of Electoral Systems is additionally analysed in order to put the German data in perspective and to check to what degree the findings can be generalized.

The book is structured along the lines of the discussion in the pages above. Correspondingly, it is divided into two parts, dealing with *increasing heterogeneity of voting* (part II) and *increasing complexity and voting* (part III). Within the parts, each of the aspects of heterogeneity and complexity discussed above is dealt with. Part II includes contributions about the heterogeneity of the vote function, which take into account voters' characteristics, characteristics of political objects, institutional aspects, and campaign features as producers of such diversity. Part III includes contributions on how voters can deal with complexity and how complexity affects voting. Specifically, the chapters deal with the aspects discussed above: characteristics of social structure, political information flows, agendas and issues, and the declining role of norms and loyalties. Part IV entails a concluding chapter.

Part II

Increasing Heterogeneity of Voting

2

Voter Fragmentation and the Differentiation of Vote Functions*

Jan Eric Blumenstiel

2.1 INTRODUCTION

In standard models of electoral behavior it is assumed that all voters come to their decision in exactly the same way. But voters are not all alike. Some might be policy-driven in their electoral choices; others perhaps put a special emphasis on party leaders or routinely follow their long-term partisanship. Consequently, the "homogeneity assumption" has been increasingly challenged recently as scholars focused on various characteristics of voters that could explain variance in voting calculi. Yet these findings have not been integrated both into a comprehensive theory and into a general model of heterogeneous voting behavior.

Therefore, the purpose of this chapter is to provide a theoretical and empirical framework that allows systematic study of voter heterogeneity. Section 2.2 discusses what previous research has already uncovered about why not all voters assign the same weight to all considerations and what analysing these differences can add to the understanding of political behavior. In section 2.3, possible moderators of the importance of vote predictors at different levels are discussed. Then, in section 2.4, it its demonstrated how the heterogeneity assumption can be integrated into existing explanatory models of vote choice. After briefly describing the data and measures that are used in section 2.5, the derived hypotheses are empirically assessed from two different perspectives. First, in section 2.6, the 2009 German federal election is used as a case study for analysing whether and why voters apply different calculi in electoral decision-making. Section 2.7 then focuses on the temporal dimension of heterogeneity, asking whether the supposition of an increasingly heterogeneous

---

* The author wishes to thank an anonymous reviewer for helpful suggestions and Konstantin Gavras for various assistance in editing the manuscript.

electorate is justified and whether there is intrapersonal homogeneity between subsequent elections at the individual level. In this way, the chapter adds to the explanation of voter heterogeneity by incorporating previous approaches into a more general theoretical and empirical model and by making first steps to uncover the so far mostly neglected temporal dimension of heterogeneity at both the aggregate and the individual level.

2.2 HETEROGENEITY AND THE STUDY OF VOTING BEHAVIOR

When empirical electoral research emerged as a subdiscipline of political science, one of its primary interests was to explain why voters decide as they do. Such explanations should not in the first place be narrative descriptions of the specific setting of a given election, but rather take the form of general theoretical models with more or less universal validity. Whether the focus was more on social (Lazarsfeld, Berelson, and Gaudet 1944) or attitudinal (Campbell et al. 1960b) attributes, the common approach was to identify a number of predictors of electoral choice and to integrate these into some sort of causal structure or equation that was applicable to the electoral decisions of the entire electorate. As is the nature of general models, this came at a price: The specifics that are unique to each individual decision had to be largely disregarded. In seeking parsimony, the models could not allow for what is referred to as voter heterogeneity, namely that some explanatory elements might be of greater or lesser importance to specific subgroups of the electorate.

However, this is not to say that the early scholars were unaware of possibly heterogeneous voting calculi. As Roy (2009, 2011) notes, individual differences in decision-making have already been stressed by Berelson and colleagues as early as 1954 (313): "The tendency in democratic literature to work with an image of 'the' voter was never justified." But, first things first, the main focus of the early studies of electoral behavior was obviously to devise general models before refining them. Nonetheless, if we think of the cross-pressured citizens first described by Lazarsfeld, Berelson, and Gaudet (1944), who are torn between two parties by their social predispositions, this is one of the first descriptions of voter heterogeneity. The authors of the *American Voter* later argued for attitudinal sources of cross pressures and introduced the notion of levels of conceptualization. Ideologues were found to be less likely to defect from an existing partisan identification when compared to the group with the lowest level of conceptualization (Campbell et al. 1960b: 264), indicating heterogeneity in the influence of long-term psychological party attachments.

That electoral scientists nevertheless by and large have continued to ignore heterogeneity in voters' calculi is what might be called the homogeneity

Voter Fragmentation and the Differentiation of Vote Functions   19

paradox: Although it has been known for a long time that voters indeed are *not* all alike as to how they weight different considerations to derive their party preferences, we often keep assuming that they are. While the homogeneity assumption more often than not is made implicitly, we can also find examples where it is made explicitly:

> The Rule involves an important assumption that is counterintuitive namely, that all the considerations which enter into a voting decision are weighed equally.... Almost certainly, the nonintuitve assumption that voters weigh all considerations equally does not always hold true (Kelley 1983: 12–13).

This being said, why should we be interested in studying voter heterogeneity at all? What theoretical insight does it possibly provide to know how voters differ in their voting calculi? The hazards of the homogeneity assumption are most distinctively summarized by Rivers (1988: 737):

> While such procedures might be justified if one's goal was to explain election outcomes, they turn out to be unsatisfactory if one's goal is to characterize voter decision processes.... In fact, if two voters have identical policy preferences and demographic characteristics, then any of the standard methods of analysing voting behavior would predict that the two would cast identical votes. Yet it is easy to think of situations where such a prediction would be unwarranted. If issues have different levels of salience to voters, then identical policy preferences do not necessarily imply identical (or even similar) voting patterns.

The following example devised by Bartle (2005: 654) illustrates this argument: Think of two parties, A and B, and two voters, V1 and V2. Let the probability of voting for A in an election be

$$p(A) = 0.1 + (0.05 \times \text{Candidate}) + (0.1 \times \text{Issue})$$

Now assume that both voters have identical attitudes toward party A, say Candidate = 7; Issue = 4. Under the traditional homogeneity condition, our prediction for both voters is that they vote for A

$$p(A) = 0.1 + (0.05 \times 7) + (0.1 \times 4) = 0.85$$

If we now drop the homogeneity assumption and instead assume V1 to be a pure candidate voter and V2 to be a pure issue voter our prediction changes to

$$V1 : p(A) = 0.1 + (0.05 \times 7) + (0 \times 4) = 0.45$$

$$V2 : p(A) = 0.1 + (0 \times 7) + (0.1 \times 4) = 0.5$$

The numerical illustration of heterogeneity in this example and the rather mathematical term "calculus" should of course not be taken too literally. To assume that consideration weights are represented in voters' heads in any numerical form similar to regression weights is unrealistic. Calculus heterogeneity should rather be thought of as mental dispositions to prioritize certain aspects in thinking about or acquiring information about elections, political parties, politicians, or policies.

Furthermore, although different voting calculi should be associated with differences in party preferences, calculus heterogeneity is neither a necessary nor a sufficient condition for different decisions between any two voters. At the individual level, changes in attitudes can cause a change of party preference despite entirely stable calculi, and changing calculi can be irrelevant for vote choice. Therefore, increasing the predictive power of explanatory models is but one of many motives for studying calculus heterogeneity. More importantly, it has been argued that, from a theoretical perspective, ignoring the individual weights of the explanatory variables is the most severe blind spot of the Michigan model (Rudi and Schoen 2005). Furthermore, even if there are enough reasons to assume that the electorate has never been homogeneous, the argument has been fostered further by the finding of declining social determination of voting decisions (Butler and Stokes 1969; Särlvik and Crewe 1983; Dalton 1984, 2008). According to Dalton (2008: 184–5), partisan dealignment is accompanied by increasing electoral volatility, a tendency of voters to delay their vote decision, and growing importance of short-term factors such as issues and candidates, so that party choice for most voters now actually is a decision rather than a predetermined routine. Many Western societies are witnessing a period of increasing social differentiation and electoral volatility. Traditional family structures or single-employer careers become less frequent while new lifestyles develop and migration makes societies more multifaceted. Recent elections in Germany and other democracies were characterized by increasing volatility, unpredictability, as well as higher party system fragmentation, erosion of traditional party camps, and generally greater competition between parties (Niedermayer 2008). Both phenomena could be related. Alliances between social groups and parties have changed, but the German social structure still remains largely politicized (e.g. Pappi and Brandenburg 2010). The electorate thus has become even more heterogeneous over time.

In sum, the assumption of homogeneous calculi makes explanatory models theoretically imperfect, can lead to wrong predictions, and means ignoring potential sources of volatility and explanations for the supposedly growing importance of short-term factors in consequence of partisan dealignment and social differentiation. What we might gain by studying individual variance in the importance of considerations is not limited to avoiding these pitfalls. An enhanced understanding of voter heterogeneity can also help to explain seemingly "incorrect" decisions (see Chapter 10). Any decision that seems to be inconsistent with a prediction based on predispositions and beliefs could in fact appear more reasoned once heterogeneous calculi are included in the prediction. Moreover, to the extent that intra-individual heterogeneity exists over time (Blumenstiel and Plischke 2012; Peterson 2005), this can yield new insights into the study of campaign effects.

Based on findings about declining social determination of voting decisions and beginning with the seminal article of Rivers (1988), research has started questioning the homogeneity assumption more insistently. Some scholars dealt with the questions concerning how voters differ in terms of information processing and how they cope with incomplete information in electoral decision-making, for instance by using heuristics (Lau and Redlawsk 2006; Lupia 1994; Popkin 1991; for Germany: Glantz 2011). Others have more directly focused on heterogeneous consideration weights, that is, on differences between voters in the importance that specific aspects such as candidate or issue orientations have on their electoral choices (Bartle 2005; Glasgow 2005; Rivers 1988; Roy 2009; 2011; Peterson 2005; Sniderman, Brody, and Tetlock 1991; for Germany: Blumenstiel and Rattinger 2012). Evidence about voter heterogeneity is still largely scattered, though. Apart from Bartle's (2005) valuable distinction of two types of heterogeneity,[1] attempts to systematize possible explanatory variables of heterogeneity are rarely to be found. Most previous studies are either highly specific in terms of the independent variable, focusing on specific aspects of voting, such as the effects of issues (Fournier et al. 2003), economic voting (Gomez and Wilson 2001), or candidate-orientations (Bartle 2005). Or a more general research design as to the dependent variable makes it necessary to narrow the independent variable down to information (Roy 2009, 2011). Still others have primarily concentrated on how to identify heterogeneity (Rivers 1988; Glasgow 2001; Blumenstiel and Rattinger 2012), thereby only marginally touching possible explanations for heterogeneity. The dynamics of voter heterogeneity are also unknown since hardly any longitudinal research exists, assessing heterogeneity over time by studying intra-individual change and stability in the style of decision-making.

In this chapter two research questions will guide the analysis. First, the most fundamental question reads "Why do individual voting calculi differ?" It picks up the fragmentary theoretical framework, the study of voter heterogeneity has hitherto suffered from, seeking to develop a scheme to classify possible explanations for variance of consideration weights between voters. Second, as the absence of longitudinal analyses is a major shortcoming of previous research,

---

[1] Type 1 heterogeneity means "that voters place different weights on considerations", type 2 heterogeneity that "they think about politics in different ways" (Bartle 2005: 654). In this chapter, the focus is exclusively on type 1 since type 2 heterogeneity is far more difficult to study and would probably require experimental research designs.

it will be discussed whether heterogeneity has indeed increased since 1998 and how homogeneous voting calculi are at the individual level over time.

2.3 QUESTIONING THE HOMOGENEITY ASSUMPTION—THEORETICAL CONSIDERATIONS AND HYPOTHESES

A general theory to explain differences in voting calculi is still missing. As a starting point toward a more general theory, notice that heterogeneity can occur at different levels. From specific to general, heterogeneity might be explained by the characteristics of a voter, by qualities or functions of political parties, by the specific setting of a given election, and by rules or attributes of an electoral system (Table 2.1). This chapter focuses on the influence of voter characteristics, whereas in following chapters some moderators of heterogeneity that are related to the supply side (Chapters 3 and 4) and to institutional factors (Chapters 6 and 7) are discussed.

Which voter characteristics could explain differences in consideration weights? To the extent that calculi are relatively stable predispositions over time at the individual level so that the likelihood of a, say, candidate-oriented vote decision at t_1 is predictive of a similar calculus at t_2, this might be the result of relatively stable characteristics of the voter such as social characteristics. Affective characteristics, such as conflicts or ambiguities between individual attitudes within a voter's belief system could contribute to the explanation of differences in the voting calculi, too. Cognitive abilities have most often been stressed in previous studies as a predictor of heterogeneity. Increasing complexity of electoral choice situations could have the consequence that the

Table 2.1 Possible moderators of voter heterogeneity at different levels

Level	Sublevel	Possible moderators of calculus heterogeneity
Demand side	Voter	Sophistication, personality, attitudinal cross-pressures, ambivalence, salience of attitudes
Supply side	Party	Size, government participation, extremity, ambiguity, coalition options
Institutional aspects	Election	Issues emphasized during the campaign by media and/or parties. Candidate-constellation (incumbency, polarization etc.), economic situation
	Electoral system	Electoral rules, number of parties, parties' or candidates' positions

electorate becomes more heterogeneous over time, while voting calculi should be somewhat more stable at the individual level.

Demographic variables have been discredited as predictors of electoral choice (Achen 1992). Electoral behavior, the argument goes, is a function of voters' beliefs, which are influenced by social characteristics. Hence the latter have no actual causal link to vote choice—for one thing, it is not formal education that matters in the voting booth, but the amount of actual political knowledge and the extent to which one's belief system is constrained, for which education is, at best, one predictor among others. Nonetheless, some social characteristics might indirectly be related to voting decisions by means of influencing the weights voters assign to specific decision criteria. Social group memberships could still affect the aspects voters base their choice upon. Among the demographic variables that could cause heterogeneous calculi are age, religion, occupation status, and region of origin.

Age. Older voters presumably have participated in a large number of elections. This electoral experience strengthens and stabilizes existing partisan predispositions (Converse 1976; Gluchowski 1983). Citizens who had the chance to collect political experience for several decades are also less likely to change their preferences between any two elections (Schoen 2003b). We can therefore assume that long-term aspects, and especially party identification, have greater weights for the electoral decisions the older voters get.

Hypothesis 1: Partisanship is of greater importance for older voters.

Church attendance and social class. The religious cleavage as well as the cleavage between owners and workers explained the emergence of party systems in Germany and other Western societies (Lipset and Rokkan 1967a). The assumption that cleavage structures have shrinking influence on voting decisions (Dalton 2008) hitherto does not hold for the German case (Elff and Roßteutscher 2011; Pappi and Brandenburg 2010). Social cleavages remain a structuring element of voting behavior (although in changing patterns) and might also affect the voting calculi of specific social groups. For citizens who regularly attend church service or for blue-collar workers the value systems that have traditionally been associated with these cleavages might persist. As value orientations are relatively stable characteristics, these voters can be assumed to assign higher weights to long-term aspects in their decisions, especially to ideology.

Hypothesis 2a: Regular church attenders assign higher weight to ideological orientations.
Hypothesis 2b: Working-class members assign higher weight to ideological orientations.

Unemployment. Another social group whose voting behavior could deviate from the average population is the group of citizens who have had direct experience of unemployment (Pappi and Brandenburg 2010). Gainful employment not only ensures the material means of existence but also social reputation and integration. Unemployment has been perceived in Germany and in other democracies as the most important issue that governments have to solve in recent decades. The perceived importance of unemployment should obviously be even greater among those who do not have an occupation. Hence, these voters possibly assign a higher weight to their perception of party competence.

Hypothesis 3: Experience with unemployment is positively related with the weight of party competence ratings.

East German socialization. Finally, German unification has created a new cleavage between the East and West German electorates in terms of their socialization experiences (Weßels 1991). Although differences between East and West are generally reducing over time, the differences in early socialization might still persist in relatively stable characteristics such as value orientations (Elff and Roßteutscher 2011). Voters who were born in Eastern Germany might still be influenced by a certain conception of the welfare state and therefore more strongly weight socioeconomic issues in their choices.

Hypothesis 4: The socioeconomic dimension is more important for the choices of East Germans.

Issue salience. If we think about what factors might be most predictive of a voter's behavior, probably the most intuitive assumption is that attitudes which are important to the voter matter more. As important attitudes tend to be more accessible and increase the likelihood of citizens to perceive greater differences between alternative objects, such as parties or candidates (Krosnick 1988), important attitudes should provide stronger guidance for decision-making. Issue salience has repeatedly been included in analyses of voting behavior (RePass 1971; Rabinowitz, Prothro, and Jacoby 1982; Krosnick 1988; Wlezien 2005; Bélanger and Meguid 2008). It has been demonstrated that issue orientations do exert a stronger influence on vote choice for voters to whom these issues are more salient (e.g., RePass 1971; Fournier et al. 2003; Bélanger and Meguid 2008).

Hypothesis 5: Higher issue salience increases the weight of issue distances for vote choice.

Ambivalence. Just as the study of voter heterogeneity in general, attitudinal ambivalence has for a long time been disregarded in electoral research, although the concept was first described quite some time ago (e.g., Festinger 1957; Scott 1966, 1968). Attitudinal ambivalence means holding "equivalently strong positive and negative evaluations" toward an attitude object (Thompson, Zana, and Griffin 1995: 367). Here, the focus will be on ambivalence between multiple attitude objects, meaning that two or more parties are evaluated similarly positively. Ambivalent attitudes have been shown to be more instable over time (Craig, Martinez, and Kane 2005), to generally reduce the attitude–behavior relation (Armitage and Conner 2000; Lavine 2001), and to reduce the influence of party identification on vote choice (Basinger and Lavine 2005). The hypothesis for the following analyses regarding ambivalence thus is that the vote choices of voters with ambivalent preferences are generally less predictable.

Hypothesis 6: Ambivalence reduces the attitude–behavior relationship (so that the explanatory power of the vote function is lower for ambivalent voters).

(Attitudinal) cross-pressures. As mentioned above, the description of cross-pressures by Lazarsfeld and colleagues (1944) is one of the first accounts of voter heterogeneity. If the emphasis in the Erie County study was on social cross-pressures, the authors of the *American Voter* picked up the concept and shifted the attention to attitudinal sources of conflicting predispositions. If, for example, a voter favored the Republican candidate but reported a long-term identification with the Democratic Party, she was considered to be cross-pressured. The difference between ambivalence and cross-pressures is that while the former refers to short-term attitudinal conflict, the latter involves conflicting short- and long-term preferences. From the little of what is known about the impact of attitudinal cross-pressures on vote choice, it seems that although cross-pressured voters predominantly tend to stay with their identification party, they are still relatively more likely to electorally defect from their identification party (Willmann 2011). Thus, party identification should have lower importance in the calculus of cross-pressured voters and again the attitude-relationship should generally be weaker.

Hypothesis 7: Cross-pressures between long-term predisposition and short-term evaluations reduce the attitude–behavior relationship (so that the explanatory power of the vote function is lower for cross-pressured voters).

Political sophistication. The one independent variable that most previous research has focused on to explain calculus heterogeneity is cognitive abilities, mostly operationalized by political sophistication (e.g., Andersen, Heath, and Sinnott 2002; Bartle 1997, 2005; Basinger and Lavine 2005; Gomez and Wilson 2001; Roy 2009, 2011). Luskin (1987: 860) defines political sophistication as "the extent to which [...a political belief system] is large, wide-ranging, and highly constrained." The reasoning why sophistication should be related to calculus heterogeneity is straightforward. Sophisticated voters do have higher cognitive capacities that enable them to process political information more systematically and more efficiently so that their subjective rationality is less bounded than that of the politically unaware (Roy 2009; Simon 1957). Generally speaking, the more information a voter possesses, the higher the quantity and complexity of aspects she potentially can consider.[2]

In fact, it has been shown that more sophisticated voters differ in a number of aspects from the ill-informed. Among other things, sophistication is positively associated with attitude consistency and stability over time (Bartle 2000). Regarding electoral choice, knowledgeable citizens differ in terms of economic voting in that they better understand the complexity of economic conditions (Gomez and Wilson 2001), consider a higher number and more demanding aspects in their voting decision (Roy 2011), generally ascribe more importance to political issues (Andersen, Heath, and Sinnott 2002) and less importance to candidate orientations (Bartle 2005; Krosnick 1988) as well as to party identification (Campbell et al. 1960b). Regarding the outcome of the reasoning process, political sophistication also leads to different decisions (Bartels 1996). Generally speaking, we can hypothesize that sophistication should be positively associated with the weight of more demanding considerations (especially issue distances and party competence) and reduces the weight of less demanding considerations, especially leader evaluations. Furthermore, the decisions of more sophisticated citizens should generally be better predicted by their attitudes.

> *Hypothesis 8a: Political sophistication strengthens the attitude–behavior relationship (so that the explanatory power of the vote function is higher for the most sophisticated voters).*
> *Hypothesis 8b: Political sophistication increases the weight of issue orientations.*
> *Hypothesis 8c: Political sophistication reduces the weight of candidate orientations.*

Increasing complexity: Heterogeneity over time. Voter heterogeneity so far has primarily been discussed from a cross-sectional perspective, asking how voters differ in their consideration weights at one given election. However, there is reason to assume that voting decisions have become more heterogeneous over time. At the aggregate level, partisan dealignment has been suggested to come along with the erosion of stable alliances between social groups and parties. Recent elections in Germany produced massive shifts in the party system. During the 1980s and 1990s the effective number of parties was both relatively low and stable, but increased between 2002 and 2009 from 3.2 to 4.7. Coalition building has also become considerably more complicated. With a clear division of the party system in a center-Right camp of CDU/CSU and FDP and a center-Left camp of SPD and the Green party, the situation seemed relatively easy up to 1998: it was either the one camp or the other which would win the election and build the government. Less than a decade later the situation is far more complicated. The first grand coalition for almost forty years had been

---

[2] As Sniderman, Brody, and Tetlock (1991: 173) put it: "[…] the better informed voter tends to take account of nearly everything including the kitchen sink."

Table 2.2 Expected directions of associations between heterogeneity predictors and elements of the vote function

	Party identification	Ideology	Party competence	Candidate	Issue	R^2
Age	+	+				
Church attendance	+	+				
Working class	+	+				
Unemployment			+			
Ambivalence	−	−	−	−	−	−
Cross-pressures	−	−	−	−	−	−
Issue salience					+	
Political sophistication			+	−	+	+

formed in 2005, and the Left enjoyed a comeback that was as unexpected as successful. The era of two-party coalitions suddenly seemed to be over, new coalition options were discussed, and in several federal states new parties (such as Free Voters and the Pirate Party) have entered state parliaments and will compete with the established parties in future elections.

As the complexity of a choice situation increases with a higher number of alternatives, greater dissimilarity between alternatives, and increasing inter-dependencies between alternatives (Luhmann 2009), electoral choice has certainly become more complex in Germany since the 1990s. This could have contributed to an increasingly heterogeneous electorate not only in terms of ticket-splitting or party change (Lachat 2007) but also in terms of voting calculi. More precisely, since political sophistication increases the capability of dealing with complex choice situations, the gap in explanatory power of the vote function between voters with low and high political sophistication should have widened.

At the individual level, we know little to nothing about the stability of consideration weights. Vote choices have become more volatile recently, but it is unclear whether this is caused by fluctuating calculi. Short-term considerations have been suggested to be of growing importance, but the evidence is far from conclusive. To the extent that relatively stable (social) characteristics determine these weights however, it seems plausible to expect at least some stability of voting calculi over time, so that candidate voters at t_1 should also be relatively more likely to be candidate voters at t_2.

> Hypothesis 9: *The sophistication gap in explanatory power of the vote function has widened over time.*
> Hypothesis 10: *At the individual level, voting calculi are relatively stable.*

2.4 A MODEL OF HETEROGENEOUS VOTING CALCULI

To test the hypotheses outlined above and summarized in Table 2.2, corresponding interaction terms between predictors of electoral choice with variables measuring the identified heterogeneity indicators can be calculated. The vote function applied in this chapter is inspired by the work of Miller and Shanks (1996). They introduce a multistage explanatory model which builds on the classical Michigan model presented in the *American Voter*, but includes findings of other theoretical approaches. Miller and Shanks describe the voting decision process with six temporally ordered stages. In each stage explanatory variables of comparable temporal distance to vote choice are grouped together. Earlier stages therefore contain long-term factors (such as social characteristics in stage 1 or party identification in stage 2), and later stages contain short-term factors (e.g., policy preferences in stage 3, retrospective evaluations in stage 4, personal qualities of the candidates in stage 5, and prospective evaluations in stage 6). The model is used as a framework here since it is more inclusive than the model presented by Campbell et al. (1960b). While the general idea of the model to include variables which represent different causal stages will be replicated, not all specific explanatory variables are strictly adopted.

Party identification is the single most important variable in the original Michigan model and also occupies a central position in stage two of the revised model presented in *The New American Voter*. It captures the political experiences a citizen has made during her political socialization process, structures the evaluation of candidates or policies, and constitutes the most important long-term political predisposition. Another relatively stable predisposition is the ideological position of an individual on a Left–Right scale which is also located at stage two. This generalized scale allows voters to relatively easily compare their own positions with those of the parties to determine which of the alternatives best matches their preferences without referring to more detailed information. If measured as distance between a respondent's own position and her perceived party position, this variable connects the social-psychological approach of the Michigan school to the rational choice approach of Downs (1957b).

Ideology and partisanship are treated as given for a specific election. Additional to these long-term factors, the following stages of the model consider short-term aspects which affect the final voting decisions. In stage three and four policy preferences and retrospective evaluations are located. The importance of issue orientations for electoral choice is advocated in both spatial and directional theories of voting. The idea is that voting is mostly guided by self-interest and that issue positions provide information to decide how much a party represents a voter's interest (Enelow and Hinich 1984b). Here, these stages are displayed by average distance scores from the voters' own positions to the perceived parties' positions on two positional issues (the socioeconomic dimension on taxes and welfare benefits,[3] as well as immigration laws),[4] so that again measures that originate from rational choice models are integrated into the *American Voter* framework. Stage 5 is occupied by candidate orientations which are measured with scalometer ratings for the front-runners of each party. Front-runners are the most visible figures in electoral campaigns that have become large media events. Whether or not the importance of leaders is increasing as is sometimes suggested, evaluations of the parties' principal representatives clearly matter for vote choice. Finally, stage 6 is about prospective evaluations of the parties' performance. This stage is operationalized by the valence issue: which party is best able to handle the two subjectively most important problems.[5] The perceived competence of parties has already been an important predictor in the original Michigan model. If an individual has confidence that a party can find a solution to the problems she perceives as most pressing, she obviously is more likely to give her vote to this party.

Technically, it is easy to include interaction terms between the heterogeneity factors identified above and these predictors of vote choice. But what is the theoretical justification for amending the model in such a way? First, Miller and Shanks (1996: 206) discuss the inclusion of variables, capturing individual weights of the predictor variables but refraining from this option simply for a perceived lack of appropriate measures. Theoretically, the logic of their model suggests that not all stages are of equal importance to all voters. Second, other models designed to explain different forms of behavior explicitly include individual weights of certain aspects. One such model is the Theory of Reasoned Action (TORA) by Fishbein and Ajzen (1975). The most basic premise of TORA is that a behavior is influenced by a behavioral intention to perform that behavior (although not equivalent to it). This intention in turn is a function of attitudes and social norms. Behavior is assumed to be reasoned in the sense that attitudes are generally based on characteristics of the attitude object. Most intriguingly, TORA assumes the relative importance of each factor to vary between individuals. The model is theoretically open to

---

[3] "And now we come to several controversial political issues. Some people would like to see lower taxes even if that means some reduction in health, education and social benefits; others would like to see more government spending on health, education and social benefits even if it means some increases in taxes. In your view, using a scale from 1 to 11, what is the position of the political parties on this issue?"

[4] "We now turn to the issue of immigration. Should laws on immigration be relaxed or be made tougher? In your view, using a scale from 1 to 11, what is the position of the political parties on this issue?"

[5] Applying a suggestion by Kellermann and Rattinger (2005: 197), party competence for the two subjectively most important issues is measured with the following scale: 0 = party not perceived as competent for any of the two issues, 1 = party competent only for second most important issue, 2 = party competent only for most important issue, 3 = party competent to handle most important and second most important issue.

other approaches as each specific explanatory theory and its corresponding variables can easily be included into the model as subspecifications of the attitude and social norms component (Behnke 2001; Rudi and Schoen 2005). If we think of TORA as a theoretical framework in which the multistage model of Miller and Shanks can be integrated as a specification of the beliefs of voters relevant for their electoral choices, then including weights for the predictors is not only possible but necessary.

2.5 DATA AND MEASURES

Data. For the analyses presented in section 2.6, data from the German Longitudinal Election Study (GLES) 2009, component 1 is used (face-to-face pre-election and post-election cross-section, ZA5302, N = 4288). The analyses in section 2.7 additionally draw on data of the face-to-face cross-section surveys of the German Election Studies 1998–2005[6] (1998: ZA3066, N = 3337; 2002: ZA3861, N = 3263; 2005: ZA4332, N = 2540, post-election survey only) and on two three-wave face-to-face panels covering the elections 1998–2005 and 2002–2009, respectively (GLES component 7, long-term panel, ZA4662 (1998–2005), N = 1847 panel respondents participating in at least two waves; ZA5320 (2002–2009, N = 1107 panel respondents).

Social characteristics. All respondents aged sixty-five or above are classified as "old" voters. Regular church attenders are those who are members of a Protestant or Catholic church and attend religious services at least once a month. The working class encompasses all respondents with a blue-collar occupation.

Affective characteristics. Attitude importance usually is measured using subjective self-reports (Krosnick et al. 1993). Thus, issue salience is measured as the average subjective importance of positional issues on five-point scales from not at all important to very important.

Measures for ambivalence have mostly been developed in the US context (Thompson, Zana, and Griffin 1995) and are not easily transferable to the German multiparty system. Most importantly, without knowing the consideration set of a voter it is nearly impossible to decide which parties to include in the construction of ambivalence measures since attitudes toward parties not included in the consideration set should be irrelevant. Therefore, a simple dummy variable will be used based on the generalized party scalometer ratings indicating whether a voter is tied between two or more parties, that is, if she assigned the highest value to more than one party.

---

[6] A longer period would of course be desirable to study the temporal dimension of heterogeneity. While data are available for the elections in 1990 and 1994, these studies unfortunately do not contain several variables which are necessary to measure the elements of the vote function.

The term 'cross-pressures' in this chapter is defined as inconsistency between long-term and short-term determinants of vote choice. Voters who give their highest rating to a party other than their identification party are classified as cross-pressured.

Cognitive abilities. Finally, the index of political sophistication combines an objective and a subjective measure, thus reflecting the multidimensional structure of sophistication (Neuman 1986). The objective measure includes two factual knowledge questions about the German electoral system (electoral threshold and the more important of the two votes in the two-vote system), for each correct answer a value of 0.5 is assigned. The subjective component is represented by political interest, which is measured with a five-point scale, recoded to a range from 0 to 1. Voters scoring 1.5 or higher on the combined index ranging from 0 to 2 are classified as the most sophisticated.

2.6 HETEROGENEITY IN THE 2009 GERMAN FEDERAL ELECTION

As a starting point for the analyses of calculus heterogeneity, the described vote function in this section will be applied to the 2009 Bundestag election. In a first step corresponding interaction terms for Hypothesis 1 to Hypothesis 8 are estimated in a conditional logit model[7] so that a single model can be estimated for all parties rather than estimating a separate binary logistic model for each party, which would make the interpretation far more complicated. The results are presented in Figures 2.1–2.6. The coefficients of the interactions are displayed together with the 95%-confidence intervals. The values of the interaction coefficients are to be interpreted relative to the coefficient of the corresponding reference group. For instance, for the coefficient for the interaction between age and party identification, the reference is the coefficient of party identification for younger voters.[8]

In Figure 2.1, interactions with partisanship are displayed. Older voters assign greater weight to their party identification, as stated by Hypothesis 1. For church attenders and workers, the interaction coefficient also suggests somewhat greater influence of partisanship on vote choice, but the coefficients of the reference groups are in both cases included in the confidence intervals. Ambivalent and cross-pressured voters clearly rely less on their identification in their decisions, as follows from Hypothesis 6 and Hypothesis 7, respectively.

---

[7] To this aim, the dataset was transformed to a stacked format so that for each voter there are as many rows as there are parties to be evaluated. As control variables, party identification and dummy variables for the choice alternatives are included in all models.

[8] To facilitate interpretation, all coefficients have been recoded so that positive values signify greater importance. Distance variables thus indeed were transformed into measures of proximity.

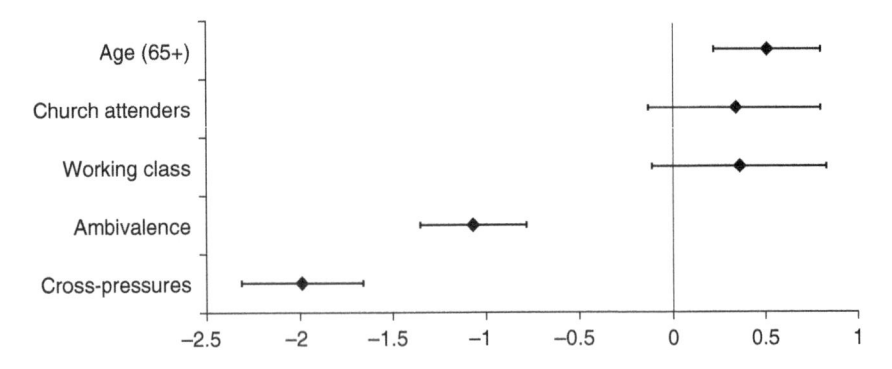

Figure 2.1 Interaction terms for weight of party identification
Note: Conditional logit coefficients and 95% confidence intervals.

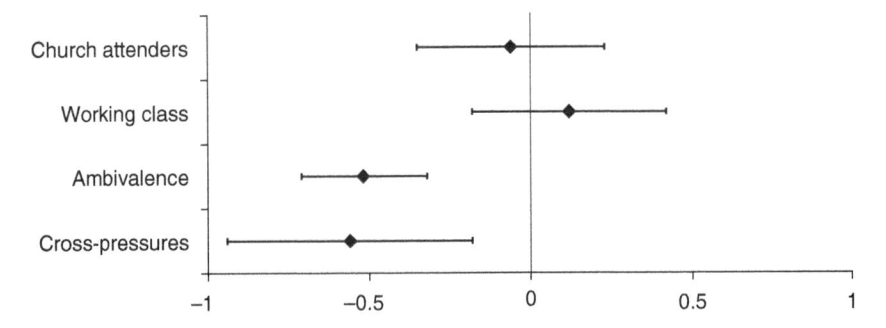

Figure 2.2 Interaction terms for weight of ideological distance
Note: Conditional logit coefficients and 95% confidence intervals.

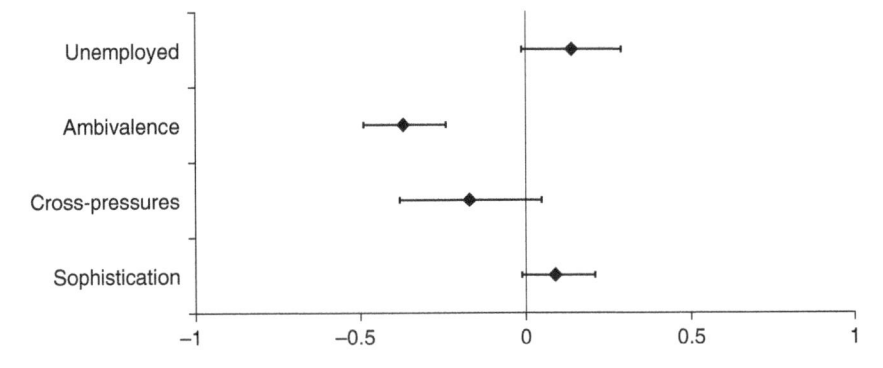

Figure 2.3 Interaction terms for weight of party competence
Note: Conditional logit coefficients and 95% confidence intervals.

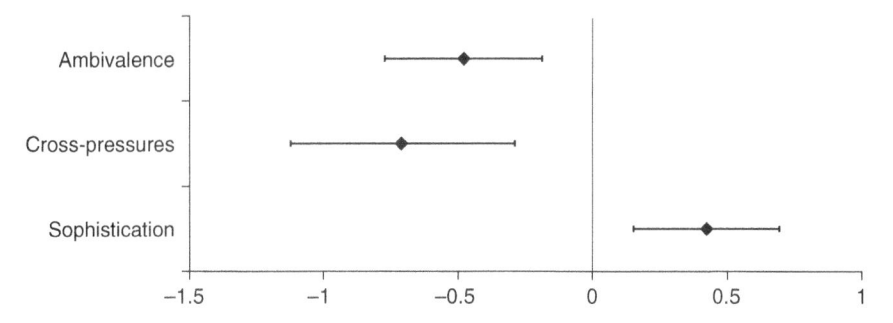

Voter Fragmentation and the Differentiation of Vote Functions   33

Figure 2.4 Interaction terms for weight of candidate evaluations
Note: Conditional logit coefficients and 95% confidence intervals.

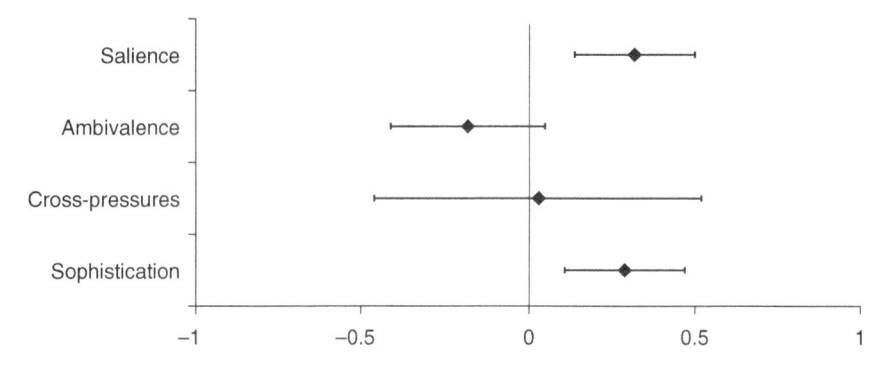

Figure 2.5 Interaction terms for weight of issue distances
Note: Conditional logit coefficients and 95% confidence intervals.

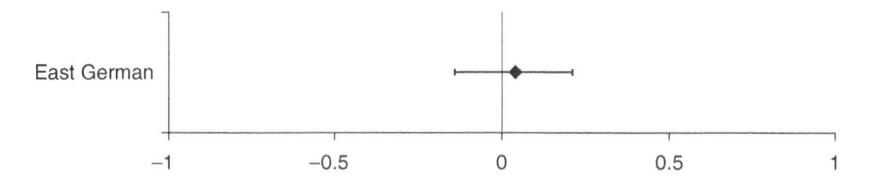

Figure 2.6 Interaction term for weight of socioeconomic issue
Note: Conditional logit coefficient and 95% confidence interval.

The results of interactions with Left–Right distances are shown in Figure 2.2. Hypothesis 2a and Hypothesis 2b must be rejected, as ideology does not affect the vote choices of workers or church attenders more heavily. Again, the interaction terms for ambivalent and cross-pressured voters are strongly negative indicating that Left–Right distance is far less predictive of the choices of these voters. For both long-term factors of the vote function we can thus state that while there are some differences in weights for elder and more experienced voters, most differences we found are due to attitudinal characteristics of the voters, namely ambivalence and cross-pressures.

Regarding perceived party competence, Hypothesis 3 and Hypothesis 8b can be confirmed (Figure 2.3). Both sophisticated voters and the unemployed assign greater weight to the competence evaluations. For ambivalent voters, the influence of party competence on vote choice is significantly lower than for the nonambivalent. By contrast, the coefficient for cross-pressured voters is only slightly smaller than for all other voters.

The consideration weights for candidate orientations are displayed in Figure 2.4. The electoral choices of ambivalent and cross-pressured voters are also comparatively less associated with evaluations of the parties' front runners. Contrary to Hypothesis 8c, the most sophisticated voters do not rely less but more on candidate evaluations. What seems surprising at first glance might, however, not be all that implausible. Indeed, previous findings as to the direction of the association between sophistication and candidate-oriented voting are not all that clear. Some authors argue that candidate orientations are the more important the less sophisticated a voter is (Bartle 2005; Luskin 1990; Krosnick 1988); others find the opposite effect (Miller, Wattenberg, and Malanchuk 1986; Roy 2009). Given the high visibility of candidates during the campaign and in TV news, it makes sense to assume that, if anything, orientations toward the front-runners can explain how the least informed voters come to their decision. However, why should the better informed not rely equally strongly, or even more strongly, on their opinions about candidates? The contradicting findings could simply stem from the confusion of *relative* and *absolute* importance. Assume that the only significant predictor of vote choices of the most unaware voters was candidate orientations, whereas the decisions of the highly informed were similarly related to candidate *and* issue orientations. Relatively speaking, candidates then would be more important for the uninformed but might still be less predictive of vote choice in absolute terms than for the best-informed voters.[9]

In terms of issue distances, the results presented in Figure 2.5 match the expectations formulated in Hypothesis 5 and Hypothesis 8b: Issue salience and political sophistication are positively associated with the weight of issue orientations on voting decisions. Interestingly, the interaction terms for ambivalence and cross-pressures are not significantly negative. Voters who perceive attitudinal ties of some sort, it seems, base their decisions rather on short-term than on long-term factors and on issue orientations especially.

---

[9] Or, put in another way: The minimal proportion of explained variance in this scenario would be higher for the low information group, but the maximum proportion of explained variance would be higher for the better informed.

Voter Fragmentation and the Differentiation of Vote Functions   35

Table 2.3 Model-fit of vote function for groups of voters

		McFadden's adjusted R^2
All voters		0.600
Only voters with…	…high sophistication	0.690
	…cross-pressures	0.296
	…ambivalence	0.382

Finally, Figure 2.6 reveals that Hypothesis 4 must be rejected. East Germans do not assign higher weight to the socioeconomic issue in their choices. Summing up these first analyses, heterogeneity was present in 2009 for the effects of all long- and short-term predictors of the vote function. While some of these differences are due to demographics, most variance in consideration weights we observed was caused by attitudinal characteristics or cognitive abilities.

This impression is reinforced by differences in model-fit of the vote function between different groups of voters. According to Hypothesis 7 and Hypothesis 8a, choices of the ambivalent and the cross-pressured voters should be least predictable by their attitudes, while the decisions of the most sophisticated should be most strongly associated with their attitudes. The results presented in Table 2.3 confirm these expectations. For all voters in the data set, the model reaches a high value of McFadden R^2 of 0.6, suggesting that the applied vote function explains voting decisions very well. For the highly sophisticated, this value increases to 0.69. By contrast, model-fit is much lower for the groups of cross-pressured and ambivalent citizens, for whom the attitude–behavior relationship indeed is weakened due to their conflicting beliefs.

Little surprising as these findings might be, they suggest that the homogeneity assumption indeed hides sizable differences between voters in their decision calculi. Furthermore, for some voter groups not only the effects of single predictors vary, but our explanatory models are not very well suited to explain the decisions of these voters at all. How voters who have equally strong feelings for more than one party or who have conflicting short- and long-term preferences decide certainly needs attention in future research. Moreover, the list of possible predictors of heterogeneity at the voter level is certainly not exhaustive. Other characteristics, such as voters' personality, might just as well be related to heterogeneous consideration weights.

2.7 HETEROGENEITY OVER TIME

In the remainder of the chapter, the perspective is now changed from a cross-sectional one to a longitudinal one. The question is how voter

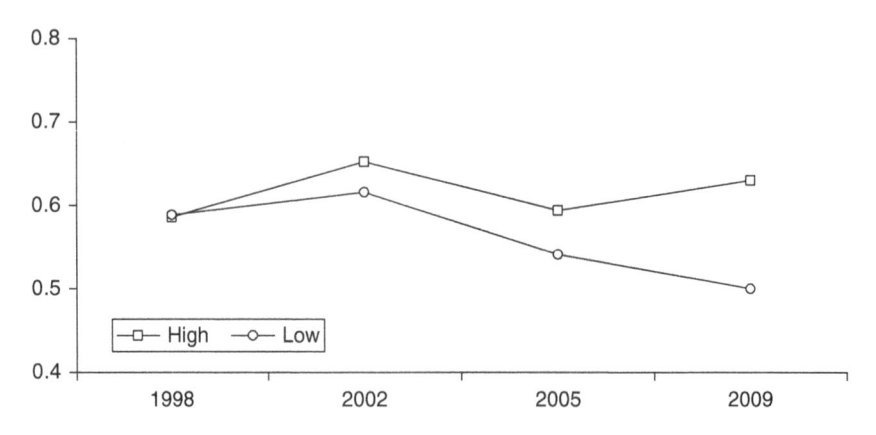

Figure 2.7 Model-fit of vote function for voters with low or high sophistication 1998–2009

Note: McFadden's adjusted R^2.

heterogeneity develops over time. Hypothesis 9 expresses the expectation that the increasingly complex choice situation in recent German elections has led to more heterogeneous calculi in the electorate. At the individual level consideration weights might be more stable, as suggested by Hypothesis 10. These two hypotheses are to be tested in this section.

The argument that heterogeneity is assumed to rise rests on the increasing complexity that has emerged in recent German elections. This development is reflected in an increase of cross-pressured voters (from 4.8% in 1998 to 7.3% in 2009) and of ambivalent voters (from 18.6% in 1998 to 23.5% in 2009). In terms of voting calculi, more complex choice situations are cognitively more demanding, so that the differences between highly and less sophisticated voters are likely to become larger. More politically sophisticated voters should be better able to adapt to the increasingly complex information environment. To test this proposition, Figure 2.7 presents the model-fit of the vote function for the two sophistication groups in the past four elections.[10] In 1998, electoral decisions of less sophisticated citizens could just as well be predicted by their attitudes as the decisions of the more sophisticated. Until 2009, the gap in explanatory power has risen to a 0.13 difference in terms of McFadden's R^2, confirming Hypothesis 9. The increasing complexity makes the decisions of less sophisticated voters more difficult to explain. These voters are more likely to make idiosyncratic choices or to be unable to cope with a choice situation that is less clear than a decade ago. For the highly sophisticated in contrast, the model-fit remained almost unchanged between

---

[10] As candidate orientations are not available in appropriate form for 1998, 2002, and 2005 this predictor was also excluded in 2009. For 2005, issue distances are not available.

Table 2.4 Stability of heterogeneity predictors over time 1998–2009

	Panel 1998–2005		Panel 2002–2009	
	1998–2002	2002–2005	2002–2005	2005–2009
Cross-pressures	0.03**	0.02*	0.06***	0.03
Ambivalence	0.05***	0.08***	0.10***	0.03
Political sophistication	0.45***	0.39***	0.20***	0.66***

Notes: phi coefficients; * $p < 0.05$; ** $p < 0.01$; *** $p < 0.001$.

1998 and 2009, suggesting that voters with higher cognitive abilities get along better with the changing political environment.

The last question that remains to be answered is to what extent there is intra-individual homogeneity over time, that is, how stable the consideration weights are over time at the individual level. To the extent that calculus heterogeneity is a function of social characteristics, differences in consideration weights can be assumed to be relatively stable as demographics typically are stable over time. However, we have seen that large parts of the variance in consideration weights are due to cognitive abilities or attitudinal characteristics. Table 2.4 displays the stability of these variables over time in two long-term panel data sets. While sophistication is rather stable in longitudinal perspective, cross-pressures and ambivalence are not. Obviously, attitudinal ties between parties are specific to a given election.

These are only indirect tests for the individual stability of consideration weights, though. To obtain a more direct assessment, the Pregibon's beta (1981) influence statistic can be used.[11] It is a measure of leverage similar to Cook's distance in linear regression and indicates the influence of each case by calculating how much the overall coefficient would change if this case was left out of the estimation. In a bivariate conditional logit model with a significant predictor this simply means to identify voters who make unexpected choices, such as voters who elect a party which is not closest to them in terms of Left–Right distance. The statistic can neither be interpreted as a self-contained measure of consideration weights nor does it provide theoretical explanations of any kind. However, it helps identifying those individuals who most strongly discount a given predictor of vote choice.[12] Table 2.5 shows phi coefficients for the association of dummy variables indicating the first quartile of most influential cases for all elements of the vote function in long-term panel data from 1998 to 2009. All coefficients are positive and significant, suggesting that voters who

---

[11] The statistic can be calculated in Stata with the option "gdbeta" of the command "predict."
[12] If conditional logit models are estimated only for the first quartile of the most influential cases, the effect of the elements of vote functions disappears or even reverses.

Table 2.5 Stability of most influential cases over time 1998–2009

First quartile of most influential cases for…	Panel 1998–2005		Panel 2002–2009	
	1998–2002	2002–2005	2002–2005	2005–2009
Party identification	0.11***	0.09***	0.10***	0.08**
Ideology	0.26***	0.18***	0.10***	0.10**
Party competence	0.17***	0.16***	0.14***	0.21***
Issue distance	0.25***	0.26***	0.28***	0.16***

Notes: phi coefficients; *p < 0.05; **p < 0.01; ***p < 0.001.

discount a predictor in an election at t_1 are also more likely to discount this predictor in election at t_2. The size of the correlations is relatively constant for all elements of the vote functions, with associations for issue distances being strongest. Hypothesis 10 is therefore supported by the results. The calculus of voters certainly is not a perfectly stable characteristic. But there clearly are tendencies for some groups of voters to systematically assign higher or lower weights to specific aspects of the vote function. This tendency of intrapersonal homogeneity should be studied in greater depth in further research.

2.8 SUMMARY AND CONCLUSIONS

This chapter was motivated by three basic aims: incorporating existing approaches to the study of voter heterogeneity into a more general theoretical and empirical framework, discussing moderators of the influence of considerations on vote choice at the voter level, and to bring the temporal dimension of calculus heterogeneity into the debate. It was argued that the homogeneity assumption of equal voting calculi should be abandoned in favor of more refined models. This makes explanations more complicated, but also more realistic. Heterogeneity can occur at very different levels. In this chapter, voter characteristics were discussed as predictors for variance in consideration weights. Social and attitudinal characteristics as well as cognitive abilities were hypothesized to influence how much voters rely on a specific aspect of the vote function. Using data from the 2009 German election it was shown that all three aspects contribute to the explanation of heterogeneous choice patterns for both short- and long-term predictors of voting decisions. Demographics such as age or church attendance primarily explain which voter groups are strongly guided by long-term aspects, whereas attitudinal characteristics and cognitive abilities account for variance in reliance on both long- and short-term considerations. Highly sophisticated voters, for example, tend to assign higher weights to issue orientations whereas cross-pressured voters rely less on partisanship. Generally, the attitude–behavior relationship is strongest for the highly sophisticated and lowest for voters holding conflicting beliefs about the parties.

Since the 1990s, the electoral choice situation has become considerably more complex in Germany. Increasing social differentiation, a changing party system, and complicated coalition building are likely causes of an electorate that becomes increasingly heterogeneous. While the most sophisticated voters are better able to adapt to this increasing complexity, the decisions of less sophisticated voters have become less predictable since 1998. At the individual level, voting calculi were shown to be stable to some extent. Those who rely on issue orientations in a given election are more likely to do so in the next election as well.

Overall, the findings strongly support the need of heterogeneity to be considered within standard models of electoral behavior. If homogeneous models were never quite appropriate to the actual complexity, they are now even less suited to explain vote choices in increasingly complex choice situations. The list of possible predictors of heterogeneity discussed here is certainly not exhaustive. For one thing, personality could possibly explain variation between voters in voting calculi, as well as stability within voters over time. This temporal dimension of heterogeneity had been almost completely overlooked by previous research. Both at the aggregate and at the individual level longer time frames and more in-depth analyses are needed to better understand inter- and intrapersonal heterogeneity in voting calculi from a longitudinal perspective.

3

Party-Specific Vote Functions

Aiko Wagner

3.1 INTRODUCTION

It is said that the way in which voters make up their mind is getting more complex. This relates to different evaluation criteria of the political supply as well. Although the idea "that the political parties created democracy and that modern democracy is unthinkable save in terms of the parties" (Schattschneider 1942: 1) is widely accepted, the characteristics of the parties only rarely come into view when studying voting behavior. The main approaches of electoral behavior seem to assume that all voters use the same criteria to assess the parties: Party identification does relate equally to all parties and a spatial utility is maximized in the same way, irrespective of the parties' features. Over the course of the last years, however, the literature challenging that view of "evaluation homogeneity" has been growing. The main thrust is that the criteria used to evaluate parties may vary across parties. This chapter will address this idea of *voting complexity as heterogeneity in the decision-making process*. Guided by the major idea of saliency theory (Budge and Farlie 1983; Petrocik 1996), the existing literature on party specificities in the components of the electoral decision will be summarized and integrated. Saliency theory tells us that not all political issues are of equal importance for all parties. Some parties are associated with a certain issue, whereas other parties are not. We will here extend this idea of systematic variance in issue importance to other elements of a general vote function: evaluation of party leaders and the parties' retrospective performance, ideological standpoints, and problem-solving capacities. In the following sections, we will discuss which characteristics of political parties may have an impact on the reasons why citizens vote for them.

Concerning different factors responsible for variations in the impact of the elements of a vote function, two kinds of argument can be distinguished. The first line of reasoning argues from a broader rational choice perspective: When is it rational to focus on which evaluation and choice criteria? If, for example, a party will presumably name the head of government, the evaluation of this party's top candidate should play a larger role than for a smaller party. Likewise, if a party proposes to implement a rather drastic and far-reaching policy change, the policy stands of this party vis-à-vis the voter's policy ideal would be expected to have a larger influence.

The second kind of argument is based on an information-processing perspective. Here, the focus is on the accessibility of information. The performance of the government is, for instance, easier to evaluate than that of opposition parties, because voters experience the results of the government's activities, whereas opposition policies are largely hypothetical.

After describing the hypotheses, they will be examined using data from the German Longitudinal Election Study (GLES) for the 2009 Bundestag election as the test case. In order to check whether the findings can be generalized, a subset of the hypotheses will be examined with data from the third module of the Comparative Study of Electoral Systems (CSES).

3.2 FACTORS SHAPING THE PARTY-SPECIFIC VOTE FUNCTIONS

By now, there is a variety of studies showing how the importance of different elements of the vote function varies across parties. However, there is no encompassing attempt to (comparatively) test existing hypotheses on party-specific differences in the impact of these elements. The following sections therefore summarize existing hypotheses on reasons why parties get their votes. Five factors proved to be of importance: party size, issue ownership, and government participation, as well as extremity and ambiguity of issue and ideological positions.

With regard to party size, three observations can be distinguished: Leaders and past performances are more important for larger parties for which issues and ideology tend to play a minor role. Firstly, it is argued that the voting calculi for larger parties may "be linked more strongly to the evaluation of their political leadership since it is more likely that these politicians are potential candidates for prime minister" (Kroh 2003: 213; Schmitt and Ohr 2000). This argument makes a lot of sense at first glance: If a person is politically more important the overall attitude towards this person should play a larger role in the choice process. Additionally, smaller parties have a special characteristic regarding the function of issues for their electoral fortune. Their core electorate tends to be more homogenous and, therefore, they do not have to compromise in order to avoid frightening off voters, but can state their points of view rather unequivocally (M. Wagner 2011b). Consequently, issue and ideological considerations can play a major role in voting for or against smaller parties.

Moreover, it has been found that larger (government) parties suffer more from bad economic performance (van der Brug, van der Eijk, and Franklin 2007). The same holds true for coalition governments: Larger coalition partners receive both more credit and more blame with regards to economic performance (Anderson 1995; Kroh 2003: 213).

Taken together, we hypothesize that for larger parties:

...*leaders are more important. (H1)*
...*issues and ideology play a minor part. (H2)*
...*evaluations of past performance are more important. (H3)*

Two prominent theories object the view of a monotonous issue and ideological influence for all parties. Saliency theory tells us that parties "do not compete by arguing directly with each other, but by trying to render their own areas of concern most prominent" (Budge and Farlie 1983: 23). Political parties try to appeal to the voters by highlighting "their" issues in the campaign. Association of certain parties with certain issues is a function of the parties' "performance in office, of the traditional interests of their core electorate, and of their issue emphases during electoral campaigns" (Lachat 2009: 2). An obvious example is the association of ecological issues with green parties. A related argument is made by Petrocik's issue ownership approach (Petrocik 1996; Petrocik, Benoit, and Hansen 2003), according to which parties have an issue-handling reputation, i.e., they are ascribed an "ability to resolve a problem of concern to voters. It is a reputation for policy and program interests, produced by a history of attention, initiative, and innovation toward these problems, which leads voters to believe that one of the parties (and its candidates) is more sincere and committed to doing something about them" (Petrocik 1996: 826). An "owned" issue obviously has to be of importance to the voters as well in order to become electorally decisive (Bélanger and Meguid 2008; Tavits 2008). Even though the notion of an issue being completely owned by one party only is not undisputed (Thurner, Mauerer, and Binder 2012), there is some evidence in favor of the issue ownership and saliency theory. Van der Brug (2004); de Vries (2010); Thurner, Mauerer, and Debus (2011); and Lachat (2009) found for different countries that issues relevant for the respective party have larger effects on voting. Furthermore, issue ownership is closely related to the idea of issue competence. It "refers to the classic idea that some parties are considered 'better' to solve a problem" (Walgrave, Lefevere, and Tresch 2011). In this respect, the issue-ownership hypothesis that built upon Stokes' work on the role of valence issues (1963) was verified in the sense that vote choice was found to be strongly associated with a party's ability to solve the most important problem (Clarke et al. 2009a; Klingemann 1973). Our hypotheses are quite straightforward here: "Owned" issues should be more important to the "owning" party. This relates to the spatial *(positions—H4)* as well as the valence *(problem-solving capacity—H5)* perspective of issues.

Whether a party is part of a government can impact the roles performance evaluations, ideology, and issues play. Government participation "forces parties to compromise and to accept ideologically unappealing choices as the best among available alternatives" (Bawn and Somer-Topcu 2012: 433), whereas opposition parties should raise issues for discussion challenging the government (Benoit 2007). Additionally, opposition parties have, by definition, no chance to prove their abilities in government. This is why they, firstly, stress issue and ideological positions more strongly while governments tend to "'celebrate' their successes" (Thurner, Mauerer, and Debus 2011: 2). Secondly, while voters can judge the performance of the governing parties in leading the country for the recent years, they have to rely more heavily on other factors as evaluation criteria for opposition parties. That is why Green and Jennings (2012) have found "support to a classic issue reward-punishment model for incumbents" but not for opposition parties (for similar findings see Bartle 2003; Stevens 2007).

Thus, for parties in government:

...issue and ideological positions are less important. (H6)
...evaluations of past performance are essential. (H7)

Building on the work of Stokes (1963), Rabinowitz and MacDonald (1989) stressed the role of extremity of the parties' political positions. They argued that issue[1] positions have to be differentiated into direction and intensity (cf. de Vries 2010). Only if the intensity of issue stands is sufficiently high do they translate into vote choices. Otherwise, "when parties occupy a centrist position on an issue they are not evaluated on the basis of that issue" (Macdonald, Listhaug, and Rabinowitz 1991: 1107). Additionally, Schmitt and Holmberg brought up that "the more extreme the ideological position taken by a party, the more likely is it to attract true believers rather than volatile pragmatists" (1995: 118). As true believers would hold similar positions as the party, the average proximity of the voters to this party should be higher than to other parties and, hence, the impact of proximity on voting stronger (cf. Kriesi and Sciarini 2004; Thurner, Mauerer, and Binder 2012). This reasoning is underscored by research on niche parties, i.e., parties that emphasize a (often noneconomic) policy neglected by other parties (B. Miller and Meyer 2011; M. Wagner 2011a). Niche parties are found to have a better chance of success if they stick to their more extreme positions and, hence, do not respond to shifts in public opinion in the same way as mainstream parties (Adams et al. 2006; Ezrow et al. 2011). Because they tend not to be in the center of the political spectrum, this refers likewise to the expectation that the more extreme the party's issue or ideological position is the larger its effects on voting should

---

[1] Although Left–Right ideology and issues are different concepts, some of the arguments relate to both; for this reason they are dealt with in common here.

be. Beyond raising the importance of issues, extremity has an impact on the significance of a party's perceived competence to solve the most important problems of a country. If parties are lumped together in the center of the ideological space and are hard to distinguish regarding their policy preferences, competence evaluations play a larger role in the electoral process (Green and Hobolt 2008). Moreover, it is often found that the electoral fortune of extremist and populist parties depends highly on the popularity of their leaders (Eatwell 2003; Müller-Rommel 1998).

In short, it is hypothesized that voting for and against more politically extreme parties depends more on:

...leader evaluations. (H8)
...issue and ideological proximities. (H9)
...the perceived capacity to solve important problems of the country. (H10)

The last factor concerns the level of clarity or ambiguity of the party's platform and its impact on the role of ideology and issues. One argument originates from the debate about catch-all parties and their lack of clarity concerning political positions (Gunther and Diamond 2001). Since they want to attract voters from different social backgrounds, ideology plays a subordinate role (Lobo 2008). But if a party platform is ambiguous in terms of issues and ideology, these criteria can hardly be used by the voters when they make up their mind. Due to this fuzziness of positions, the decision-making process of the voters has to rely on different criteria. One of those would be the personnel of the respective party (Gunther and Diamond 2003; Vetter and Gabriel 1998).

Ambiguous parties rely:

...more heavily on leaders. (H11)
...less on ideological and issue positions. (H12)

Table 3.1 summarizes these twelve hypotheses concerning the elements of the vote function that are expected to have differing impacts for different parties. Beyond that, the table allows us to see things from another perspective. Instead of looking at the party characteristics, we can examine the varying reasons to vote for the respective parties: leader evaluations, issue and ideological positions, and prospective as well as retrospective performance evaluations. These five elements of a generic vote function can also be found in the "Funnel of Causation" by Miller and Shanks (1996) that combines long-term and short-term factors. Furthermore, it covers the most relevant microlevel determinants of party competition (Bartolini and Mair 1990: 58) and of party choice (van der Eijk and Franklin 1996).

The fact that the electoral importance of leader characteristics and evaluations varies between parties is undisputed (Lobo 2008; van Wijnen 2000). If we focus on the "conditionality of leader effects" (Barisione 2009), three

Table 3.1 Elements of the vote function and factors according to which their impact may vary

Party characteristics	Elements of a vote function				
	Leader	Issues	Ideology (Left–Right)	Competence	Performance
Party size	+	–	–	+	+
Government participation		–	–		+
Extremity	+	+	+	+	
Importance		+		+	
Ambiguity	+	–	–		

party-related dimensions of the variation of leader importance can be distinguished: party size as well as extreme and ambiguous party platforms. Policies and political issues are undoubtedly central to democracy: In nearly all theories of democracy, parties are thought to be, to some extent, policy seeking (Katz 2006). Consequently, parties have to communicate their positions—on specific issues as well as on broader ideological scales. Both issue and ideological positions are assumed to be more important for smaller, more extreme, unambiguous, and opposition parties. Above that, this topic is an important factor for parties that are associated with a certain issue.

The last two elements relate to the parties' performance. From a democratic-theory perspective, a party's past performance should have a crucial impact on voting. If people are unsatisfied with the government's past performance they should simply vote it out of office. This very basic thesis is especially thoroughly tested in the field of economic voting (Lewis-Beck and Paldam 2000; Lewis-Beck and Stegmaier 2007). Past performance is especially important for larger and government parties. Theories emphasizing valence issues or party competence regarding certain policy areas found that capabilities to solve important problems play a major role for larger and more extreme parties as well as for parties that stress the respective policy area.

On a more specific level, the vote function applied empirically in the subsequent sections consists of the following variables: Firstly, even though parties are at the center of the analysis here, they are represented by politicians. Therefore, overall evaluations of party leaders (sympathy scales) as well as generalized party evaluations are included. The second section explains vote choice on the basis of a spatial model in which ideological proximities are used as overall utility measures (Downs 1957a). In addition to this rather long-term stable factor, specific issues of an election are considered in two ways. Firstly, in line with the rational-choice approach, political issues are analysed with a spatial model of issue distances (Enelow and Hinich 1984b). Secondly, issues play a role regarding the prospective evaluation of the parties' ability to deal with the most pressing problems the country is facing. Whereas this perspective focuses on the prospective competence, an encompassing or wide vote function must also comprise retrospective evaluations of the parties' performances in the last election period. As party identification has been found to be an important predictor of party choice—the "standing decision"—and as a control for endogeneity effects, it is included in every equation, too. To avoid a kitchen sink model, the five elements are analysed separately.

The following section will test the hypotheses for the German parliamentary election of 2009, determining to which degree the choice process of the German electorate differed across parties and can be characterized as complex in this sense. Afterwards, as many of our hypotheses as possible will be tested comparatively. Thereby, we can combine an in-depth test of all hypotheses for a single election with insights from testing some of those hypotheses for a plurality of elections.

3.3 PARTY-SPECIFIC EXPLANATIONS OF VOTING IN THE 2009 GERMAN BUNDESTAG ELECTION

The German election 2009 took place under unusual circumstances. The grand coalition, which was in office since the election in 2005, faced one of the most severe economic crises that was, however, not homemade (Bieber and Roßteutscher 2011). The coalition partners had to work together during the campaign, which might be the reason why it seemed "bland" and to bring forth only a "tame campaign rhetoric" (Rohrschneider and Jung 2012: 2). As the two largest, rather moderate parties were part of the coalition, the effects of party size, extremity, and governing status should overlap to a degree. This should be kept in mind when interpreting the results.

The data originates from the post-election cross-section data set of the German Longitudinal Election Study (GLES). The evaluation of the leaders of the five parties in the German Bundestag[2] was measured on an eleven-point like–dislike scale. The same applies to the generalized evaluation of the parties. To measure party identification we used the CSES standard measure ("Do you usually think of yourself as close to any particular party?" followed by "Which party do you feel closest to?").

---

[2] CDU and CSU are treated as one party because they form a single parliamentary group in the German Bundestag. Whereas CSU competes solely in Bavaria, CDU does so in all other *Länder*. Accordingly, evaluations and positions relative to the CSU and its top candidates were used for respondents from Bavaria.

The Left–Right distance is calculated as the squared distance between the voter's and the perceived parties' positions on an eleven-point Left–Right scale. The same is true for the three political issues. The first concerns the redistribution of income, constantly a pivotal topic for the German party system. Given that the 2009 election took place in times of an economic crisis, this issue gained additional importance. The endpoints of the eleven-point scale are "lower taxes/less government spending on health, education and social benefits" and "more government spending on health, education and social benefits/higher taxes," respectively. The second issue question deals with the subject of immigration laws and asks whether these laws should be relaxed or made stricter. Thirdly, respondents were asked to place themselves as well as the parties on a scale measuring attitudes towards nuclear power stations ("more nuclear power stations should be built" versus "all should be closed down today").

Competence of parties is measured by the response to the question on the perceived ability to solve the (again subjectively perceived) most important issue. Past performance measures how satisfied the respondent was "with the work of the following political parties over the last four years" (again on an eleven-point scale with the endpoints "totally dissatisfied" and "totally satisfied"). The dependent variable is (reported) vote choice for one of the parties in the Bundestag. Nonvoters and voters for the minor parties have been excluded from the analyses. All continuous variables have been standardized.

To avoid simply pooling all variables in an apples-and-oranges way, five different models have been calculated for the 2009 election. In all of them, party identification has been used as a control variable due to the fact that the feeling of being close to a party still proves to be a very strong predictor of voting behavior in Germany (Schmitt-Beck 2011), despite trends of de-alignment (Dalton 2012; Dassonneville, Hooghe, and Vanhoutte 2012).

Conditional logistic regression models with party-specific parameters (Thurner, Mauerer, and Binder 2012; van der Eijk and Kroh 2008) have been estimated on the basis of a "stacked" data matrix (van der Eijk et al. 2006). To model the party specificity, interaction terms of party dummies and the respective variable have been included in the model. The first question concerning all models is to which degree the elements of the vote function contribute differently to explaining vote choice for the five parties. If variances can be discovered, the second question asks for the reasons.

The Impact of Leader Evaluations in Germany, 2009

The model for assessing the impact of leader evaluations of party choice consists of party dummies (p_2 to p_5), the interactions of party dummies and party identification (PI), party dummies and leader evaluation (Leader),[3] and party dummies and party evaluation (Party Liking).

$$\text{Logit}(\text{Party Choice}) = \beta_1 \times p_2 + \beta_2 \times p_3 + \beta_3 \times p_4 + \beta_4 \times p_5 + \beta_5 \times p_1 \times \text{PI} + \beta_6 \times p_2 \times \text{PI} + \beta_7 \times p_3 \times \text{PI} + \beta_8 \times p_4 \times \text{PI} + \beta_9 \times p_5 \times \text{PI} + \beta_{10} \times p_1 \times \text{Leader} + \beta_{11} \times p_2 \times \text{Leader} + \beta_{12} \times p_3 \times \text{Leader} + \beta_{13} \times p_4 \times \text{Leader} + \beta_{14} \times p_5 \times \text{Leader} + \beta_{15} \times p_1 \times \text{Party Liking} + \beta_{16} \times p_2 \times \text{Party Liking} + \beta_{17} \times p_3 \times \text{Party Liking} + \beta_{18} \times p_4 \times \text{Party Liking} + \beta_{19} \times p_5 \times \text{Party Liking} + \varepsilon$$

The leaders of CDU/CSU were rated best (mean of 7.1 on the 11-point scale), followed by the SPD chancellor candidate (6.3). The leaders and candidates of the FDP and the Greens were evaluated similarly with an average value of 5.6 and the candidates of the Left the worst (4.9). But how did these evaluations contribute to the electoral fortune of the parties? Figure 3.1[4] shows the coefficients (triangles) and the 95% confidence intervals for party-specific effects of party and leader evaluation. Most importantly, it clearly shows that there is virtually no variance in the absolute importance of party leaders.

But Figure 3.1 illustrates at the same time that the importance of generalized party evaluations varies considerably. As the coefficients of generalized leader and generalized party evaluations are representing how important the personnel is vis-à-vis the party as a whole, the proportion of both—the leader-party ratio—can be interpreted as a measure of personalization (Wagner and Weßels 2012). All those five ratios lie well below one, pointing to the fact that parties are still more relevant as evaluation criteria than their leaders. For SPD and CDU/CSU the ratios are nearly identical at 45%, for FDP they are 40%, for the Greens 28%, and the Left 52%. Table 3.2 shows the distribution of the four independent variables of the second stage as well as the coefficient ratios of leader to party evaluation.

The evaluations of the Green candidate Renate Künast and FDP party leader Guido Westerwelle did not have as much influence as the evaluations of SPD and CDU/CSU leaders, which supports the idea that leaders matter more for larger parties. On the other hand, the ratings of the fairly polarizing top candidates of the Left—Oskar Lafontaine and Gregor Gysi—had the strongest impact on voting, comparatively. In terms of extremity of the

---

[3] If more than one candidate or party leader per party was evaluated, the mean of both evaluations was used. Again, for CDU/CSU, the values for CSU were used in Bavaria and for CDU in all other *Länder*.

[4] Because presenting 19 coefficients alongside with confidence intervals etc. in tables would be too confusing graphs are used to present the most important findings.

Party-Specific Vote Functions

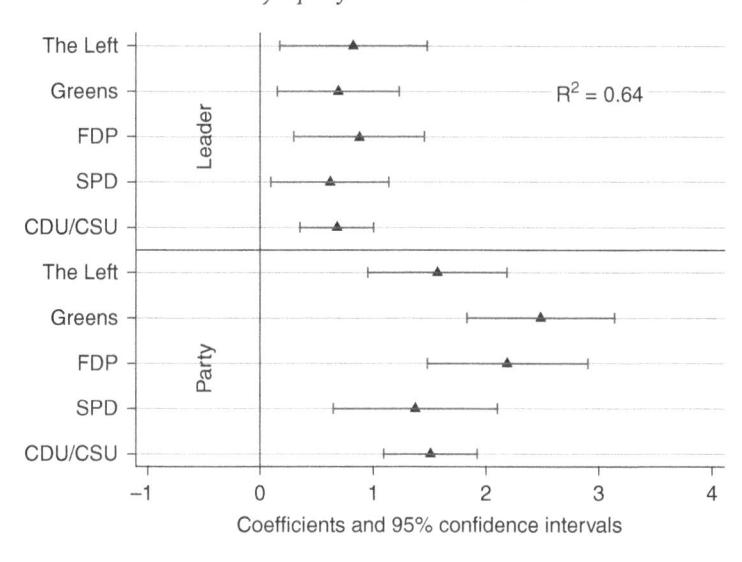

Figure 3.1 Regression results of the leader-evaluation model

Table 3.2 Party size, ambiguity, extremity, government participation, and leader-to-party impact ratio

Party	Party size	Left–Right ambiguity	Left–Right extremity	Government participation	Leader–party ratio
CDU/CSU	33.8	1.48	1.46	1	0.45
SPD	23.0	1.28	1.42	1	0.45
FDP	14.6	1.54	0.74	0	0.40
Greens	10.7	1.41	1.76	0	0.28
The Left	11.9	1.24	3.83	0	0.52

party's position, the results do not lead to a rejection of the hypothesis. Whereas the other four parties deviate less than two points from the midpoint of the Left–Right scale, the perceived average position of the Left is nearly four points left of the center. But again, this relationship is far from linear, especially with the Green candidate exerting such a low (relative) effect on vote choice. With respect to ambiguity, the hypothesis cannot be corroborated at all. The ambiguity of the ideological positions of the main parties—measured as the standard deviation in the people's perceived party positions—is rather low. If anything, the relationship is reversed: The Left and SPD as the two least ambiguous parties exhibit the strongest leader impact. In sum, we find only support for the claim that for more extreme parties leaders are more important.

The Impact of Ideological and Issue Distances in Germany, 2009

Ideology is one of the main sources of a party's utility for a voter. In the Downsian conception of democratic competition, the proximity of the parties to the voter determines the utilities arising from the voting act. The main axis of political competition is generated by the ideological Left–Right or liberal–conservative spectrum (Fuchs and Klingemann 1990). Therefore, (squared) distances between the Left–Right position of a voter and the perceived positions of parties proved to be an excellent explanatory variable for party choice (Dalton 2011). The following rather simple party-specific spatial model includes squared Left–Right distances, party identification, and party dummies as nonideological control variables.[5]

Left–Right distances explain party choice in the German 2009 election quite well (Figure 3.2). As expected, the coefficients of ideological distance are negative for all parties and statistically significant—the higher the squared distance, the lower the probability of voting for the respective party. This means that ideological similarities of voters and parties were important predictors of party choice in this case. However, there are differences between parties: Whereas the coefficients of ideological proximities for CDU/CSU, SPD, FDP, and the Left are rather similar, voting for the Greens seems to be driven to a larger extent by ideological proximity considerations.

Although the Greens were part of the opposition and one of the smaller parties, the hypotheses of weaker ideological effects for larger and governing parties cannot be confirmed, because the effects of the other small and opposition parties—FDP and the Left—are virtually indistinguishable from these of the larger and governing parties. The hypotheses concerning extremity and ambiguity do not achieve any support either. Firstly, the effect of ideological proximity for the most extreme party in terms of distance to the neutral point—the Left—is the same size as the effect for the center parties FDP and CDU/CSU. Secondly, regarding the (lack of) clarity of positions, the Greens do not stand out. Taken together, none of our hypotheses seems to provide an explanation as to why ideology did play a larger role for the Greens than for the other parties in 2009.

The second spatial model tested is an issue-position model. Here, squared distances between voters and the parties on the three mentioned issues—taxes and welfare state spending, immigration laws, and nuclear power stations—have been used in interaction with party dummies as independent variables. The model again comprises party identification interactions.

---

[5] The equation resembles the previous one on leader effects, with ideological distances instead of generalized party and leader evaluations.

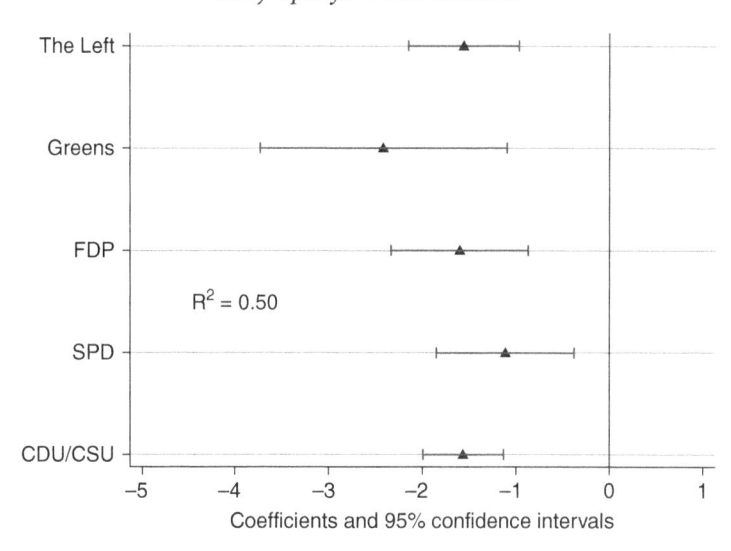

Figure 3.2 Regression results of the ideology model

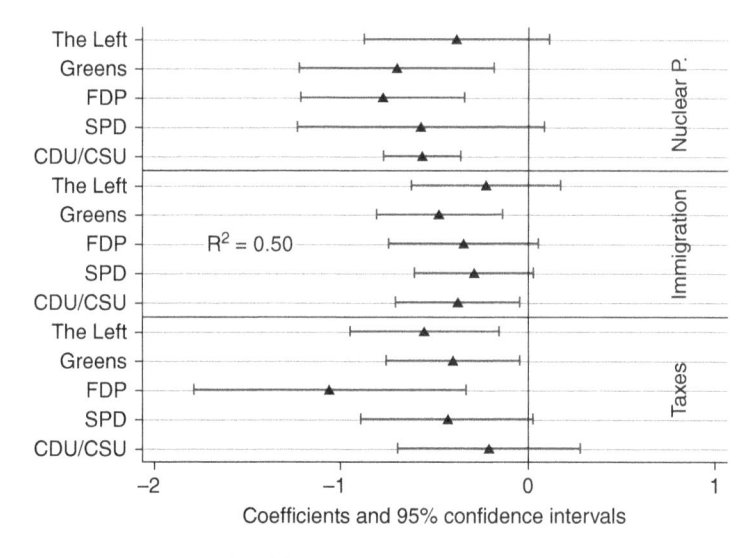

Figure 3.3 Regression results of the issue model

The results clearly show the varying importance of different issues for different parties (Figure 3.3). Parties' positions vis-à-vis the voters' own positions on the socioeconomic issue do not significantly contribute to the explanation of voting for SPD or CDU/CSU. In contrast, the position concerning tax increase or relief evidently played a role for voting for or against the Greens and the Left and a key role for the FDP. Even though immigration was not a major issue in

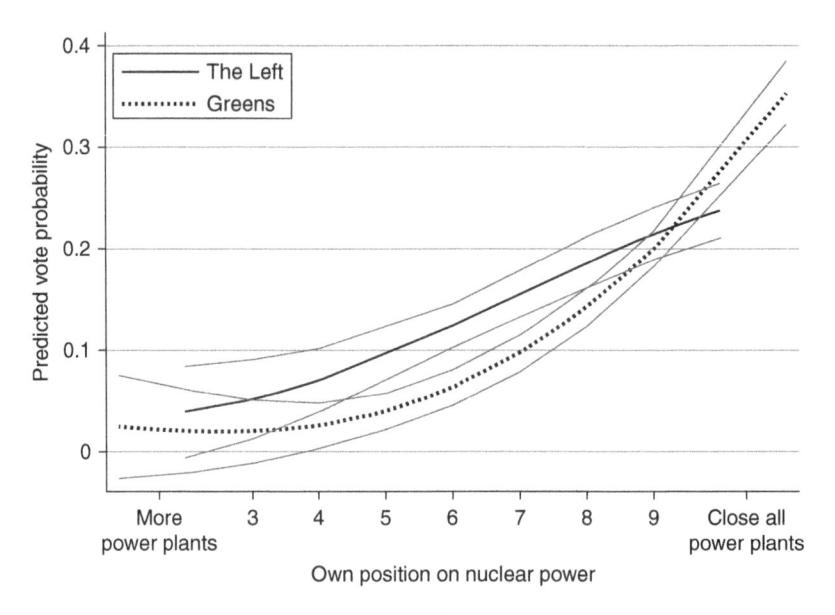

![Figure 3.4]

Figure 3.4 Example of the differing impact of issue position on voting

the 2009 Bundestag election, significant effects can be traced for the Greens and CDU/CSU. Concerning the further use of nuclear energy, statistically reliable effects are found for CDU/CSU, FDP, and the Greens, but not for SPD and the Left. This last difference is exemplified in Figure 3.4 in which the predicted probabilities to vote for the Greens or the Left are depicted against the voter's own position on the issue of building more versus closing down all power stations. The average perceived position of the Left on this issue is at 8.3 and that of the Greens at 10.2; both parties were in favor of closing down power stations, but the position of the Green party is much more pronounced. While the probability to vote for the Left increases with the voter's own position moving towards the anti-nuclear power pole, this relationship is much more distinctive for the Greens. The same is true regarding repulsion effects: The steepness of the probability curve points to the fact that for a moderate supporter of nuclear power stations voting for the Left is still probable, but voting for the Greens is very unlikely.

Can the proposed explanations account for this remarkable difference? Whereas in socioeconomic terms issue effects are only significant for the smaller parties, it seems to be exaggerated to state that issues generally matter more for small than for larger parties. Since the smaller parties were also opposition parties in 2009, the same applies for the hypothesis concerning governmental status.

Table 3.3 summarizes the values of issue extremity—measured as the absolute distance of the average perceived party position from the midpoint of

Table 3.3 Issue extremity and issue ambiguity

Issue	Party	Extremity	Ambiguity
Socioeconomic issue	CDU/CSU	1.09	2.24
	SPD	0.95	1.67
	FDP	*1.88*	*2.23*
	Greens	*1.08*	*1.98*
	The Left	*1.75*	*2.68*
Immigration issue	CDU/CSU	*1.68*	*2.27*
	SPD	0.70	1.80
	FDP	0.92	2.00
	Greens	*1.78*	*2.22*
	The Left	0.97	2.89
Nuclear power issue	CDU/CSU	*2.17*	*2.07*
	SPD	1.25	1.77
	FDP	*1.66*	*2.18*
	Greens	*4.17*	*1.55*
	The Left	2.26	2.06
	Mean of significant cases	2.02	2.14
	Mean of insignificant cases	1.16	2.06

the scale—and issue ambiguity—measured as the standard deviation of the perceived position of parties on the three scales. It shows the extremity and ambiguity of parties with a significant (in italics) and insignificant coefficient. The figures speak for themselves. Voters do use parties' positions in relation to their own as a yardstick for making their choice and all the more if parties occupy more pronounced issue positions (the difference between 2.02 and 1.16 reaches the 95% significance criterion). But whether a party's position is unambiguous is of no importance to the voters.

For testing the issue-ownership approach for German parties, the Manifesto data (Volkens et al. 2011) have been used.[6] There, the salience of a certain issue is measured as the share of statements on this issue in the party's manifesto. With respect to immigration laws, no fitting Manifesto coding category was found. Environmental protection (category 501) matches best for the issue of nuclear power. Not surprisingly, the Greens put twice as much emphasis on this issue as the other parties. Several categories may fit regarding the economy. Concerning controlled economy, welfare state, and Keynesianism

---

[6] The MARPOR project uses quantitative content analyses of parties' election programs to measure their political preferences. For more information see <https://manifesto-project.wzb.eu/information/information> accessed October 29, 2013.

(categories 412, 504, and 409, respectively), the Left can be differentiated from all other parties, while both SPD and the Left stressed labor market topics (701) more often than the other three parties. FDP (and to a lesser degree CDU/CSU) put emphasis on freedom of markets (414). Hence, we can further specify our hypothesis: Nuclear power should be especially important for the Greens, whereas socioeconomic topics should be particularly important for the Left and FDP; to a lesser degree for SPD and CDU/CSU; and the least for the Greens.

The first expectation does not hold true. The issue of nuclear power stations was important for voting decisions concerning the Greens, but also concerning FDP and CDU/CSU. CDU/CSU and FDP were the proponents of lifetime extensions for nuclear power stations (at least until the Fukushima nuclear disaster) and the Greens were strictly against it.

The question of taxes and welfare state expenditures was central for the FDP, but important for the Left, too. Although the effect just reaches the 95% significance criterion for the Greens and slightly misses it for SPD, the overall pattern fits with the expectation. If the topic of taxation, welfare state, and government intervention in the market is stressed in a manifesto, these issue positions do play a larger role for voting behavior. This amounts to a mixed overall picture: For the issue of taxation, the emphases in the platforms do play the expected role, but not so for nuclear energy.

The Impact of Prospective and Retrospective Performance in Germany, 2009

The issue-ownership theory suggests as well that different parties are associated with different issue areas in which they are perceived to be more competent than others. As past research has found (e.g., Lachat 2009) and we have seen in the last section, parties' manifestos express these differences. Whereas the last section analysed this topic in a framework of spatial models, we will now turn to a valence perspective concerning the most important problem the country is facing, and which party is thought to be best able to solve this problem. Do different perceptions of problem-solving capacities have different impacts on party choice? Again, the vote function we use consists of the party dummies and party identification, as well as the interactions with the competence to solve the most important problem (yes/no for the respective party) and evaluation of past performance.

Figure 3.5 shows the key results of such a model of prospective expectation of problem-solving competence and retrospective evaluation of the performance of the parties. The coefficients vary considerably referring to different mechanisms of how perceived competence translates into party choice. Whereas the impact was rather low for the longer-established parties—CDU/CSU, SPD, and

Party-Specific Vote Functions 55

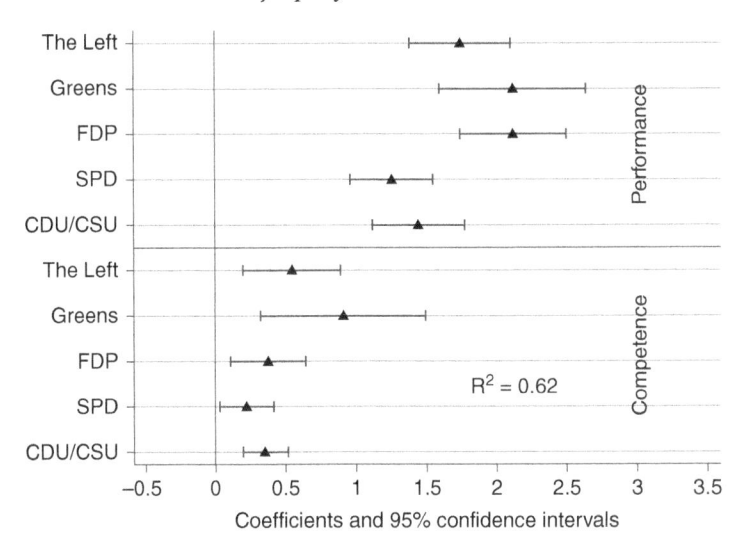

Figure 3.5 Regression results of the competence and performance model

FDP—the Left and the Greens could profit more from appearing competent. Overall, the effects for the larger parties tend to be a little less distinctive than those for opposition parties. But although these differences are rather small and hardly statistically significant, they point to the opposite direction than expected. The proposition of a stronger impact for extreme parties finds support, however. Competence on voting has a stronger influence for ideologically less moderate parties (the Left and the Greens) than for CDU/CSU, SPD, and FDP.

Regarding the assessment of the parties' past performance, clear patterns can be recognized. The influence of the performance measure on party choice is clearly higher for the smaller parties that were in the opposition as well. This may be the case because there was a grand coalition government and the economic crisis was believed not to be homemade (Beckmann, Trein, and Walter 2011). The economy went bad, but no one was to blame, and both large parties were in charge, as Anderson and Hecht (2012) put it. This special situation may have mixed up the previously found effects.

All in all, we find a considerable degree of variation in the importance of the single elements of the vote function between parties. However, only a few of the hypotheses brought forward on party-specific vote functions by the recent literature could be confirmed. On the basis of the results presented in Table 3.4, three dimension of interpretation can be distinguished: by the elements for which impact varies (I), by the factors explaining the variation (II), and by parties (III).

I. The hypotheses on the varying impact of leaders, issues, and problem-solving abilities are partly confirmed. Party leaders tend to be more

Table 3.4 Overview of confirmed and rejected hypotheses

Party characteristics		Elements of a vote function				
		Leader	Issues	Ideology (Left–Right)	Competence	Performance
Party size		partly confirmed	rejected	rejected	rejected	rejected
Government participation			rejected	rejected		rejected
Extremity		partly confirmed	confirmed	rejected	confirmed	
Importance			partly confirmed		confirmed	
Ambiguity		rejected	rejected	rejected		
Deviance: predicted minus reported vote shares	CDU/CSU	5.0	6.7	11.1	4.7	
	SPD	0.0	−0.8	−0.8	0.5	
	FDP	−3.4	−0.7	−5.4	−3.5	
	Greens	−1.5	−3.4	−3.6	−1.5	
	The Left	−0.1	−2.5	−1.4	−0.2	

important for larger and more extreme parties. Issue proximity of the party and the voters plays a more pronounced role if a party takes a more extreme stand on an issue and/or if this issue is of crucial importance to this party. The same is true for the party's perceived competence in solving important problems. On the other hand, variation in the influence of ideology and retrospective performance on voting in the 2009 German election could not be explained on the basis of the existing literature.

II. Concerning the factors explaining the variance it was argued that voters should give their vote to large and small parties for rather distinct reasons: Leaders and expected as well as past performances should be more important for larger parties, whereas issue and ideological distances should play a more important role for voting for smaller parties. But our results show that party size had just a minor impact on vote choice in the German case.

According to the literature, parties in government should be assessed more on the basis of their performance in the preceding legislative period and less on the basis of issue and ideological congruence in comparison to opposition parties. But instead, government participation showed no impact at all. With regard to moderate versus extreme parties, it was expected that the former's electoral success would rely more heavily on their leaders, their issue and ideological stances, and their ability to deal with apparently serious problems. For the German election 2009 it was shown that more extreme issue positions affected the relevance of issue proximity and problem-solving competence, whereas ideological extremity had only a slight impact on the importance of leader evaluations and none on the explanatory power of ideological proximity. The function of the importance of certain political topics is clear, though: The more relevant an issue or a problem is to a party, the more relevant it should be for the party's support. This proved to be true only for problem-solving competence, which co-varied strongly with the parties' reputation. But the importance and/or salience of a political topic exerted no systematic influence when issues were used as independent variables of party choice in a spatial-model framework. At last, ideological and issue ambiguity of a party was supposed to lead to a lesser impact of ideology and issues as well as to a pronounced effect of leader evaluations, but ambiguity showed no impact at all.

III. Looking at the differences between observed vote shares, i.e., the reported voting behavior in the survey, and predicted vote shares on the basis of the models allows us to make statements about which party's election result is explained best on the basis of which elements of the vote function. All in all, the vote share of the CDU/CSU is underestimated in all models. According to the vote functions applied, the chancellor's party was expected to gain more votes, on average 6.9 percentage points, than it got in the election. The opposite is true for the FPD, which gained more support than the models can explain (average 3.3% percentage points). This effect can be attributed to coalition-targeted voting. In 2009, supporters of a bourgeois coalition wanted to make sure that their vote did not end up supporting another grand coalition. Therefore, the optimal choice for them seemed to be voting for the liberal party (Weßels and Wagner 2011). In contrast, the explanation of the vote shares of the SPD comes close to perfection—irrespective of the model used. For the FPD, the issue model's predictions are closest to the observed voting behavior. The electoral fortune of the Greens depends on their positions on all three issues, whereas for the Left only their stance regarding taxes and welfare expenditure is of significant importance. For the Greens and the Left, leader evaluations and the parties' (retrospectively and prospectively evaluated) performance explain the electoral behavior best. And whilst the popularity of the SPD candidate may make a difference, the election outcome of the FDP depends to a lesser degree on their leader. These differences have, of course, major implications for our understanding of political competition in Germany.

Summing up, for four parties, CDU/CSU, SPD, the Greens, and the Left, the leader, party evaluation, and competence-performance models provide the best explanations for actual party choice. As this applies to two small opposition parties and two big, moderate government parties, no clear pattern can be distinguished. Is this the case because the German parliamentary election in 2009 took place under unusual circumstances and is, therefore, atypical? In order to answer this question, we now turn to a comparative analysis.

3.4 PARTY-SPECIFIC EXPLANATIONS OF VOTING: COMPARATIVE PERSPECTIVES

As we have seen in the previous section, the election in Germany in 2009 was characterized by some peculiarities—above all the severe economic crisis and the grand coalition. On the one hand, this led to special and partly unusual voting patterns (Banaszak and Doerschler 2012). On the other hand, this caused an overlap of some of the explanatory factors for the variance of vote functions: party size, government participation, and, to some extent, extremity of parties. Hence, not all reasons for variation could be selectively tested. To ensure generalizability of the present findings, we will concisely examine a broader sample of elections in the last step. For this purpose, we use the third module of the Comparative Study of Electoral Systems (CSES III). There we find questions on Left–Right positions of the voters as well as the perceived platform positions of the main parties. Information on the evaluation of party leaders and their parties, on perceived closeness to a certain party, and on ascribed problem-solving capacity is available as well. Data on twenty-two elections between 2005 and 2009 from twenty countries can be used for our purposes.[7] This number of elections allows us to apply statistical tests to inspect the hypotheses. A two-step approach will be applied (Achen 2005; Franzese 2005; Jusko and Shively 2005). In the first step, party-specific vote functions will be estimated for each country and element (leaders, ideological proximity,

---

[7] The following elections were used (including abbreviations): Australia 2007 (AUS_2007); Austria 2008 (AUT_2008); Switzerland 2007 (CHE_2007); Czech Republic 2006 (CZE_2006); Germany 2005 (DEU_2005) and 2009 (DEU_2009); Finland 2007 (FIN_2007); France 2007 (FRA_2007); Croatia 2007 (HRV_2007); Iceland 2007 (ISL_2007) and 2009 (ISL_2009); Israel 2006 (ISR_2006); South Korea 2008 (KOR_2008); Mexico 2009 (MEX_2009); The Netherlands 2006 (NLD_2006); Norway 2005 (NOR_2005); New Zealand 2008 (NZL_2008); Poland 2005

Table 3.5 Hypotheses to be tested comparatively

Party characteristics	Elements of a vote function		
	Leader	Ideology (Left–Right)	Competence
Party size	+	–	+
Government participation		–	
Extremity	+	+	+
Ambiguity	+	–	

and prospective competence expectation) using conditional logistic regression analyses and including party identification as a control. The results will be explained in the second step. There, the coefficients of, for example, competence evaluation for the different parties in all analysed elections will constitute the dependent variables which will then be regressed on the appropriate factors, in this case ideological extremity and party size. Table 3.5 summarizes the nine hypotheses that will be tested comparatively, including the expected direction of influence.

The first set of hypotheses looks again at the relative importance of leader vis-à-vis party evaluations. To ensure comparability of the coefficients across the different models (Mood 2010), our analysis does not straightforwardly focus on the coefficients of leader sympathy rating (β_{Leader}) but on a leader-party ratio ($\beta_{Leader}/\beta_{Party}$). Thereby, the model-specific bias in the coefficient is controlled for (Auspurg and Hinz 2011). Figure 3.6 shows a considerable degree of variation between the impacts of leaders of different parties at each single election.[8]

According to Table 3.6, we find no support for the assertion that leaders are more important for extreme parties.[9] However, party size and ideological ambiguity do relate to the relative impact of leaders in the expected manner.

(POL_2005) and 2007 (POL_2007); Portugal 2009 (PRT_2009); Sweden 2006 (SWE_2006); and Thailand 2007 (THA_2007). The study parts from Belarus 2008, Brazil 2007, Hong Kong 2008, Ireland 2007, Japan 2007, and Mexico 2006 had to be excluded from our analysis because of missing data on the most relevant variables (vote choice and party identification) or because the covered election was not a lower house election.

[8] Insignificant (relative) leader effects were recoded to zero. The same applies to the effects presented in Figures 3.7 and 3.8.
[9] A multilevel model was estimated because the eighty-eight parties are nested within eighteen elections (for some of the CSES countries, information on leader evaluations are missing). The pseudo-R^2 values are based on an OLS regression with clustered standard errors within each election. The impact of the leader evaluation of the French Front National is fifteen times as high as the impact of the party's assessment. For this case, the hypotheses of extremity and size are confirmed. However, such an extreme outlier would bias the analysis of the second stage. Therefore, the Front National has been excluded from the analysis as four other unduly influential outliers (according to the Cook's distance).

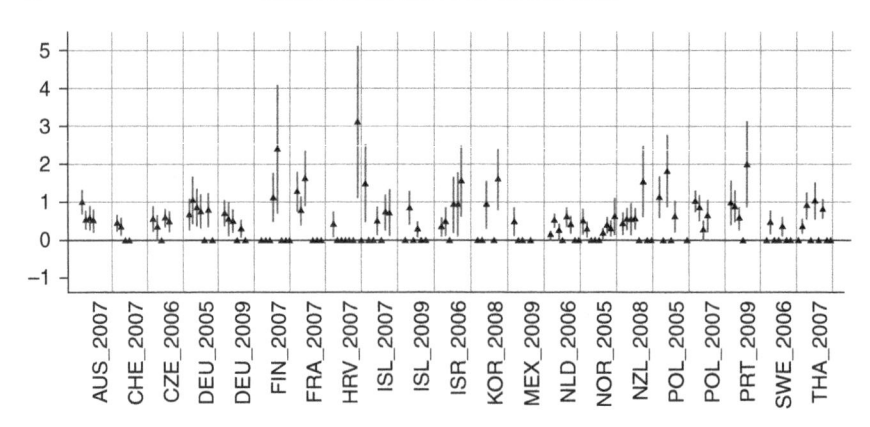

Figure 3.6 Distribution of relative leader impact on voting in twenty-one elections

Table 3.6 Multilevel regression results for coefficients of leader–party ratio

Variable	Coefficient (standard error)
Extremity	−0.01 (.60)
Party size	0.007* (.004)
Ambiguity	0.21+ (.12)
Constant	−0.13 (.22)
LogLikelihood	−38.92
Pseudo-R^2	0.09
N	88 parties, 18 elections

Notes: + = significance on 10% level; * = 5%.

The larger or the more ambiguous the party regarding its ideological stance, the more personalized is the calculus of its voters (and nonvoters). The weak explanatory power of the model points to the fact that large parts of the origins of the observable heterogeneity of the impact of political personnel are still unknown.

Turning to the impact of Left–Right proximity on voting we find again a large amount of variation both between and within each country (see Figure 3.7). For two of the seven parties in the Austrian election, for example, ideological proximity did not play a significant role (and was set to zero) and the impact for the first party is only about a third of that of the fourth party. For each election, the proximity coefficients were calibrated in relation to the largest one. The resulting values reach from zero—no and/or insignificant impact—to a maximum of one. This results in a proportionate-importance

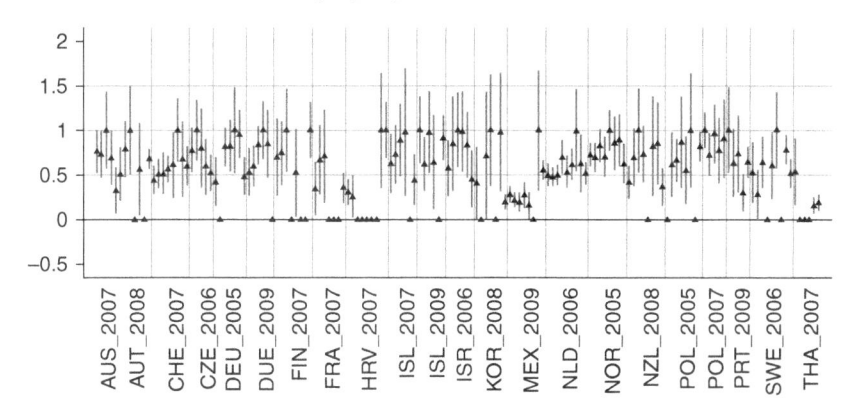

Figure 3.7 Distribution of Left–Right impact on voting in twenty-two elections

measure assessing how important Left–Right proximity was for a certain party in the respective election in relation to the party to which it showed to be most important. Again, variance is not only found between countries[10] but as well within countries across different parties.

Can this variance be attributed to the proposed factors of party size, extremity, ambiguity, and government participation? The results presented in Table 3.7 point to a rather stable influence of ideological proximity on voting, which is independent of a party's size, its level of clarity of standpoints, and of the question of whether it is part of the government or opposition. Extremity exerts a significant impact on the importance of Left–Right distances. If a party is perceived as rather extreme, its ideological position does play a larger role for voting, underlining the distinct character of niche parties. The exact position of moderate parties, on the other hand, seems to be of lesser importance. The proportion of explained variance is not overwhelmingly high (17%). But this is also no particularly weak result when we take into account that no country-specific variables have been included, although the importance of Left–Right is country-specific.

The perceived ability of parties to solve a country's most important problem is the last element of the vote function that will be analysed comparatively. Figure 3.8 shows once more a noticeable degree of variation between parties. Yet again, there are differences between elections as well.[11] Whereas for some

---

[10] The existence of significant variance on the upper level, i.e., elections, above the included factors, supports earlier findings on the differing relevance of ideology (Klingemann and Weßels 2009; Kroh 2003). Again, two parties yielding an exceptionally high bias were excluded.

[11] This time, variance across elections does not reach the usual thresholds for significance. This underlines the relevance of party-specific in contrast to country-specific reasons for the variation in the impact of competence on party choice.

Table 3.7 Multilevel regression results of rescaled Left–Right distance coefficients

Variable	Coefficient (standard error)
Extremity	0.06** (0.02)
Party size	0.27 (0.21)
Ambiguity	−0.07 (0.10)
Government participation	0.05 (0.06)
Constant	−0.13 (0.22)
LogLikelihood	−17.20
Pseudo-R^2	0.17
N	103 parties, 20 elections

Note: ** Significance at 1% level.

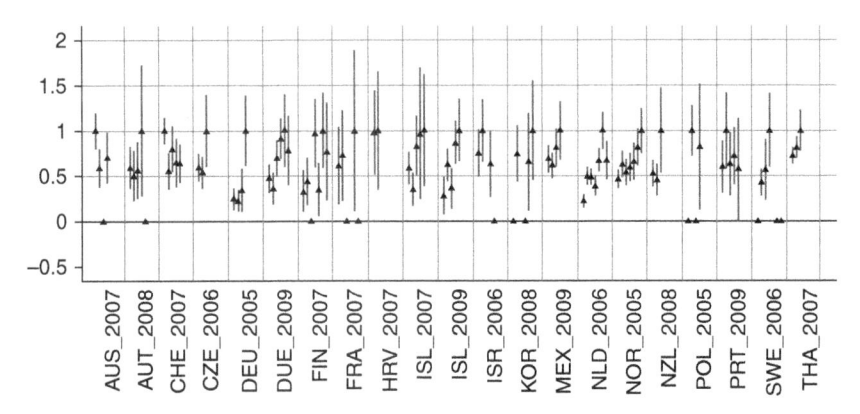

Figure 3.8 Distribution of competence impact on voting in twenty-one elections

elections, e.g., in Thailand, the perceived ability to deal with the country's pressing problems was of similar importance for all parties, its impact varies considerably in other countries such as the Netherlands.

The hypotheses suggested that variation across parties is caused by the parties' size and extremity. Based on the model's results, the extremity conjecture must be rejected (see Table 3.8). The most interesting finding, however, is that party size matters for the extent to which competence translates into party choice, but its influence runs counter to the hypothesis. As for the 2009 election in Germany, competence proves less important for larger parties in the comparative analysis. The smaller parties profit most from appearing to be able to solve the problems a country is facing.

What the comparative perspective amounts to is somewhat sobering: Only three out of nine hypotheses are confirmed. The most central findings are,

Table 3.8 Multilevel regression results of rescaled competence coefficients

Variable	Coefficient (standard error)
Extremity	0.02 (0.03)
Party size	−0.01** (0.004)
Constant	0.79** (0.08)
LogLikelihood	−8.74
Pseudo-R^2	0.18
N	59 parties, 15 elections

Note: **Significance at 1% level.

firstly, that parties of different sizes get their votes for different reasons. Whereas leader evaluations are more important for larger parties it is, surprisingly, the other way around for problem-solving competence. The reason may be that such ability is expected from the larger parties anyway. Secondly, ideological proximity plays a larger role for extreme than for moderate parties. Thirdly, when parties' positions are ambiguous with regard to Left–Right scales, evaluations of party leaders gain importance. The two last points can be related to some contemporary populist parties. If these manage to leave the voters in the dark about their extreme positions in order to avoid deterring potential voters, they may profit from the charismatic appeal of their leaders (van der Brug and Mughan 2007).

3.5 CONCLUSION

In this chapter, we have asked whether all parties are evaluated on the same grounds, as implicitly assumed in most theories on electoral behavior, or whether there is such a thing as party-specific vote functions. Specifically, we looked at the reasons why parties get their votes. After a short overview of the most relevant, scattered literature on this topic, a series of hypotheses was explicated. Based on the results of the German parliamentary election of 2009, the main question can be evidently answered: The causes of party choice are not identical for different parties. Regarding the explanations of this heterogeneity, only some hypotheses derived from the literature could be confirmed. In particular, the importance of issues for a party and its moderateness or extremity helped to explain why some issues and problems were more relevant for the electoral fortune of certain parties. After investigating all hypotheses on one election, we turned to a comparative test. Analysing twenty-two elections of the third CSES module showed that the heterogeneity of vote functions is ubiquitous. However, only one-third of the hypotheses passed the tests. The most important results point to the role of party size and extremity of party positions. If the trend towards more ambiguity of party positions proves to be true, leaders will gain more importance for the electoral decision-making process. But this does not necessarily imply a trend towards a personalization of politics as contemporary party systems are rather characterized by fragmentation than by concentration, and larger parties dominating the party system are becoming rare. With smaller parties and, thus, a decrease of leader importance on the one hand and more ambiguous party positions and an increased relevance of the parties' personnel on the other hand, there should be conflicting trends at the same time.

Besides, it appears that the results found in analysing the German election of 2009 cannot be generalized easily. Whereas ideological extremity did not play a role for the impact of ideological proximity in Germany, it clearly does in the comparative analysis. On the other hand, the hypothesis that problem-solving competence is more important for larger parties was rejected for the German case as well as comparatively. This emphasizes the advantages of comparative inquiry, while the fact that the varying impact of issues could not be analysed comparatively underlines the relevance of case studies.

There is not only an abundance of factors shaping electoral behavior, they are multidimensional as well. One of these dimensions is that most of the factors have a significantly different magnitude of influence on different parties—there are different reasons for the electoral fortune of large and small parties, of extreme and moderate parties, of programmatically ambiguous parties and parties with unequivocal positions. We took a first step to overcome the mainly fragmented research by combining the relevant but specialized perspectives on issue ownership, personalization, and performance evaluation. It seems that voting behavior is more complex than most theories assume. Yet, more work needs to be done in order to define this complexity more closely in terms of reasons for the variation in the impact of different elements of vote functions. As mentioned above, national-level factors like the polarization and fragmentation of the party system have been found to play a role and should be considered as well. Therefore, the next step toward a thorough answer to the question of the origins of complexity may be to develop a theory that integrates the roles of macro- and meso-factors for party-specific decision-making processes of individuals.

4

Coalitions and Voting Behavior in a Differentiating Multiparty System

Sascha Huber

4.1 INTRODUCTION

In multiparty systems voters face not only more difficult decisions, as there are more options than in two-party systems, but they are also confronted with higher uncertainty about the future government. Compared to plurality systems, where party choices translate more directly into the formation of a government, voters in proportional representation (PR) systems are confronted with a more complex decision environment. If they want to select a future government, voters will have to take into account and evaluate coalitions that might be formed after the election. Until now, voting research has not dealt much with such evaluations and their impact on electoral behavior. Although most countries with parliamentary systems are governed by coalitions, voting research—originating in the Anglo-Saxon world of two-party systems—has been focusing almost exclusively on parties or candidates. Coalition considerations of voters were ignored most of the time—also in research dealing with electoral choices in multiparty systems. Even though Downs (1957a) indicated early that voters in multiparty systems shall take coalitions into account, he was at the same time very skeptical about whether voters actually do. Only recently, coalition considerations of voters are systematically investigated (see Blais et al. 2006; Hobolt and Karp 2010; Duch, May, and Armstrong 2010).

In this chapter, it will be examined whether vote choices in the German multiparty system are guided not only by party and leader evaluations but also by coalition evaluations. It is argued that coalitions are meaningful political objects for voters in multiparty systems that can have effects on vote choices independent from party and leader evaluations—not only for sophisticated voters. With a growing number of parties and an increasingly complex party system over time, coalition considerations might have become even more important—as political objects and as cues for voting behavior.

4.2 THEORY

Vote Choices in Multiparty Systems

Most of the literature on voting behavior has focused on two political objects: parties and candidates. Naturally, there was not much talk about coalitions in the classic American literature (Berelson, Lazarsfeld, and McPhee 1954; Campbell et al. 1960a). In a presidential, two-party system coalitions just do not occur. In parliamentary systems with PR and multiple parties, however, coalitions can be meaningful political objects. Voters will, for instance, relate to a government that is most of the time made up by more than one party, and they will also relate to an opposition that often contains more than one party. Still, adaptations of the classic literature on voting behavior to other countries with multiparty systems often neglected coalition considerations altogether.

Early on, Downs (1957a: 147) emphasized the different and more complex decision environment that voters face in multiparty systems: "each vote supports a party which will have to compromise its policies even if elected; hence the policies of this party are not the ones which a vote for it actually supports. Instead the vote supports the policies of whatever coalition the party joins." That is, instrumental voters should not only keep in mind what each party stands for but they should also anticipate which coalitions might be formed after an election and which compromises might be implemented by possible coalitions.[1] This involves much more uncertainty and complexity. Downs was therefore very skeptical about the chances of instrumental voting in multiparty systems: "In systems usually governed by coalitions, most citizens do not vote as though election were government-selection mechanisms" (Downs 1957a: 300). According to this view, voters in multiparty systems will not so much vote in order to select a government but rather in order to be represented by a party or to express a preference for a party. Being confronted with the uncertainty of various potential coalitions, they will stick to a more simple calculus involving only parties and candidates.

---

[1] The theoretical literature on electoral and governmental decision-making in multiparty systems often assumed that voters will anticipate or react to outcomes of the coalition formation process (e.g., Austen-Smith and Banks 1988) and coalition and inter-branch bargaining (e.g. Alesina and Rosenthal 1995, Persson and Tabellini 2000).

Instrumental and Expressive Motives of Coalition Voting

A growing literature on strategic voting in PR systems suggests that this view was maybe a bit too skeptical and that voters also apply instrumental coalition considerations in multiparty systems (Cox 1997; Duch, May, and Armstrong 2010). Bargsted and Kedar (2009) showed that coalition expectations were a significant factor of voting behavior in Israel. Carman and Johns (2007) examined elections for the Scottish Parliament and found hints for ticket-splitting based on coalition preferences. Irwin and van Holsteyn (2003) demonstrated for the Netherlands that voters adapt vote choices to different coalition scenarios. For Austria, the interplay of expectations and coalition preferences was found to have an effect on voting (Meffert and Gschwend 2010). In Germany, it has been demonstrated that coalition considerations did have an influence on vote choices (Gschwend 2007, Bytzek and Huber 2011) and that especially small parties like the FDP can benefit from coalition voting (Shikano, Herrmann, and Thurner 2009; Huber et al. 2009). These strategic voting studies were naturally focusing on the strategic component of vote choices. That is, they were concentrating on the interplay of coalition expectations and coalition preferences. If voters were only instrumentally motivated, the impact of coalition preferences in PR systems would depend on expectations. Preferences for coalitions would only be important if specific expectations about the outcome are met (e.g., Bowler, Karp, and Donovan 2010). One example is the so-called "coalition insurance strategy" that was proposed for the German party system with two big parties and various small parties. The strategy takes into account the thresholds, not the parties (e.g., Pappi and Thurner 2002): If the potential small coalition partner of a preferred big party is in danger of not exceeding the threshold, supporters of this big party may deviate from their first preference and vote for the small potential partner in order to secure the formation of this coalition. This deviation from the preferred party is thus conditional on the expectations about the result of the election and the following coalition bargaining process.

However, it is obvious that voters with instrumental motivations will face a very difficult vote decision in multiparty systems and that not all voters actually will be capable or willing to engage in a rather complicated calculus including expectations about the outcome of elections, the perception of coalition signals sent out by parties, and the anticipation of the coalition formation after the election. Even though there are now interesting results suggesting that some voters do apply this logic, Downs' skepticism does not seem to be entirely unreasonable. In this chapter, I will argue that Downs was probably not too wrong with his skepticism about how many voters will instrumentally select governments in multiparty systems, but he was probably mistaken when expecting that voters facing the complexity of the decision environment will always fall back to simple party voting. Voters might still have coalition preferences and they may want to express them with their vote, independent from complex instrumental reasoning weighing expectations and coalition signals. That is, vote choices might be not only influenced by instrumental coalition considerations but also by expressive coalition considerations.

According to theories of expressive voting, voters have not only instrumental goals like selecting a government, but they are also motivated by just expressing their preferences (e.g., Brennan and Lomasky 1993). Expressing one's own preferences might be a good in itself providing utility independent of the policy outcomes of a future government. In his comprehensive account of expressive choice, Schuessler (2000: 15) used the metaphor of a jukebox that people will not only use in order to hear a song but also to establish an identity: "Participation is not only a means for me to create the Frank Sinatra outcome on the jukebox—it is also a way for me to establish, reaffirm, demonstrate, and express my Frank Sinatra*ness* to the rest of the world, as well as to myself." Theories of expressive choice thereby focused on parties and candidates. By voting for a party or a candidate one can express something about oneself. In this perspective, voting for Obama in 2008, for instance, would generate direct utility by demonstrating a tolerant and antiracist attitude. Or voting for the Green party in Germany would demonstrate that one is a "good" person, being conscious about environmental issues.

Expressive motives will not be restricted to parties and candidates. In multiparty contexts, one may also find it attractive to express coalition preferences. Having stronger preferences for coalitions than for parties may signal that one is adapting to the changing political supply and the performance of government; that one is flexible and maybe more "individual" and "complex" than just sticking to one party or candidate once and for all. Take, for instance, a supporter of the SPD in Germany. She may think of herself as being "social" and "caring for the poor." As a self-concept, this may still be a bit narrow and one-dimensional. So she may also want to express that she is "tolerant" and "idealistic." One way of demonstrating these dimension of one's self-concept is to vote based on coalition preferences (here, for instance, SPD–Greens), because the coalition preference represents a fuller or more attractive picture of oneself. Or to reformulate the metaphor of Schuessler (2000), it may be appealing to demonstrate the own "Sinatraness" all the time at the jukebox, but it may be even more appealing to demonstrate a more complex or nuanced picture by sometimes choosing another artist. One may choose Sinatra one time and, say, Radiohead another time. Or even better, if possible, one may choose two songs: Sinatra and Radiohead.

The Case of the German Electoral System: Incentives for Coalition-Directed Voting

The German electoral system with two ballots exactly provides for this possibility—choosing two "songs" at the same time. Voters can split their vote and choose a candidate of one party with the first vote ("Erststimme") and another party with the second vote ("Zweitstimme"). This two-vote system should suit expressive coalition motives as voters have the easy opportunity to express themselves. If there was only one vote, a defection from the preferred party would always come with some psychological costs and voters would have to trade off the utility they would gain by expressing some coalition preference— by voting for a junior partner of the preferred party for instance—against the utility they would gain by expressing their party preference. With two votes at hand, one can easily express both, demonstrating both the identity that is associated with the party preference and the identity that is associated with the coalition partner. One does not need to choose between one's "Sinatraness" and one's "Radioheadness"; one can express both and maybe demonstrate an even richer personality than the sum of the parts.

For instrumental reasoning the German election system is not that easy. The mixed member proportional system (MMP) with two ballots combines single member district representation with proportional outcomes, and is therefore often described as the "best of both worlds" (Shugart and Wattenberg 2001). From an instrumental voter's view, however, MMP systems can be quite challenging. Voters first need to know the different meaning of the two votes: the first vote using a majoritarian logic of choosing a local candidate and being the less important one and the second vote for a party list using a proportional logic for determining the composition of the parliament and thus being the more important one.

Second, they need to consider different strategic considerations for both ballots. For the first vote ("Erststimme") or candidate ballot, voters need to follow the logic of a majoritarian election and assess the chances of the various candidates of winning the district. Voting for candidates with no chances of winning the district will be a wasted vote. Therefore, there is the incentive to restrict choices to the viable candidates in the district, normally the candidates of the big parties. For the second or party list vote ("Zweitstimme"), voters need to follow the logic of a proportional election, keeping in mind potential thresholds and possibly considering coalition signals in multiparty systems. As outlined above, voters who want to influence government formation may not only consider which party comes closest to their political views but also try to anticipate the chances of the various parties of entering parliament and forming a specific coalition. Considering the strategic incentives for the two votes together, a relatively clear pattern of potentially insincere voting emerges. For the plurality ballot of a local candidate, there will be a tendency of small party supporters to deviate. For the party list PR vote, it might be rather the supporters of big parties who vote insincerely in order to help a potential coalition partner to exceed the threshold. As the relative strength of the parties in Parliament is almost entirely determined by the PR pillar, the consequences are quite different: Insincere voting on the plurality ballot for local candidates will not weaken the preferred party, but insincere voting on the party list ballot will weaken the own party.

Finally, instrumental voters should cast the two ballots independently. Having made a decision for one vote should not influence the decision for the other. As MMP is not a preference voting system, in which one might indicate the first preference with the first vote and the second preference with the second vote, it does not make sense just to split votes between the first two preferred parties. Similarly, it is not possible to indicate a preferred coalition by splitting the votes between coalition partners. As votes in the two pillars are counted separately, this potential signal will not reach any political actor and the coalition formation process will not be influenced by the amount of votes that were split between any of the parties. Therefore, instrumental voters should make decisions separately for each of the two votes.

Expressive voters, on the other hand, will not care too much about the institutional logic of the electoral system. They might be satisfied with the opportunity to cast two votes and thereby possibly express more of their personality and identity. There is some evidence that voters actually are often influenced by the existence of a second vote. Cox and Schoppa (2002) showed that parties presenting a candidate in the plurality pillar will increase their chances of votes in the party list PR pillar. Hainmueller and Kern (2008) analysed contamination effects of the incumbency of local candidates on the share of votes in the party list PR pillar in Germany and found that the share of *Zweitstimmen* was increased about 1.4 to 1.7 percentage points, if the local candidate of the plurality pillar was the incumbent. Ferrara, Herron, and Nishikawa (2005) examined the consequences of the mixed electoral system for the Italian Senate and found interaction effects between both votes. For New Zealand, Karp (2009) showed that the popularity of local candidates had an influence on the evaluation of parties. Contamination effects have also been shown for the Ukraine, Lithuania, and Russia (Herron and Nishikawa 2001; Ferrara, Herron, and Nishikawa 2005). These effects are not necessarily based on expressive motives. There might also be other reasons for these results, like a lack of electoral knowledge. Still, contamination effects are the expected outcome if voters do mainly care about preference expression.

Differentiation of Party Systems and the Number of Parties

The number of alternatives will generally influence the complexity of voting decisions and they may also have an impact on coalition-directed voting. In general, judgments between alternatives should be easier in a two-party system than in a five-party system. The more alternatives there are the more information is needed to discriminate between them. This holds whether voters use substantive information or whether they rely on heuristics and simple cues. Take, for instance, the easy heuristic of Left and Right: if a voter wants to vote for a "Left" party, in a two-party system it is enough to know which of the two parties is "Left" and which party "Right." In a multiparty system with more than one "Left" party, this simple heuristic is no longer decisive and more cues or substantial information are needed. The difficulty of an instrumental voting decision might therefore increase with the number of alternatives. In psychology, there is growing evidence that too many options actually do pose a problem for decision-making. Experimental research has shown that people are more likely to feel capable of choosing when there are small numbers of alternatives and that they are also more likely to be satisfied about the decision afterwards (e.g., Iyengar and Lepper 2000). This applies in particular when people have no clear preferences (Chernev 2003) and when decisions are complex (Greifeneder, Scheibehenne, and Kleber 2010). These findings also correspond to results of participation research in political science. Comparative studies repeatedly find a negative impact of the number of parties on turnout (e.g., Blais 2006, Jackman 1987). One possible reason of these results is the higher demands of multiparty systems with many alternatives.

These demands may even get higher when voters not only care about the various parties but also care about the resulting coalitions. If all parties in a system would potentially form a coalition with each other, the possible coalitional outcomes of an election would be exponential to the number of parties. Often, however, parties signal their willingness or unwillingness to engage in a particular coalition before an election, which will reduce the number of feasible coalitions and therefore also the complexity of instrumental coalition voting. A rather manageable coalition context would be, for instance, a four-party system with two camps, one camp to the Left and one to the Right. If parties form only coalitions within these two camps, voters might still be able to calculate the various coalition outcomes. If, however, one party would change its coalition preferences, things would become more complicated again. With the entrance of a fifth party into the system, coalition dynamics would become even more complicated as a parliamentary majority is harder to reach for two parties alone. A case in point is the 2005 election in Germany when the CDU/CSU and the SPD did not reach a majority with their favorite small coalition partners. Neither of them wanted to form a coalition with the fifth party, the former communist party, and eventually they had to form a grand coalition. Thus, instrumental coalition considerations will usually become much more complex when the number of parties increases.

At the same time, expressive coalition reasoning might become even more pronounced with an increasing number of parties in a system. Just as one might rather choose different songs out of a jukebox when the number of songs in that jukebox increases, voters might also express more nuanced views with their vote when there are more parties in the system. The more coalitional options there are, the more tempted voters might be to split their vote.

Splitting might also be an easy way out of the decision dilemma that voters face with a big number of party alternatives. If a voter wants to express that he is leftist and liberal, but he is not sure which of two parties would signal this best and is maybe also not willing to get more information on the particular parties, he could just express a preference for a combination of these parties. That is, he would have a strong preference for a coalition of these parties. And with the German two-vote system he could even vote for both.

The skepticism of Downs regarding the capability of voters to vote instrumentally in multiparty systems already showed that even rational choice scholars acknowledged the complexity of instrumental coalition considerations. There is some evidence that it is often mainly sophisticated voters who have the capacity and the knowledge to weigh coalition considerations strategically (e.g., Meffert et al. 2011). Unsophisticated voters, on the other hand, do often lack the capability and the necessary knowledge concerning, for example, reasonable expectations about the election outcome and coalition signals. According to this view, differences between sophisticated and unsophisticated voters should be even more pronounced as the number of parties increase and the decision environment grows more complex. Contrary to instrumental coalition voting, expressive coalition voting does not need a lot of capability and political knowledge. If voters have expressive motives, they can easily follow them without any further calculus. And they would also not need any more complicated calculus when the number of parties rises. Therefore, one would not suspect any differences between sophisticated and unsophisticated voters in the amount of expressive coalition voting. When looking at trends of voting behavior over time, political sophistication can thus be used as a rough proxy to distinguish between potential instrumental and expressive motivations of actors. If one finds sharp differences in deviating from the preferred party between sophisticated and unsophisticated voters, this would indicate rather instrumental motivations. If one finds no differences between the two groups, this could be a clue for the relevance of expressive motivations.

Research Questions

This theoretical discussion has led to various expectations about coalition voting: In multiparty systems voters will find coalitions to be meaningful political objects; they will therefore base their voting decisions not only on party and leader evaluations but also on coalition considerations; these coalition considerations do not need to be only instrumental but may also be purely expressive; and, finally, the differentiation of the German multiparty system might have led to a growing importance of coalition considerations over time.

In the remainder of this chapter, three specific research questions will be addressed consecutively. First, what effects did the differentiation of the German multiparty system have on the influence of coalition considerations? It will be examined whether there has been a growth of coalition-directed voting over time. Two indicators will be used for this task: the amount of split-ticket voting in German elections and the amount of deviation from the party preference with the PR vote. Political sophistication will be used as a proxy to get some preliminary insight whether a potential increase in coalition-directed voting is driven by instrumental or expressive motivations. Second, do voters actually see coalitions as distinct political entities that they relate to? The preference structure for different political objects—parties, leaders, and coalitions—will be examined to gain some insight into the role that coalitions play as a guiding factor for voting behavior. The traditional proposition is that coalition evaluations are just derivations of party evaluation. Here the hypothesis is tested that coalitions are more than the sum of their parts and that voters can actually prefer coalitions over their constituent parts. Third, if there are distinct coalition preferences, do they also have an independent effect on vote choices in multiparty systems? It will be examined whether coalition preferences have an impact on top of party and leader evaluations and whether this impact is moderated by coalition expectations, as one would expect from an instrumental point of view, or whether there is also an independent main effect of coalition preferences, as one would expect from an expressive perspective.

4.3 DATA

Different data sets are used for the analysis. To address the longitudinal questions three data sources are used. The first source is the "representative election statistic" since 1961. It is published by the German Federal Statistical Office and includes the combination of first and second votes in German elections. This data source thus gives a pretty accurate description of split-ticket voting in Germany over time. Second, I use pre-election studies since 1961 that included party preferences and often also some coalition preferences.[2] These surveys are used to further investigate whether an increase of split-ticket voting can be—at least partially—explained by a growing importance

---

[2] All election studies used in this chapter are available via GESIS data archive, Cologne: 1961: ZA0056; 1965: ZA0556; 1969: ZA0426; 1972: ZA0635; 1976: ZA0823; 1980: ZA1053; 1983: ZA1276; 1987: ZA1537; 1990: ZA1919; 1994: ZA3065; 1998: ZA3066; 2002: ZA3861; 2005: ZA4302; 2009: ZA5303.

of coalition-directed voting over time. Finally, for the cross-sectional in-depth analysis of the preference structure of voters and the impact of coalition preferences on vote choice, the preelection GLES face-to-face survey for the 2009 election is used (ZA5300) as it includes the most extensive battery of coalition preferences and expectations.[3]

4.4 RESULTS

Split-Ticket Voting and Deviation from the Preferred Party

A first indirect way to examine a potentially growing influence of coalition considerations is to look at the amount of split-ticket voting over time. Figure 4.1 shows the amount of vote splitting with the two ballots since 1961. There has been a sharp increase in split-ticket voting. The share of voters voting for a different party with the first vote and the second vote went up from about 5% in 1961 to 27% in 2009. From 1961 to 1976 there were only some fluctuations, staying below 10%. After that and the establishment of the Greens as a fourth party there was a steady rise to almost 15% in 1987. After German unification in 1990, the former communist party of the GDR entered the party system, first as a regional East-German party and later with a new name it also became established in West Germany. This seems to have led to another increase in split-ticket voting, culminating in more than one-quarter of voters splitting their vote in the most recent 2009 election.

Besides the rising number of parties, there are several other potential explanations for this upswing. First, processes of partisan dealignment may have led to more voters distributing their votes to different parties and candidates respectively. Second, voters might have learned more about the electoral rules and become more used to the different strategic logic of the majoritarian first vote for a candidate and the proportional second vote for a party list. Third, elections might have become more personalized at the local level with more voters basing their first vote on the personalities of the local candidates and less on their party affiliation. Finally, coalition considerations might have become more important over time—either for instrumental or for expressive reasons. Voters might have either behaved more strategically with their party vote of the PR pillar or they might just have used the German two-vote system as an opportunity to express their coalition preferences, splitting their vote between the two partners of that coalition.

---

[3] The 2009 studies (ZA5300, ZA5303) used in this chapter were conducted as part of GLES. Principal investigators were Hans Rattinger, Sigrid Roßteutscher, Rüdiger Schmitt-Beck, and Bernhard Weßels.

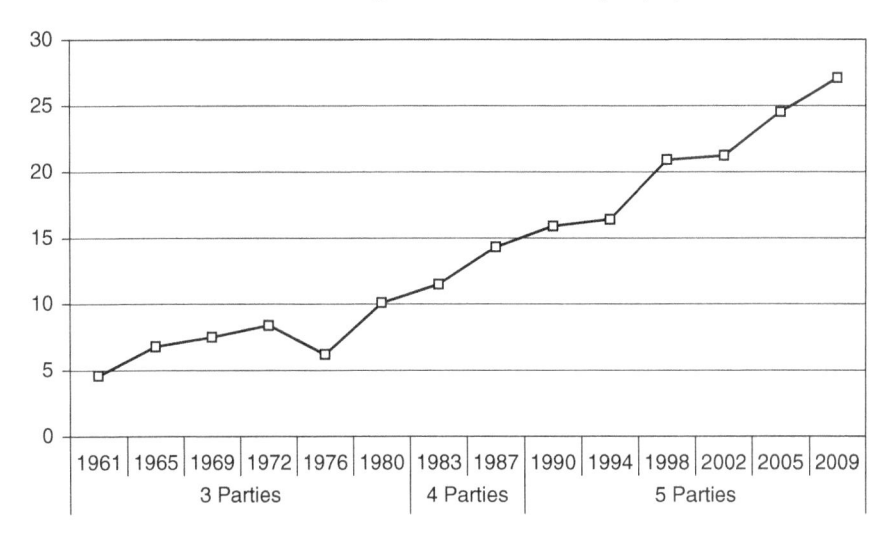

```
30
25
20
15
10
 5
 0
    1961 1965 1969 1972 1976 1980 1983 1987 1990 1994 1998 2002 2005 2009
           3 Parties              4 Parties            5 Parties
```

Figure 4.1 Share of vote splitting 1961–2009
Source: Representative Election Statistic, Federal Statistical Office.

These different reasons are not necessarily exclusive. It is reasonable to assume that all of them did play a role and that they interacted with each other to produce the sharp increase in vote splitting. For the argument of this chapter, however, it is important to disentangle those explanations based on the first vote (increasing personalization and strategic voting with the first vote) and those based on the second vote (dealignment and growing importance of coalition considerations). This cannot be done with the representative voting statistic as it only contains actual vote choices. One needs to look at the party preferences of voters. Only if voters increasingly deviate from their party preference with their PR vote, one may infer that dealignment processes and coalition considerations did play a bigger role over time.

Using German election study data since 1961, Figure 4.2 displays the share of voters deviating from their preferred party with their PR vote. This party preference is measured via scalometer ratings of the various parties. Deviation is operationalized as voting for another party than the one with the highest rating.[4] For comparison, Figure 4.2 also shows the share of voters deviating from their preferred coalition. This coalition deviation is operationalized as voting for a party that is not part of the preferred coalition.

The share of voters deviating from their preferred party increased from about 6% in the 1960s to around 15% in the most recent elections. On the other hand,

---

[4] If voters have ties on the highest rating, voting for each of those parties with the highest rating are counted as "sincere", that is, not deviating from the preferred party.

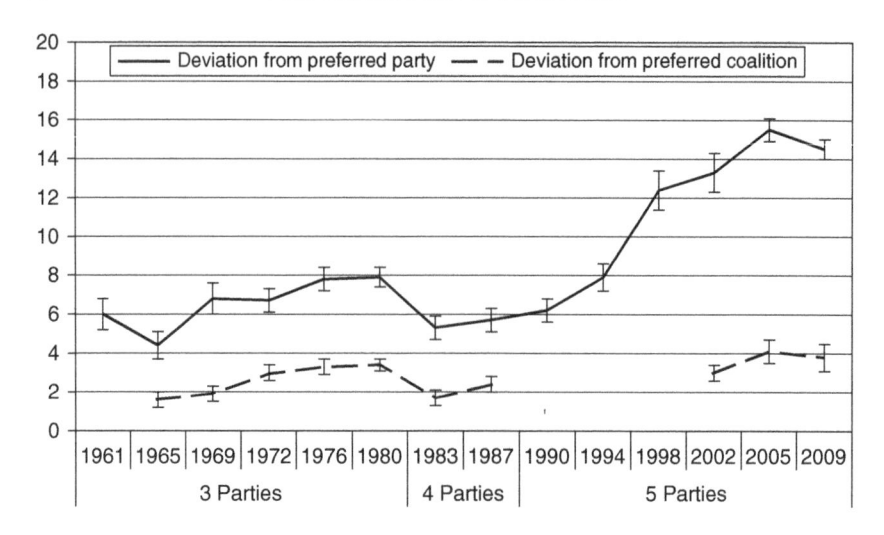

Figure 4.2 Deviation from first preference with party vote 1961–2009

Notes: Share of deviation from first preference, standard errors. Preelection studies 1961–2009; in 1961, 1990, 1994, and 1998 no questions were asked about coalition preferences.

the share of voters deviating from their preferred coalition stayed rather stable between 2 and 4%. Thus, voters more often voted for another than their preferred party, and the party they voted for instead was part of their preferred coalition. That is, coalition considerations seem to have become more important over time. Interestingly, this increase has not been steady over the last decades.

After a small rise in the 1970s, there was a sharp decline in 1983. A potential explanation for this decline is the coalitional switch of the FDP in 1982, when the FDP dropped out of the long-lasting coalition with the SPD and formed a new government with the CDU/CSU under Helmut Kohl. Voters with a preference for a SPD–FDP coalition might have been irritated about this change, and SPD supporters might have stopped voting strategically for the FDP. At the same time, CDU supporters were probably not yet convinced that the FDP would stick to a CDU–FDP coalition and therefore still voted sincerely for their preferred party, the CDU. From 1983 to 1994 deviation rose again to the levels of 1980. Since 1998 it increased sharply, possibly a reaction to the new dynamics of a five-party system and the growing importance of the PDS/Linke in the German Parliament. Thus, a good part of the increase in vote splitting as shown in the official voting statistics can be traced back to higher deviation levels from the preferred party with the PR party vote. Possible reasons are both a further partisan dealignment and a stronger influence of coalition considerations.

In order to get some insights into the question whether these coalition considerations have rather instrumental or expressive foundations, Figure 4.3

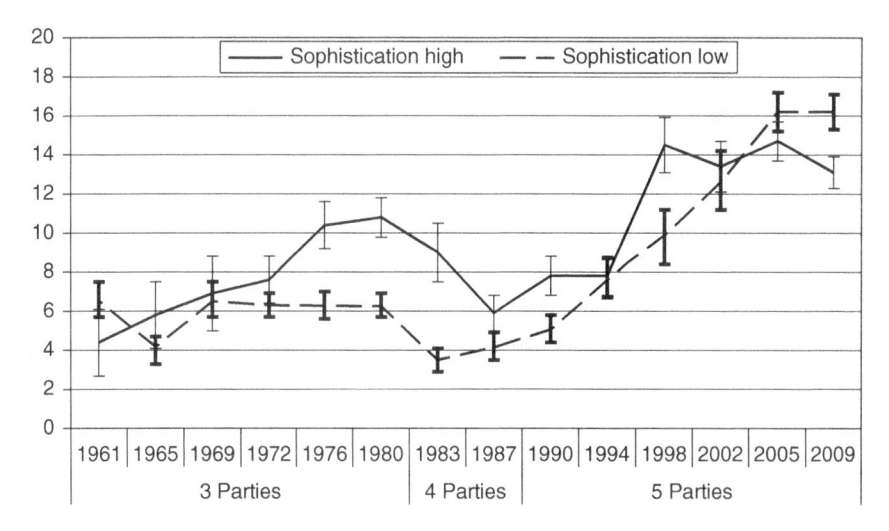

Figure 4.3 Deviation from first preference with party vote 1961–2009, level of sophistication

Note: Share of deviation from first preference, standard errors.

illustrates the share of deviation from the preferred party for voters with high sophistication and voters with low sophistication.[5] If, on the one hand, voters are instrumentally motivated, one would expect that highly sophisticated voters are more inclined to deviate than voters with low sophistication who might just stick to a simple party-based calculus. If, on the other hand, voters are rather expressively motivated, there should be no difference between these groups. Voters with high sophistication should be as prone to expressive motivations as voters with low sophistication.

Figure 4.3 reveals an interesting and changing pattern. For a long time—in particular during the 1970s and 1980s—highly sophisticated voters were more likely to deviate from their first preference than less sophisticated voters. For eight of twelve elections until 1998 this difference was also statistically significant. After 1998 this picture changed fundamentally, and in 2009 it was voters with low sophistication who were more likely to deviate from their party preference. A possible interpretation of this pattern is that in the 1970s and 1980s party deviation was still mainly instrumentally driven—with sophisticated voters showing more of that behavior. However, that seems to have changed

---

[5] Sophistication is operationalized by formal education (low: Volksschule/Hauptschule/Mittelschule/Realschule; high: Fachschule/Abitur/Fachhochschulreife). Using formal education is one of the standard approaches to operationalize the concept (see Luskin 1987; Sniderman, Brody, and Tetlock 1991). Measuring it more directly via political knowledge is not a viable option as the various cross-sections that are used in the analysis do not always have knowledge questions.

in the 1990s and 2000s, and expressive motivations, as indicated by the sharp increase of deviation of less sophisticated voters, have gained ground. Taking the last four elections together, there is no significant difference between more and less sophisticated voters anymore. Given that an instrumental vote calculus based on coalition considerations became even more complex in the five-party system of recent elections, it is not too surprising that deviation levels of highly sophisticated voters stagnated. It is more surprising that deviation levels of voters with low sophistication increased so strongly.[6] The changes between 2005 and 2009 are a case in point. After the election of 2005, the fifth party in the system, the PDS, was for the first time strong enough to prevent a coalition of either the SPD and Greens or the CDU/CSU and FDP, and forced the two big parties in Germany, the CDU/CSU and SPD into a so-called grand coalition. For voters, this illustrated the complexity of the five-party system quite impressively. Sophisticated voters reacted with less deviant voting in 2009. As the complexity of instrumental coalition voting increased, they voted more often for their preferred party. On the other hand, the level of deviation stayed constantly high for unsophisticated voters.

Overall, Figures 4.2 and 4.3 indicate that coalition considerations have increased quite tremendously over time. Dealignment processes, the differentiation of the party system, and the increasing number of parties are plausible explanations for this trend. Given the greater complexity of instrumental coalition voting in five-party systems compared to three-party systems, purely instrumental motives can hardly account for the sharp increase of party deviation. Expressive coalition considerations may also have played an important role. The findings of the separated analysis of sophisticated and unsophisticated voters affirm this interpretation to some degree, as there is mainly an increase of deviation for voters with low sophistication.[7]

Preferences for Parties, Candidates, and Coalitions

Standard accounts of voting behavior have only examined parties and candidates as political objects. It seems natural that voters relate to parties and candidates and generate evaluations and preferences about them. Apparently,

---

[6] A potential explanation besides more expressive motivation is that the less sophisticated voters and maybe also the high sophisticated voters were just thinking they acted instrumentally although sticking to their own party would have been more beneficial to them (see Linhart and Huber 2009).

[7] By no means does the analysis suggest that expressive motivations are tied to unsophisticated voters and instrumental motivations are tied to sophisticated voters. Still, it is informative that the sharp differences in vote deviation that existed between sophisticated and unsophisticated voters in the 1970s and 1980s decreased in the 1990s and 2000s. As the complexity of instrumental coalition voting increased over time, the share of deviation increased more for unsophisticated voters than for unsophisticated voters.

for many researchers it seemed less natural, or at least less consequential, that voters also generate evaluations and preferences about coalitions. Earlier, it was argued that coalitions are discrete political objects and not just derivations of party preferences. To test this claim, a very simple analysis may help. The GLES data for the German election in 2009 asked respondents to rate parties, candidates, and coalitions on the very same thermometer scales ranging from –5 to +5. This provides the opportunity to compare the ratings of the various political objects. One can compare the ratings of the preferred party with those of the preferred candidate and those of the preferred coalition. If coalition evaluations were only derivations from party evaluations, the rating of a specific coalition should just be the (weighted) mean of the ratings of the parties that are part of this coalition. That is, the rating of the preferred party should always be higher than the ratings of the preferred coalition that consists of this party and another party. If, however, coalitions are discrete political objects that voters relate to, voters may also rate a coalition higher than the parties it is composed of. Figure 4.4 shows the average ratings of the preferred party, the preferred candidate, and the preferred coalition.

On average, voters rate their preferred coalition significantly higher than their preferred party. The mean rating for the preferred party is 2.6 and for the preferred coalition 3.1. Apparently, many voters judge coalitions as being more than the sum of their parts. They assess their preferred coalition more positively than their preferred party. Interestingly, they also evaluate their preferred coalition more positively than their preferred candidate. Given that

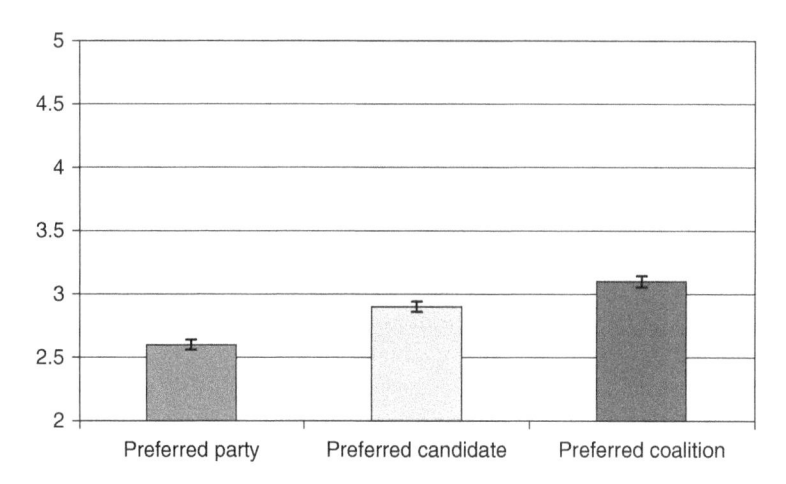

Figure 4.4 Average scalometer ratings for preferred parties, candidates, and coalitions 2009

Notes: Means of ratings, standard errors.

Table 4.1 Share of voters with highest rating for parties, candidates, and coalitions 2009

Highest rating for	All voters	Voters with high sophistication	Voters with low sophistication
Party	10.4	10.4	10.3
Candidate	16.4	13.6	22.9
Coalition	25.9	28.0	21.1
Tie party and candidate	12.4	11.6	14.2
Tie coalition and party	7.7	8.7	5.1
Tie coalition and candidate	10.3	9.9	10.9
Tie coalition, party, and candidate	16.9	17.5	15.3

candidates as persons usually elicit stronger feelings—positive and negative—than abstract entities like organizations and associations, this is quite surprising. Apparently, voters relate pretty strongly to coalitions and give them the most positive evaluations.

Table 4.1 additionally reports the share of voters evaluating the various political objects highest on the scalometers. About 26% of voters rate their preferred coalition higher than their preferred candidate and their preferred party. A share of 16% favors a candidate above the preferred party and the preferred coalition. And only about 10% evaluate their preferred party higher than their preferred coalition and candidate. In addition, there is a fair amount of voters giving the same rating to various political objects, producing ties between the preferred party, the preferred candidate, and the preferred coalition.

The pattern of preferences is also quite stable across sophistication levels[8], though some differences are noteworthy. While 28% of voters with high sophistication rate coalitions highest, only about 21% of those with low sophistication do so. The sharpest difference appears for candidates: while it is only 14% of highly sophisticated voters who rate them highest, it is about 23% of voters with low sophistication. Taking the ties into account as well, voters with high sophistication do rate coalitions a bit higher than voters with low sophistication, but overall the differences are not too pronounced. It is not only voters with high sophistication who relate to coalitions. Both highly and less sophisticated voters do care about coalitions and generate strong preferences that are not just plain derivations of party evaluations.[9]

---

[8] With political knowledge questions at hand in the GLES data for 2009, political sophistication is now measured by a simple additive index of the three knowledge questions asked. Respondents who answered two or more of the three questions correctly were classified as having a "high" political sophistication.

[9] The generation of strong coalition preferences is also quite stable across other variables: 27% of men and 25% of women rate coalitions highest; 25% of those respondents who have a party

Coalition Preferences and Vote Choice

It is one thing that voters express strong evaluations of coalitions when they are asked about them specifically in surveys; it is another thing whether these evaluations also translate into vote choices. Voters cannot simply vote for a coalition, they need to vote for parties or candidates. Still, coalition considerations might influence vote choices in multiparty systems. In the remaining part of this chapter, I will test the effects of coalition preferences in the German Federal election of 2009. First, it is examined whether coalition preferences have an explanatory value for vote choice—in addition to party and leader evaluations. Second, possible moderating effects of coalition expectations will be tested. According to an instrumental voter view, coalition preferences should only be of importance if expectations suggest that a coalition-directed vote is more beneficial than a straight party vote. Thus, there should be a strong interaction effect of coalition preferences and coalition expectations but no direct effect of coalition preferences. If, on the other hand, voters are also expressively motivated one would also expect a distinct main effect of coalition preferences.

In order to test for effects of coalition preferences and expectations on vote choice, a simple comprehensive model is calculated in a first step. As one can assume that coalition preferences have effects on all potential vote choices and not only for particular parties, modeling all potential vote choices in one model offers a general picture of effects of coalition evaluations. Thus, the data set is expanded by the number of parties of the German Bundestag (CDU/CSU, SPD, FDP, Greens, and the Left). In this stacked data set, vote choice for the respective party serves as dependent variable, with each respondent contributing five observations. Since these observations are not statistically independent, all observations based on a single respondent are treated as a "cluster", and robust standard errors, corrected for clustering, are reported.

The baseline model includes evaluations of the political objects that are traditionally seen as the only relevant ones: party evaluations on the one hand and leader evaluations on the other hand. For party evaluations, the first measure indicates whether a respondent prefers the respective party to all other parties and the second measure indicates the party rating of all the respective parties. If political parties were the only political object that voters care about, those two measures should already explain vote choices to a very large extent. The second measure, the ratings of all respective parties, should also control for evaluations of other parties in the system that can be potential coalition

---

identification rate coalition highest and 29% of those having no party identification; 27% of respondents with low political interest and 24% of those with high political interest; 25% of "Left" voters and 27% of "Right" voters; 29% of "younger" voters (< = 55 years) and 23% of "older" voters (>55 years old); and 24% of respondents with low and 30% with high *need for cognition*.

partners. With regard to leader evaluations, I include whether the leader of the respective party is preferred over the leaders of the other parties. As it has been frequently shown that party leaders have a distinct impact in addition to that of party evaluations, a significant effect on vote choice of the respective party is assumed.

In model 2, coalition preferences are added to this baseline model of voting behavior. Coalition preference in this model indicates whether the respective party is part of the coalition that is preferred by the respondent—measured via coalition ratings. In model 3, the interaction of coalition preferences and coalition expectations are included. Coalition expectation in this model indicates whether the respondent expects the respective party to be part of the future government coalition after the election. If voters were instrumentally motivated, one would expect a negative interaction effect as voting based on coalition considerations should decrease when voters expect that the respective party of the preferred coalition will be in government anyway. Or to put it differently, if one expects that the preferred coalition is formed anyway one can stick to one's party preference; if one thinks the preferred coalition might be at risk to gain the majority one might be tempted to vote based on these coalition preferences trying to improve the chances of that coalition. Thus, if voters were only instrumentally motivated a strong interaction effect is expected, and if voters are also expressively motivated a distinct main effect of coalition preferences is expected.

In model 4 the moderating effect of sophistication is examined. If only voters with low sophistication act on expressive coalition motives, there should be a strong interaction between coalition preferences and sophistication. If, on the other hand, also highly sophisticated voters have expressive coalition motivation, there should be no interaction. Finally, in model 5 it is examined whether expressing coalition preferences is particularly important for supporters of big parties. As supporters of big parties might particularly feel the need to express a more nuanced picture of them than just voting for a catch-all party—that is possibly perceived as indistinct—they might be tempted to deviate with one of their votes and indicate their coalition preference.

Table 4.2 presents the results of the five models. To assess the relative explanatory power of the five models, McFadden's Pseudo-R^2 and the Akaike Information Criteria (AIC) are presented (Burnham and Anderson 2004).

As expected, the baseline model 1 with party preference, party rating, and leader preferences explains vote choice already quite well, with all three factors having strong significant effects. However, adding coalition preferences in model 2 improves the model again. Coalition preferences have a significant effect on vote choice: Whether a party is part of the preferred coalition or not increases the chances of voting for that party. With the inclusion of coalition preferences Pseudo-R^2 rises from 0.56 to 0.58 and the AIC value decreases considerably, indicating a better model-fit of the coalition model. Model 3 tries to capture the instrumental component of coalition voting by the interaction

Table 4.2 Coalition preferences and vote choice 2009

	Vote choice for respective party				
	Model 1	Model 2	Model 3	Model 4	Model 5
Party preference	2.98 (0.14)***	2.92 (0.14)***	2.94 (0.14)***	2.92 (0.14)***	2.95 (0.14)***
Party rating	4.04 (0.21)***	3.60 (0.23)***	3.53 (0.23)***	3.62 (0.23)***	3.55 (0.23)***
Candidate preference	1.22 (0.14)***	1.16 (0.15)***	1.16 (0.15)***	1.17 (0.15)***	1.16 (0.15)***
Coalition preference		.85 (0.07)***	1.21 (0.11)***	0.74 (0.16)***	0.83 (0.12)***
Coalition expectation			0.43 (0.13)**		
Coalition preference × coalition expectation			−0.82 (0.18)***		
Sophistication				−0.66 (0.12)***	
Coalition preference × sophistication				0.22 (0.22)	
Preference for big party					−0.40 (0.08)***
Coalition preference × big party preference					0.08 (0.13)
Constant		−5.14 (0.14)***	−5.26 (0.15)***	−4.77 (0.15)***	−4.93 (0.14)***
McFadden's Pseudo-R^2	0.56	0.58	0.58	0.58	0.58
AIC	0.437	0.428	0.426	0.427	0.427
N (Respondents)	1416	1416	1416	1416	1416
N (Observations)	7029	7029	7029	7029	7029

Source: GLES preelection (ZA5300).
Notes: Cells contain logit coefficients of the stacked data set with robust standard errors in brackets. All variables are transformed to an interval from 0 to 1. * $p < 0.05$, ** $p < 0.01$, *** $p < 0.001$.

of preferences and expectations. This interaction has the expected negative effect and is significant. Apparently, voting based on coalition considerations is more frequent when voters are not sure whether their preferred coalition parties will actually form the government. However, this instrumental component of coalition voting is not the dominant one. As a comparison of model 2 and 3 indicates, there is almost no increase of R^2 and almost no decrease of AIC. Thus, coalition preferences seem to have an impact on vote choices that is quite independent from expectations about the winning coalition. The results of these models suggest that at least some of the coalition-directed voting is based on expressive motivations. Additionally, the results of model 4 indicate that these expressive motivations are not restricted to voters with low sophistication. Coalition preferences have similar effects on vote choices of voters with high and low sophistication. According to Model 5 the effects of coalition considerations are also not moderated by the preference for a big or small party. Coalition preferences are equally important for supporters of big catch-all parties and supporters of small parties.

In order to substantiate the findings of distinct coalition effects, Table 4.3 reports the results of a further analysis. In the previous paragraphs it has been shown that many voters do generate strong preferences for coalitions and that many voters evaluate their preferred coalition more highly than their preferred party. One of the arguments proposed in this chapter was that coalitions are distinct political objects voters actually do care about and therefore evaluations of these objects should have an impact on vote choice. If this argument holds, coalition preferences should have a particularly strong effect for those voters who have strong coalition preferences and rate their preferred coalition higher than their preferred party. To test this expectation, Table 4.3 presents the results of separated models for voters with strong and weak coalition preferences. Voters who rate their preferred party higher than their preferred coalition should vote more according to party considerations, and voters who rate their preferred coalition higher than their preferred party should vote more according to coalition considerations.[10]

The separated models 1 and 2 show quite some variation. There is a stronger impact of coalition preferences among voters who evaluate their preferred coalition higher than their preferred party. At the same time, they are less influenced by party evaluations. And there is a stronger impact of party evaluations among voters who evaluate parties higher than coalitions. These effects also show in the full model for all voters. Testing the moderating effect of the preference structure directly with interactions, all three interactions are significant. Voters who expressed higher ratings for their preferred coalition than for their preferred party are more likely to be influenced by their coalition preferences, less likely to vote according to their party preference, and also less likely to vote based on party ratings. Thus, the preference structure does in fact moderate the impact of party and coalition preferences. These results affirm the general argument that voters relate to coalitions in multiparty systems and that coalition preferences can have an independent effect on vote choices. They also affirm the argument that expressive motivations do play a role—in

---

[10] The operationalization of strong and weak coalition considerations thus builds on the analysis in Table 4.1 and thereby focuses only on party and coalition ratings. Ties between party and coalition preference ratings are coded as "weak" coalition considerations.

Table 4.3 Coalition preference and vote choice 2009: Strong and weak coalition preferences

	Vote choice for respective party		
	Model 1 Voters with weak coalition preferences	Model 2 Voters with strong coalition preferences	Model 3 All voters
Party preference	3.82 (0.31)***	2.66 (0.28)***	3.74 (0.29)***
Party rating	3.38 (0.47)***	1.85 (0.38)***	3.34 (0.47)***
Candidate preference	0.50 (0.29)	0.92 (0.27)**	0.72 (0.19)***
Coalition preference	1.53 (0.19)***	2.49 (0.26)***	1.51 (0.20)***
Strong coalition preference			0.82 (0.37)*
Strong coalition preference			
× coalition preference			1.00 (0.32)**
× party preference			−1.02 (0.39)**
× party rating			−1.47 (0.50)*
Constant	−6.16 (0.28)***	−5.32 (0.25)***	−6.14 (0.27)***
McFadden's Pseudo-R^2	0.70	0.57	0.65
N (Respondents)	606	371	977
N (Observations)	3022	1852	4879

Source: GLES preelection cross-section (ZA5300).
Notes: Cells contain logit coefficients of the stacked data set with robust standard errors in brackets. All variables are transformed to an interval from 0 to 1. * $p < 0.05$, ** $p < 0.01$, *** $p < 0.001$.

addition to instrumental motivations. Voters who have a strong preference about a party (and not so much about coalitions) may want to express and demonstrate this preference, and voters who have a strong preference about a coalition (and not so much about parties) may want to express that preference.

4.5 CONCLUSION

One of the key changes on the supply side of politics in Germany has been the differentiation of the multiparty system. This has led to more options for voters and a more complex decision environment. With the number of parties, the number of potential coalitions has also increased. On the one hand, this has arguably resulted in higher media attention on coalition politics. On the other hand, this has left voters who primarily want to select a government with a highly complicated task. It was Downs (1957a) who pointed out that instrumental voters in multiparty systems need to take coalitions into account. At the same time, he was highly skeptical whether voters have the capacity to do so. His conclusion was that voters will fall back to simple party considerations and neglect coalitions altogether. In this chapter, it was argued that voters in multiparty systems do have distinct coalition preferences and that these preferences also affect vote choices. This impact can not only be based on instrumental motivations as Downs and the strategic voting literature are suggesting. It may also be based on expressive motivations. According to this view, coalitions might be ideal political objects for voters to demonstrate and affirm a more nuanced and complex picture of their identity. And as society and politics is differentiating, coalition-directed voting might become even more attractive, as one can signal individuality and distinctiveness to others and to oneself. Coalition-directed voting might then be not only based on instrumental reasoning but also on expressive considerations.

Overall, the analysis in this chapter has confirmed the general proposition that coalitions are meaningful political objects for voters and that they can have a distinct impact on voting decisions. Contrary to instrumental arguments, the differentiation of the German party system has not led to less coalition-directed voting but to more. The longitudinal analysis of split-ticket voting has revealed a sharp increase in splitting over time. The more detailed analysis with election surveys since 1961 has shown that this increase can be—at least partially—explained by higher levels of deviation from the party preference with the party vote of the PR pillar. Political sophistication was then used as a proxy to get some insight into the question whether the increase in coalition-directed voting is driven by instrumental or expressive motivations. The pattern among voters with high and low sophistication suggests that the increase—in particular since the late 1990s—was rather driven by expressive motivations. The analysis of the preference structure of voters further revealed that voters do care about coalitions and, quite surprisingly, that they often care more about them than they do about parties and candidates. Coalition evaluations are thus not just derivations of party evaluations; voters often see coalitions as being more than the sum of their parts. Finally, the analysis of voting choices in 2009 revealed an independent impact of coalition preferences. This impact was slightly moderated by coalition expectations. The analysis of vote choices thus confirms both possible motivations for coalition-directed voting to some degree: instrumental and expressive.

Multiparty systems may be complex for instrumental voting. Still, coalition evaluations can play a role for voting decisions as voters might also be expressively motivated. Overall, the differentiation of the German party system and the growing number of potential coalitions seem to have led to more and not to less coalition-directed voting. Expressive considerations might be one reason: When voters in multiparty systems stand in front of the "electoral jukebox" (Schuessler 2000), some voters opt not always for the simple statement of their "Sinatraness." They opt for a more complex statement of their identity, choosing rather a combination of songs. And as the party system is getting differentiated and more complex, more voters may want to express a more differentiated political statement.

The German two-vote system will definitely help with this expressive motivation as voters have the opportunity to distribute votes to different parties. At the jukebox this provides for the opportunity to choose two songs. And instead of choosing two songs of Sinatra, they might rather choose one Sinatra and one other song. If voters have only one vote, not choosing one's preferred party comes at a cost which might prevent expressive coalition voting. The results of this chapter therefore seem to be a promising starting point for future comparative research on the impact of not only instrumental but also expressive coalition voting.

Another promising route for research will be a closer investigation of the different motives to vote for a coalition. Most of the literature on coalitions and voting behavior assumes an instrumental voter. In this chapter, it was argued that there might also be expressive motives at work. The reported results do—to some degree—affirm such an interpretation. Still, the indicators are very indirect, and the analysis presented in this chapter can only be a first explorative step. With traditional survey measures it will be generally difficult to disentangle different motivations of coalition voting. One possibility would be the inclusion of new measures of instrumental and expressive motivations in voting studies. Experimental research might be another possible path to obtain more detailed insight into the motivations and conditions of coalition voting in multiparty systems.

5

Voting Complexity in a Multilayered System
Or: How Voting Choices in Second-Order Elections Impact the Stability of Party Identification

Sigrid Roßteutscher, Ina Bieber, and Philipp Scherer

5.1 INTRODUCTION

The voter is increasingly unpredictable. Voters shift between parties more than ever; the percentage of nonvoters is rising. The voting decision is often postponed to the final moments of the campaign. Germany is a prime example, but by no means an exception within the realm of established Western democracies. While searching for an explanation for this trend, the answer repeatedly arises as a reference to the dissolution of the stable cleavage structures which characterized European party politics for many decades. As a result, it is said that we are witnessing the decline of lasting party–voter alliances and the long-term attachments which linked individuals' location in the social structure to the party system (see Chapter 8 in this volume for a more in depth account on cleavage voting). Modernization is the responsible process behind this development. According to the dominant narrative, changes in the economic structure eroded the stable milieus of both the working class and Catholicism. A profound value change resulted from increasing levels of material well-being and social security in the aftermath of the Second World War, when the economy was blossoming and a densely knit social welfare state was established. Consequently, a growing number of individualized voters began to seek political expression beyond the elite-driven "old" mass parties.[1] Their loyal voter base eroded and they were to become "parties without partisans" (Dalton and Wattenberg 2000b).

---
[1] See e.g., Inglehart 1990; Norris 2000; Dalton 2002.

That said, this chapter seeks to add an explicitly political perspective to this essentially socioeconomic explanation for declining voter–party alignments. In particular, it points to two related facets which contribute to a decline in party identification and dealignment—beyond the forces of (anonymous) economic changes and individualization processes. *First*, the voter plays an active role. By consciously deciding whether to vote or to abstain, or whether to cast the vote sincerely or to defect from one's "own" party, the individual voter contributes actively to the (in-) stability of his/her party identification and thus, as an aggregate pattern, to declining levels of partisanship in the electorate. *Second*, multilevel electoral systems introduce a different quality of elections. So-called second-order elections, which are perceived to be of lesser importance compared to the national first-order election, and of which the European Parliament (EP) election is the prime example (see also Chapter 6 in this volume), offer opportunities for abstaining or voting differently at an apparently "low cost." By not voting, or voting differently, however, older attachments fade away. We argue that party defection at second-order elections is as consequential as party disloyalty at first-order elections. Therefore, multilevel voting is a significant force towards rising volatility and the decline of stable party identification.

This chapter thus relates to relevant literature by taking up the older controversy of party identification as either a long-term effective part of a person's identity, or a shaky and easily reversible attitude. It adds to this debate by arguing that electoral choices are a significant moderating factor in deciding whether an individual's party attachment remains stable or becomes volatile. By focusing on "deviant" choices, this chapter creates a new perspective and argues that nonvoting and voting differently are equally important for explaining shifts in party identification. Finally, it relates the debate about stability of party identification to the literature on second-order elections by arguing that vote choices at second-order elections are as consequential as choices at first-order elections.

In the subsequent section, we will develop this theoretical link between electoral choices, multilevel voting, and dealignment processes. Thereafter, the different data sets used will be introduced. An empirical assessment of the hypotheses spelled out below, will conclude this chapter.

5.2 LINKING ELECTORAL CHOICES AND MULTILEVEL VOTING TO DECLINING PARTISANSHIP

Voting Choices and Party Identification

In the classic formulation of the Michigan school, party identification is formed during early socialization processes and stabilized during life-long practices of voting (see e.g., Converse 1969; Jennings 1990; Miller and Shanks 1996). As a kind of psychological party membership, it is a part of a person's individual identity (Campbell et al. 1960a). The party identification of an individual is a "standing" decision, a strong predisposition which parties can easily mobilize and turn into countable votes. Changes in party identification were only conceptualized as responses to dramatic changes in the fortunes of the nations (such as war, or hunger crisis) or in the individual's life cycle, such as death of partner, loss of job etc. (Campbell et al. 1960a: 145ff.). During the life cycle, a person's identity is stabilized through a process of habituation and the experience of iterative loyal party vote. In other words, voting for one's party is a crucial and necessary part of remaining a party identifier (Markus and Converse 1979; Johnston and Pattie 1999). The classic Michigan approach would accept that, for various idiosyncratic reasons, voters might once in a while vote against their standing decision (see e.g., Markus and Converse 1979). In fact, the difference between partisan vote and non-partisan vote was conceptualized as a measurement of how strongly short-term factors, such as issues and candidates, produce deviations from a so-called "normal vote" (e.g. Converse 1966). However, since the late 1970s, the static notion of the Michigan school came under heavy criticism. Based on European data, scholars have claimed that party identification was conceptually indistinct from voting behavior. In other words, party identification and voting choices are not projected along a causal chain (Budge, Crewe, and Farlie 1976; Thomassen 1976; Thomassen and Rosema 2009, see also Clarke et al. 2009b: 92ff.). From a rational choice perspective, such "attitudes" are largely a product of issue preferences and retrospective performance evaluations (Fiorina 1981; Adams 2001). The most extreme variant suggests that party identification is nothing more than a rather fluid response to choices at the ballot box (see e.g., Asher 1983: 342f; Franklin and Jackson 1983). In a nutshell: "you become what you vote" (Grofman, Wayman, and Barreto 2009: 69, similar Thomassen and Rosema 2009: 52) In this revisionist perspective, party "identification" is no longer the long-term stable part of a person's identity, but rather a fugitive attitude that may change and adapt at short notice.[2] In both conceptions, however, vote choices play a pivotal role. In the tradition of the Michigan school (see also Chapter 13 in this volume) party identification structures and predetermines votes and stabilizes through party-loyal voting decisions. Deviant voting may occur, however, under normal circumstances partisanship remains "unmoved." From the perspective of

---

[2] This revisionist approach is criticized on the grounds of methodology (see e.g., Green and Palmquist 1990; Green and Schickler 2009). The main criticism concerns the ignorance of measurement errors which produces an exaggerated picture of partisan instability and a false impression of the impact of short-term factors on party identification (Green and Palmquist 1990, 1994).

its competitor, party "identification" is understood as an attitudinal component of the individual's mind, which changes in response to factual decisions at the ballot box. Recently, scholars of party identification point to the supposedly heterogeneous sources of partisanship and suggest that party identification is both a socialized part of personal identity for some voters and a rather fluid and adaptive attitude for others (e.g., Erikson, MacKuen, and Stimson 2002: 115ff.; Bartle and Bellucci 2009: 17; Box-Steffensmeier and Smith 1998). If so, how strongly deviant choices at the ballot box really impact party identification is precisely the subject of this chapter.

Furthermore, we argue that the stability/instability generating effect of voting choices is amplified through second-order elections. In principle, campaigns are effective means of political mobilization and should thus increase the strength and impact of "fundamentals" such as party identification (see Converse 1969 for the classical account, but also Chapter 10 in this volume). However, in electoral systems where second-order elections hold prominent roles, the mobilization impact of campaigning may be less straightforward. Compared to the traditional, nation-state centered "first-order election," "second-order elections" (the term was originally coined by Reif and Schmitt 1980) are supposed to be of minor importance for both parties and voters. Turnout is chronically low (see for example Franklin, van der Eijk, and Oppenhuis 1996; Steinbrecher, Huber, and Rattinger 2007) and parties invest a fraction of the sum of which they tend to invest in national first-order campaigns. Campaigning is less intense, the media coverage rather modest, and mobilization is thus less effective than in first-order elections (Marsh 1998). It can be therefore acknowledged, that multilevel systems encourage "deviant" behavior because the elections, and the outcome of the elections, are perceived as insignificant. Not voting, or voting differently, are seemingly easier decisions and are attached with lower "psychological" costs than at national first-order elections. The motivation for deviant voting may be diverse and idiosyncratic, i.e., including motives such as sanctioning parties in national government (e.g., van der Eijk, Franklin, and Oppenhuis 1996), signaling dissent and dissatisfaction with national politics (Anderson and Wood 1996), "voting by the boot" (see Oppenhuis, van der Eijk, and Franklin 1996) or simple "voter fatigue" originating from too many election campaigns (Jackman and Miller 1995: 482f., see also Franklin 1996; Boyd 1986, 1989; Lijphart 1997).[3] However, if it is true that choices matter and that voting for one's party is a crucial ingredient for long-term party attachments, such "deviant" behavior, independent of a voter's motivation, should leave traces, no matter

---

[3] For a more in-depth account on voting motivations at second-order elections, see also Chapter 6 in this volume.

whether it occurs at the first- or the second-order election. We thus arrive at the first set of hypotheses:

> H1: *Deviant choices weaken party identification and....*
> H2: *Deviant choices are easier to make and thus, more frequent at second-order elections, therefore multilevel systems contribute significantly to declining partisanship.*

Is this the case for all types of voters? We expect that individuals with very strong party identification will be less susceptible to the "second-orderedness" of elections. As party attachment is a profound part of an individual's personal identity (or, in line with the revisionist approach, at least a very determined attitude), strong identifiers will use any election to express their political identification, and nonvoting, as well as voting differently, should not frequently occur. Moreover, as they are less concerned with considering strategic/coalition aspects of voting, it may even be the case that strong identifiers more often vote sincerely, or "from the heart," in second-order elections in comparison to first-order elections (Schmitt, Sanz, and Braun 2009). This difference might be particularly relevant for multiparty systems, such as Germany's, where coalition governments are the rule and where the 5% threshold provides strong incentives for shifting votes strategically between major and minor parties (see Chapter 4 in this volume). On the other hand, those parts of the electorate, possessing no party identification, could be particularly prone to nonparticipation (Campbell et al. 1960a). In any case, voting will not irritate a nonexisting party attachment but could, in certain instances, produce new party sentiments. Therefore, we expect that voters who identify with a party, but who feel that this attachment is rather weak, will be especially receptive to the second-orderedness of elections. The party's mobilization efforts may not reach this part of the electorate. Moreover, while strong identifiers feel an urge to confess party belonging through loyal party vote, such a need is presumably less developed and pressing among weak identifiers. Indeed, evidence shows that weak identifiers vote inconsistently far more often, i.e., not in line with their party identification (Thomassen and Rosema 2009: 50f.; Green and Schickler 2009: 187). In order to regain cognitive consistency, weak identifiers are thus particularly prone to revising their party identification in light of such deviant choices (Bartle and Bellucci 2009: 16; Grofman, Wayman, and Barreto 2009: 69). We will thus introduce a third hypothesis:

> H3: *The effects of deviant choices are particularly visible for voters with weak party identification.*

5.3 DATA

The main argument put forward above claims that deviant choices, i.e., nonvoting and voting insincerely, generally harm a person's party identification (henceforth PID). Furthermore, it is argued that deviant choices in second-order elections are 1) from an individual perspective, as harmful as deviant choices at first-order elections, and 2) from an aggregate perspective, even more harmful because deviant choices are mass phenomena compared to first-order national elections where deviant choices, particularly nonvoting, are far less common practice. In order to assess the impact of voting decisions on the development of individuals' PID, panel data is mandatory. There should also be measurements concerning voter intentions in second-order elections. The German Longitudinal Election Study (GLES, see http://www.gles.eu) consists of three data sets which meet these criteria to different extents, which were conducted in different modes (online, telephone, and face-to-face), and which stretch across different time spans, as well as a multiple number of elections. We will conduct a robust test of the hypotheses spelled out above by using all three data sources and comparing the respective results.

The core data set for assessing the impact of voter choices in second-order elections is the so-called Multilevel Panel which was particularly designed to follow individuals across the diverse layers of the multilevel system.[4] It made use of the extraordinary occasion when certain German voters were called to the ballot box three times within a short time span preceding the Federal elections of 2009. On June 9, all Germans were asked to vote in the election for the European Parliament. On August 30, there were state elections in three German *Bundesländer* (Saxony, Thuringia, Saarland). Parallel to the Federal election on September 27, the electorates of two further regions (Schleswig-Holstein[5] and Brandenburg) were called to the ballot box. The study was designed as a three-wave panel and followed individual voters across the layers of the multilevel system. The first wave of the panel was conducted directly before the elections of the European parliament (May 27 to June 7). In each state with upcoming state elections, 500 interviews were conducted. In addition, a control group from regions without state elections (N = 500) completed this quasi-experimental design. The second wave of the panel was administered between August 21 and August 31 (i.e., in the run-up to the state elections in Saxony, Thuringia, and Saarland). The third and final wave took place between September 18 and September 27, directly before the Federal election and the two state elections in Schleswig-Holstein and Brandenburg. All interviews were conducted online.[6]

---

[4] Multi-Level Panel (GLES 2009). Principal investigators: Hans Rattinger, Sigrid Roßteutscher, Rüdiger Schmitt-Beck, Bernhard Weßels. GESIS Data Archive, Cologne. ZA5304 Data file Version 2.1.0 (GLES 2011b).

[5] Schleswig-Holstein is a special case because elections had to take place after Parliament was dissolved ahead of schedule. This was not clear when the basic design of the study was decided upon. Therefore, voters from Schleswig-Holstein took part only in the last two waves of this three-wave panel.

[6] See Study Materials 2011/95 at http://www.gesis.org for details concerning case selection, recruitment of panelists, quota sample, etc.

Considering the arguments spelled out above, deviant choices should generally weaken PID. The role of multilevel systems, it is argued, amplifies these general effects because deviation from the "standing" decision is seemingly easier and involves lower costs, particularly for voters with an already weak PID. That said, the effectiveness of voting decisions should be visible beyond the peculiarities of second-order elections. Therefore, two further data sets, both focusing on first-order elections, shall be employed to test the overall validity of our general argument.

To begin with, starting sixty days before the Federal election day, a Rolling Cross-Section Survey was fielded. Every day, a representative slot of 100 respondents was interviewed via telephone.[7] The RCS design was completed by a post-election panel wave which was conducted directly after the Federal election on September 22. Both surveys, pre- and postelection, contain measurements of PID. Although there are no questions concerning participation and voter choice at the state elections, which took place while the RCS was in the field, there is information concerning the regional origin of the interviewees. We can therefore deduce whether respondents experienced an additional second-order election. Moreover, the panel design of the RCS combines preelection voter intentions with postelection voting decisions. The data is, therefore, useful to assess whether executed decisions in comparison to decision intentions, have a different impact on the persistence or instability of PID.

However, both data sets, the Multilevel Panel and the Rolling Cross-Section, might be suboptimal for assessing the long-term effect of deviant choices. Both were fielded during the so-called super-election campaign of 2009 (Bieber and Roßteutscher 2011: 17) when the German electorate was called to the ballot box at least twice within a rather short period of time (the June EP election and the September Federal election). Analysing longer time intervals will serve as a hard test for our hypotheses concerning the impact of voter choices. Short-term shifts in PID may also be caused by measurement error or meaningless fluctuations with little lasting effect (see e.g., Green and Schickler 2009) because "individuals return rapidly to their personal equilibria, which rarely change" (Green and Yoon 2002: 3). We will therefore employ a third dataset, which stretches across a longer time period and thus provides an insight into the long-term impact of decision trajectories. This last data set is the third wave of a Long-Term Panel, conducted in face-to-face mode, which started at the 1998 election campaign. Here, we will focus on panelists who participated in the 2005 and 2009 postelection surveys.[8] By combining these three different data sets, we

---

[7] Rolling Cross-Section Campaign Survey with Post-election Panel Wave (GLES 2009). Principal investigators: Hans Rattinger, Sigrid Roßteutscher, Rüdiger Schmitt-Beck, Bernhard Weßels. GESIS Data Archive, Cologne. ZA5303 Data file Version 5.0.0 (GLES 2011d).

[8] Long-term Panel 2005-2009-2013 (GLES 2009). Principal investigators: Hans Rattinger, Sigrid Roßteutscher; Rüdiger Schmitt-Beck, Bernhard Weßels, Steffen Kühnel, Oskar Niedermayer, Bettina Westle. GESIS Data Archive, Cologne. ZA5321 Data file Version 1.0.0 (GLES 2012b).

Table 5.1 Description of the data sets

	Multilevel Panel (MLP)	Rolling Cross-Section (RCS)	Long-Term Panel (LTP)
Time frame	June–September 2009	60 days before September 22	2005–2009
Mode	Online	Telephone	Face-to-Face
No. of panel waves	3	2	2
No. of campaigns covered	2 (min), 3 (max)	1 (min), 2 (max)	2 (min), 4 (max)
No. of cases	1017	4027	1121
No. of cases, max. campaigns	824	675	116
No. of cases, min. campaigns	193	3352	188
Time 1	Vote Intention EP 2009 (preelection survey)	Vote Intention Federal 2009 (preelection survey)	Vote decision Federal 2005 (postelection survey)
Time 2	Vote Intention Federal 2009 (preelection survey)	Vote decision Federal 2009 (postelection survey)	Vote decision Federal 2009 (postelection survey)

can test the impact of choices in multiple ways, thereby cross-checking the validity of results in a particularly concise manner.

In order to compare results across the various data sets, Time 2 always remains the panel wave concerning the 2009 Federal election. With regard to T1, the panels differ. In the case of the MLP, T1 refers to the June EP election, while in the RCS T1 refers to the first wave preelection voting intention. Finally, in the case of the Long-term Panel, T1 is the reported voting decision in the 2005 Federal election. In all three data sets, a variable is created to account for the number of additional second-order elections which occurred between T1 and T2. Table 5.1 presents basic information concerning the three data sets.

5.4 ASSESSING THE LINK: EMPIRICAL ANALYSES

Voter Trajectories from Second- to First-Order Election

The empirical analysis focuses on present-day Germany. Note, however, that the argument is of a general nature. PID is in decline in almost all countries (see e.g., Schmitt and Holmberg 1995; Dalton 2000; Dalton, McAllister, and Wattenberg 2002b, for comparative evidence). Due to the process of

96 Voters on the Move or on the Run?

(a) Having a PID

(b) Strength of PID

- ■ Loyal partisans
- □ Shifting voters
- ▲ 1st-order voters
- △ 2nd-order voters
- ● Nonvoters

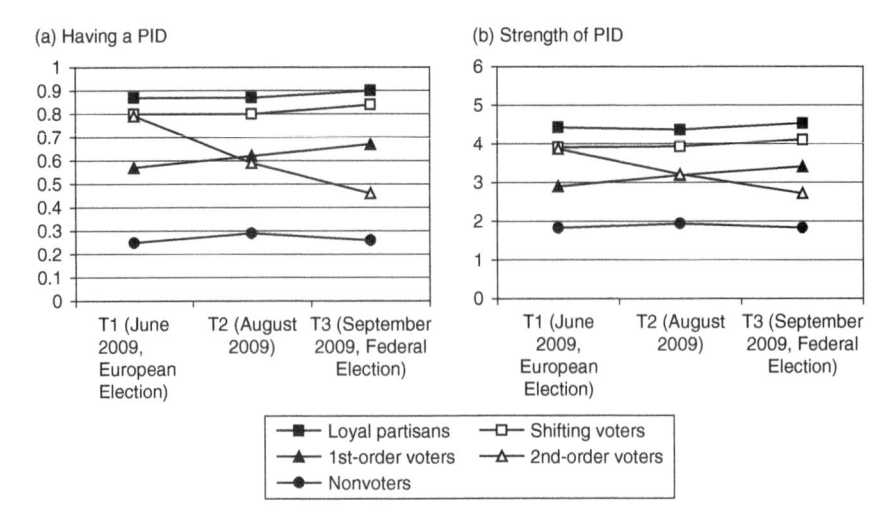

Figure 5.1 Party identification and strength of attachment by voter type

Notes: Party Identification 0 "no," 1 "yes"; Strength of PI from 1 "no PI" to 6 "very strong PI." Loyal partisans: Voted for the same party at the EP and Federal election; shifting voters: voted for different parties at the EP and the Federal election; first-order voters: no vote, or no valid answer for EP but party vote for Federal election; second-order voters: no vote, or no valid answer for Federal but party vote for EP election; nonvoters: no vote, or no valid answer for EP and Federal election.

Europeanization, there are regular second-order elections in all European Union member states. Therefore, the evidence of this chapter should shed light on the link between electoral choices at second-order elections and partisanship beyond the idiosyncratic single case.

Based on this chapter's core data set, the Multilevel Panel, Figure 5.1 presents primary evidence concerning the choices made at two subsequent elections and the development of PID.[9] Figure 5.1 portrays the relationship between combined voter choices at the EP and the Federal election with the existence and strength of PID. Clearly, voters who participated at both second- and first-order elections and decided in favour of the same party (i.e., loyal voters), possess very stable and high levels of PID. Somewhat surprisingly, the same is true for voters who took part in both elections but shifted between parties (note, however, that parts of this subgroup have shifted their

---

[9] The measurement for having a party identification is straightforward. Those who reply that they feel attached to a party are coded as "1" and those who claim that there is no party they feel close to received the value "0". The measurement concerning strength of identification is a combination of two distinct questions. Individuals without party attachment are coded as "1", those who admit to feeling close to a party but claim that the attachment is very weak, rather weak, or moderate received the codes 2, 3, and 4, those with rather strong or very strong attachment are coded 5 and 6. The resulting scale thus scans from "1" (no party identification) to "6" (very strong party identification).

loyalty from one party to another). Those who abstained from both elections, on the other hand, are very stable as well. However, nonvoters are characterized with extremely low levels of PID. By contrast, two voter groups demonstrate high levels of fluctuation. Both groups, however, abstained from one of the elections and participated in the other, even though their PID trajectories follow opposite paths. First-order voters, i.e., those who abstained from the EP election but voted at the Federal election, demonstrate a clear increase in party identification, both in terms of having one and in terms of its strength. The reversed pattern emerges with regard to so-called second-order voters, voters who took part in the EP election but did not participate in the Federal election. Across time, there is a strong decline in PID with regard to both indicators.

While this first piece of descriptive evidence suggests that the decision to not vote impacts PID more significantly than shifting choices, we cannot distinguish whether (past) voting choices at the EP election or the shadow of future choices at the Federal election cause these clear upward and downward trends. We will again employ the core data set, the Multilevel Panel, in order to document actual voter trajectories. Table 5.2 presents the precise choice combinations of voters from the EP to the Federal election. According to the argument spelled out above, the electorate is divided into three distinct groups: voters who report strong PID; voters who claim that they are attached, but rather weakly; and nonidentifiers.[10]

To begin with, those of the electorate, who were identified as strong partisans at T1, could basically choose three different trajectories of voting (loyal voting, shifting voting, and electoral abstention). Note that at T1 there is no significant difference concerning strength of identification. Scholars have, rightfully so, cautioned us to take survey responses simply at face value without correcting for measurement error, especially if a variable is supposed to measure a latent construct such as PID and if this measurement is obtained by a single survey response (Green and Palmquist 1990: 877; Green and Schickler 2009: 184). However, there is no convincing reason to expect that such measurement errors are unevenly distributed among strong identifiers, i.e., if there is error it should be equally present in all trajectories (concerning the assumption of randomness in measurement errors, see also Green and Palmquist 1994: 441).[11] Hence, we can be sufficiently confident that shifts in PID are substantially related to choices taken at two subsequent elections.

---

[10] Strong identifiers: responses "rather strong" or "very strong". Weak identifiers: "very weak", "rather weak", and moderate. Nonidentifiers: those who say that they are not attached to a party.
[11] By contrast, it may be plausible that there is a difference in the size of measurement error between strong and weak identifiers, because the survey question might cause greater irritation among the latter. Again, however, errors should be distributed randomly within the subgroup.

Table 5.2 Trajectories of voting—from the EP to the Federal election

	Decision at T1	In %	Mean PI	Decision at T2	In %	Change in PI (T1–T2)	Change in Strength (T1–T2)
Strong N = 429	Party vote	72.0	5.21	Party vote	77.3	−4.6**	−0.27***
				Vote other party	17.2	−7.5*	−0.51**
				No vote	5.5	−29.4*	−1.59**
	Vote other party	9.6	5.15	Party vote	51.2	0.0	−0.23*
				Vote other party	43.9	−16.7+	−0.89*
				No vote	4.9	—[1]	—[1]
	No vote	18.4	5.05	Party vote	51.9	−9.8*	−0.32
				Vote other party	26.6	−14.2+	−0.81+
				No vote	21.5	−29.4*	−1.18*
Weak N = 262	Party vote	38.9	3.96	Party vote	72.5	−10.8**	+0.18
				Vote other party	18.6	−5.3	+0.32
				No vote	8.8	−77.8**	−2.00**
	Vote other party	18.7	3.92	Party vote	24.5	−8.3	+0.75+
				Vote other party	69.4	−11.8*	−0.03
				No vote	6.1	−66.6	−1.33
	No vote	42.7	3.86	Party vote	34.2	−21.1**	−0.24
				Vote other party	44.1	−30.6***	−0.55*
				No vote	21.6	−45.8***	−1.21**
None N = 327	Party vote	27.6	1.00	Party vote	54.4	+63.2***	+2.14***
				Vote other party	36.7	+51.5***	+1.67***
				No vote	8.9	+37.5+	+1.50+
	No vote	72.4	1.00	Party vote	48.1	+49.6***	+1.73***
				No vote	51.9	+13.0**	+0.38***

Notes: T-Test for paired samples: + < 0.10; * < 0.05; ** < 0.01; *** < 0.001. [1] only two cases left. Arrows for dominant paths are bold; marginal paths indicated by dotted arrows.

Looking at strong identifiers, roughly three-quarters participated in the second-order EP election and decided in favour of "their" party. Only a minority (18%) abstained, and even fewer voted for another party. Of those who opted for their own party, 77% also remained loyal voters during the first-order Federal election, while nonvoting (5%) and party shifting (17%) concerned only small fractions of strong identifiers. Voting "from the heart" is clearly the dominant pattern among strong identifiers who voted loyally in the second-order election. Regarding strong identifiers using the EP election for deviant choices, this pattern of sustained loyalty is much less obvious. Only half of this group decided in favour of "their" party at the Federal election (i.e., party shifting and nonvoting at the first-order election is more frequent amongst strong identifiers who decided not to vote for "their" party at the second-order election).

As we turn to weak identifiers, we see that the distribution of choices at the EP election is clearly different. Party vote and nonvoting are equally prominent choices and voting differently is twice as frequent as in the case of strong identifiers. However, of those weak identifiers who decided in favour of their party, the largest fraction (72%) stayed with the party during the Federal election (i.e., behaved exactly as strong identifiers with loyal party vote in the EP election). In contrast, among those who shifted party at the EP election, roughly 70% also voted against their "standing decision" at the Federal election. Of the weak identifiers who abstained from participating in the second-order election, more persons voted differently or abstained, rather than voting for their party (34%). Finally, 72% of the nonidentifiers did not participate in the EP election. Roughly half of them decided later, in the Federal election, to cast a vote. Of the smaller fraction of nonidentifiers who participated in the second-order election, more than 50% stayed with the chosen party at the Federal election, roughly 40% decided in favour of another party, and only very few chose to not participate at all.

The last two columns of Table 5.2 display net changes in PID (second last column) and the strength of the attachment (last column) per voter trajectory. With regard to both strong identifiers, who voted loyally for "their" party, and nonidentifiers, who never cast a vote (first and last trajectory), we observe clear ceiling and floor effects. PID was so strong (close to the maximum value of "6") or so depressed (at the minimum value of "1") that further rises or declines were impossible and the shift of only very few individuals impacted the group's mean values; in a negative direction in the case of loyal party identifiers and in a positive direction in the case of abstaining nonidentifiers. The more interesting cases, however, are those individuals with less unwavering behavioral patterns. Clearly, nonvoting has a depressing impact on PID, even amongst strong identifiers. No matter how they decided in the EP election, not voting in the Federal election results in a 30% drop in PID and a significant decline in the strength of the attachment. This pattern is even more pronounced with regard to weak identifiers. Abstention at the Federal election produces a drop in identification between 46 and 88 percentage points. With regard to both strong and weak identifiers, the decision to not vote has a far more dramatic impact on party attachment than the decision to vote for another party. Finally, voting decisions can also increase PID. This is particularly clear with regard to nonaffiliated individuals who voted at T1 and T2 for the same party. Sixty-three per cent of the individuals with this pattern report having a PID at T2, and we also witness an extraordinarily strong increase in attachment strength. Moreover, among independents, a party-switching voting pattern produces a significant upward trend in identification.

In short, these first descriptive analyses of voter trajectories, during the time between the EP and the 2009 Federal election, suggest a nuanced picture: Those who are strongly attached to a party demonstrate a very high probability of loyal party vote across the multilevel electoral system. By contrast, those whose attachment is weaker are far more often susceptible to deviant choices, in particular during second-order elections. If, however, identifiers, strong or weak, start to "toy" with their vote and if they, in particular, choose to abstain from elections, the PID suffers. Moreover, loyal party voting in the federal first-order election is clearly conditioned by previous choices at the second-order election. Independent of the strength of the party attachment, if the second-order election is used for sincere voting, the likelihood of loyal voting at the subsequent Federal election is very high. If, by contrast, both strong and weak identifiers decide to vote in a deviant manner, the chance is high that deviant voting continues in the first-order election.

In order to test our hypotheses in a more concise manner, we will now turn to multivariate approaches.

Explaining Shifts in Party Identification

We will now make use of all three data sets in order to cross-validate the findings obtained on the basis of our core data set, the Multilevel Panel. As the data was collected in different modes and cover highly different time spans (from four years to sixty days, see Table 5.1), we will not interpret the size of the coefficients, but rather compare the significance and direction of the effects.

Dependent Variables

The construction of the dependent variables is straightforward and mirrors the logical options of how PID can change between two points in time: it can lose or gain in strength; it can shift from one party to another; individuals might abandon their PID and end as nonidentifiers and; finally, individuals can gain an identification and swap from independence to identification.

Voting Complexity in a Multilayered System 101

Table 5.3 Patterns of stability and change between Time 1 and Time 2

	Types of Election/Effect					
	Multilevel Panel		Rolling Cross-Section		Long-Term Panel	
	Second-order short-term		First-order short-term		First-order long-term	
Trends in PID:						
Loyal partisans	49.4	72.5	49.5	75.5	54.5	70.0
Shifting party ID	9.4	13.9	8.0	12.3	14.1	18.1
Opt-out party ID	9.2	13.6	8.0	12.3	9.3	11.9
N Partisans		692		2635		873
Consistent Nonpartisans	19.8	61.8	19.8	57.4	7.7	34.7
Opt-in party ID	12.2	38.2	14.7	42.6	14.4	65.3
N Nonpartisans		325		1386		248
N Total	1017		4021		1121	
Trends in PID Strength:						
Up 2 or more	13.0		16.5		14.9	
Up 1 step	13.5		11.7		15.8	
No change	54.4		52.3		42.5	
Down 1 Step	8.4		10.0		15.3	
Down 2 or more	9.8		9.5		11.5	
N Total	1017		4021		1120	

Table 5.3 presents the distributions of the dependent variables in the different data sets. Considering the diverse survey modes and time span covered, the basic distributions are very similar. The two short-term panels, the MLP and the RCS, particularly converge at a high degree. Looking at the entire electorate, roughly 50% remain loyal partisans, slightly less than 10% (MLP and RCS) and 14% in case of the LTP shifted between parties, and again less than 10% shifted from partisanship to independence. With regard to both short-term panels, roughly 20% were consistent nonpartisans and slightly more than 10% gained a PID between T1 and T2. With regard to nonpartisans, the LTP produces different distributions and the percentage of consistent nonpartisanship is extremely low (less than 8%). Accordingly, the size ratio amongst nonpartisans is reversed. With regard to the short-term panels, remaining independent is the dominant pattern (roughly 60:40). The LTP, by contrast, contains a majority of individuals who gained a PID between 2002 and 2005, while only 35% remained

independent. Moreover, the long-term panel at T1 (2005) consists of relatively few nonpartisans. Only 22% (248 of 1121) of the respondents claim to be independent, compared to 32% (MLP) and 35% (RCS). There is a further peculiarity of the LTP at T1 that should be mentioned before starting the multivariate analyses. Presumably due to deviations in question design and wording (e.g., no separate question for electoral participation), the proportion of nonvoters is extremely low, at 8.4%.[12] Even taking the typical under-reporting of nonvoting in surveys into account, this deviation from "true" participation is immense. The deviations concerning nonpartisans and nonvoters in the LTP at T1 should be kept in mind, as we cannot exclude if they have any impact on the subsequent analyses.

The Baseline Model

In order to test the voting choice model as thoroughly as possible, the theoretically relevant variables are added in a second step to a baseline model. This model consists of indicators which impact the stability of PID, as previous research has shown.[13] Subsequently, we will briefly describe the motivation for the inclusion and the respective construction of these indicators. However, not much emphasis will be given to their substantial contribution in explaining changes in PID. The analyses focus on what individual choices add to our understanding on top of these standard explanations. To begin with, measurements concerning respondents' age and the period of time in which they identify with a specific party account for the established finding that the likelihood of shifts in PID diminishes across individuals' life cycle and with the time in which individuals feel attached to a party (see e.g., Converse 1969; Schoen and Weins 2005; Kroh and Selb 2009; Ohr and Quandt 2012, but see Green and Yoon 2002 for a refutation of the age thesis). To account for the massive shifts in the German party system from the 1980s onward, a dummy variable was created which sets all respondents socialized during the heydays of stable cleavage politics and durable party competition constellations (Grofman, Wayman, and Barreto 2009: 64), apart from those respondents who experienced political socialization under the conditions of the newer four- or five-party system (i.e., were born after 1970 and experienced political socialization in the 1980s or later). A dummy variable that distinguishes East from West Germans acknowledges the fact that, for historical reasons, respondents

---

[12] Of those who already entered the three-wave panel in 2002, only nine respondents confess electoral abstention. Among the new panelists of 2005, there were seventy-eight nonvoters.

[13] Hence avoiding, as much as possible, the "omitted variable bias" which lies at the core of methodological criticism against revisionist approaches (Gerber, Huber, and Washington 2010: 722ff.).

who grew up in the former GDR less often identify with political parties, and that attachments are generally less stable than in West Germany (see e.g. Weßels 2007; Rattinger 2000; Schmitt-Beck and Weick 2001; Arzheimer and Schoen 2005). Education enters the basic model as a measurement of political sophistication. With regard to the classic dealignment account, sophisticated voters are less dependent upon party cues and are the first to desert party affiliation (Dalton and Wattenberg 2000b, for Germany). However, Kroh and Selb (2009: 177) find insignificant effects of educational levels once the impact of political socialization is controlled for. Kroh (2012: 221) and Arzheimer (2006: 799ff.) even show that rising educational levels result in increasing party attachments and partisan stability).[14] A dummy variable accounts for the fact that German women report a more stable PID than males (e.g., Schmitt-Beck, Weick, and Christoph 2006). Moreover, the traditional cleavage structure, with its partisanship fostering character (Schmitt 2009: 76f.; see also Chapter 8 in this volume), entered the models, first, by distinguishing the identifiers of the traditional cleavage parties, the Social Democrats (SPD) and the Christian Democrats (CDU/CSU), from adherents of the smaller parties (e.g., Schmitt-Beck, Weick, and Christoph 2006); and, second, by taking into account the sociostructural features of the old cleavage parties' core clientele (i.e., working-class background, Union membership, Catholicism, and active church involvement). In Germany, these characteristics of primary group membership (Campbell et al. 1960a; Grofman, Wayman, and Barreto 2009: 66) historically constituted the link between social groups and political parties (Müller and Klein 2012; Elff and Roßteutscher 2011; Roßteutscher 2012; see also Chapter 8).[15] Finally, two measurements are included in order to capture the degree of political mobilization at T1; political interest and frequency of political conversations with significant others (Campbell et al. 1960).[16] As with education, there are opposing ideas about their potential impact. While advocates of the dealignment thesis (Dalton 1984; Dalton and Wattenberg 2000b) expect that political involvement renders partisan cues obsolete and relate high interest to declines in partisanship, others argue, as well as prove with evidence, that political involvement results in stable political attitudes, including stable party sentiments (Schmitt-Beck, Weick, and Christoph 2006; Arzheimer and Schoen 2005). In order to keep control for

---

[14] Formal secondary education is measured on a four-point scale from 1 'no school qualification" to 4 'highest degree (i.e., Fachhochschule/Abitur).

[15] In the case of class, union membership, or denomination, dummy variables were constructed with workers, union members, and Catholics coded "1"; all others "0". For church involvement we employ a five-point scale ranging from "never attend church" (1) to "attend church more often than once a week" (5).

[16] Political interest is measured on a five-point scale ranging from (1) "no interest" to (5) "very high interest". Frequency of political discussion is measured on an eight-point scale from (1) "no day" to (8) "seven days a week".

the potentially mobilizing impact of campaigning (Farrell and Schmitt-Beck 2002; Schmitt-Beck, Weick, and Christoph 2006; see also Chapter 9 in this volume), both measurements will also be used as trend measurements (i.e., indicating shifts in political interest and discussion frequency which occurred between T1 and T2).[17] In the case of the Rolling Cross-Section, the point in time in which the interview of the first panel wave was conducted, is entered as an additional control variable in order to account for the fact that changes in orientations are less likely the closer to election day.

The Choice Model

With regard to the theoretically important variables, the relevance of second-order elections is captured by a variable which accounts for the number of elections that occurred between T1 and T2. In the case of the Multilevel Panel and the Rolling Cross-Section, this is a simple dummy variable which discriminates between respondents who experienced an additional state election (1) and those who did not (0). In the case of the longer time span covered by the Long-Term Panel, the variable ranges from a minimum of two additional second-order elections to a maximum of four (see Table 5.1 above). A dummy variable separates those with weak PID from persons with strong or no identification in order to assess whether weak identifiers are particularly susceptible to shifts in PID. Individual choices are modeled, per election, as a series of dummy variables reflecting the potential voter trajectories documented in Table 5.2 (i.e., loyal voting and variants of deviant voting in terms of party identifiers) and voting or abstaining, in terms of independents.

Results

Before examining the impact of choices on diverse aspects of partisan instability, some brief comments regarding the impact of the variables of the baseline model are necessary. It is obvious that the longer individuals possess a PID, the less likely it is that this PID would change or lose strength. The results across data sets are not fully consistent, but in general, the PID of small parties' adherents is less stable than the PID of the classic cleavage parties. The evidence concerning political sophistication and political involvement supports previous findings for Germany (see e.g., Arzheimer 2006; Kroh 2012) and

---

[17] The trend measurements were constructed by subtracting the T1 measurement from the T2 measurement, thus, positive values signal an increase in interest or political conversations, negative values mean a decline, while values of "0" mean that interest and conversations remained on an identical level during the two points in time.

contradicts the cognitive mobilization thesis of dealignment theories; education and, in particular, political interest relate clearly and positively to stable partisanship. Campaigning matters insofar as individuals, who experience an increase in political interest and/or an increase in political discussions between T1 and T2, are less susceptible to shifts in PID. In regard to the age, the political socialization, and social background of the respondent, there are no consistent findings across the three different data sets and the different dependent variables. Very clearly, however, the choice models add grossly to our understanding of shifts in PID (see explained variance in Tables 5.4–5.7). Subsequently, we will discuss the impact of second-order elections, weak identification, and electoral choices on deterioration of PID in more detail.

Table 5.4 shows the findings concerning shifts in PID strength that occurred between T1 and T2. Consistent across data and election types, weak identifiers have a modest tendency to increase the intensity of their party sentiments between two points in time. Looking at the relevance of electoral choices, the diverse data sets suggest very similar findings. Insincere voters at T2, i.e., the first-order election, are likely to experience a downward trend in PID strength. Moreover, clear upward trends in identification occur with regard to non-identifiers who participated in both elections. This is a clear and strong case for independents who chose the same party in both second- and first-order elections, but also visible for those who decided in favour of different parties. There are several instances, however, where findings are less consistent. With regard to the impact of nonvoting at T2, two data sets, the MLP and the LTP, suggest a significant negative impact on the strength of party identification. The RCS data, however, shows a very modest but opposite effect. Vice versa, nonvoting at the 2005 Federal election has a positive impact on the development of PID strength (no significant effects appear with regard to the other data sets). This counterintuitive result could be explained by assuming that nonvoting at first-order elections signals a severe crisis in the relation between party and adherent, which, however, recovered in the course of time.[18]

Turning to shifts in party identification from one party to another (Table 5.5), deviant voting choices, at both points in time, matter significantly. A vote against the standing decision increases the likelihood that individuals transfer their attachment from one party to another. Nonvoting, by contrast, produces inconsistent findings: Based on the MLP, neither nonparticipation at the EP election nor nonparticipation at the Federal election exerts significant effects. However, the RCS data (and partly also the LTP) portrays nonvoting as a predictor for shifting party identification. As this difference appears not only with regard to T1 but also at T2 when all data sets refer to the same Federal election, the multilevel background of the MLP cannot provide an explanation for this

---

[18] Note however, the problematic measurement of nonvoting in the 2005 election panel (see above).

Table 5.4 Explaining changes in party identification: strength of identification T1 to T2

	MLP Basic	MLP Choice	RCS Basic	RCS Choice	LTP Basic	LTP Choice
Controls:						
Time	–	–	−0.00	−0.01	–	–
Age	−0.07	−0.03	0.06*	0.07**	−0.05	−0.01
Cohort 1970	−0.09+	−0.05	0.03	0.01	−0.04	−0.03
East Germans	−0.04	−0.07+	0.07***	0.05**	0.03	−0.05
Gender	−0.02	0.01	−0.03	−0.02	0.02	0.00
Education	0.02	−0.01	0.05**	0.04**	0.05	0.03
Worker	−0.03	−0.03	0.02	0.02	0.00	0.01
Union membership	−0.03	−0.02	−0.06***	−0.04**	−0.03	−0.04
Catholic	−0.03	−0.02	0.02	0.00	−0.02	−0.02
Frequency church visits	−0.01	−0.01	−0.02	0.02	0.04	0.02
Time having PID	0.39***	0.20***	–	–	–	–
PID small parties	0.02	0.02	−0.21***	−0.07***	−0.14***	−0.02
Political interest T1	0.04	0.02	−0.05**	−0.01	−0.01	0.05
Political conversation T1	−0.04	−0.02	0.02	0.02	–	–
Change in interest (T1 to T2)	0.15***	0.11**	–	–	0.01	0.05+
Change in conversation (T1 to T2)	−0.01	0.01	0.01	0.02	–	–
Test Variables:						
Additional second-order election		0.03		0.01		−0.01
Weak PID at T1		0.07*		0.07***		0.09***
Shifting vote T1		0.02		−0.00		−0.04+
Vote without PID T1		0.11*		0.10***		0.26***
No vote T1		0.01		0.01		0.13***
Shifting vote T2		−0.06+		−0.07***		−0.14***
Party vote without PID, T2		0.30***		0.41***		0.28***
Vote other party without PID, T2		0.07+		0.18***		0.19***
No vote T2		−0.10*		0.05*		−0.09**
Intercept	−1.47**	−0.87+	0.13	−0.91***	0.24	−0.60
R^2adj.	0.16	0.28	0.05	0.27	0.01	0.36
No. of cases	941	941	3917	3917	1105	1105

Notes: Changes in PID strength: Continuous variable stretching from −5 to +5. Cell entries: beta coefficients of an OLS regression model; Reference categories: Vote decision T1 and T2: loyal partisans, i.e., voting in line with PID at T1. Levels of Significance: + < 0.10; * < 0.05; ** < 0.01; *** < 0.001.

Table 5.5 Explaining changes in party identification: shift of party identification T1 to T2

	MLP Basic	MLP Choice	RCS Basic	RCS Choice	LTP Basic	LTP Choice
Controls:						
Time	–	–	1.00	1.00	–	–
Age	1.03*	1.06**	1.00	1.00	0.98	1.00
Cohort 1970	1.83	3.05*	1.04	1.30	0.87	1.32
East Germans	1.03	1.05	1.17	1.00	1.43	1.15
Gender	1.08	1.25	1.16	1.17	0.64*	0.83
Education	1.08	0.90	0.71***	0.67***	0.94	1.00
Worker	1.00	1.12	1.95***	1.76**	0.51+	0.48+
Union membership	1.24	1.16	0.62**	0.75	0.71	0.80
Catholic	1.21	1.36	1.11	1.07	0.53*	0.51*
Frequency church visits	0.81	0.84	0.97	0.98	0.94	1.01
Time having PID	0.61**	0.61**	–	–	–	–
PID small parties	0.93	1.26	2.41***	3.52***	1.27	2.39**
Political interest T1	1.19	1.27	0.89+	1.01	0.94	0.98
Political conversation T1	1.10	1.06	1.05	1.02	–	–
Change in interest (T1 to T2)	1.03	1.03	–	–	1.06	1.11
Change in conversation (T1 to T2)	1.03	1.04	1.04	0.96	–	–
Test Variables:						
Additional second-order election		1.05		1.35		1.09
Weak PID at T1		1.51		1.49**		0.94
Shifting vote T1		2.09*		3.50***		2.29**
No vote T1		0.64		2.94***		1.33
Shifting vote T2		8.24***		3.36***		12.60***
No vote T2		0.23		2.94***		10.04***
Intercept	−2.67*	4.75**	0.32*	0.05***	0.68	−2.92**
Nagelkerke R^2	0.07	0.32	0.08	0.24	0.07	0.25
No. of cases	657	657	2658	2658	866	866

Notes: PID Shift between T1 and T2: 1 = Shift between parties, 0 = PID with same party, No PID = missing. Cell entries: log odds (Exp(b)) resulting from binary logistic regressions. Reference categories: Vote decision T1 and T2: loyal partisans, i.e., voting in line with PID at T1. Levels of significance: + < 0.10; * < 0.05; ** < 0.01; *** < 0.001.

Table 5.6 Explaining changes in party identification: opt-out party identification T1 to T2

	MLP Basic	MLP Choice	RCS Basic	RCS Choice	LTP Basic	LTP Choice
Controls:						
Time of interview	–	–	1.00	1.00	–	–
Age	0.99	0.98	1.00	1.00	1.00	1.02
Cohort 1970	0.97	0.94	1.37	1.44	2.52*	3.67**
East Germans	2.01*	2.77*	1.02	1.14	1.84*	1.26
Gender	0.76	0.58+	0.97	0.98	1.00	1.12
Education	0.69	0.72	0.88+	0.91	0.84	0.84
Worker	1.66	1.21	0.86	0.75	1.44*	1.35*
Union membership	1.06	1.14	1.46**	1.80***	1.37	1.73+
Catholic	1.66	1.74	1.24	1.20	1.67+	1.79*
Frequency church visits	0.96	0.97	0.93	0.98	0.88+	0.86+
Time having PID	0.66**	0.77+	–	–	–	–
PID small parties	0.89	0.99	1.46**	1.70***	0.83	1.02
Political interest T1	0.66*	0.80	0.71***	0.83*	0.66**	0.79
Political conversation T1	1.05	1.14	0.98	0.97	–	–
Change in interest (T1 to T2)	0.52**	0.60*	–	–	0.75*	0.78+
Change in conversation (T1 to T2)	1.06	1.11	0.91**	0.91**	–	–
Test Variables:						
Additional second-order election		0.95		0.82		0.88
Weak PID at T1		2.11*		1.99***		2.79***
Shifting vote T1		0.84		1.23		1.61
No vote T1		2.09*		2.24*		0.71
Shifting vote T2		1.53		1.91***		3.34***
No vote T2		6.91***		2.98***		9.84***
Intercept	1.99	−0.38	0.25	0.09***	−0.48	−2.69
Nagelkerke R^2	0.11	0.25	0.05	0.15	0.06	0.16
No. of cases	658	658	2658	2658	865	865

Note: Opt-out PID: 1 = those with PI at T1 and without PID at T2, 0 = those with PID at T1 and T2, missing: no PID at T1. Cell entries: log odds (Exp(b)) resulting from binary logistic regressions. Reference categories: Voting decision T1 and T2: loyal partisans, i.e., voting in line with PID at T1. Levels of significance: + < 0.10; * < 0.05; ** < 0.01; *** < 0.001.

Table 5.7 Explaining changes in party identification: opt-in party identification T1 to T2

	MLP Basic	MLP Choice	RCS Basic	RCS Choice	LTP Basic	LTP Choice
Controls:						
Time	–	–	0.99*	0.99*	–	–
Age	0.98	0.99	1.03***	1.03***	0.99	1.00
Cohort1970	0.71	0.64	1.36	1.37	0.60	0.76
East Germans	0.80	0.50	1.30+	1.62*	1.00	0.82
Gender	0.57*	0.66	0.76*	0.76*	1.62	1.47
Education	1.08	0.68	1.02	1.01	0.99	0.92
Worker	0.97	1.04	1.21	1.25	1.22	1.37
Union membership	1.33	0.91	0.79	0.80	0.71	0.69
Catholic	0.84	0.92	1.15	1.09	1.25	1.39
Frequency church visits	0.98	0.93	1.07	1.06	1.12	1.08
Political interest T1	1.39+	1.06	1.02	0.91	1.35	1.19
Political conversation T1	1.00	0.99	1.11**	1.07*	–	–
Change in interest (T1 to T2)	2.01**	1.71*	–	–	1.18	1.11
Change in conversation (T1 to T2)	1.06	1.07	1.06+	1.03	–	–
Test Variables:						
Additional second-order election		2.90*		0.75		1.04
Vote without PID T1		2.23*		1.62***		0.62
Party vote without PID, T2		7.47***		3.56***		4.31**
Vote other party without PID, T2		4.13*		2.51***		5.48***
Intercept	−0.37	−0.39	0.17***	0.08***	−0.27	−0.79
Nagelkerke R^2	0.13	0.33	0.07	0.16	0.04	0.10
No. of cases	238	283	1252	1252	241	241

Notes: Opt-in PID: 1 = those without PID at T1 and with PID at T2, 0 = those without PID at T1 and T2, missing: PID at T1. Cell entries: log odds (Exp(b)) resulting from binary logistic regressions. Reference categories: Voting decision T1 and T2: No vote. Levels of significance: + < 0.10; * < 0.05; ** < 0.01; *** < 0.001.

discrepancy. Therefore, the evidence concerning the effect of electoral abstention is inconclusive. Voting insincerely at second- or first-order elections, however, provokes consistent, as well as strong PID shifts from one party to another.

Table 5.6 presents predictors concerning the opt-out option, or in light of the dealignment perspective, the most relevant trend. There is a very clear and consistent impact of weak identification. Those who started with a weak party identification at T1 are far more susceptible to opt-out than individuals with strong attachments. Looking at the impact of decisions, nonvoting at T1 and, in particular, nonvoting at T2 are very potent predictors of opt-out patterns. Voting against one's party at T1 has no impact on the persistence of party identification, while deviating choices at T2 seem to exert negative effects on holding one's attachment. In short, with regard to losing one's party identification, nonvoting is the dominant predictor.[19]

Among the logical options that individuals could experience during electoral campaigns, there is finally the option to turn from independence to partisanship. Table 5.7 presents the respective analysis. Note, the sample is now restricted to individuals without party identification at T1. For the first time, the MLP data suggests a clear and significant impact of additional second-order campaigns. Campaigns mobilize individuals into party attachments. The effect is not validated by the other two data sets. However, the quasi-experimental design of the MLP is set up precisely to distinguish a treatment group (an additional second-order election) from a control group (no additional election) and might thus be a particularly credible witness for additional campaign effects. With regard to the voting decision, non identifiers had only two options: to vote, or to not vote (see trajectories in Table 5.2). The relevant contrast category is therefore nonvoting. Clearly, voting (compared to electoral abstention) matters. There are strong effects for all party voting decisions in both subsequent elections. The effect is particularly visible with regard to former nonidentifiers who chose the same party at the occasion of both the EP and the Federal elections. With one exception (the T1 voting decision in the case of the LTP data[20]), all data support these findings.

5.5 ASSESSING THE ROLE OF WEAK IDENTIFICATION

So far, the third hypothesis of this chapter has not been appropriately tested. Individuals with a weak PID, we argued, are particularly likely to adopt their party attachment in response to deviant decisions. The models discussed

---

[19] The long-term panel deviates from the short-term panel evidence insofar as T1's (2005) nonvote decision has no impact on losing one's PID. Whether this is the case because of the problematic measurement of nonvoting at T1 or whether this result is substantially meaningful, cannot be answered conclusively.

[20] This might again be caused by the massive under- and misrepresentation of nonvoters at T1.

above included the main effects of weak PID. However, our argument basically demands an operationalization via an interaction between weak PID, on the one hand, and deviant voting, on the other. The last empirical section of the chapter will turn to this issue. Consequently, all models are recalculated as specified above, but are complemented by additional interaction terms.[21] Only statistically significant interactions ($p < 0.10$) are discussed.[22] Considering the very high consistency of evidence concerning the impact of weak identification across different data sets, these final analyses are again restricted to the core data set, the Multilevel Panel. The marginal effects of the interaction terms are calculated, while all other variables are set to their mean value. In two instances (shift of PID from one party to another and loss of a PID), the main effects presented in Tables 5.5 and 5.6 are a sufficiently correct description of the effect of weak PID. The additional interaction term is insignificant. That is, weak identifiers are somewhat more likely to shift between parties and clearly more at risk of losing party affiliation altogether, independent of whether they vote sincerely or in a deviant manner. By contrast, the change in strength of PID is conditioned on weak identifiers' decision to abstain from electoral participation (see Figure 5.2).

Nonvoting exerts an additional depressing effect on weak identifiers.[23] This is the case for nonvoting concerning both the September Federal election and the June European Parliament election. While for strong identifiers and non-identifiers abstention at the European Parliament election is irrelevant or even results in a modest increase of PID strength between T1 and T2, this is clearly not the case for weak identifiers. In terms of strength, the decision to not vote in the second-order election depresses PID by roughly 0.7 scale units (compared to weak identifiers who participated in the election). With regard to the Federal election, strong and nonidentifiers' party attachment is not affected by nonvoting. In other words, their attachment remains roughly the same, independent of whether they cast a vote or abstained. If, however, weak identifiers chose to not participate, we witness a clear negative development (1.3 units on the trend scale) compared to weak identifiers who chose to vote for a party. In short, nonvoting in both elections impacts weak identifiers, but not individuals with or without strong party sentiments.

---

[21] Note that the opt-in model (Table 5.6) includes only respondents without PID. Therefore, no interactions with weak PID can be calculated.

[22] The interpretation of the statistical significance concerning interaction terms in logistic models is not unproblematic. However, in order to apply a common criterion to all dependent variables, we will apply the significance criterion of OLS models where its interpretation is straightforward.

[23] The interaction terms regarding voting insincerely are not significant.

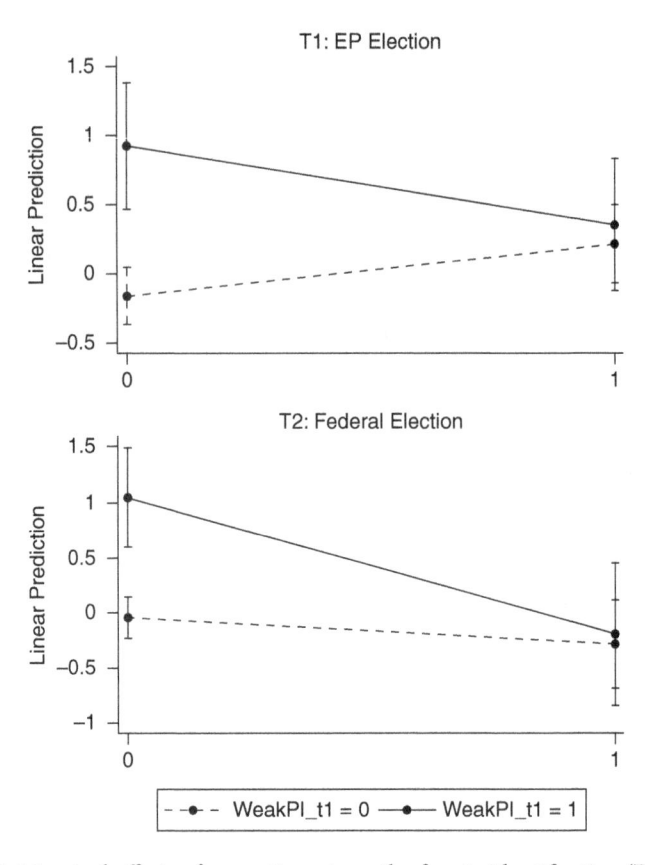

Figure 5.2 Marginal effects of nonvoting: strength of party identification (T1 to T2)

5.6 CONCLUSION

After extensive analyses of trends in partisanship, Green and Yoon conclude: "Like a buoy anchored to the floor of a harbor, partisanship drifts with the current but, in calm waters, returns to its usual position" (Green and Yoon 2002: 19). The claim is that short-term shifts are simply noise, because the dominant long-term nature of PID is characterized by very high intra-individual stability. Indeed, our analyses also reveal that stability is the dominant pattern for individuals with strong or very strong party sentiments! For weak identifiers, you rather toss the dice. Whether they stay with their party, or whether they defect, is preconditioned on their voting behavior. If, during elections, they decide to stay with their party, the likelihood that their partisanship remains intact and even increases in strength is very high. If, however, they decide differently, partisanship suffers. Amongst the deviant choices, nonvoting is particularly harmful. Only shifts between parties are more strongly related to insincere voting. Recall, however, that also strong identifiers who chose the nonvoting option experience clear setbacks in their PID—both in terms of having one and in terms of its strength (see Table 5.2).

However, the development of PID is no one-sided downward trend. Under specific conditions, voting choices push individuals from independence, or indifference, to partisanship. Again, the central mechanism is electoral participation (instead of nonvoting). Individuals who cast a ballot and, in particular, individuals who do this repeatedly and for the same party, can rather quickly develop a sentiment of party belonging. In this respect, PID is a direct response to decisions at the ballot box. Therefore, this chapter's evidence also supports the notion of party identification as a relatively fluid and adaptive sentiment that is challenged, if not reactivated, through actual voting decisions, and becomes stabilized through loyal party votes. With that said, two of the data sets employed in this chapter capture a rather short time span between the June EP election and the September Federal election of the "super-election-year, 2009." Hence, one could argue that the data measures individuals' short-term fluctuations, which may, after some time, fall back into their original PI position. However, the Long-term Panel data, which stretches across a four-year period, supports the general validity of decision effects: Deviant choices, in the context of the 2005 Federal election, still impact the strength and the stability of party identification at the time of the 2009 Federal election.

To sum up, this chapter formulated two hypotheses concerning the relationship between the decline in partisanship and electoral choices, and their particular impact in second-order elections. Moreover, we proposed that weak identifiers are particularly susceptible to the "second-orderedness" of elections and their own deviant choices. The relevance of electoral choices is strongly and consistently supported with evidence. Among the deviant choices, nonvoting is a particularly powerful predictor of a decline in party identification. Weak identifiers are generally more susceptible to deviant choices, particularly electoral abstention, than strong identifiers. Weak identifiers are also highly at risk to lose their PID. Choices matter, independent of whether they relate to second- or first-order elections. Moreover, multilevel systems induce a different quality of elections. Second-order elections are perceived as relatively insignificant and therefore offer ample opportunities for deviant choices. These seemingly easy and cost-free violations of party sentiments, however, leave their imprint on party identification and are hence, of primary importance to the future development of loyal partisanship in Germany as well as elsewhere. Looking at the impact of nonvoting in combination with the particularly low and shrinking turnout rates at second-order elections, the conclusion is straightforward: Multilevel systems provide a significant and politically effective gateway for electoral volatility, instability, and decline of PID. Nonvoting is very frequent and abstention weakens party attachments.

Not only voters, but parties and political elites alike treat second-order elections, in particular elections for the European Parliament, as less important. Campaigning is less intense, the party's top personnel less involved, and a fraction of the sum spent for national first-order is invested in mobilization. With regard to the perception of "second-orderedness" there is a strong voter–elite-party alliance of relative indifference. However, our evidence suggests that parties and political elites are well advised not to ignore the effects of seemingly less important electoral choices at second-order elections. Taken for granted that parties have an interest in loyal partisanship, nonvoting is particularly harmful to their strongholds. As they mobilize halfheartedly by failing to convince the public of the importance of such non-national elections, they actively contribute to low turnout.

Hence, we conclude that the dominant narrative, which points to processes of modernization and individualization, tells only parts of the story. There is a particular political facet to the story of decline. First, individuals' choices matter significantly and deviant voting harms party attachment. This is particularly the case for electoral abstention. Second, political parties are not only innocent "victims" of anonymous sociostructural changes, but by accepting and "living" the second-orderedness of some election types, they put up with low, as well as declining, turnout rates. However, toying with nonvoting and toying with turnout has a cumulative impact: individual party identification weakens, and parties lose their most loyal voters.

6

Contextualizing Turnout and Party Choice
Electoral Behavior on Different Political Levels

Heiko Giebler

6.1 INTRODUCTION

There is a long research tradition regarding elections in different contexts. Most of the literature focuses on cross-country or cross-time comparisons. Here, electoral institutions, party systems, and societal developments are described as relevant contextual factors shaping political attitudes, political behavior, and, in consequence, electoral results. A smaller but nevertheless important strand of research deals with the comparison of different kinds of elections, most prominently and systematically of European vs. national elections, on-year vs. off-year congressional elections in the US, or regional vs. national elections within a single country. These studies apply a different logic of comparison. In short, they contrast the behavior of the same electorate in different types of elections. Previous studies comparing the aforementioned sets of elections identified significant differences, especially regarding aggregated figures of both turnout and party vote shares (Campbell 1960; Reif and Schmitt 1980). In general, the periods between those elections are too short to assume a significant impact of, for example, societal developments. Party system differences and diverse electoral systems can also not fully account for the variation. In other words, context matters, but the set of relevant contextual factors in these studies differs from those in cross-country or cross-time comparisons.

All democracies are, more or less, multilayered systems—albeit to different degrees. Representative institutions are located on different political levels and have specific competencies both in terms of legislation and in terms of administration. This results in a certain hierarchy of local, regional, national, and even supranational bodies that plays a crucial role for individual electoral behavior. As Reif (1997: 117) puts it in the context of European and regional elections: "All elections (except the one that fills the most important political office of the entire system and therefore is the first-order election) are 'national second-order elections', irrespective of whether they take place in the entire, or only in a part of, the country." Similarly, Campbell (1960) distinguishes between low- and high-stimulus elections, the latter being congressional elections held at the same time as presidential elections.[1]

The nature of an election affects turnout as well as party choice. Following a classical rational-choice argumentation, relevance should have a direct effect on individual turnout. In general, the benefits of casting a vote are very small because the probability of casting the decisive vote is close to zero. The benefit is even lower if the election is perceived to be of less importance (Franklin 2001). Moreover, political parties invest fewer resources in mobilizing individuals for second-order elections for similar reasons. But, although turnout is lower in second-order elections, there is still a substantial number of citizens casting a ballot. There must be other motivations to turn out in such elections. Further, second-order voters tend to vote "differently" in comparison to more important elections. For example, they are assumed to use less relevant elections as barometer elections, i.e., as a possibility to punish governing parties, or to vote free of strategic constraints (van der Eijk, Franklin, and Oppenhuis 1996). In sum, in addition to low turnout, we expect different rationales of voting and, consequently, different electoral results for second-order elections.

This chapter addresses the question as to whether there are truly different rationales of electoral behavior depending on the electoral level or type of election by applying a rigid but promising research design. Specifically, this paper asks whether there is level-specific electoral behavior or not. The German Longitudinal Election Study (GLES) provides ideal data for such a comparison: Individual-level data are available for regional, national, and European elections in Germany and all those elections are covered by a short-term panel study (Rattinger et al. 2011). Drawing on this data, this study can provide a true comparison of electoral behavior on different political levels (regional vs. national vs. European) based on the same sample of respondents. Following prior work on turnout and vote functions, we identify potential variations between the levels that are induced by the electoral level itself.

The paper is organized as follows: First, we summarize some of the prominent approaches to second-order elections. This is used to develop hypotheses regarding varying determinants of turnout and party choice in regional, national, and European elections. After a brief description of the data and

---

[1] For the sake of simplicity, whenever possible, second-order national elections, low-stimulus elections, and any other less important elections are here subsumed under the term "second-order election."

the operationalization, we present results on individual turnout. The second empirical part deals with party choice. Finally, the results are discussed and implications for the second-order model based on level-specific electoral behavior are presented.

6.2 APPROACHES TO SECOND-ORDER ELECTIONS

There is only one first-order election in each democracy. It is defined as the election filling the most important political office (Reif 1997: 117) and, as such, it generates a high stimulus for both voters and parties. First-order elections have a structuring effect on other elections taking place in the multilayered system (Franklin and Weber 2010: 676). Therefore, every other election in the same democracy is by definition a second-order election. It is reasonable to further differentiate between these second-order elections because some of them might show more second-order electoral behavior regarding turnout and party choice than others.

We can look at Germany as an example. In Germany, people vote at the local, regional, national, and European level. Obviously, the national election is the most important and, for this reason, the first-order election. But what about the three types of second-order elections? Research on the impact of national factors on regional elections shows that this effect not only varies between regions but is also weak (Müller and Debus 2012; Völkl et al. 2008: 31).[2] In a comparison of all member states for the 2009 election, de Vries et al. (2011) showed that EP elections in Germany are characterized by EU issue voting far beyond the average of all countries. Nevertheless, with respect to many other aspects, Germany is not an exception when it comes to the second-order nature of EP elections (for example: Giebler and Wüst 2010, 2011b; Oppenhuis 1995). These findings point to some relevance and independence of EP elections, confirming at the same time a certain dependence from, and subordination to, the first-order election.

Putting the three election types into a hierarchy, European elections show more second-order characteristics than regional elections, while the latter are independent or at least relatively independent from national elections.

Hence, we propose one additional specification to the aforementioned definition of second-order elections: The distinction between first- and

---

[2] Research on the "second-orderness" of local elections in Britain supports these findings to a certain degree. Rallings and Trasher (2005) show that local elections are less dependent on national elections than EP elections. Heath et al. (1999) point out that electoral behavior in local elections is more similar to behavior in national elections than to behavior in "true" second-order elections.

second-order or low- and high-stimulus elections should not be based on a mere dichotomy but should be understood as a matter of degree. In line with Marsh and Mikhaylov (2010: 16), research should focus on degrees of second-orderness linked to specific characteristics of different second-order elections.

In addition to voters and parties, the media perceive second-order elections as less important (Cayrol 1991; de Vreese, Lauf, and Peter 2007; Maier and Tenscher 2006; Weber 2007; Wüst and Roth 2005). As a consequence, the expected benefits of winning the election are reduced making individual turnout, intense and expensive election campaigns, as well as extensive media coverage less likely (Marsh 1998: 593).[3] In other words, these elections take place in an "inhibiting" context. They are therefore characterised by lower turnout, losses for governing and bigger parties, and vote gains for smaller and/or radical parties. In the case of EP elections, this pattern has been more or less stable for three decades (Hix and Marsh 2011).

> Many voters cast their votes in these elections not only as a result of conditions obtaining within the specific context of the second-order arena, but also on the basis of factors in the main political arena of the nation....Perhaps the most important aspect of second-order elections is that there is less at stake (Reif and Schmitt 1980: 9).

Comparing EP and first-order elections, the gap between turnout levels and the deviation of vote shares on the aggregate level can be explained by the first-order electoral cycle (Reif and Schmitt 1980). This finding has been substantiated in many studies, most prominently by Franklin (2001), Schmitt (2005), as well as Hix and Marsh (2011). EP elections "'borrow' some importance as means for commenting on national politics in the member countries" (Franklin 2001: 316). First-order elections have a structuring effect on all other elections taking place in the multilayered system; the magnitude of the effect is higher if second-order elections are conducted shortly before or after national elections (Franklin and Weber 2010: 676).

With only few exceptions (e.g., Carrubba and Timpone 2005; Giebler and Wagner 2011; Rohrschneider and Clark 2008; Schmitt, Sanz, and Braun 2009), scholarly analysis of electoral behavior in EP elections does not take a comprehensive perspective of both acts linked to voting—namely, turning out and casting a ballot. However, there are other approaches to second-order elections that stress that turnout and party choice are specifically connected with variations in electoral results.

---

[3] Regarding electoral campaigns, Giebler and Wüst (2010) have identified vast differences between candidates, political parties, and countries concerning campaign intensity as well as campaign style. On the other hand, a direct comparison of campaigns in European and national elections in Germany shows that differences might primarily be caused by the institutional setting and not by the perceived importance of the election (Giebler and Wüst 2011b).

"Surge and decline" developed by A. Campbell (1960) and revised by J. E. Campbell (1997) is probably the most prominent approach in this context. In on-year elections, the US congressional election takes place simultaneously with the presidential election. Off-year or midterm elections are held independently and, hence, described as less relevant. There are certain similarities between the findings on European vs. national and on- vs. off-year elections in terms of the emerging patterns. J. E. Campbell (ibid.: 7) wrote:

> Whether the president has been a Republican or a Democrat, serving in the nineteenth or twentieth century, midterm elections have virtually always been at the expense of his party.

Another similarity is the vast gap in turnout (McDonald 2010: 127) that occurs between presidential and midterm election years. Scholars explain these patterns by highlighting two different types of voters: core voters who are generally interested in politics and show a stronger attachment to one of the two parties and peripheral voters who are neither very much interested in politics nor have a strong party identification (PID). On-year elections are high-stimulus elections mobilizing not only core but also peripheral voters. A. Campbell (1960: 400) argued that a low-stimulus election is not simply the "smaller version" of a high-stimulus election because core voters are not identical to peripheral voters. They are not only different regarding their basic characteristics but also in their decision-making rationale. Hence, variation in electoral results is a somewhat natural consequence linked to behavioral rationales.

6.3 WHAT TO EXPECT? LEVEL-SPECIFIC ELECTORAL BEHAVIOR

The underlying assumption of this paper is that electoral behavior can only be explained on the micro level in order to prevent ecological fallacy.[4] In a nutshell, the literature on EP as well as on midterm elections assumes that individual behavior is either directly determined by the relevance of the electoral level itself or indirectly by contextual effects like mobilization levels which are a function of the respective electoral level. For example, a voter might cast a protest vote against the government in a second-order election because of the lower importance of this election (direct effect). Alternatively, political

---

[4] In one of the most advanced approaches to tackling the problem of ecological fallacy when analysing individual behavior on the basis of aggregated data King (1997: xv) argues that "no method of ecological inference, including that introduced in this book, will produce precisely accurate results in every instance."

parties might put less effort into their campaigns, thereby decrease the probability that citizens will turn out, and this might lead to lower turnout levels as well as systematic differences of parties' vote shares (indirect effect). In other words, microlevel explanations are crucial for any endeavor to explain individual electoral behavior, but this behavior depends on contextual factors at the same time.

But which kind of behavioral patterns or rationales do we expect to identify? What justifies the assumption that there is level-specific electoral behavior distinguishing first- from second-order elections? In the remainder of this section, we deduce hypotheses for turnout as well as party choice.[5]

Turnout

First and foremost, second-order elections are defined by the fact that "less is at stake." EP elections, for example, do not result in the formation of a government and even the impact of electoral results on policies is hard to identify due to the specific institutional setting (Schmitt and van der Eijk 2008: 210). Building on this perspective, Weßels and Franklin (2009) even argue that the real puzzle of turnout on the European level is not why it is that low, but why it is that high.

The benefits of turning out are lower in comparison to first-order elections. Individuals attributing lower relevance to an election and its results should be less inclined to participate. In addition, the congruence of demand (citizens' preferences) and supply (parties' policy positions) is more than just a classical tool of judging the quality of representation. If no relevant party represents a citizen's preferences, there is no real use in casting a ballot. The degree of citizens' alienation from the supply side determines the potential benefits of turning out. Finally, benefits not fully captured by rational calculations have an impact as well. It seems reasonable to assume that a lasting attachment to a political party can be seen as at least partly based on bounded rationality (Jones 1999). This seems to be in line with the findings of A. Campbell (1960); citizens showing a stable party identification participate to a higher degree even in less important elections. They are habitual voters because they are more closely attached to the political system (Franklin and Hobolt 2011) and

---

[5] At this stage, it is necessary to highlight two things. First of all, the focus of this paper is not on comparing the explanatory power of different theoretical approaches to second-order elections. Hence, we do not have to link each hypothesis explicitly with one of the approaches. Secondly, there is no need to include additional explanatory approaches. We are not interested in providing a "perfect" explanatory model but in testing specific assumptions concerning microlevel electoral behavior in less important elections.

party identification is a valid shortcut in gathering information on political platforms (Aldrich 1993: 263), in consequence, on whether to turn out or not.

H1: The more second-order an election is, the higher is the effect of cost–benefit calculations on individual turnout.

Several studies have shown that political interest is an important factor in studying second-order elections (de Vries et al. 2011; Hobolt 2005; Hobolt and Wittrock 2011; Oppenhuis 1995). There are two arguments why political interest is crucial: (1) Citizens interested in politics are able to evaluate the relevance of a political level more correctly. It seems important to note that none of the elections under research in the literature cited above is completely unimportant—it is merely a matter of degree. The power of the EP has increased significantly over time (Rittberger 2012) and divided government as a result of midterm changes can—under certain circumstances—lead to a complete gridlock in the US system (Burden and Kimball 2002: 6ff.). Nevertheless, this relevance is less visible than the formation of a (new) government after a first-order election and, hence, people more interested in politics might be more aware of this specific relevance. (2) Political interest is a good indicator of psychological involvement fostering turnout (Blais 2000: 13f.). First of all, psychological involvement decreases the costs of voting because the individual already has enough information on political parties, candidates, and the election itself to come to a decision. More importantly, there is a stable connection between political interest and the sense of duty to vote (ibid.: 97).

H2: The more second-order an election is, the higher is the effect of political interest on individual turnout.

"The less the efforts made to inform and mobilize the electorates, the less the turnout" (Weßels and Franklin 2009: 616). During an electoral campaign, political actors have to distinguish themselves from competitors as well as to (re-)establish the citizens' attachment to the political system. What does this mean for the impact of campaign mobilization efforts in elections of varying importance? Basically, mobilization is less crucial in first-order elections because their relevance ensures high media coverage (for a discussion, see Schuck et al. 2011) and brings people to talk more often about the upcoming elections in their social networks. There is not such a strong "state of awareness" in second-order elections.

H3: The more second-order an election is, the higher is the effect of campaign mobilization efforts on individual turnout.

The literature on European as well as on off-year elections assumes that there is at least one basic benefit of second-order elections: Citizens can signal their dissatisfaction with the national government in a highly formalized way. While the election itself might not feature prominently in the media, dramatic losses by the government or the emergence of a new party in those elections will definitively dominate the news for quite some time. Analogously to the work on EP elections—and certainly influencing it—there is a referendum theory of midterm elections. "The midterm is neither a mystery nor an automatic swing of the pendulum; the midterm vote is a referendum" (Tufte 1975: 826). Moreover, people dissatisfied with the president have a higher probability to vote in an off-year election (Kernell 1977). Hence, we expect that the population actually voting is varying in second-order elections depending not only on the election type but also on the proportion of voters holding less favorable evaluations of the government.

H4: The more second-order an election is, the higher is the effect of negative government evaluations on individual turnout.

Party Choice

There are large deviations of a party's vote shares in elections on different political levels. The most successful approaches to explaining these deviations are concentrated on the macro level (Hix and Marsh 2011). We know much less about the validity of the underlying microlevel assumptions because existing microlevel studies do not apply a truly comparative design but analyse party choice in second-order elections only. For example, scholars have shown that attitudes towards the EU matter for vote-switching between national and European elections (Hobolt, Spoon, and Tilley 2008) or that EU issue voting has become a relevant factor (de Vries 2010; De Vries et al. 2011). In other words, there are factors beyond the national electoral cycle shaping electoral behavior in EP elections. But, and this is crucial for the underlying analysis, this research is not comparative in the true sense because it deals with electoral behavior on only one political level or suffers from severe memory effects. In contrast to this, we are able to formulate and test microlevel hypotheses linked to different political levels relying on the GLES panel survey where systematic differences in party choice can be traced back to different rationales of voting (Giebler and Wagner 2011; Marsh and Mikhaylov 2010; Oppenhuis, van der Eijk, and Franklin 1996).

One assumption regarding electoral behavior in second-order elections is rather straightforward: The magnitude of sincere voting—or "voting with the heart"—should be higher (Schmitt, Sanz, and Braun 2009). In this context, "sincere" means casting one's vote for the party whose portfolio is the closest to one's preferences. As a result, ideological proximity and party identification should be more relevant for party choice. Van der Eijk and Franklin (2009: 135) put it like this: "[They] vote for the party whose policies or personnel they like best, not paying attention to questions of government formation or other consequences of election outcomes."

> H5: *The more second-order an election is, the more dominant for party choice is 'voting with the heart.'*

With the declining importance of long-term factors, evaluations should more and more become the driving forces of party choice. Less important elections can be used as barometer elections to signal dissatisfaction with the national government's performance. Voters primarily articulate their discontent with the government's performance under the assumption that this may pressure parties to change national policies.[6] Second-order elections provide a vent for uttering dissatisfaction without risking blockades of government formation or extreme and ill-suited governments on the most important political level. This increases the probability of "voting with the boot."[7]

> H6: *The more second-order an election is, the more important for party choice is 'voting with the boot.'*

If "voting with the heart" and "voting with the boot" are the more prominent the more second-order an election is, then strategic voting cannot play a major role in these elections[8]—neither regarding the psychological effects of electoral systems (Cox 1997; Duverger 1963; Wagner 2011) nor government or coalition formation (Bargsted and Kedar 2009; Meffert and Gschwend 2010). Put differently, strategic voting would either result in worse model performance of indicators linked to "voting with the heart" or "voting with the boot" or in a direct impact of the ascribed relevance of the respective electoral level on party choice.[9]

Obviously, parties and candidates compete for votes not only by establishing different stances on political issues but also by communicating their ideas and goals to a wider public. Due to dealignment, electoral research has

---

[6] There is also a smaller body of literature following Fiorina's (1996) argument of "balancing" which he developed to explain split-ticket voting and divided government in the US. Empirically, there seems to be no proof for such behavior in EP elections. This is not surprising: The power of the EP is still too weak to be able to balance out the policies of national parliaments or the Council of Ministers. Hence, Fiorina's argument is not further taken into account here.

[7] One might argue that such behavior is similar to the basic idea of economic voting (Lewis-Beck and Stegmaier 2007). However, the performance of governments is not restricted to economic development but relates to a more general evaluation.

[8] Strategic voting, in this case, is defined by Cox in the following (1997: 71): "Some voter, whose favorite candidate has a poor chance of winning, notices that she has a preference between the top two candidates; she then rationally decides to vote for the most preferred of these top two competitors rather than for her overall favorite, because the latter vote has a much smaller chance of actually affecting the outcome than the former."

[9] One might argue that casting a protest vote is strategic behavior. Generally speaking, this is true. But it is not strategic behavior in the meaning of the term outlined in the literature on rationales of electoral behavior.

focused more and more on this feature of electoral campaigns (Schmitt-Beck and Farrell 2002). "If long-term anchors like class and partisan identification have eroded,...strategic communication represents the most plausible candidate [for electoral success]" (Norris et al. 1999: 9). It is safe to assume that mobilization efforts are less frequent in second-order elections. At the same time, whenever mobilization of an individual takes place there should be a positive effect on the probability to vote for the respective party. In first-order elections, on the contrary, a bevy of political advertisements and mobilization efforts might overwhelm citizens and, thereby, decrease the effectiveness of such efforts.

H7: The more second-order an election is, the more important for party choice is mobilization by parties and candidates.

We argue that second-orderness is a matter of degree. The same holds true for the impact of the described factors on turnout, party choice, or both. Hence, we do not assume, for example, that party identification has no effect on turnout in first-order elections. Nevertheless, we should witness a growing impact of these factors with an increasing second-orderness of an election. Before we can test this empirically, it is necessary to address questions of data and operationalization.

6.4 DATA AND OPERATIONALIZATION

Interestingly, the number of studies comparing electoral behavior between levels in an appropriate way is rather small. Most analyses are only conducted on one political level, for example, explaining turnout or party choice in European elections. Typically, a second step then compares these results to expectations regarding other levels without testing these expectations empirically. Therefore, findings on the general impact of second-orderness on electoral behavior are inconclusive at best. Other studies neglect problems of model specification or the inappropriateness of comparing model coefficients under certain circumstances.

We use a unique data source in this chapter. GLES provides a three-wave panel study on voting behavior in European, regional, and national elections in Germany. It was conducted as preelection online surveys and respondents were recruited online as well as offline.[10] The first wave focused on the elections

---

[10] Hence, this study analyses the impact of different independent variables on the intention to vote and vote intention. There are advantages and disadvantages associated with preelection survey. None of these factors can bias our analysis because effects should be identical on every political level.

to the European Parliament, the second wave covered three regional elections (Saarland, Saxony, and Thuringia), and the last wave dealt with the national election. All elections took place in 2009.[11]

We are well aware of problems linked to online surveys, e.g., concerning representativeness. Likewise, and this is a feature of all panel studies, there are problems related to panel mortality as well as missing information on some of the crucial variables.[12] However, we endeavor to ensure the validity of any results that are presented. For example, we calculate adjustment survey weights based on an iterative proportional fitting algorithm (raking) in Stata to increase the validity of our results.[13]

The analytical potential of the survey is tremendous. One of the biggest problems of existing research on second-order elections is the lack of panel studies measuring electoral behavior in elections on different political levels (Marsh and Mikhaylov 2010; Weber 2011). Any comparison based on typical datasets on second-order electoral behavior, for example the European Election studies, is tainted by memory and social desirability effects as well as by efforts to ensure cognitive consistency. Respondents might not be able or willing to remember correctly whether they voted in the last first-order election or for which party. Similar problems occur with questions about turnout probability and vote intention. Hence, even if vote functions are compared between elections, classical data sources do not provide good preconditions to do so. For this purpose, it would be feasible to compare models estimated on different samples, for example based on EES and CSES data. But, while this would solve the aforementioned problems, scholars were then confronted with all the problems linked to comparing estimations based on different samples. Fortunately, none of this is a problem with the panel data set under analysis here.

Table 6.1 presents the variables and their codings as used in this chapter. Additionally, it allocates the variables according to the different hypotheses presented above. All variables are election-specific, meaning that each of the variables was part of the questionnaire for each survey and they were framed in the context of the respective electoral level.

---

[11] Further details on the survey can be found in the study description (GLES 2011b).
[12] The panel started with about 3,500 respondents and ended with about 1,500. Unfortunately, many of these respondents cannot be included into the analyses because there were no regional elections in their *Bundesland* or these elections took place at the same time as the national election. Moreover, a significant number of respondents was added only after the EP election (still a part of the first wave) or at the beginning of the second wave. In other words, the number of "usable" respondents is much lower than the figure given above even if we don't take into account item nonresponse. To deal with the latter, we applied list-wise deletion as a simple but adequate—though not perfect—way to deal with missing values (Allison 2002: 12).
[13] The weights are based on gender, education, age (in categories), and regions. This represents the classical weighting strategy of offline surveys. For more information on the computation see Bergmann (2011).

Table 6.1 Description of variables and codings

Name	Description	Coding	Hypothesis
Dependent variables			
Turnout	Does the respondent intend to vote in the election?	1 = yes; 0 = no; respondents are coded as "1" if they are either more or less sure that they will participate or have already cast a postal vote.	—
Party choice	Which party does the respondent intend to vote for?	1 = votes for the respective party; 0 = votes for one of the other parliamentary parties	—
Independent variables			
Turnout model			
Electoral level	What type of election?	1 = national; 2 = regional; 3 = European	—
PID	Does the respondent have a party identification?	1 = yes; 0 = no	H1
Interest	Is the respondent interested in politics in general?	1 = yes; 0 = no; respondents are coded as "1" if they are at least strongly interested in politics.	H2
Mobilization	How many times was the respondent in contact (active and passive) with a party or a candidate?	Continuous variable	H3
Utility	What is the highest utility of a respondent to vote for one of the major parties?	Continuous variable; highest proximity to any of the major parties on the Left–Right dimension	H1
Relevance	How relevant are the electoral results for the respondent?	1 = relevant; 0 = irrelevant; respondents are coded as "1" if they say that the election results are at least important to them.	H1
Government evaluation	How well does the national government (CDU/CSU and SPD) perform?	Continuous variable; average of the evaluations of all parties in government; high values indicate good performance.	H4
Party choice model			
PID	Does the respondent have a party identification?	1 = yes; 0 = no	H5
Left-Right proximity	What is the proximity of the respondent to the respective party?	Continuous variable; linear distance between ego's position and subjective party's position; high values indicate high proximity.	H5

(*Continued*)

Table 6.1 Continued

Name	Description	Coding	Hypothesis
Mobilization	How many times was the respondent in contact (active and passive) with a specific party or one of their candidates?	Continuous variable	H7
Relevance	How relevant are the electoral results for the respondent?	Continuous variable	H5/6
Government evaluation	How well does the national government (CDU/CSU and SPD) perform?	Continuous variable; scale-mean-centered evaluation of party performance in government for all parties in government; scale-mean-centered average of the evaluations of all parties in government multiplied with −1 for all opposition parties; high values are associated with a higher probability to vote for the respective party.	H6

For the party choice model, the variable "relevance" had to be transformed into a party-specific variable before it could be included in the conditional logistic regression model. We applied a technique developed by van der Eijk, Franklin, and Oppenhuis (1996: 348) that uses y-hats from party-specific logistic regression models as an individualized measure of the impact of the variable on the probability to vote for a specific party. Unfortunately, any coefficient can no longer be interpreted in a directional way. But it is possible to link the results of the party-specific models to the results in the conditional logistic regression model which allows at least for some tentative conclusions regarding the directional nature of the relationship between relevance and party choice.

6.5 EMPIRICAL FINDINGS

Turnout

Turnout levels vary significantly between the different elections in Germany. The average turnout rate in the sample was 58.7% for the three regional elections under research, 68% for the national election, and 53.1% for the European

Table 6.2 Individual turnout patterns and turnout levels (percentage of respondents; N = 581)

Elections respondents participated in	Turnout of respondents
RPE, NPE, and EPE	71.6
RPE and NPE	11.0
NPE only	4.1
NPE and EPE	4.0
RPE only	1.2
RPE and EPE	0.4
EPE only	0.2
No participation	7.4
Type of election	Turnout of respondents
RPE	85.6
NPE	90.8
EPE	76.4
No participation	7.4

Notes: All figures are weighted. RPE = regional parliament election; NPE = national parliament election; EPE = European Parliament election.

election.[14] Table 6.2 gives an overview of the turnout rates. The vast majority participated in all three elections while only 7.4% did not participate at all. The numbers presented in the right-most column are significantly higher than the official turnout figures. This is common in election surveys and caused by over-reporting as well as by the fact that citizens that are voting have a higher probability to take part in such a survey. Nevertheless, this is without consequence for the identification of different rationales of individual turnout on the three different levels because we are interested in differences only.

Are there election-specific differences in the explanation of turnout (differences) in European, national, and regional elections? To answer this question, we estimate a logistic regression model.[15] We constructed a stacked data matrix (van der Eijk et al. 2006). As we are analysing three different elections from three different panel waves, each respondent is represented by three election-specific rows

---

[14] The overall turnout for Germany was higher for the national election (70.8%) and significantly lower for the European election (43-%).

[15] The detailed results are presented in Table 6.4 in the appendix to this chapter. We control for the data structure by using clustered standard errors in all analyses (clustered by respondent and/or region).

Contextualizing Turnout and Party Choice

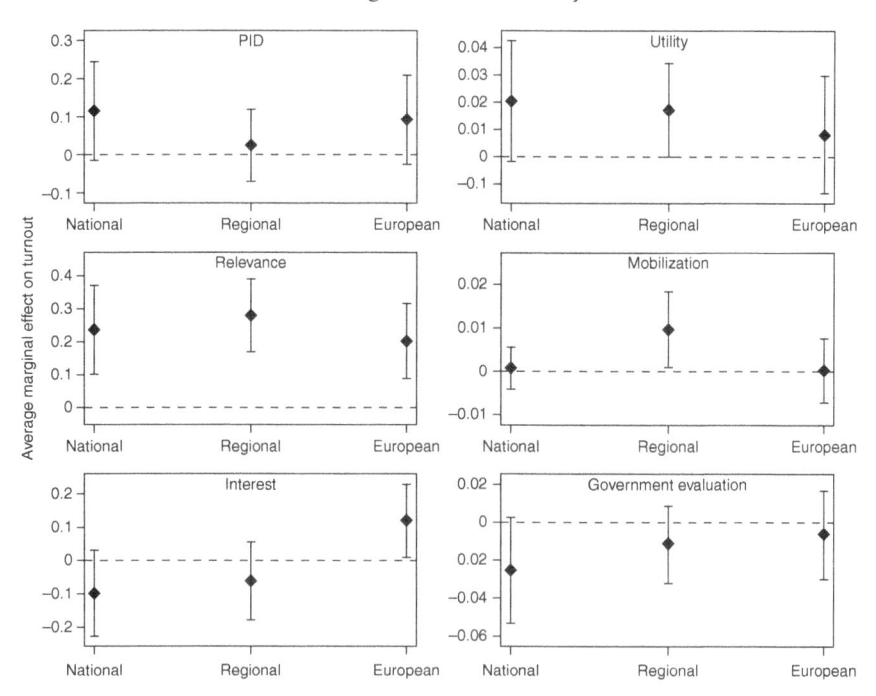

Figure 6.1 Average marginal effects on turnout for each electoral level (N = 1743 [581])

Notes: The dots represent the average marginal effects holding all other variables to their empirical mean. The whiskers represent the 95% confidence intervals.

in the data set. Election-specific effects are estimated by including interaction terms; each predictor is interacted with the electoral level (Debus 2012; Long and Freese 2006: 293ff.; Thurner, Mauerer, and Binder 2012).[16] Differences regarding the determinants between elections should point to a significant impact of the election type on turnout. As indicated above, a comparison of coefficients between models or—as in this case—between groups based on interactions is not appropriate due to unobserved heterogeneity (Mood 2010). However, it is possible to calculate marginal effects that are not only easier to interpret than logistic coefficients or log-odds but also have the advantage of being directly comparable.[17] The average marginal effects (AME) are presented in Figure 6.1.

At first glance, two things become obvious. The AMEs are rather similar: In all six subplots the whiskers representing the 95% confidence intervals are

---

[16] The model has to include dummy variables representing the electoral levels. Here, the national level is used as base category.

[17] There is a debate whether or not marginal effects suffer from unobserved heterogeneity as well (Mood 2010). This should be unproblematic here because we control for relevant group effects (the political level on which the election is conducted).

overlapping indicating that none of the point estimates is significantly different from any of the other point estimates. Additionally, the number of significant AMEs is rather low. This does not mean that the overall predictive power of the model is weak or that the different independent variables have no impact on turnout in general.[18] It simply shows that the impact of the six independent variables is seldom conditional on the electoral context. However, there are differences regarding the predictors and a closer look is necessary to confirm or reject the hypotheses presented above.

Party identification, utility, and ascribed relevance are three different ways to address the validity of H1. If a respondent has a strong party identification, a high utility of voting for at least one relevant party, or ascribes high relevance to an electoral level, his or her benefits of voting increase. Consequently, the respondent should show a higher probability to vote. In other words, the more second-order an election is, the stronger the effect of PID, utility, and attributed relevance should be. Unfortunately, there is no evidence for this claim. All AMEs for PID and utility are insignificant on the 5% level. Even comparing the effect size does not show the assumed effect. The ascribed relevance has a significant impact on all three levels with a more or less identical effect on national and European elections (the probability increases by 20% ranging from unimportant to very important) and a slightly larger one for regional elections (about 30%). Nevertheless, this speaks only in favor of characterizing regional elections as second-order while the other elections have to be classified as elections of the same order.

H2 relates to the increased relevance of political interest in second-order elections. Indeed, the AME for political interest in European elections is the largest and, more importantly, the only significant estimate. Being interested in politics increases the probability to turn out in EP elections by about 12%.[19]

Mobilization only shows a significant impact in regional elections. For each contact with a party or a candidate, the probability of participating increases by 1%. Regarding national and European elections, the AMEs are not only insignificant but also very small. Therefore, H3 holds for regional but not for European elections.

Finally, we expected a negative effect of positive government evaluation on turnout in less relevant elections (H4). Although all AMEs are indeed

---

[18] In fact, the model performs rather well in regard to explained variance. The Nagelkerke R^2 is 0.31. As this is a very conservative measure and the model does not include a full set of other predictors associated with turnout (for example, age), the model actually performs very well. The same is true for the proportion of correctly classified cases.

[19] This can also be interpreted as a weak confirmation of H1. We argued that high levels of political interest decrease information costs. This has a favorable impact on the cost-benefit calculations of citizens. As all other indicators linked to H1 do not confirm the hypotheses and as political interest in itself is an important indicator linked to various concepts (for example habitual voting), it seems justified to reject H1 nevertheless.

negative, the subplots show no significant estimates. Moreover, the effect is the largest for national elections, which leads to a clear rejection of H4. Dissatisfied citizens do not turn out with a higher probability in second-order elections.

All in all, there is only weak evidence of different behavioral rationales based on the second-order approach. Political interest is far more relevant in EP elections, while mobilization is more important in regional elections. Nevertheless, none of these second-order elections is truly deviating from the first-order behavioral pattern regarding turnout.

Party Choice

This section examines the determinants of party choice. As a first step, Table 6.3 gives an overview of vote switching. About two-thirds of the respondents voted for the same party in all three elections. This is a surprisingly low figure, especially when we take into account that all elections took place within a short period of time. Due to the lack of panel studies covering different political levels, it is only possible to compare these figures with the proportion of quasi-vote switchers.[20] The proportion of vote switchers between the European and the national election is close to 25%. Van Egmond (2007: 38) has shown that the number of quasi vote switchers was traditionally much lower in Germany: It ranged from 11.8 to 16.9% for the EP elections in 1989, 1994, and 1999. We calculated the number of quasi-vote switchers for the 2009 EP election using the 2009 EES voter survey (EES 2009). The proportion is significantly smaller, about 15%; if we restrict the sample to respondents living in the three regions under research here, it even drops to a mere 12%. It is important to highlight that relying on quasi-vote switching seems to underestimate individual volatility to a large degree.[21] Thus, it becomes even more important to understand the, potentially divergent, driving forces of party choice on different political levels.

Before presenting the results of the explanatory model, it is necessary to describe again the data structure and the model specifications. Party choice is estimated with a conditional logistic model applied to a stacked data matrix.[22] Unfortunately, there is—to our knowledge—no possibility to estimate a combined model that includes choice sets for more than one election

---

[20] Quasi-vote switchers are defined as voters stating that they will vote for a different party in the next election, normally the next national election.

[21] It is very unlikely that this gap is completely caused by the fact that we are comparing vote intentions closely before an election and not reported party choice with vote intention.

[22] In contrast to the data structure used to estimate turnout, the design of this stacked data matrix follows the more common design of parties nested in respondents. There is information regarding five parties in the survey and we constructed three data sets, one for each election.

Table 6.3 Vote switching between regional, national, and European elections (percentage of respondents; N = 202)

Vote intention	Proportion of respondents
For the same party in all three elections	67.2
EPE ≠ NPE	24.3
RPE ≠ NPE	21.3
EPE ≠ RPE	21.2
For different parties in all three elections	1.3

Notes: All figures are weighted. RPE = regional parliament election; NPE = national parliament election; EPE = European Parliament election.

if the number of higher level units is too small to run a multilevel model. Hence, we calculated separate explanatory models for each election, including an identical set of predictors holding the sample constant. This makes it impossible to compare coefficients directly in a meaningful way because they are based on separate estimations. As Mood (2010) points out, one of the most reliable ways to compare the effects of predictors between models is to calculate ratios. The amount of unobserved heterogeneity is fixed in each model. Therefore, dividing all coefficients by another coefficient taken from the model eliminates this distortion. To meet criteria of model specification, our model includes only relevant variables. As a consequence, following the "ratio approach" would prevent us from comparing all coefficients between the three models because one coefficient would have to be used to standardize the remaining coefficients. We solve this problem by including an additional variable that is only used to calculate the ratio.[23] This "benchmark variable" has to be uncorrelated with all other variables (including the dependent variable) in order to measure the unbiased effects of all "true" predictors. Hence, the variable is randomly drawn for each model, while the correlation matrix is fixed to the "true" correlations in the survey for all "true" variables and to zero for the benchmark variable.[24]

The standardized coefficients are presented in Figure 6.2;[25] hollow markers represent insignificant coefficients (95% level). The substantial number of significant coefficients and the high Nagelkerke pseudo-R^2

---

[23] By adopting this strategy, we lose one degree of freedom. Comparing the models with and without the "benchmark variable" leads to tiny differences for coefficients or p-values (about 0.001).

[24] Again, a detailed regression table can be found in the appendix (Table 6.5).

[25] The figure does not present the results for the benchmark variable because they are of no substantial interest.

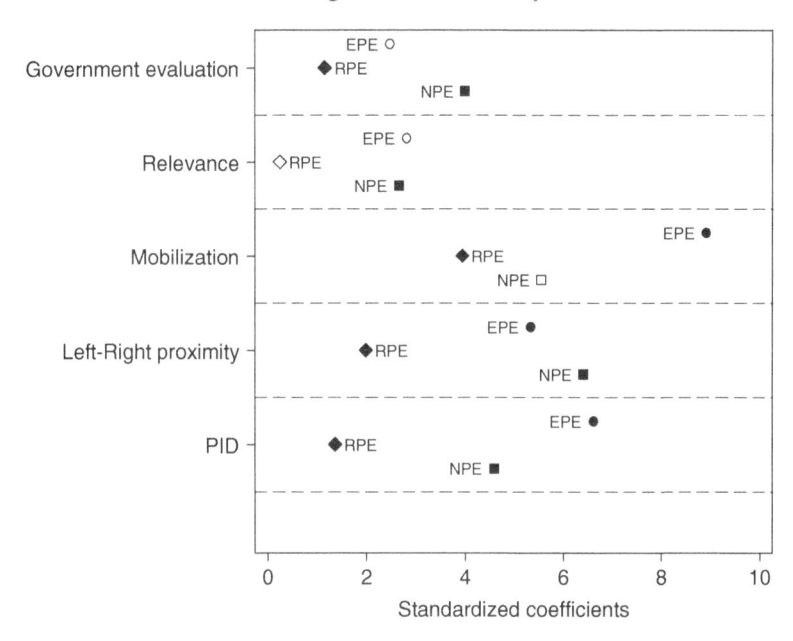

Figure 6.2 Standardized conditional logistic regression coefficients

Notes: Hollow markers represent insignificant coefficients (95% level). RPE = regional parliament election; NPE = national parliament election; EPE = European Parliament election.

values (EPE: 0.66; RPE: 0.71; NPE: 0.61) underline the quality of the parsimonious models. The model predicting party choice on the national level performs worst. This can be interpreted as an indication of more strategic voting in national elections because the model does not include features linked to strategic electoral behavior. However, the gap is only moderate, especially in comparison to the EPE model. Moreover, and in contrast to the assumptions, the RPE model shows the highest proportion of explained variance—meaning strategic electoral behavior is the least relevant on this level. Based on this finding, regional elections are more second-order than European elections that are, in turn, more second-order than national elections.

As expected, PID and the Left–Right proximity have a positive and significant impact on party choice in all models. According to Hypothesis 5, more sincere voting should take place in less relevant elections. There is no convincing evidence supporting this hypothesis. Indeed, party identification has the strongest effect in European elections, but it is only moderately higher than the standardized coefficient for national elections.

Moreover, the small coefficient for regional elections indicates that sincere voting does not really matter on this level. Left–Right proximity is also the least relevant in regional elections. In contrary to party identification and the theoretical assumptions, it matters the most for national elections.[26] Taking both measures of sincere voting together, there is slightly more "voting with the heart" in European elections than in national elections. But, even if we neglect the findings regarding regional elections, this small difference is only a weak confirmation of one of the core assumptions of the second-order approach.

When we look at the amount of "voting with the boot," it ultimately becomes clear that regional elections are not at all typical second-order elections. The respective coefficient is far smaller than the coefficient for national elections. Government evaluations play no role in European elections, which leads to a clear rejection of H6.

Regarding mobilization, European elections are truly second-order. The standardized coefficient is close to twice as high as the other two coefficients. In line with H7, the lower relevance of European elections combined with the overall lower level of campaigning make individual mobilization much more effective. Once again, regional elections seem to resemble a first- much more than a second-order election. This confirms prior findings on the independence of regional elections in Germany.

Finally, the impact of electoral relevance, which is only significant for national elections, is relatively small. It is by a clear margin the smallest coefficient predicting party choice in national elections. The mere ascription of relevance to a political level is far less important than other factors not directly linked to a political level. As mentioned above, the interpretation of the effect is not straightforward: It can only be interpreted in relative terms, e.g., by comparing the average effect for each of the five parties in the model predicting party choice in the national election. This effect is the largest for the Greens and the smallest for the Left; the effect for the other three parties is more or less identical. In other words: This does not point to a clear pattern, either in regard to party size or incumbency.

---

[26] Due to data limitations, we are not able to include any other spatial measure of voter/party coherence. Especially in the context of EP elections, this is far from ideal. More recent studies have shown that the issue of Europe or European integration has some relevance for electoral choice (de Vries et al. 2011; Hobolt, Spoon, and Tilley 2008). Nevertheless, the impact of the Left–Right super issue is still superior (de Vries et al. 2011: 23) and, more importantly, universal, meaning relevant on all political levels.

6.6 DISCUSSION

Comparative research on electoral behavior focuses on either differences or similarities over time, space, or political levels. Comparisons of political levels or types of elections are rare, especially on the micro level. Using a rather unique panel dataset covering regional, national, and European elections in Germany 2009, we compared determinants of turnout and vote choice to identify level-specific differences of behavior. For that purpose, we developed hypotheses from the literature on second-order elections.

Overall, the findings shed some doubts on the microlevel assumptions of second-order approaches. In contrast to theoretical expectations, the effects of cost–benefit calculations do not differ significantly in relation to turnout. There is weak evidence that regional elections are more second-order, but individual rationales do not differ between European and national elections. The same is true for mobilization effects. Additionally, behavioral patterns cannot be distinguished according to dissatisfaction with the government. Nevertheless, there is one finding supporting the deduced micro-foundation of second-order elections: Political interest is a strong predictor of participation in EP elections. This finding is consistent with earlier research on second-order elections. At the same time, it is the only finding also present in other studies that holds if panel data is used and turnout functions are compared directly.

One of the core assumptions of the second-order approach—more sincere voting in less important elections—is confirmed, but only weakly. People tend slightly more to vote with their hearts, but the differences are small. There is some evidence, though, for less strategic behavior, particularly in European elections. "Voting with the boot" in regional or European elections is shown to be irrelevant. Party choice is not determined by expressing dissatisfaction with the government's performance.

As in our analysis of turnout, only one hypothesis could clearly be confirmed. Mobilization has a strong effect on party choice in regional elections and an even stronger effect in European elections, while the overall high visibility of national elections seems to depress the effect of mobilization efforts. In addition, the analysis of party choice provided one very interesting finding: Quasi-vote switching is significantly lower than the real amount of volatility. This makes it even more important to understand the driving forces behind individual electoral behavior on different levels.

Going beyond Reif's definition of a second-order election by understanding second-orderness as a continuous rather than a binary concept seems reasonable. Regional elections are very similar to first-order elections, but show some characteristics of second-order elections as well. Nevertheless, it would be incorrect to define them as second-order elections to the same extent as

European elections. Even for the latter, we demonstrated that only certain assumptions connected with second-order elections hold if tested with a rigorous and valid design. Political interest has a divergent impact on turnout; the same is true for mobilization efforts to a larger and "voting with the heart" to a smaller degree. This defines European elections as second-order national elections. If we assume that second-order elections should show all the characteristics presented in the theoretical section, European elections in Germany figure as something in between.

These findings have to be interpreted with caution. We sacrificed universality in favor of a panel design by looking only at elections in Germany in 2009. However, this study highlights the importance of a clearly spelled out micro-level hypothesis and an appropriate research design. Some of the constraints applied here have to be relaxed if scholars want to conduct similar analyses comparing different countries or points in time. In any case, data availability and computational methods have improved significantly, and it seems reasonable to ask for more attention to these issues.

Level-specific explanations, as tested here, can point out some differences between regional, national, and European elections. Nevertheless, considering the vast gaps in turnout and party performance, it would be rather bold to assume that these differences constitute sufficient conditions.

One strand of arena-specific behavior in the context of European elections was not taken into account here. As Carrubba and Timpone (2005) or Hobolt, Spoon, and Tilley (2008) argue, citizens link different policy areas to different political levels. For example, the success of ecological parties could be based on the supranational nature of environmental protection (Curtice 1989). Similar arguments are made regarding anti-European parties (Hobolt, Spoon, and Tilley 2008) or European integration in general (de Vries 2010; de Vries and Hobolt 2012). If this is truly the case, we are confronted with level-specific behavior that is not determined by second-orderness but rather by policy seeking. The weak performance of the second-order approach in our analyses clearly calls for a broader research agenda going beyond classical work in regards to both theory and methodology.

Appendix

Table 6.4 Determinants of individual turnout (logistic regression)

DV: Turnout (1 = yes)	Coefficient	Robust Std. Error
PID	1.47 *	0.72
× regional election	−1.20	0.69
× European election	−0.80	0.74
Interest	−1.27	0.83
× regional election	0.61	0.76
× European election	2.22 ***	0.74
Mobilization	0.01	0.03
× regional election	0.09	0.06
× European election	−0.01	0.05
Utility	0.27	0.17
× regional election	−0.09	0.18
× European election	−0.21	0.17
Relevance	3.65 ***	0.92
× regional election	−0.02	1.09
× European election	−2.17 ***	0.81
Government evaluation	−0.34	0.21
× regional election	0.21	0.23
× European election	0.29	0.18
Regional election	−1.15	1.19
European election	−1.37	1.06
Intercept	1.41	1.12
Observations	1743 (clustered in 581 respondents in 3 regions)	
Pseudo-R^2 (Nagelkerke)	0.31	
Log pseudolikelihood	−531.91 (null model: −773.55)	

Notes: *** $p < 0.001$; ** $p < 0.01$; * $p < 0.05$. "National elections" are used as the base category for the dummy variables as well as the interactions. The data is weighted (see above).

Table 6.5 Determinants of individual party choice (conditional logistic regressions)

DV: Party choice (1 = yes)	Regional election (RPE)		National election (NPE)		European election (EPE)	
PID	3.04 ***	(0.47)	2.34 ***	(0.41)	3.13 ***	(0.31)
Left–Right proximity	4.43 **	(1.58)	3.28 ***	(0.54)	2.53 *	(0.99)
Mobilization	8.78 **	(3.21)	2.84	(3.83)	4.23 **	(1.55)
Relevance	0.52	(0.48)	1.36 **	(0.43)	1.33	(0.85)
Government evaluation	2.57 ***	(0.73)	2.04 **	(0.63)	1.17	(0.64)
Benchmark variable	2.23	(1.49)	0.51	(1.01)	0.47	(1.45)
Observations	\multicolumn{6}{c}{1010 (nested in 202 respondents nested in 3 regions)}					
Pseudo-R^2 (Nagelkerke)	0.71		0.60		0.66	
Log pseudolikelihood	−94.6 (null model: −115.3)		−128.6 (null model: −149.4)		−111.6 (null model: −129.8)	

Notes: *** $p < 0.001$; ** $p < 0.01$; * $p < 0.05$. "National elections" are used as the base category for the dummy variables as well as the interactions. The data is weighted (see above). Robust standard errors are provided in brackets.

7

Does Personal Campaigning Make a Difference?

Heiko Giebler, Bernhard Weßels, and Andreas M. Wüst

7.1 INTRODUCTION

Recently, local campaigning of candidates has gained more and more attention. This is true for majoritarian electoral systems like in Britain (Denver and Hands 1993; Denver et al. 2003; Denver, Hands, and MacAllister 2004; Johnston and Pattie 1995; Pattie, Johnston and Fieldhouse 1995) as well as for proportional electoral systems like in Finland and Spain (Karp, Banducci, and Bowler 2007; Gschwend and Zittel 2012; Shugart, Valdini, and Suominen 2005) and mixed-member electoral systems like in New Zealand and Germany (Karp 2009; Gschwend and Zittel 2012; Zittel and Gschwend 2007, 2008). Two general research questions characterize these analyses: First, whether local campaigning has become more important and changed its character. Second, whether local campaigning affects voting behavior. Our chapter focuses on the latter research question. Specifically, we contribute to the discussion as to whether and how local, particularly personal, campaigning affects voters' decision-making. The answer to this question seems self-evident in majoritarian voting systems where candidates run in single-member districts (SMDs) and campaign for themselves. In PR systems, in particular those with closed party lists, local (personal) campaigning seems less likely not only because of larger district magnitude but also because voters opt for a party list.[1]

Mixed-member electoral systems like Germany's, entailing a proportional, thus, list-tier and a plurality component of SMDs, may reveal mixed effects since neither do all candidates run in a district nor do all district candidates

---

[1] If preference voting is possible, the campaign strategies of the list candidates are expected to be personalized because preference votes may be decisive for getting elected (Bowler and Farrell 2011; Giebler and Wüst 2011a).

have to win in their districts in order to gain representation (Wüst et al. 2006: 424). The German electoral system distributes seats according to the proportional component, i.e., party list votes, but half of the members of the German Bundestag are elected in SMDs by a plurality of nominal votes. The founders of this electoral system held the firm belief that the plurality element would introduce incentives for more personalized politics at the grassroots level (Scarrow 2001). It is less clear whether this intention, embedded in the institutional design, is effective. In a review on findings by Farah (1980: 191–2), Kaase (1984: 163–4) concluded that

> ...the initial expectations in designing the personalized proportional representation system (PR) with respect to citizen-deputy ties have certainly not materialized, despite obvious efforts by the deputies to establish firm roots in their constituencies.

Nohlen, an expert on German election law, supported this perspective and made an argument based on the specific institutional feature that allows candidacy in a district and on a party list at the same time. He argued that because of the high share of dual candidacies, it makes little sense to distinguish between members of parliament who were elected in a SMD and those elected via party list (Nohlen 1978: 305–6). Proverbial wisdom claims that in single-member districts even broomsticks ("Besenstiele") could successfully run for office because only the party label counts. This speaks against a local campaigning effect and, specifically, against an effect of personal campaigning on the nominal vote. Under these circumstances, candidates' campaigning should clearly be "bowling for the party."

However, authors like Kaase, Farah, and Nohlen referred to times before the mid-1980s. Since then, a number of relevant factors have changed, i.e., vote switching and ticket splitting has increased. This process, which began in the 1980s and has accelerated after German unification, led Zittel and Gschwend to argue that due to developments of political parties and voter markets earlier characterizations may no longer fit (Zittel and Gschwend 2008). Findings of Klingemann and Weßels (2001) for the national elections 1998 suggest that a candidate's performance in the district has an effect on vote shares. In particular, perceived performance of a candidate makes a difference. If citizens think that a candidate has done a good job in the constituency, they will reward the candidate with a higher vote share. Performance-driven vote choice can affect the electoral performance of candidates in two ways—both of which result in a higher vote share for the local candidate: The first possibility is that a voter will choose to vote for a candidate whose party allegiance matches the voter's party vote. The second possibility is that a voter "defects" from his or her party-list vote in the SMD vote because of the good performance of a local candidate. In this case, ticket splitting is rather a result of candidate performance than of strategic considerations. For strategic decisions like splitting to the advantage of a coalition, performance aspects should not matter much. Evidence from Klingemann and Weßels (2001), however, suggests that candidate performance matters. Yet, their study relies only on voters' perceptions. The study does neither consider candidates' activities during the campaign nor voters' perceptions of candidates' campaigns. Hence, the question remains: Does local campaigning matter? Furthermore, does the strategy of campaigning—personal vs. partisan—make a difference for the success of district candidates in gaining personal votes? Do candidates "bowl alone" or "bowl for the party"?

We address these questions from two angles: candidates and voters. From the candidates' angle, we investigate whether and to what degree district campaigning matters. From the voters' angle, we ask for the degree to which the perceived and evaluated action of the candidate matters for the personal vote. The chapter proceeds as follows: First, we report the state of research on local campaigning and derive hypotheses. In a second step, we investigate candidates' campaigning: the resources used and its style as well as the effect on personal voting in the districts. Thirdly, we investigate the match between candidates' reporting of campaign activities and voters' perceptions of these efforts. Next, we estimate the impact of perceived campaign activities on the individual vote choice. Here, we answer three questions: Does a candidate profit from her effort, does the party profit from her effort, and can a candidate's efforts help to explain split-ticket voting? A final section summarizes the results and reflects on their implications for the literature as a whole.

7.2 STATE OF RESEARCH AND HYPOTHESES

Different types of electoral rules reflect different ideas of political representation (Huber and Powell 1994). In personalized voting systems, direct election of candidates should strengthen the linkage between voters and their representative more than in list-vote systems. This was, exactly, the expectation of the founding fathers of the Federal Republic of Germany after World War II. The personal component in the voting system should allow for a stronger tie between citizens and representatives in the district. In contrast, Nohlen (1978: 305–6) argued that there is no effect of local candidates on the vote due to the extremely high proportion of candidates running in the district and on a party list simultaneously. Even common knowledge says that local campaigns are largely irrelevant for pure majoritarian systems with single-member districts due to the high centralization of the campaigns in national elections, which is a result of party discipline, electronic media, and the prominent role of top candidates (Carty and Eagles 1999: 70; Denver, Hands, and MacAllister 2004).

These findings are surprising because theories on incentives in electoral systems clearly argue that district magnitude is the trigger that does or does not lead to the "cultivation of the personal vote" (Carey and Shugart 1995) and, thus, to the degree to which candidates engage in local and personalized campaigning. Studies examining nomination criteria for single-member districts and party lists show clear and expected effects. Porter (1995) found that, for Germany, the ability to win votes and a candidate's performance in the constituency matter most for the nomination at the district level and much less for nomination on a party list. Conversely, the political position within the party matters much more for list than for district nomination (Porter 1995). This raises the question as to whether candidates are only pleasing the "selectors" or whether there is more to local campaigning.

Results seem to support the latter. Inconclusive and incompatible findings may be a consequence of different measurements of campaigning and of differences in the strategic use of campaign resources and their outcomes. Carty and Eagles (1999), for example, reported findings from Jacobson for the US showing that the more incumbents spent, the less they gained in terms of votes. This seemingly paradoxical finding could be a result of candidate vulnerability as candidates that are more vulnerable may spend more in order to avoid defeat. It is not easy to demonstrate the counterfactual, but those candidates might actually have gained even fewer votes with less investment.

There is little doubt that campaigning matters for turnout (Krassa 1988). This holds true in comparative perspective. Differences between electoral systems are as expected: The impact of campaigning on turnout is strongest in the US and Britain and rather weak in proportional systems like the Netherlands and Sweden (Karp, Banducci, and Bowler 2007). Results also support the idea of directional effects of campaigning—but not consistently. Whiteley and Seyd (1992), for example, found an effect of campaigning on the vote in British elections. However, they used a poor measure of campaigning, i.e., membership density of parties in the districts, and ran their analysis exclusively on the aggregate level (Whiteley and Seyd 1992). Later studies confirmed directional campaign effects but showed that these effects vary for different parties (Denver et al. 2003: 556). Pattie and colleagues concluded that local campaigning seems to be much more valuable for challengers than for incumbents (Pattie, Johnston, and Fieldhouse 1995). Therefore, there is generally reason to assume that local campaigning not only exerts an influence on turnout but does so in a directional manner, although the effect may vary due to characteristics like incumbency or party affiliation of candidates. A general expectation or hypothesis is, therefore, that there is a positive relation between campaign efforts, i.e., campaign intensity, and voters' support for a candidate.

What are the actual characteristics of campaign intensity? Indicators for campaign intensity range from simple measures of district membership density to refined measures differentiating between traditional and modern means

(Whiteley and Seyd 1992; Fisher and Denver 2009; Norris 2000). Many studies use the amount of money spent during the campaign (Pattie, Johnston, and Fieldhouse 1995; Pattie et al. 1994). However, as Carty and Eagles stressed, a local campaign has to serve at least three purposes—organizing support, communicating the message of the candidate, and mobilizing voters—for which the money spent alone may not be a sufficient indicator of intensity. Instead, they propose to consider two basic campaign resources, namely money and people (Carty and Eagles 1999). Denver, Hands, and MacAllister (2004: 291–2) constructed a campaign-intensity index based on the number of campaign workers involved, the extent of door-to-door and telephone canvassing, the number of leaflets delivered, the use of computers, and the organization of the campaign team. Not focusing on the effects of campaigns but on the determinants of campaign intensity and the use of specific means, Giebler and Wüst (2011a) differentiated between duration, money, and time spent in order to measure intensity as well as the difference between classical and postmodern means and instruments. They showed that a broad set of factors ranging from systemic to party to individual-level characteristics impact campaign intensity and that there is no universal pattern predicting the different measures of intensity.

There also is no clear answer to the question as to which means and resources matter most for getting votes. Research indicates, however, that despite all efforts of parties to modernize their campaigns "modern campaign techniques seem to be regularly less effective than traditional ones" (Fisher and Denver 2009: 207). Furthermore, research results seem to suggest that traditional methods show stronger effects than modern campaigning. Whether the style of campaigning, i.e., more personalized or more party-centered, makes a difference is uncertain. Research on campaign styles is a new development and has, so far, been investigated only with regard to the existence of different styles and their explanation and not to the effect of those styles on outcomes (Zittel and Gschwend 2008). Comparing different measures of local campaign intensity, Pattie and colleagues came to the conclusion that local campaign spending is a quite good measure of campaign effort (Pattie et al. 1994). Denver and Hands (1997), however, argued that intense campaigning is a result of prevalent canvassing, which is more closely related to the availability of volunteers. Thus, one could argue that an intense campaign needs sufficient money, sufficient volunteers, and sufficient time resources of actors. As previous research has indicated that money is the universal indicator of campaign intensity, our expectation is that money shows the strongest effect on candidates' success in terms of vote shares.

The effect of campaign styles on outcomes is not yet clear. A general conclusion and expectation in terms of hypotheses is hard to draw from the findings alone. Considering also theoretical arguments, the following expectations or hypotheses seem plausible: (a) Financial resources help to win votes, but the effect of traditional canvassing might be stronger because it leads to direct contacts and (b) personalized campaigning should trigger a personal vote to a higher extent than party-centered campaigning. This expectation follows from the observation that local campaigning matters for candidates and that it is not only the party that matters. Consequently, if a candidate wants to improve her vote share, she should focus on a personalized campaign.

7.3 DATA AND DESIGN

The primary aim of this chapter is to identify the effect of local campaigning on electoral success in SMDs. The easiest way to address this question is to link candidates' efforts and behavior to their district vote share. In contrast to other studies that rely on aggregate data or official statistics regarding the spending of candidates, we have derived the amount of candidates' efforts from the candidates themselves in a postelection candidate survey. Hence, we have much more detailed information, especially on the kinds of efforts used in the campaign or its overall style and orientation. This information can be related to a measure of the dependent variable (personal vote share) that is free from measurement or sampling errors because it represents official election outcomes.

Unfortunately, such a research design has its drawbacks. The design cannot exclude the possibility that the correlations between campaigning and the individual vote are the spurious product of an unmeasured causal relationship, known as ecological fallacy. There are advanced estimation techniques addressing this problem, for example those developed by King (1997), that make ecological fallacy less likely but not impossible. We choose two strategies to guard against ecological fallacy. Following the considerations of Carty and Eagles (1999), the model of electoral fortune of candidates in the districts includes additional basic variables affecting parties' vote shares. Including those effects diminishes the likelihood that the effects estimated for campaign efforts are spoiled. The second strategy is an approach related to the "Coleman Bathtub." Originally, Coleman's approach deals with the problem of ecological fallacy by validating macro–macro relations with microlevel models. In other words, the bathtub represents a macro–micro–macro model of the underlying phenomena (Coleman 1990: 7–10).

Our research design does not fully reproduce the bathtub, which would include a direct test of the effects of macrolevel variables on the independent variables at the micro level, the microlevel model, and a test whether microlevel outcomes in sum reproduce the dependent variable on the macro level. The result is rather a triangle than a bathtub (Figure 7.1). Arrow 1 represents the model with individual-level data from the candidates and macro

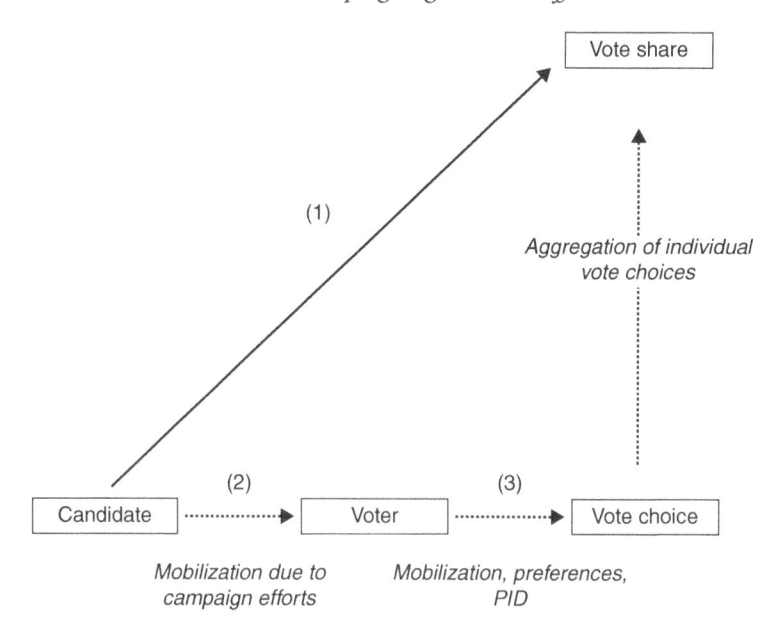

Figure 7.1 Research design

Diagram: Candidate →(2) Voter →(3) Vote choice; arrow (1) from Candidate to Vote share; "Aggregation of individual vote choices" from Vote choice up to Vote share. Labels: "Mobilization due to campaign efforts" under arrow (2); "Mobilization, preferences, PID" under arrow (3).

outcomes. For a proper test, the micro level of voters is needed. Thus, we have to operationalize and test the "bottom" of our triangle as well. We have to show that there is an effect of candidates' behavior on voters and, in consequence, an effect of mobilization on the citizens' vote choice (arrow 3). In order to complete our bathtub model, arrow 2 has to be investigated. Due to lack of data, the test of the impact of the actions reported by the candidates on the perception and evaluation of the candidates by the voters cannot be fully integrated into the microlevel explanatory model. For the same reason, we can't perform the last step of the bathtub, namely reproduce the macrolevel outcome by the summed outcomes of the microlevel model.

We have divided the empirical section into three analytical steps. First, we present an explanatory model for arrow 1: Is there an impact of candidates' behavior on vote shares and, if so, which factors determine electoral success? The two regression models applied use information from the GLES 2009 candidate survey (GLES 2011a), constituency results for the personal vote, and some contextual factors regarding the constituency.[2] They test two dependent variables, namely vote share in the constituency and difference between constituency vote share and party-list vote share in the district.

---

[2] Detailed descriptions of the variables we used as well as of their codings can be found in the appendix to this chapter (see Tables 7.6 to 7.8).

It seems rather common to predict separate models for each (relevant) party running in the election. While this is no big problem in OLS models, it is an invalid strategy for any models with, for example, binary outcomes. More important in the context of our analysis, separate models would not account for the dependency of a candidate's result on the result of another candidate. The success of one candidate is directly linked to the failure of at least one other candidate in the constituency. Hence, simultaneous estimation should be more appropriate[3], that is, running a model with all cases and taking the dynamic nature of political competition into account. We follow this strategy by using a "stacked" data matrix (van der Eijk et al. 2006).

The second step investigates the relationship between campaign activities reported by candidates and the voters' perception in the districts. Thirdly, we estimate an individual-level model to investigate the validity of arrow 3. It tests to which degree the perception of candidates' efforts and performance contributes to vote choice. This model uses data from the voter study only. As with the analysis at the candidate level, the data matrix represents a stacked data matrix.

7.4 CANDIDATES' CAMPAIGNING AND ELECTORAL SUCCESS

The general hypothesis of this chapter is that local campaigning matters for vote choice. We want to minimize the risk of incorrectly rejecting the null hypothesis by falling into the trap of ecological fallacy and therefore include contextual variables known to have an impact on voting behavior in the model. We use a simple linear regression model with clustered standard errors for constituencies to test the impact of individual-candidate behavior and efforts on their respective electoral success. The dependent variable is the candidate's personal vote share. Overall, there is information for 510 candidates and 267 constituencies. This sample represents about 35% of all constituency candidates and 90% of all constituencies. Moreover, candidate population characteristics like age, gender, or party affiliation are well represented in the sample.

---

[3] If the vote share or electoral success (candidate has won a mandate or not) is used as a dependent variable and the model includes information on all candidates in the constituency, it is no longer sufficient to estimate a "combined" model. The values of the dependent variable are conditional in such a scenario. However, conditional models are available for both binary outcomes as well as proportions.

Such models are not necessary for our analyses because (1) there are only three constituencies for which we have a full set of candidates and (2) their vote shares do not sum up to 100% due to the exclusion of candidates running for parties without parliamentary representation.

Nevertheless, all analyses in this section apply poststratification weights (see study description).[4]

The results for candidate-specific variables on campaign resources, i.e., money spent in the campaign, the number of people engaged in a candidate's campaign, and the time a candidate applied to her campaign, show that money has a strong positive and statistically significant effect (Table 7.1). People and time show positive effects, too, but they are not statistically significant. The second set of candidate-specific variables refers to the campaign modus and the campaign style. Regarding modus, prior research has indicated that traditional means of campaigning are still more effective in terms of electoral success than modern ones (Fisher and Denver 2009). In our analysis, the coefficient has the expected direction, but the standard error of the coefficient is so large that it would be quite bold to conclude that traditional campaigning has a stronger effect than modernized campaigning. Diversification of the mean mix of campaign instruments (leaflets, e-mails, contacts, posters, etc.) also does not count. Concerning campaign style effects, i.e., more personalized or more partisan campaigning, research suggests that money not raised by the party and the emphasis of constituency issues contribute to the success of candidates in SMDs (Gschwend and Zittel 2012). Theoretically, personalized campaigning should be more effective for getting votes because the object of choice of the personal vote is a person. This expectation is supported by the direction of the coefficient and its statistical significance.

The last candidate-specific variable is incumbency, which is known to be a strong predictor of campaign intensity (Giebler and Wüst 2011a). We differentiate between four types of candidates: candidates running for the first time in the constituency and without a mandate in the last election in 2005 (the base category), candidates that ran unsuccessfully in the constituency in 2005, candidates who won a list mandate in 2005, and the incumbents in the constituency. It is no surprise that incumbency has a very strong positive effect on the vote share of a candidate in a district. This confirms prior findings that, regardless of campaign intensity and performance, holding an office is the best predictor for vote share (Klingemann and Weßels 2001). Based on our findings, this statement needs to be qualified. The coefficient for candidates who won a list mandate in 2005 is positive but insignificant, meaning that only the specific office of being the constituency representative in the parliament increases the personal vote share in the following election.

Turning to structural and contextual factors, some remarks on their specific utility are necessary. It seems reasonable to assume that certain

---

[4] As mentioned above, only a very low number of constituencies is represented in our sample by all candidates running. However, there are three or more candidates for about one-third and at least two candidates cover another 40%. Hence, we are confident that the results presented here are valid even regarding electoral competition.

Table 7.1 Determinants of nominal constituency vote shares

	Coefficient	95% confidence interval	
Campaign intensity			
Ressources: money (sqrt)	0.02***	0.01	0.03
Ressources: time (sqrt)	0.09	−0.15	0.33
Ressources: people (sqrt)	−0.02	−0.29	0.25
Campaign modus and style			
Campaign modus (traditional)	1.10	−0.96	3.16
Diversity of means	−0.06	−0.16	0.04
Campaign style (personalized)	0.20**	0.02	0.39
Incumbent (base category = new candidate)			
Unsuccessful in 2005	0.27	−0.39	0.93
List mandate in 2005	0.57	−0.56	1.70
Constituency mandate in 2005	6.13***	3.86	8.41
Structural/contextual factors			
Unemployment rate			
SPD candidate	1.24***	0.49	1.99
CDU/CSU candidate	−0.86***	−1.29	−0.43
FDP candidate	−0.36***	−0.55	−0.16
Bündnis 90/Grüne candidate	−0.16	−0.36	0.04
Linke candidate	0.39***	0.22	0.55
Population density			
SPD candidate	−0.38	−1.12	0.35
CDU/CSU candidate	−2.02***	−3.10	−0.94
FDP candidate	0.05	−0.40	0.50
Bündnis 90/Grüne candidate	1.26***	0.77	1.76
Linke candidate	−0.51**	−1.01	−0.01
Turnout			
SPD candidate	−0.09	−0.56	0.38
CDU/CSU candidate	−0.13	−0.45	0.19
FDP candidate	−0.09	−0.24	0.06
Bündnis 90/Grüne candidate	0.32***	0.17	0.47
Linke candidate	−0.13**	−0.25	−0.01
East Germany			
SPD candidate	−17.4***	−23.3	−11.5

(*Continued*)

Table 7.1 Continued

	Coefficient	95% confidence interval	
CDU/CSU candidate	−2.69	−7.05	1.67
FDP candidate	0.11	−1.59	2.81
Bündnis 90/Grüne candidate	1.03	−0.75	2.81
Linke candidate	15.1***	12.7	17.5
Party (base category = SPD)			
CDU/CSU candidate	29.6	−15.4	74.7
FDP candidate	−4.52	−43.1	34.1
Bündnis 90/Grüne candidate	−36.8*	−75.7	2.19
Linke candidate	−7.64	−46.6	31.4
Intercept	20.1	−17.6	57.7
Observations	510 (in 267 constituencies)		
R-squared	0.94		

Notes: *** $p < 0.01$; ** $p < 0.05$; * $p < 0.1$. Robust standard errors (clustered by constituency); weighted data.

contextual factors have party-specific effects on the fortune of candidates regardless of individual efforts. For example, there are still significant party-specific differences comparing West and East Germany, even after two decades (Gabriel 2011). Measuring these tendencies can help to shed even more light on the underlying research question but it makes it necessary to "individualize" the determinants. This can be done by interacting the structural determinant with variables measuring a candidate's party allegiance (Long and Freese 2006: 293ff.; for practical examples in the field of electoral research: Debus 2012; Thurner, Mauerer, and Binder 2012).[5] As a result, we get coefficients for candidates running for the SPD, the CDU/CSU, the FDP, etc.

The context variables include unemployment rate, which we know to be especially important for the Social Democrats and the Left. Indeed, results show that both parties gain more in areas with higher unemployment in comparison to Christian Democrats, Liberals, and the Greens. Population density is relevant because in urban areas the Green Party is more successful due to student and alternative milieus in larger cities, in particular in university cities. Our results support these earlier findings. Turnout as contextual variable has been shown to have small and significant partisan effects. In general, Social

[5] The model has to include dummy variables measuring a candidate's party allegiance. Here, the SPD is used as a base category. The model does not include the constitutive contextual variable because this would make it impossible to estimate all five coefficients due to reasons of overspecification.

Democrats suffer more from low turnout than other parties (Kohler 2011). This general finding is not supported regarding the success of local candidates. If any party suffers it is the Left; if any party gains it is the Greens. Overall, this results in a stunning R^2 of 0.94. If our model was limited to the first seven candidate-specific predictors it would still have an R^2 value of 0.70. Therefore, the explanatory power is based not only on party-specific contextual factors but also on the indicators measuring candidates' behavior and efforts.

Overall, the model performs very well and supports some of the expectations regarding the campaign variables: Money counts and so does personalized campaign style. Campaign modus, i.e., traditional or modern, makes no difference; neither do resources beyond money and the diversification of means. This supports the results of Gschwend and Zittel (2012: 387) for the 2005 national elections, although their findings are not comparable because they looked for effects of these factors that are relevant for individual personal vote and did not investigate district vote share.

Obviously, the presented model can only give information on the level of personal vote share. Due to the mixed-member electoral system and the strong role of political parties, spillover effects are plausible. Although the results indicate that personal campaigns are of relevance, the success and failure of candidates might still be determined by their party affiliation. We address this question with a second model. Here the dependent variable is the difference between personal and party vote share in the constituency. Positive values indicate a larger share of personal votes. The predictors are identical to those used in the first model, with the exception of contextual variables and party dummies. The effect of these variables is covered by using the party vote share in our calculation of the dependent variable. We present the results in Table 7.2.

Clearly, individual and campaign characteristics can explain differences between personal and party vote shares. Not only is the R^2 close to 0.5, but also seven out of nine predictors have significant coefficients.

All indicators measuring campaign resources have a valid impact on the dependent variable. The more resources a candidate has or spends, the more personal votes she will gain in relation to her party's vote share. For example, a candidate campaigning for ten hours per week increases his relative vote share by 1.4 percentage points in comparison to a person who does not campaign at all. The campaign style exhibits the expected effect as well: Personalized campaigning helps winning personal votes at the cost of party votes. This finding speaks for a strategic usage of "bowling alone" versus "bowling for the party."

Incumbency returns the expected effect, too. Again, we use new candidates as the base category. While unsuccessful candidates do not profit significantly from their status, holding a mandate is very helpful to win a larger share of personal votes. Holding everything else fixed, we found that the candidate who won the constituency seat in 2005 would win 5-percentage points more personal than party votes.

Table 7.2 Determinants of constituency vote share differences (nominal minus party list)

	Coefficient	95% confidence interval	
Resources: money (sqrt)	0.02***	0.01	0.02
Resources: time (sqrt)	0.43***	0.21	0.65
Resources: people (sqrt)	0.32***	0.14	0.50
Campaign modus (traditional)	−0.41	−2.98	2.16
Diversity of means	−0.22***	−0.34	−0.11
Campaign style (personalized)	0.28***	0.14	0.42
Incumbent (Base category = new candidate)			
Unsuccessful in 2005	0.38	−0.43	1.19
List mandate in 2005	1.61***	0.58	2.64
Constituency mandate in 2005	5.04***	3.88	6.20
Intercept	−3.65***	−6.34	−0.96
Observations	510 (in 267 constituencies)		
R-squared	0.51		

Notes: *** $p < 0.01$; ** $p < 0.05$; * $p < 0.1$. Robust standard errors (clustered by constituency); weighted data.

However, there is also a rather surprising result: Traditional campaigning, such as canvassing or public debates, is negatively associated to winning constituency votes compared to list votes. Although the coefficient is clearly insignificant, it is interesting to see that several aspects linked to personal contacts between candidates and voters do not lead to an increase in personal vote share. Finally, heterogeneous campaigns, meaning campaigns relying on a large set of different instruments, decrease personal vote share. One could argue that relying on a large set of instruments decreases the quality of each instrument in terms of resources. As a result, voters might not be able to absorb all information due to inadequate campaign efforts. But the basic information—for which party the candidate is running—is always easy to understand and this might increase the party but not the personal vote share.[6]

---

[6] We also tested interaction effects between the number of instruments used and the three indicators measuring resources. Indeed, comparing the marginal effects leads to the finding that more resources in the case of time and personnel decrease the negative effect of using more instruments—but only to a very small degree. The effects always remain negative. Regarding financial resources, the more money a candidate spends, the more its negative impact grows—but again only marginally. However, the inclusion of these interaction terms does not improve the model substantively. Hence, we stick to the simple model presented in Table 7.2.

This section has shown two things: The absolute level of personal votes depends, significantly, on local campaigning and individual characteristics. Furthermore, contextual factors are relevant and some conditions are more favorable for a candidate—especially her party affiliation. "Bowling alone" helps the candidate to succeed, but "bowling for the right party" is also important. Additionally, we showed that local campaigning can account for the differences between a candidate's personal and her party's vote share. Investing more resources in the personal campaign and focusing the campaign on the candidate increase vote-share differences tremendously.

7.5 VOTERS' PERCEPTIONS OF CANDIDATES' EFFORTS

In order to avoid a gap between aggregate data analysis and a micro model of vote choice, we have to (a) show that voters' perceptions of candidates' campaigns matter and (b) link these perceptions to candidates' actions. Thus, before estimating a micro model explaining vote choice determined by candidates' efforts as perceived by voters, it is prudent to check the relationship between what candidates reported and voters perceived. It is clear that efforts and activities of candidates are only indirectly connected to electoral success. Indirectly, in this case, means that their effect is conditional on whether potential voters are aware of and reached by these efforts. The voter data is taken from the 2009 GLES preelection survey (GLES 2011c).

In the voter survey, respondents were asked whether a specific candidate made personal contact with them or whether they had received or seen campaign material of the candidate. The candidate survey provides information on the campaign instruments used by a candidate. Given this, we can investigate whether the usage of, for example, personal leaflets by a candidate was successful in terms of having reached voters in her constituency.

One measure of success is whether voters remember a candidate's name.[7] The expectation is that receiving personalized campaign information, seeing campaign posters with the candidate, and having contact with a candidate should help to increase recognition of her.[8]

---

[7] Citizens were asked to give the name of each party's direct candidate to measure recognition. There was no filter from this question regarding the campaign activity questions. Hence, citizens were asked whether they received campaign material from the constituency candidate of the SPD, the CDU/CSU, etc. without stating the name.

[8] Pinpointing causal direction in this case is difficult. If a citizen is familiar with a candidate he or she might be able to remember more easily any activity by this candidate. At the same time, having received a personal flyer or having seen a campaign poster makes it much easier to remember the name and, therefore, to recognize the candidate.

Does Personal Campaigning Make a Difference?

Table 7.3 Campaign activities and their reception by candidate recognition in percentages (N = 3,497)

Campaign activities	Candidate recognition	
	No	Yes
Received campaign information of candidate		
No	95.4 (2727)	83.1 (535)
Yes	4.7 (133)	16.9 (109)
Has seen campaign poster of candidate		
No	77.6 (1921)	47.8 (284)
Yes	23.4 (554)	52.2 (310)
Has been contacted by candidate		
No	98.9 (2826)	93.6 (597)
Yes	1.2 (33)	6.4 (41)

Notes: This table includes only information on those candidates who actually used the respective campaign instruments, meaning those who provided personal campaign information material, used personalized campaign posters, or contacted citizens directly. The frequencies are provided in brackets.

The results show, first, that candidates could not get through to all voters. The maximum proportion of voters reached by an activity was about one-third. However, Table 7.3 also reveals that campaign information, posters, and contacts make a difference. Voters who have seen campaign posters of candidates have more than the twice the proportion of candidate recognition than those who have not. Effects are even relatively (not in absolute terms) larger for campaign information and contacts. For those that had these experiences, the proportion of recognition is four times as high as for those who had not (Table 7.3).

A second test checks whether intensity of the campaign matters for the recognition of the campaign measures. From the analysis of the effects of candidate campaigning on the vote share in the districts, we already know that the amount of money spent has a large effect. Thus, campaign intensity is here measured in terms of money. The relationship should be a very simple one: the more money, the more campaign information material or posters are provided. Based on averages, Figure 7.2 shows that there is a clear relationship between campaign intensity in terms of money spent and having received information about the candidate, recognizing posters of the candidate, and having been contacted. In all cases, the mean value of money spent is higher for the "yes" category. If candidates spend more money, there is a higher probability that

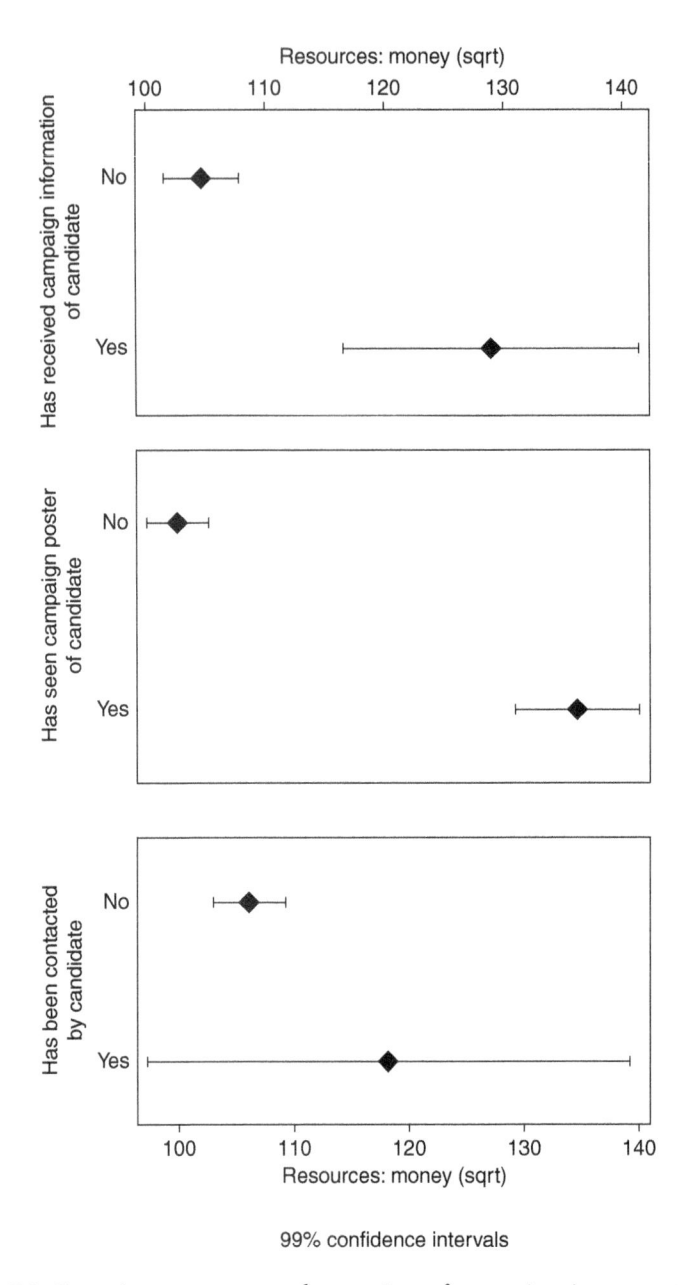

Figure 7.2 Campaign resources and reception of campaign instruments (mean comparisons)

Notes: Each dot represents the mean of money spent (sqrt) by candidates. A distinction is made whether a citizen has received campaign material, seen a campaign poster, or had contact. The calculations are based on the stacked data matrix including 3,549 observations.

voters in their constituency actually receive campaign information regarding these candidates. A comparison of the 99% confidence intervals shows that the difference is highly significant for the first two indicators (received campaign material and saw a personalized campaign poster). The difference is not significant for contacts, which may simply indicate that money cannot buy time for a candidate to make contacts.

We can conclude that there is a relationship between campaign activities and the voters' perception of these activities. Thus, we can argue that if we find a relationship between voters' perception of campaign activities and their vote choice this is not just a projection. We expect that perceptions relate positively to candidates' activities as reported by them. But is there a measurable effect of campaigning on vote choice on the micro level at all?

7.6 VOTERS' CAMPAIGN PERCEPTIONS AND THEIR VOTE

Thus, the last step in our analysis examines whether we can establish an explanation of the personal vote from a voter perspective. Gschwend and Zittel (2012) recently presented results on this very question linking aggregate information on candidate activities at the constituency level with voter data. We deliberately refrain from this strategy for the following reasons: Due to data restrictions, only a limited number of constituencies would be covered,[9] and even for those constituencies information is only available for a small number of candidates. This would result in a highly unrepresentative model burdened by incomplete data. At the same time, a vote for a specific candidate is conditional on not voting for the remaining candidates. Gschwend and Zittel (2012: 387) used a stacked data matrix but applied an unconditional logistic model, which gives rise to serious doubts regarding their findings. Confidence intervals get larger when conditional models are applied. More importantly, as the predicted probabilities of vote choice are conditional, they sum up to one. High probability to vote for one candidate goes hand in hand with low probabilities of voting for the remaining candidates. Obviously, both factors significantly influence the regression results. Therefore, we limit our analysis to the micro level of voters and do not include candidates' reports on their activities. We already established that there is a relationship between candidate activities

---

[9] Missing information on constituencies and low numbers of respondents in many constituencies also make it impossible to validate the last step in Figure 7.1. This last step would consist in testing how well the individual-level model of vote choice can mirror the aggregated results for a constituency. With a sample size of 2,200 respondents (not taking into account missing values for the relevant variables) and 299 constituencies, it is not possible to get representative electoral results that could be compared to the official constituency results.

and the perception of these by voters. Furthermore, we think that there is no reason to assume that candidates' activities exert a direct influence on voters' calculus. Voters have to perceive something before they can use this information as a relevant element of their decision-making. Thus, our model includes perceptions of candidates' activities and evaluations.

One feature of mixed-member systems is the combination of two different components—personal vote and party-list vote—and there is much debate as to the degree of independence between these components (Gschwend, Johnston, and Pattie 2003). There is evidence of so-called contamination effects, and it is assumed that the direction of contamination is from party to candidate (Nohlen 1978: 305–6). This is the reason for the "broomstick hypothesis" referred to in the introduction. In order to evaluate whether a candidate and her activities make a difference, we must control for such contamination. Our model includes two variables that can be used for this means: the like–dislike scale for the party of the candidate and the party-list vote of the respondent. In total, the model consists of variables related to the intensity of the campaign (receiving information, seeing posters, direct contacts), evaluative measures (like–dislike, proximity), and information on the campaign strategy.

Going beyond the debate about one-sided contamination, i.e., from party-list vote to nominal vote for the constituency candidate, we also test a second model investigating contamination in the opposite direction. The reason is simple and has been highlighted by Gschwend and van der Kolk (2006: 167). They ask "why do so many parties present candidates in the constituency contest of mixed systems although they are clearly doomed to lose?" and argue that parties improve their vote shares in the list contest if they present a candidate (viable or not) in the constituency. Our second model includes the same variables as the first but party-list vote as the dependent variable and nominal vote as the second control variable for contamination effects.

Our hypotheses are straightforward and the same as with the above models, just based on perceptions: (1) The more intense a candidate's campaign is, the more likely it is that she will profit from it; 2) the more positively a voter evaluates a candidate, the more likely it is that the candidate will receive a vote from this voter; and (3) the more a candidate emphasizes herself as a person from the voter's perspective, the more likely it is that a personal vote is triggered.

The model is a conditional logistic regression applied to a stacked data matrix in which each personal vote alternative for the five parties of the German Bundestag represents a case, coded 1 when choice is in favor of the candidate and 0 if not. Table 7.4 presents the results. For the nominal vote, model estimates show that having received information from a candidate and having seen posters matter. Furthermore, positive evaluations in terms of candidate like–dislike and proximity exert a positive influence on the personal vote. This holds true even after controlling for party like–dislike and party-list vote. Interestingly, direct contacts with a candidate and campaign style do

Table 7.4 The impact of the perception of the campaign and the candidate on the nominal and party-list vote

	Nominal vote		Party-list vote	
	Coefficient	Std. error	Coefficient	Std. error
Information from candidate	1.288 ***	0.192	−0.018	0.220
Posters of candidate	0.412 ***	0.159	0.197	0.137
Direct contact with candidate	0.012	0.470	1.270 ***	0.420
Evaluation of candidate	0.376 ***	0.073	0.210 ***	0.052
Proximity to candidate (Left–Right scale)	0.104 ***	0.022	0.058 ***	0.016
Campaign style (personal vs. party)	0.075	0.056	−0.201 ***	0.046
Party like–dislike of candidate's party	0.282 ***	0.023	0.152 ***	0.021
Party-list vote	1.941 ***	0.155	–	–
Nominal vote	–	–	1.954 ***	0.156
No. of observations		6,995		6,995
Prob > chi^2		0.000		0.000
Pseudo R^2		0.618		0.545

Notes: *** $p < 0.01$; ** $p < 0.05$; * $p < 0.1$. Robust standard errors (clustered by constituency); weighted data.

not matter. The latter result contrasts with the results of Gschwend and Zittel (2012), who found a positive and significant effect. As mentioned, they most likely overestimated the effect and its statistical significance by applying an unconditional model to a stacked data matrix.

Thus, even after controlling for contamination effects, candidates' campaign efforts make a difference for their vote share. Surprisingly, those variables often assumed to indicate most strongly the effort for a personal vote, i.e., getting in direct contact with voters as well as presenting oneself primarily as a person and not as a party soldier, do not show significant effects. Is this finding an indicator that candidate's campaign efforts are rewarded but personalized campaigning is not? This would imply that candidates' efforts count for their vote share but stressing one's own personality too much and leaving one's party aside, i.e., "bowling alone," is not helpful.

Results for the impact of candidates' campaigning on party-list vote seem supportive of this argument. In this model, candidates' efforts to provide the voters with information about themselves (information brochures, posters) do not increase the party's vote share, whereas direct contact matters considerably, as do the other candidate-related variables. Campaigning for the party helps the party's vote share. Therefore, the model for party-list vote suggests that a candidate and her contact with voters matters if she stands for the party.

Concerning the strength and direction of spillover effects from party to candidate or vice versa, results show that the variance in the nominal vote can be explained better than variance in party-list vote. Furthermore, factors that benefit the candidate's vote share and those that are conducive to the party's vote share show different patterns, meaning that we cannot easily make a general claim. Results seem to suggest that voters make a clear distinction between the two choices and that this differentiation also depends on how a candidate campaigns.

These results suggest that there is an independent impact of candidate's activities and voters' candidate evaluations on the personal vote, but we can further disentangle candidate and party by looking to those voters who split their vote between candidate and party and those who voted a straight ticket. This model includes interactions of evaluations of the candidate and like–dislike of the candidate's party with vote splitting. We select evaluations because if contamination by party preferences is driving personal vote choice, this should culminate in different evaluations by those voting a straight ticket and those who choose to split. If there are only strategic reasons for splitting between party and personal vote, there should be no significant difference between the impacts of candidate evaluations regarding split- and straight-ticket voters. But if the performance of the candidate is the reason for splitting, evaluations should, on average, perform better with split-ticket voting than with straight-ticket voting, as defection from party preference that is not purely strategic requires a good reason.

We use interactions similar to those of the candidate-/vote-share model presented above. Hence, we receive "voter-type specific" coefficients for all relevant independent variables.[10] Results show that both evaluations have less impact in the case of splitters (Table 7.5). Moreover, the coefficients are not significantly different. This implies that vote split is not primarily driven by a preference for a particular candidate but by strategic considerations. This is also indicated by the smaller effect of the like–dislike scale for a candidate's party in case of ticket splitting.

The most interesting finding is that the effect of campaign style is significant for both groups, i.e., splitters and straight voters, but in opposite directions. A straight ticket is more likely when the campaign style is more party-oriented, a split ticket is more likely when the campaign style is more personalized. The more personalized a candidate's campaign is in the eyes of the voters, the more likely this candidate is to receive their votes. These results are a clear indication that candidates' campaigning, as well as the style of their campaigning matters, and that "bowling alone" can pay off.

---

[10] In this case, "voter-type specific" means that we get coefficients for split- and straight-ticket voters.

Table 7.5 The impact of the perception of the campaign and the candidate on the nominal vote for straight-ticket and split-ticket voters

	Coefficient	Standard error
Information from candidate	1.202 ***	0.191
Posters of candidate	0.543 ***	0.121
Direct contact with candidate	0.953 **	0.400
Evaluation of candidate		
Straight ticket	0.615 ***	0.098
Splitting personal and list vote	0.336 ***	0.113
Proximity to candidate (Left–Right scale)		
Straight ticket	0.155 ***	0.027
Splitting personal and list vote	0.105 ***	0.029
Campaign style of candidate (personal vs. party)		
Straight ticket	−0.146 *	0.076
Splitting personal and list vote	0.209 ***	0.078
Party like–dislike of candidate's party		
Straight ticket	0.436 ***	0.030
Splitting personal and list vote	0.290 ***	0.044
No. of observations		6,995
Prob > chi²		0.000
Pseudo R²		0.483

Notes: *** p < 0.01; ** p < 0.05; * p < 0.1. Robust standard errors (clustered by constituency); weighted data.

It is difficult to decide to which degree candidate evaluations by straight-ticket voters result from their party preference. Even controlling for like–dislike of the candidate's party cannot rule out that spillover from a positive view of the party might influence a voter's judgment of candidates. For those who split their ticket, however, it is safe to assume that the spillover did not work the other way round—from candidates to parties. At least the personal vote of those 25% is not "infected" by party choice. The link between candidates' efforts and the voters' perception of these efforts supports this claim.

7.7 CONCLUSIONS

Does personal campaigning matter? Do district candidates fare better "bowling alone" or "bowling for the party"? We tried to answer these complex questions via a complex design. We started with a model explaining the electoral fortune of district candidates in terms of their vote shares. Results demonstrate that about 60% of the variation in district vote shares of candidates is due to campaign resources, efforts, and campaign style. Specifically, money spent for the campaign and a personalized campaign style count. However, these are results based on aggregate data. Even controlling for a number of context variables and the vote share of the candidate's party cannot fully exclude the possibility that the underlying assumption that campaign efforts reach voters and influence the direction of their vote choice is wrong and the resulting interpretation is simply a product of ecological fallacy.

The crucial conceptual consideration regarding our questions is that there must be input, i.e., campaign efforts of candidates. These efforts have to be measured independently of perceptions, because perceptions can be wrong, merely projections, etc. There must exist a link between input, measured independently of perceptions, and the perceptions themselves. We are sure that behavior and choice are no automatic consequences of inputs. Rather, individuals have to recognize these inputs, evaluate them, and draw their conclusions after weighing different inputs against each other or against a personal yardstick.

For this reason, we have tried to reproduce Coleman's bathtub approach as far as our data allow. We checked if voters perceive the campaign efforts as reported by the candidates. This proved to be the case. Given this supportive finding, we were confident of testing a micro model of vote choice at the voters' level. The crucial design aspect here is that our measures of voters' perceptions of candidates' efforts match well with the questions we asked the candidates about their resources, activities, and campaign strategy.

The model explaining the personal vote included perceptions of campaign efforts such as: information from the candidate, posters, and direct contacts as well as a general evaluation and proximity. All variables show significant effects except for direct contacts of the candidate with voters and campaign style, i.e., whether the candidate concentrated the campaign on herself as a person or on the party. Thus, campaign efforts matter, as suggested by the aggregate model explaining vote shares.

However, perceived campaign efforts exert a smaller influence on split-ticket than on straight-ticket voters. We cannot fully exclude the possibility that there are contamination effects between party preference and the evaluation of candidates by the voters. But the findings regarding the match of reported campaign efforts of candidates and the voter's perception of these efforts support the view that this perception is not a projection from party preferences on candidate evaluation. It rather shows that there is a concrete basis for these perceptions and that input and perception are consistent to a relevant degree. We can conclude that personal campaigning helps candidates to increase their vote share beyond their party's popularity.

Does Personal Campaigning Make a Difference?

This does not mean that personalized campaigning solely focused on the candidate as a person will always be the best strategy to gain a bigger vote share. Personalized campaigning clearly has a negative effect on vote choice by straight-ticket voters. It seems that those voters wish for a "connection" between the candidate and the party. In this case, "bowling for the party" would help both the candidate and the party. On the other hand, the candidate should call attention to herself in order to win votes from ticket splitters that defect from their party vote for strategic reasons and not because of their evaluation of the candidate's performance. The best way to achieve this is by "bowling alone."

Appendix

Table 7.6 Variables used in Section 7.4

Name	Description	Coding
Dependent variables		
Nominal constituency vote shares	Nominal constituency vote share of each candidate	Percentage points
Constituency vote share differences	Constituency vote share differences for each candidate	Nominal vote share minus party-list vote share
Candidate-specific independent variables		
Resources: Money (sqrt)	Size of candidate's overall campaign budget in euros	Square root of value; high values indicate more resources
Resources: Time (sqrt)	Number of hours per week used for campaigning during the last month before the election	Square root of value; high values indicate more resources
Resources: People (sqrt)	Size of campaign team	Square root of value; high values indicate more resources
Campaign modus (traditional)	Measurement of traditional campaign instruments and efforts as proportion of all instruments and efforts used by the candidate	Values range from 0 (no traditional campaign) to 1 (purely traditional campaign). Candidates not using any instruments or efforts were set to 0.5.
Diversity of means	Number of different instruments and efforts used during the campaign	High values indicate a higher number and, therefore, diversity.
Campaign style (personalized)	Is main goal of the candidate's campaign party- or candidate-centered?	High values indicate focus on candidate while low values indicate focus on party.

(Continued)

Table 7.6 Continued

Name	Description	Coding
Incumbent	Status of respective candidate	0 = new candidate (base category) 1 = unsuccessful in 2005 2 = won list mandate in 2005 3 = won constituency mandate in 2005
Structural/contextual factors		
Unemployment rate	Unemployment rate in the constituency at the time of the election	High values indicate more unemployment; measured in percentage points.
Population density	Average number of people per km² living in the constituency	High values indicate high density.
Turnout	Turnout rate in the constituency	High values indicate high turnout; measured in percentage points.
East Germany	Region in which the constituency is located	Dummy; 1 = East Germany
Party	Candidate's party affiliation	1 = SPD (base category) 2 = CDU/CSU 3 = FDP 4 = Bündnis 90/Grüne 5 = Linke

Notes: All variables are taken from the candidate survey that provides contextual information as well.

Table 7.7 Variables used in Section 7.5

Name	Description	Coding
Source: candidate survey		
Resources: money (sqrt)	See Table 7.6	See Table 7.6
Source: voter survey		
Candidate recognition	Respondents were asked to name the candidates running in their constituency.	Dummy; 1 = yes
Received campaign information of candidate	Did the respondent receive campaign information from the respective candidate?	Dummy; 1 = yes
Seen campaign poster of candidate	Has the respondent seen a personal campaign poster of the respective candidate?	Dummy; 1 = yes
Have been contacted by candidate	Has the respondent been personally contacted by the respective candidate?	Dummy; 1 = yes

Table 7.8 Variables used in Section 7.6

Name	Description	Coding
Dependent variables (also used as control variables)		
Vote choice (nominal)	Nominal vote of the respondent	Dummy; 1 = yes
Vote choice (party list)	Party-list vote of the respondent	Dummy; 1 = yes
Independent variables		
Information from candidate	Did the respondent receive campaign information from the respective candidate?	Dummy; 1 = yes
Posters of candidate	Has the respondent seen a personal campaign poster of the respective candidate?	Dummy; 1 = yes
Direct contact with candidate	Has the respondent been personally contacted by the respective candidate?	Dummy; 1 = yes
Evaluation of candidate	Thinking highly or not highly of the candidate	11-point scale; −5 not at all, +5 highly
Left–Right proximity to candidate	Left–right self-evaluation to perceived left–right position of candidate	11 minus |Left–Right self minus Left–Right party|
Campaign style (personal vs. party)	Did candidate put more emphasis on herself as a person or on her party?	11-point scale; −5 party, +5 candidate as a person
Party like-dislike of candidate's party	Thinking highly or not highly of a party	11-point scale; −5 not at all, +5 highly

Notes: All variables are taken from the voter survey.

Part III

Increasing Complexity and Voting

8

Network Politicization and Political Integration
From Grand Cleavages to Private Network Structures

Sigrid Roßteutscher and Daniel Stegmueller

8.1 INTRODUCTION

One of the dominant theoretical strands in political science, in general and electoral research in particular, proclaims the end of grand narratives: the end of the class struggle, the decline of traditional cleavage structures that organized party politics in Europe since the 19th century and the birth of representative democracy (Clark and Lipset 2001; Lipset and Rokkan 1967a; Bartolini and Mair 1990). As a result, contemporary society is becoming increasingly individualized (Inglehart 1990). Economic growth, the security promise of mature welfare states, and the expansion of the educational system have contributed to a spread of cognitive mobilization, elite-challenging participation patterns, and the rationality of the individual self which invents and expresses itself according to narrowly defined self-interest or short-term issue-orientated forms of political activism (e.g. Norris 1999).

Mankind, however, is unlikely to exist in individualized, anonymous structures. Even if the traditional cleavage structures were indeed dissolving due to ongoing processes of secularization and structural changes in the labor market, the conclusion that we are witnessing an individualized society is premature. Political behavior is inherently social (e.g., Huckfeldt 2001; Zuckerman 2005; McPherson, Smith-Lovin, and Cook 2001) and there is no plausible explanation for why an individuals' appetite for social and political interaction should have decreased because of the advent of a cleavage-free society. More importantly, the traditional cleavage structure linked citizens from diverse educational and social backgrounds to the political party system. In this respect, cleavages were not only highly successful in producing political stability, but also in providing a high degree of political equality and integration. In this chapter we will argue that the network structure of the postcleavage society can no longer provide such egalitarian outcomes. In private networks, individuals with similar backgrounds in terms of social structure and political characteristics cluster. As a result, present-day society is increasingly split into micronetworks of highly sophisticated and politically attentive citizens with high participation rates, and networks where sophistication is low and participation is rare. Therefore, the decline of political cleavages results in increasing levels of political inequality and a decreasing degree of political integration.

This chapter focuses on present-day Germany and seeks, first, the theoretical and empirical link between grand cleavage structures and the political significance of private networks for public action. Secondly, it examines the impact of cleavages and network politicization on political equality and integration.

8.2 THE NARRATION OF INDIVIDUALIZATION AND CLEAVAGE DECLINE

By now, it is common wisdom to describe contemporary societies as highly individualized. The (post-) modern citizen, so the argument goes, is liberated from all constraints which characterized social and political life in the past. We decide if, whom, and when we marry; we choose or don't choose a religion; we plan and design our life trajectories as we wish. There are no external authorities or forces to blame and all risks are ours (see e.g., Beck 2007, for a fuller account). Moreover, as enlightened and rational actors, we seek political expression beyond the political mass organizations that guided our political behavior in former days (see in particular Inglehart 1990; Inglehart and Welzel 2005; Welzel 2006). Several long-term trends have jointly contributed to the advent of the individualized, emancipative societies typical for advanced post–Second World War Western democracies. Unprecedented levels of economic growth and the development of densely knit social security systems guaranteed previously unknown degrees of material well-being and safety. The expansion of the educational system since the 1970s greatly increased the political knowledge and competencies amongst the citizenry while changes in the economy toward an emerging service society meant a decreasing number of jobs in manual production, as well as for unskilled labor. The structure of this service, knowledge, and welfare society disempowered the collective and binding forces of both labor unions and churches.

This process of individualization, so the story continues, impacts the citizen as a political actor. Increasing educational levels resulted in cognitive mobilization and improved political skills. Cognitively and politically resourceful, more and more citizens became "self-sufficient in politics" (Dalton and Wattenberg 2002: 11). Therefore, the role of political parties diminished because the electorate questions the privileged position of (party) elites and prefers to turn to other, more self-directed, short-term and expressive forms of political action. Moreover, a fundamental value change that affected all advanced industrial societies since the 1960s resulted in a spread of postmaterialist and emancipative values which are incompatible with the nature of party discipline and elite-driven modes of political participation (Inglehart 1990; Welzel 2006; Dalton 2002). Finally, the social milieu in which stables cleavage politics are based is in a process of erosion due to increasing levels of social, generational, and geographical mobility (Dalton and Wattenberg 2002: 11). As a result, an increasingly cognitively mobilized and politically sophisticated electorate turns away from political parties and, in particular, deserts the old dominating cleavage parties of working-class and Catholic origin—the elite-driven mass parties par excellence.

The story of dealignment is supported by much empirical evidence. In many Western democracies loyal partisanship decreases, voters increasingly decide in favor of different parties, and the final decision is postponed to late, even the very last moments of an electoral campaign (e.g., Dalton, McAllister, and Wattenberg 2002a; for Germany see, e.g., Rattinger et al. 2011; Schmitt-Beck and Partheymüller 2012). In Germany, as well as in other advanced democracies, the once "frozen" party system (Lipset and Rokkan 1967a: 50) defrosted and allowed newcomers of diverse ideological backgrounds to enter the scene and gain the support of the electorate. The older cleavage parties of political Catholicism and working-class origin became the major victims of these profound changes in the nature of the party systems. This is particularly visible in Germany where the two cleavage parties, the Social Democrats und the Christian Democrats, won above 90% of the vote during the 1970s and fell to under 60% during the federal election of 2009 (Poguntke 2011: 128).

But not all parts of the individualization narrative are backed by empirical evidence. Clearly, there is a rise in educational levels and social mobility. There are also clear indications of a decline in party identification and cleavage voting (see also Chapters 5 and 13 in this volume). However, the link between both aspects is less evident. If decline in party attachments is due to rising educational levels, highly educated voters should desert the parties first. However, empirical evidence tends to indicate the opposite. Nonpartisanship is more frequent amongst the lower educated, who lack political sophistication (for Germany, see e.g., Arzheimer 2006; Kroh 2012). Moreover, the collapse of voter support for mass integration parties of Social and Christian Democrat origin is not clearly related to rising postmaterialist values. Amongst the German population, for instance, the rise of postmaterialism reached its zenith at the end of the 1980s (Roßteutscher 2013), whereas the most serious decline in electoral support for the cleavages parties appeared during the first decade of the 21st century. Finally, although educational levels are clearly rising, there is no evidence that political knowledge and sophistication increases as well. A long-term perspective on the German electorate from the 1950s to the present finds literally no change with regard to levels of political expertise (Glantz, Bathelt, and Maier forthcoming).

Hence, the narration of individualization that links a decline in partisanship to processes of modernization is deficient in terms of specifying the precise mechanism that relates both trends. This chapter argues that this is indeed the case because advocates of the individualization thesis neglect the social dynamics of politics. The dichotomy between the historically developed, grand superstructures of cleavage-based party politics, on the one hand, and the vision of an individualized, politically self-sufficient electorate, on the other, is false. There is no simple alternative between "the citizen as a lone individualist or the citizen as a joiner" (Fine and Harrington 2004: 341) and we "do not engage in the political process as isolated individuals" (Huckfeldt 2001: 426). By contrast, cleavage politics based on the micro structures of closely knit social milieus, in a very similar manner as "postcleavage" politics, is embedded in political networks of socially connected and perceptive individuals. However, the nature of political networks, we argue, has become politically more unequal. In the classic cleavage society (almost) all individuals, independent of their social background and level of sophistication, were linked to the political system. In the postcleavage society this is no longer the case. Rather, we increasingly witness a bipolar distribution of individuals with access to high competence and high participation networks and others who cluster with network partners characterized by political disinterest and apathy.

8.3 THE MEDIATING ROLE OF POLITICAL NETWORKS

The early advocates of the cleavage approach focused on macrohistorical lines of conflict and how and under which conditions these conflicts transformed into stable alliances between parties and segments of the electorate (Lipset and Rokkan 1967a). Thus, they were much less concerned about how these alliances were maintained and transcended across generations at the micro level of the voter. In contrast, Pappi (2002) applies the concepts of *Vergesellschaftung* and *Vergemeinschaftung*. The first refers to the macro level of organized interest groups who link voters to the political party, and the latter to the dense net of social relations in private networks. Accordingly, a social structure is completely politicized when societies are segmented, i.e., there is no overlap or cross-cutting relationship between both levels because all members of one local social community share the same interest group and party, while another network community belongs to a second interest group and party (Pappi 2002: 28f.). This was exactly the case during the heydays of cleavage politics. In 19th century Europe, large-scale industrialization produced a new urban class that was economically exploited and politically disadvantaged because the electoral system knew of elaborate mechanisms (census vote, class-based disproportional vote, cut of voting districts in favor of rural areas, etc.) that prevented fair representation and power sharing. Moreover, in Germany and other religiously divided countries such as Switzerland and the Netherlands, Catholics were excluded from political office and experienced the process of nation-building and democratization as an attack on their identity, lifestyle, and values. A cultural war (Kulturkampf) between state and Protestant state elites, on the one hand, and the Catholic Church and an emerging Catholic political movement, on the other, characterized these countries during the 1870s (Rémond 2000, Blaschke 2002; Roßteutscher 2009). Both minority groups responded with building closed milieu structures, a proliferation of in-group associations, their own media outlets, and the formation of political parties. In many respects, these milieus were closed defense bulwarks that served two major purposes: excluding contact with out-groups and protecting and empowering the in-group (Lipset and Rokkan 1967a). From a network perspective, such social systems are "fragmented and incoherent" because there are not even weak ties which connect individuals from diverse communities (Granovetter 1983: 202). The milieu indeed took care of its members and catered for their needs from "cradle to grave." In return, mass organizations—the Church, unions, and parties— "embodied authoritative, broad-based and distinctive values that members were expected to adopt" (Welch, Sikkink, and Loveland 2007: 24). In such an environment, social homogeneity is absolute in terms of class with regard to the Socialist milieu and in terms of religion in the case of the Catholic milieu. As the basis of the formation of social milieus was political conflict, the private networks of the cleavage society were highly politicized. This integration in a politicized social structure provided the ground for political exchange with politically homogeneous others. If networks are politically decisive in reducing "uncertainty" about the electoral behavior of others (Franklin 2004), uncertainty would have been absent in the traditional cleavage society. Naturally, milieu members had hardly any chance at communicating with persons from different social or religious backgrounds, with different political ideas and/or partisan affiliations. Thus, they were "socially insulated from disagreement," thereby minimizing the likelihood of attitudinal or behavioral change (Huckfeldt, Johnson, and Sprague 2005: 21). In these milieus there was, therefore, a very strong voting norm concerning voting for "their" party and this norm was uniformly communicated through the networks of everyday life (Lazarsfeld, Berelson, and Gaudet 1944: 137ff.). In other words, the milieu-embedded social networks from which cleavage parties recruited their support were characterized by high political homogeneity, high levels of politicization, high turnout, and high levels of loyal party vote.

Network Politicization in the Postcleavage Constellation

For quite a while, these historical milieus had lost their original reason of formation. After the final implementation of the "one (wo)man-one vote" principle, the working class and the working-class party became a major, often dominant player in the political arena after the Second World War. Likewise, Christian Democracy became a distinct force in many European countries and shaped the nature of postwar democracies in Germany and elsewhere. The processes at the heart of the individualization paradigm, for instance increasing mobility, rising educational levels, ongoing secularization, etc., contribute to a further erosion of milieu structures and the numerical decline of cleavage groups (e.g., Roßteutscher 2012). However, evidence shows that those individuals who remained within the subcultures of the milieu are still the parties' most loyal stronghold (Evans 2000; Elff and Roßteutscher 2011). In other words, the voter–party link exists, yet it applies to an increasingly tinier fraction of the electorate.

The party–voter link thus dissolves from the margins, i.e., those segments of the electorate who are most clearly affected by the dissolution of traditional milieu structures. As the traditional linkage organizations—Church and union—reach fewer and fewer individuals (Arzheimer 2006), cleavage decline is particularly visible among marginal cleavage groups, i.e., Catholics without church commitment and workers without union membership. Lacking both the clear-cut communications of the linkage organization and the mobilization environment of closed milieu structures, marginal groups are not only less loyal cleavage voters but are also presumably characterized by private networks with lower levels of politicization and participation. Indeed, with regard to cleavage voting in the past, marginals were closer to core cleavage groups than to the uncleavaged segments of society, i.e., Catholics without church involvement still voted disproportionally more often for the Christian Democrat party than secular or Protestant individuals, and workers without union membership voted more frequently Social Democrat than other classes. However, this relative "advantage" of marginal groups shrinks with regard to the religious cleavage (Pappi 2002; Elff and Roßteutscher forthcoming) and completely disappeared with regard to the socioeconomic cleavage (Pappi 2002: 40). In the absence of evidence on the network qualities of marginal cleavage groups, we can only formulate an assumption that needs empirical testing. In analogy to trends in cleavage voting, we expect that marginal cleavage groups are distinct from core cleavage groups and thus more or less indistinct from uncleavaged groups in society.

We thus arrive at our first hypotheses. In particular those who remained in the rather closed milieu structures, linked to the parties' core linkage groups, i.e., the unions and the (Catholic) Church should possess a relatively high degree of network politicization. This leads to high levels of political integration in terms of turnout, party attachment, and cleavage voting.

> H1: *The degree of network politicization and political integration is higher among core cleavage groups than among marginal cleavage groups.*
> H2: *The degree of network politicization and political integration of marginal cleavage groups is indistinct from the degree of network politicization and political integration of individuals who do not belong to political cleavages.*

These first hypotheses relate to the level of politicization and integration. However, we not only claim that the cleavage society was more politicized and integrated, but also that politicization and integration was more equal. We turn to this issue in the subsequent section.

The Egalitarian Impact of Traditional Cleavage Structures

Cleavages allied voters of different social statuses and educational levels to the party system. In the postcleavage society, this is no longer the case. Yet, to use Aristotle's famous and often quoted proverbial expression, "birds of a feather flock together." Human beings are inherently social and in choosing our companions we select partners and friends who are similar to ourselves. This so-called "homophily" principle is one of the standard truisms of empirical (network) sociology (see e.g., Berelson, Lazarsfeld, and McPhee 1954; Blau 1974; McPherson, Smith-Lovin, and Cook 2001; Marsden 1988; Granovetter 1973; Kossinets and Watts 2009) or, what economists termed the "natural aversion of heterogeneity" (Alesina and Ferrara 2002: 225; see also Costa and Kahn 2003: 104). With regard to cleavage structures, the selection mechanism is obvious; as individual milieu members had hardly any chance to meet someone different from themselves, the social and political homogeneity of micro networks was a direct result of closed milieus. For most of us, however, such closed communication environments do not (any longer) apply. Yet, even if the degree of social connectedness remained unchanged and we thus do not witness the advent of the individualized society advocated by Dalton and colleagues, the political quality of network structures changed immensely. Cognitive mobilization, the result of rising educational levels (Dalton 2002: 32), is the new dividing line in the postcleavage constellation of the present state.

The Discriminating Impact of Cognitive Mobilization

In the cleavage society levels of politicization and political integration were high. This was particularly the case when the specific constellation of conflict lines prompted strong working-class parties, i.e., a party system which also integrated individuals from lower socioeconomic backgrounds and with less political skill into the political arena. Moreover, the religious cleavage had a historically strong egalitarian facet, too. The Catholic milieu of the late-19th century emerged as a response to the foundation of the German Empire, which treated Catholics and the Catholic Church as enemies of the predominantly Protestant nation (Reichsfeinde). Its political arm, the Center party (Zentrum), mobilized Catholics of all social strata and from all educational backgrounds (Roßteutscher 2009). Therefore, authors such as Falter (1991) described the Center party as the first "Volkspartei" (catch-all party) on German soil. Although the Christian Democrat Party was founded after the Second World War in order to overcome the constraints of a pure Catholic party and positioned itself as the conservative alternative to Social Democracy open to Christians of all denominations, it never gave up its aspiration as a party beyond class appeal. In Germany, thus, the two major cleavage parties, CDU/CSU and SPD, which dominated party politics for decades, aimed at mobilizing voters from the lower classes (the SPD) and from all classes, including the lower classes (CDU/CSU). Therefore, electoral participation was high and highly equal. If the old alliances and the participatory resources provided by cleavage parties and their linkage organizations no longer reach the segments of the electorate who lack political skills and have low political sophistication, this resource poverty can only be compensated by the private networks of everyday life. However, if the homophily principle applies, it is highly likely that resource-poor individuals cluster in networks of resource-poor people.

Moreover, for unsophisticated voters in particular, partisan loyalty provided a clear and low-cost cue for voting (Dalton 2002: 21). If Dalton's argument is correct, the more sophisticated, i.e., highly educated, among the noncleavaged voters should have little problem in coming to grips with the ambiguities of present-day party politics and should find their way through the complexity of political communication. The less sophisticated, however, who lack the clear cues of a cleavage in-group might react by excluding politics from their social interaction and lean towards a withdrawal from politics, especially if their networks are resource-poor as well.

If our assumptions are correct, uncleavaged segments of the electorate are more likely to belong to private networks where politicization is low (see H1 and H2 above). However, social relations are only politically meaningful if they carry political substance, i.e., if there are discussions about political matters between network partners (e.g., Knoke 1990; McClurg 2003; Klofstad 2007). The basic idea is that political discussions bear information about how to become active, increase political curiosity, and recruit individuals into politics (Klofstadt 2007: 180). Politically active networks thus provide resources, increase the desire for participation, and promote active recruitment (Verba, Schlozman, and Brady 1996; Klofstad 2007: 181). Assuming that (almost) all individuals are socially connected, the fact that some never talk politics signals a very low significance of politics in a person's social interactions (see e.g., McClurg 2006: 745). In addition, political conversations with partners who abstain from electoral participation impact the electoral behavior of the discussant (Nickerson 2008; Schmitt-Beck and Mackenrodt 2010; Partheymüller and Schmitt-Beck 2012). In the cleavage society in which the norm of cleavage voting was omnipresent, such abstention signals were rare.

If we further assume that networks void of political talk are more prominent among persons with lower levels of education, apolitical networks contribute to an unequal distribution of participative resources. This is due to the fact that social interaction has an extra benefit as "it facilitates the application of individual resources to collective behavior" (McClurg 2003: 451). Indeed, McClurg could show that political conversations activate individuals from higher social and educational backgrounds even more than individuals with a low educational background. "High status individuals are more likely to benefit from politically-oriented social interaction than low status individuals," thus contributing to the widening of the gap between low and high status individuals (McClurg 2003: 459f.). In addition, civic duties, including the norm of electoral participation, are more widely spread among higher educated people. We therefore expect—based on the assumption that most private networks are relatively homogeneous in terms of educational background[1]—that there is more pro-participation communication and pressure in networks of highly educated individuals (Gerber and Rogers 2009: 180).

Moreover, the cleavage society assured political integration through milieu embeddedness and exposure to the communication of linkage organization and mass party. Although we expect that politicization is generally higher among core cleavage groups, we also expect it to be distributed more equally. Cleavages were (and presumably still are) able to ally individuals to the political party and the political system even if they were resource-poor and their private networks apolitical. This is the case because political communication flowed through diverse channels, i.e., mass and linkage organizations, social milieus, and private networks. Thus, if one of these communication avenues fails, there are still two other channels that secured individuals' political loyalty. By contrast, in the postcleavage society, a direct exposition to political communication of mass organizations is rare. There is no social milieu

---

[1] For the US, Marsden finds that private networks show about half the educational diversity of the general population and that 30% of personal networks are fully homophilous on education (Marsden 1987).

that enforces norms of party loyalty. Although the founding fathers of the microsociological perspective pointed to the political significance of social milieus and linkage organizations (see e.g., Lazarsfeld, Berelson, and Gaudet 1944: 20) they believed that the basic mechanism of party loyalty was provided by the social networks of everyday life (Lazarsfeld, Berelson, and Gaudet 1944: 137ff; Berelson, Lazarsfeld, and McPhee 1954: 298ff.). By contrast, we argue that all three avenues are of importance. Thus, in the postcleavage constellation, political integration depends solely on an individual's personal characteristics and the communicative impact of private networks. Therefore, we expect that the intermediating impact of education and network politicization is stronger than among core cleavage groups.

> H3: *The impact of education on network politicization is higher among uncleavaged than among core cleavage groups.*
> H4: *The impact of education and network politicization on political integration is higher among uncleavaged than among core cleavage groups.*

8.4 DATA AND OPERATIONALIZATION

Core cleavage groups are in decline; in Germany and elsewhere. Based on Germany's longest time series of cross-sections, the German Social Survey Program (ALLBUS)[2], Figure 8.1 presents trends from 1980 to the present. Figure 8.1 shows that both cleavages are indeed affected by a decline and that this decline concerns both core and marginal groups. Looking at Catholics who attend church at least once a month, they constituted above 20% during the early 1980s and fell to only modestly above 10% by 2010. With regard to unionized workers, the share diminished from clearly above 10% to roughly 5% at the end of the ALLBUS time series.[3] Note, however, that the processes at the heart of the individualization paradigm, such as educational expansion, value changes, changes in the labor market, and expansion of welfare, were set in motion long before the start of the ALLBUS time series. Hence, Figure 8.1 cannot portray the heydays of cleavage politics when a clear majority of the German population was linked to one of the two major cleavages.

Clearly, at the present time, core cleavage groups constitute only a small fraction of contemporary German society. This notwithstanding, we expect

---

[2] ZA4574, available at http://www.gesis.org/allbus/studienprofile/kumulation-1980-2010/ accessed October 30, 2013.

[3] Note that the rise of workers visible in Figure 8.1 after 1990 is caused by German unification and the fact that, social-structurally, there were higher proportions of employees in manual professions in the East compared to the West. The rise in the number of Catholics documented by the last two ALLBUS surveys is, by contrast, not supported by official statistics, which report further gradual decline (Elff and Roßteutscher forthcoming).

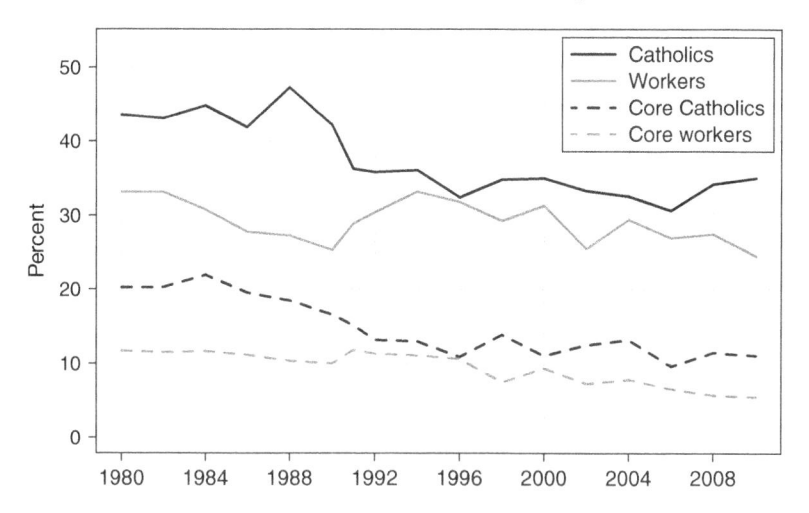

Figure 8.1 Cleavage Groups in German Society—1980 to 2010

that, in terms of their core characteristics, they are still representatives of the traditional cleavage society. For a detailed analysis of network politicization and political integration, large case numbers are mandatory. The GLES provides such a database. In a three-monthly cycle, 1,000 adult Germans from a quota sample, recruited via an Online Access Pool, were interviewed.[4] All surveys included basics concerning class background, educational level, union membership, church affiliation and involvement, electoral participation, and party vote. All surveys also provide some minimum information concerning political content of network structures, i.e., the frequency of political discussions with significant others. We will use the cumulated data from online surveys fielded directly before the 2009 Federal election, up to the final survey at the end of 2011. Case numbers accumulate to above 11,000.[5] In four of the surveys a more detailed question module on political networks was administered, including questions about the number of network partners, electoral participation, and the party choice of up to two network partners. We will use this subset with more than 4,000 realized interviews for more in-depth analyses.[6]

---

[4] Long-term Online Tracking, Cumulation 2009–2011 (GLES). Principal investigators: Hans Rattinger, Sigrid Roßteutscher, Rüdiger Schmitt-Beck, Bernhard Weßels. GESIS data archive, Cologne. ZA5357 Data file version 1.0.0 (GLES 2012a).

[5] Restriction free download available from http://www.gesis.org/wahlen/gles/daten-und-dokumente/daten/ accessed October 30, 2013.

[6] This applies to the surveys fielded in September 2009, December 2009, December 2010, and December 2011.

Dependent Variables

Network Politicization

Above we argued that network politicization is (i) lower among uncleavaged segments of the electorate (compared to core cleavage groups), and (ii) increasingly dependent upon individuals' level of sophistication in terms of education. Several indicators of network politicization, for which previous research showed that they are significantly related to political participation, will be used to test these assumptions: a general measure of discussion frequency (see e.g., Klofstad 2007; McClurg 2003; Verba, Schlozman, and Brady 1996; Knoke 1990), and network size in terms of the number of political discussion partners (see e.g., Eveland and Hiveley 2009; Kwak et al. 2005). In addition, and because we are particularly interested in network impact on political integration, two indicators capturing explicit party signals and abstention cues, which emanate from discussion partners, are included in the analyses (similar e.g., Partheymüller and Schmitt-Beck 2012).

According to our assumption that networks are increasingly bipolar, i.e., separating individuals with and without political discussant networks, the core network variable will not only be analysed as a quasicontinuous variable stretching from "0" (no political discussions) to "7" (political discussions occurring seven days a week), but also in a dichotomized version that distinguishes explicitly apolitical networks (those without any political discussions) from all networks where at least some political conversations appear (no matter whether this happens only once a week or more often).

Using the smaller, more detailed, subsample, we are also able to assess with how many network partners political discussion takes place. We explicitly asked for a first and a second discussion partner, and there is a follow-up question which asks whether there are more network partners who provide political conversations. Accordingly, the variable is constructed to range from "0" (no political discussions in private network) to "3" (three or more discussion partners). The definition of political discussion is vague and idiosyncratic to a respondent's own understanding of politics. Therefore, we are further interested in knowing whether these political discussions explicitly relate to the political party system. Hence, a variable capturing clear party signals is created. It received the value of "0" if the respondent has no political discussion partners or if the party choice of the discussion partner was unknown to the respondent. If the respondent was able to name the party choice of one discussion partner, the variable was coded "1" and if there was a further discussion partner of whom the respondent knew the preferred party, the value "2" was inserted. In order to capture explicit cues of electoral abstention, we created an additional dummy variable that distinguishes respondents who receive explicit abstention cues from their network, from those who do not.[7]

---

[7] As case numbers are very low, a finer distinction is not feasible.

Political Integration

If the argument spelled out above is correct, the postcleavage society is less successful in integrating all citizens, the sophisticated as well as those with lower educational background, into the political system. The core indicator of integration applied here is electoral participation. Turnout is a participatory act that demands very little resources. Moreover, in representative democracy it is the basic and essential form of voice. Therefore, if even this "simple" act of voting is not exercised, political integration is at least fragile. All surveys, with the exception of the first online survey conducted two weeks before the election in September 2009, contain a re-call question concerning electoral participation and vote choice at the 2009 Federal election. We created a dummy variable separating voters (coded "1") from nonvoters ("0"). As the narrative on cleavage decline proclaims a process of party dealignment, we will use party identification as a second measure of political integration. No matter whether individuals cast a ballot or not, feeling some form of identification with a party is certainly a way to relate the personal self-concept to the wider field of politics (Campbell et al. 1960a, see also Chapter 5 in this volume). We construct a dummy, which distinguishes all respondents who claim to possess a party identification, from those who say that they do not feel close to a party. Finally, as the decline of cleavages is not only related to shrinking turnout rates and decline in party identification, but also named as a reason for the relative decline of the grand cleavage parties, CDU/CSU and SPD, and the fragmentation of present-day party systems, we construct an indicator for cleavage voting in form of a dummy variable that separates Christian and Social Democrat voters from all others.

Independent Variables

Cleavage variables are constructed in two different ways. First, dummy variables were constructed for core and marginal groups of both cleavages. In the case of the religious cleavage, "core groups" are Catholics who visit church more often than once a month. "Marginals" are Catholics who visit church less regularly or never. In the case of the socioeconomic cleavage, core is defined as workers with union membership and marginal as workers without membership.[8] Secondly, and according to the argument that not one of the cleavages but rather the entire cleavage system provided for network politicization and system integration, a further indicator variable is constructed. This variable contrasts both core cleavage groups to all others who do not belong to the core of cleavage politics. The final substantively important independent variable is

---

[8] The worker category is built from current employment and previous or past employment in the case of the retired and persons who are at present not in the labor force (for whatever reason).

respondents' education as the central measure of cognitive mobilization. Since the German educational system is rather stratified—it is composed of different tracks, of which some allow access to tertiary education while others do not—we create a variable that separates the highly educated with access to tertiary education (i.e., Fachhochschulreife, Abitur, coded 1), from those without (school not completed, Hauptschule, Realschule). In all analyses, age, gender, and an East German regional origin of the respondent are included as controls.

Logic of Analyses

The analyses proceed in two steps. According to the argument spelled out above, we will first examine whether core cleavage groups, marginal cleavage groups, and uncleavaged groups are distinct with regard to their political network structures (H1 and H2). In all instances, we proceed by exploiting first the larger data set and focus the analysis on the most general or "most fundamental" (Eveland and Hiveley 2009: 215) indicator of network politicization: whether and how often individuals lead political discussions in their private networks. In the second step, we will employ the more detailed but case-poorer dataset, consisting of the four online surveys, which contain the more extensive network module.

As we are less interested in the main effects of cleavage membership, but argue that cleavages had an egalitarian impact by linking individuals, independent of their level of sophistication, to the political system, we include an additional interaction term between the cleavage variables and education. In the second part of the analysis, when indicators of political integration are the dependent variables, the network indicators are then added as further independent variables. Interaction terms with education are included as described above. Additional interaction terms are constructed in order to test whether political integration varies across cleavage groups as a function of the degree of network politicization. In all instances we estimate several model specifications. Model 1 examines the joint effect of cleavages against the uncleavaged contrast group, while Model 2 estimates the effect of both cleavage groups separately. Further models include interaction effects between cleavage membership and education (Model 3) and cleavage membership and network politicization (Model 4).

8.5 RESULTS

Table 8.1 reports descriptive evidence concerning the distribution of sociodemographics, sophistication, network politicization, and political integration among

Table 8.1 Descriptives: demographics and education. Means and standard errors (in brackets)

	\multicolumn{4}{c}{Full sample}				\multicolumn{4}{c}{Sub-sample}			
	No.	Age	Gender	East	Educ.	No.	Age	Gender	East	Educ.
Core worker	430	47.367 (0.539)	0.202 (0.019)	0.119 (0.016)	0.040 (0.009)	172	46.593 (0.890)	0.209 (0.031)	0.169 (0.029)	0.047 (0.016)
Marginal worker	1588	43.144 (0.302)	0.433 (0.012)	0.203 (0.010)	0.053 (0.006)	630	42.525 (0.480)	0.452 (0.020)	0.194 (0.016)	0.048 (0.009)
Core Catholic	307	45.625 (0.978)	0.511 (0.029)	0.046 (0.012)	0.447 (0.029)	116	44.267 (1.649)	0.517 (0.047)	0.043 (0.019)	0.505 (0.048)
Marginal Catholic	2499	41.861 (0.289)	0.511 (0.010)	0.016 (0.002)	0.256 (0.009)	1034	41.230 (0.443)	0.536 (0.016)	0.015 (0.004)	0.255 (0.014)
Core cleavage	733	46.632 (0.518)	0.333 (0.017)	0.087 (0.010)	0.208 (0.015)	286	45.584 (0.856)	0.336 (0.028)	0.115 (0.019)	0.228 (0.025)
No cleavage	10,676	42.728 (0.144)	0.512 (0.005)	0.145 (0.003)	0.286 (0.004)	4256	42.407 (0.230)	0.509 (0.008)	0.147 (0.005)	0.287 (0.007)

Notes: Age in years; Gender: 1 female, 0 male; Nationality: 1 East German, 0 West German; Educ.: 1 higher education (category 4&5, i.e., access to tertiary education, Fachhochschulreife and Abitur), 0 other).

the different cleavage groups in contemporary German society. Looking at basic sociodemographics, we see that members of core cleavage groups are on average significantly older than both members of marginal groups and the larger uncleavaged segment of contemporary society. Table 8.1 also shows a clear male dominance of the socioeconomic cleavage and an additional bias concerning East German origin, in particular for marginal workers. With regard to education, members of the workers' milieu, both core and marginal, possess by far the lowest educational level of all groups. In contrast, core Catholics have, in comparison to all other groups, a rather high educational level; higher than marginal Catholics and uncleavaged groups. Note this high educational background of core Catholics is not supported by reference data such as the German General Social Survey (ALLBUS), but is a peculiarity of the GLES Online surveys. Thus, we cannot rule out that the overrepresentation of the highly educated among core Catholics impacts our findings. Looking at the core cleavage groups compared to the uncleavaged, differences are not very large. However, members of core cleavage groups are consistently older, rather male, and of a relatively low educational background.

Table 8.2a reports means and standard errors for the dependent variables in the full sample with over 11,000 respondents. Among core workers, 76% possess politically active networks in the sense that there is political talk with network partners. Among marginal workers this applies to less than

65%. The difference between core and marginal Catholics is similarly large (86 to 72%). Looking at turnout, we find that 86% of unionized workers report electoral participation compared to 71% of workers without union membership. Among core Catholics, the participation rate is above 90% and 10% lower among Catholics without regular church affiliation. Similarly, party identification is high among core cleavage groups (78% in the case of workers and 79% for Catholics) and much lower among marginal groups (62 and 70%). Looking finally at the degree of cleavage voting, i.e., voting decisions in favor of SPD or CDU/CSU, we find relatively small differences between the two groups of workers (a 4% advantage of core compared to marginal workers), but larger differences in the Catholic milieu. Among core Catholics, 60% vote along cleavage lines compared to only 49% of marginal Catholics.

We will now briefly describe our subsample and look at the distribution of additional indicators of network politicization (Table 8.2b). Core workers have a larger network of political discussion partners and receive more party signals and less abstention cues from their network than marginal workers. Core Catholics possess more discussion partners and have a higher number of party voters and fewer abstaining partners in their networks than marginal Catholics.

Hence, the descriptive evidence is clear and consistent: Core cleavage groups are highly politicized (compared to marginal groups as well as compared to the

Table 8.2a Descriptives: network politicization and political integration in full sample. Means and standard errors (in brackets)

	Discuss. freq.	Discuss. dummy	Turnout	Party ID	Cleavage vote
Core worker	3.228 (0.092)	0.760 (0.021)	0.858 (0.018)	0.784 (0.020)	0.484 (0.026)
Marginal worker	2.671 (0.045)	0.647 (0.012)	0.706 (0.012)	0.621 (0.012)	0.434 (0.015)
Core Catholic	3.556 (0.113)	0.859 (0.020)	0.908 (0.018)	0.794 (0.023)	0.599 (0.029)
Marginal Catholic	2.929 (0.037)	0.723 (0.009)	0.800 (0.009)	0.697 (0.009)	0.487 (0.011)
Core cleavage	3.358 (0.072)	0.801 (0.015)	0.878 (0.013)	0.787 (0.015)	0.535 (0.020)
No cleavage	3.111 (0.019)	0.736 (0.004)	0.799 (0.004)	0.705 (0.004)	0.442 (0.005)

Notes: Discussion freq.: from never to seven days a week; Discuss. dummy: 1 with discussions, 0 no discussions; Turnout: 1 vote, 0 no vote; Party ID: 1 yes, 0 no; Cleavage vote: 1 vote for SPD or CDU/CSU, 0 vote for other parties, no vote.

Table 8.2b Descriptives: Network politicization and political integration in subsample. Means and standard errors (in brackets)

	No. disc. partners	Party signals	Abstention signals	Turnout	Party ID	Cleavage vote
Core worker	1.384 (0.089)	0.733 (0.063)	0.074 (0.024)	0.854 (0.031)	0.740 (0.034)	0.447 (0.041)
Marginal worker	0.986 (0.042)	0.541 (0.030)	0.129 (0.017)	0.698 (0.020)	0.628 (0.019)	0.447 (0.023)
Core Catholic	1.698 (0.102)	1.052 (0.077)	0.010 (0.010)	0.930 (0.031)	0.793 (0.038)	0.524 (0.049)
Marginal Catholic	1.231 (0.034)	0.708 (0.025)	0.063 (0.009)	0.778 (0.015)	0.685 (0.015)	0.492 (0.018)
Core cleavage	1.507 (0.068)	0.860 (0.050)	0.046 (0.014)	0.881 (0.023)	0.760 (0.025)	0.482 (0.032)
No cleavage	1.322 (0.017)	0.737 (0.012)	0.072 (0.005)	0.784 (0.007)	0.695 (0.007)	0.449 (0.009)

Notes: No. disc. partners: from 0 (no discussion partner) to 3 (three or more discussion partners); Party signals: from 0 (no party vote of discussion partners) to 2 (both discussion partners vote for a party); Abstention signals 1 at least one discussion partner is nonvoter, 0 no discussion partner is nonvoter, missing: respondents without discussion partners. For others, see note to Table 8.2a.

uncleavaged), core Catholics consistently score highest, marginal Catholics are similar to the uncleavaged segment of society, and marginal workers constitute the group of society with the lowest level of politicization and integration. Do these findings hold in a multivariate design? Do we find the expected link between education, cleavage membership, on the one hand, and network politicization and integration, on the other?

Cleavages, Education, and Network Politicization

Table 8.3 presents models with network characteristics as dependent variables in order to be explained by education and cleavage membership. Table entries are average marginal effects calculated by holding all observed variables constant at individually observed values and varying the variable of interest between two states (since our independent variables of interest are discrete). For both states, we calculate expected values of the dependent variable; the difference between these is the marginal effect.[9]

---

[9] Thus for linear models, these simply express differences in the original metric of the outcome variable, while for logit (and ordered logit) models, they represent differences in predicted probabilities. Corresponding standard errors are obtained using the delta method.

Table 8.3 Network politicization. Marginal effects and standard errors (in brackets)

	Full sample		Subsample		
	Discuss. freq.	Discuss. dummy	No. disc. partners	Party signals	Abstention signals
Core cleavage	0.126	0.047	0.012	0.014	−0.020
	(0.072)	(0.018)	(0.006)	(0.008)	(0.016)
Education	0.757	0.163	0.036	0.052	−0.016
	(0.040)	(0.010)	(0.003)	(0.005)	(0.008)
Core worker	0.029	0.009	0.002	−0.003	−0.003
	(0.094)	(0.021)	(0.007)	(0.011)	(0.017)
Core Catholic	0.261	0.101	0.020	0.022	−0.042
	(0.110)	(0.023)	(0.005)	(0.003)	(0.011)
Education	0.750	0.161	0.036	0.050	−0.015
	(0.040)	(0.010)	(0.003)	(0.005)	(0.008)
Education					
—no cleavage	0.737	0.147	0.033	0.040	a
	(0.041)	(0.008)	(0.003)	(0.004)	
—core worker	0.637	0.088	0.032	0.043	a
	(0.462)	(0.105)	(0.019)	(0.020)	
Diff. test p	0.829	0.576	0.967	0.872	
—core Catholic	1.133	0.141	0.017	−0.015	a
	(0.217)	(0.039)	(0.012)	(0.027)	
Diff. test p	0.073	0.880	0.207	0.040	
Joint test p	0.195	0.847	0.451	0.120	

Notes: Marginal effects for No. disc. partners are for Prob (y = 2), for party signals Prob (y = 1). All analyses control for age, gender, and East/West origin.
a Perfect prediction.

Looking at the main effects in Model 1, which tests the impact of cleavage membership in general, there are two marginal effects different from zero: Core cleavage membership increases the probability of moving in networks where political discussion takes place by 4.7 percentage points, and the probability of having at least a second discussion partner by 1.2%. Turning to Model 2, which separately examines the effects of both cleavage groups, we see that these general effects are exclusively caused by core Catholics. The marginal effects for workers are in no single instance different from zero. By contrast, membership in the Catholic cleavage group increases the probability of political discussions by 10 percentage points, that of having a second discussion partner by 2 percentage points, that of receiving at least one clear party signal by 2.2 points, and it decreases the probability of receiving explicit abstention cues by 4.2 percentage points; an effect that is almost three times the size of the effect of higher education. With regard to education, the marginal effects are consistently different from zero and often large: The highly educated (compared to those from lower educational background) discuss politics more frequently, possess larger discussion networks, and receive more party signals and fewer abstention cues.

Model 3 contains additional interaction terms in order to test whether cleavages mute, as hypothesized (H3), the impact of sophistication, i.e., we examine whether the effect of higher education differs between cleavage groups. Again, we calculate marginal effects for all cleavage groups, which are easier to interpret than raw coefficients. With regard to the uncleavaged group, the evidence is clear; high education leads to network politicization or, in other words, more discussions, more discussion partners, more party signals, and fewer abstention cues. Within cleavage groups the effects are generally in the same direction. However, they are smaller in size and most of the time not statistically different from zero. Furthermore, as an even stricter test, we calculate the p-value for the difference in average marginal effects between uncleavaged and the different cleavage groups.[10] This p-value is statistically significant in one instance; among the uncleavaged, higher education increases the probability of receiving a party signal by 4 percentage points while membership in the core Catholic cleavage decreases it slightly by 1.5 percentage points. The p-value of the difference test suggests that this difference is statistically significant. In other words, the effect of education varies significantly between the uncleavaged and Catholics.

Our "level" hypotheses (H1 and H2) are partially confirmed. The networks of cleavage groups and, in particular, of core Catholics, are more politicized than the networks of uncleavaged groups, even when controlling for the effects of education, gender, age, and regional origin. In a statistically strict sense, H3, concerning the egalitarian impact of cleavages, is only supported in the case of core Catholics and the reception of party signals.

Explaining Political Integration

Turning to our fourth hypothesis, we test whether the impact of education and network politicization on political integration is higher among uncleavaged than among core cleavage groups. Table 8.4a presents the results concerning our three indicators of political integration by using the complete data set. In order to increase the accessibility of the table, we refrain from documenting the main effects. However, in all instances, main effects of cleavage

---

[10] The difference follows a chi-squared distribution (with 1 degree of freedom). This test is necessary, since finding a significant and a nonsignificant effect does not necessarily mean that the difference between them is statistically significant as well (Gelman and Stern 2006).

membership are positive and often quite large.[11] Model 3 contains the marginal effects of the interaction between education and cleavage. Looking at the group of uncleavaged individuals, evidence is again clear and consistent. Higher education increases the probability of turnout by 15.4 percentage points and the probability of having a party identification by 13.2 percentge points. It depresses, though, the probability of voting in favor of one of the cleavage parties by 3.5 percentage points. In contrast, the marginal effect of higher education for Catholics is smaller, with a larger standard error, and this difference between core Catholics and the uncleavaged is statistically significant,[12] i.e., the participation enhancing effect of education is significantly stronger among uncleavaged groups in comparison to core Catholics. Looking at party identification, marginal effects of education among cleavage groups are much smaller and are even negative in the case of core workers, with large standard errors attached, rendering them insignificant. Their differences to the uncleavaged group are statistically significant, meaning that education plays a significantly different role among uncleavaged and core cleavage groups. It impacts the probability of being a party identifier among the uncleavaged segments, while it has no effect among core cleavage groups. With regard to cleavage voting, none of the p-values reaches the conventional level of statistical significance. However, we see that among core Catholics the (negative) effect of high education is much stronger than among uncleavaged groups (14 percentage points compared to 3.5 percentage points). In other words, high education decreases the probability of cleavage voting, particularly among Catholics.

Model 4 in Table 8.4a contains the interaction effects with discussion frequency, thereby testing the hypothesis (H4) that members of cleavage groups are less dependent upon the activating impact of their private networks. In order to facilitate the interpretation, we use only our indicator variable, which separates individuals who talk politics, from those who do not. We find, again, a very consistent effect of political talk among the uncleavaged. Discussion increases the probability of turnout by 17.2 percentage points; increases the probability of having a party identification by 21.4 percentage points; and decreases cleavage voting by 3.4 percentage points. In the case of cleavage groups, by contrast, discussion is hardly relevant for turnout. The marginal effects are much smaller (about 6 percentage points), standard errors are relatively large, and the effect is thus indistinguishable from zero. Difference test p-values are statistically significant, that is compared to the uncleavaged; where discussion is decisive in producing turnout among core cleavage groups, the

---

[11] Further tables including main effects available upon request.

[12] As all workers with higher education vote, the prediction is perfect and no estimates can be calculated. More advanced techniques for estimating models with complete separation exist (Gelman et al. 2008), but are beyond the aim of this chapter.

Table 8.4a Political integration. Interaction effects only, estimated average marginal effects and standard errors (in brackets), full sample

	Turnout	Party ID	Cleavage vote
Model 3			
Education			
—no cleavage	0.154	0.132	−0.035
	(0.007)	(0.009)	(0.012)
—core worker	a	−0.062	0.014
		(0.116)	(0.131)
Diff. test *p*		0.097	0.714
—core Catholic	0.080	0.031	−0.140
	(0.036)	(0.048)	(0.060)
Diff. test *p*	0.044	0.036	0.085
Joint test *p*		0.029	0.209
Model 4			
Discussion			
—no cleavage	0.173	0.214	−0.034
	(0.010)	(0.011)	(0.014)
—core work	0.060	0.172	−0.057
	(0.045)	(0.051)	(0.063)
Diff. test *p*	0.015	0.426	0.726
—core Catholic	0.055	0.177	−0.052
	(0.064)	(0.079)	(0.091)
Diff. test *p*	0.070	0.645	0.842
Joint test *p*	0.012	0.661	0.924

Note: All analyses control for age, gender, and East/West origin.
a Perfect prediction.

role of discussion is significantly different: The probability of turnout is simply independent of whether individuals discuss politics or not. By contrast, with regard to the effect of discussion on party identification, differences between cleavage groups and the uncleavaged are insignificant. The marginal effect of political talk is slightly smaller (17 percentage points compared to 21 percentage points among the uncleavaged group) and standard errors are larger. The same applies to cleavage voting, where the negative effects of political discussion are slightly larger but not distinguishable from zero. In other words, the

Table 8.4b Cleavage network interaction effects. Only p-values of tests of difference in average marginal effects displayed, subsample

	Turnout	Party ID	Cleavage vote
Model 3			
No. disc. partners			
—core worker test	0.050	0.457	0.967
—core Catholic test	0.163	0.602	0.711
Joint test	0.062	0.670	0.933
Model 4			
Party signals			
—core worker test	0.018	0.527	0.865
—core Catholic test	0.017	0.627	0.464
Joint test	0.005	0.734	0.750
Model 5			
Abstention signals			
—core cleavage test	0.804	0.547	0.571

Note: All analyses control for age, gender, and East/West origin.

egalitarian impact of cleavages is very clear with regard to turnout, but less effective with regard to party identification and cleavage voting.

We will, finally, turn to our richer subdata set and examine the discriminating impact of further network characteristics (Table 8.4b). To save space, table entries are only p-values of the tests for differences in average marginal effects. Beginning with turnout and looking at network size, the difference in marginal effects between core workers and uncleavaged groups is statistically significant (see Figures 8.2 and 8.3 below for a substantive interpretation). With regard to party signals, all differences are statistically significant. Concerning abstention cues, the findings are inconclusive. The joint test for cleavage groups, in general, is insignificant. Separate tests cannot be calculated because of perfect predictions, i.e., being a core worker who receives an abstention signal predicts turnout perfectly. Looking at party identification and cleavage vote, none of the p-values reaches the level of statistical significance. In other words, there is no systematic difference in the effect of network politicization between cleavage groups and the uncleavaged.

In the remainder of this section we turn once more to the core results and present two versions of graphical visualization of our findings. As turnout

Network Politicization and Political Integration 189

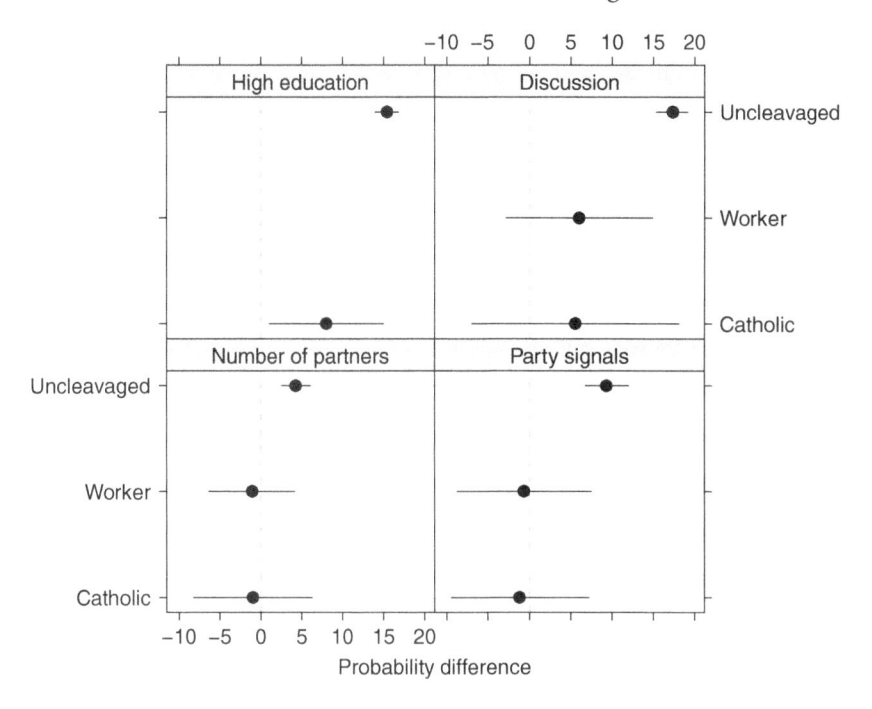

Figure 8.2 Probability differences in turnout depending on sophistication and network politicization

is the most basic and essential indicator of political integration and also the dependent variable which produces the most consistent findings, we restrict this final step to turnout.

Based on the findings in Table 8.4a and 8.4b, Figure 8.2 portrays differences in predicted probabilities of turnout due to education and network politicization among cleavage groups. Looking at education, among the uncleavaged, the difference in predicted turnout between the low and highly educated is very high (about 10 percentage points). By contrast, among Catholics, the difference is much smaller and standard errors are large, however, the effect is still statistically different from zero. Whether the difference would be clearer if the educational distribution within core Catholics would be less biased is a question open to further research. With regard to network politicization, however, probability differences are clear and consistent. Politicization is extremely effective with regard to uncleavaged individuals and increases the probability of turnout by more than 15 percentage points with discussions, more than 5 percentage points with network size, and about 10 percentage points in the case of party signals. For core workers and Catholics, the probability differences are much smaller (discussions) or close to zero (number of partners, party signals), standard errors are large, and the effects are indistinguishable from zero.

The same information is depicted from a different angle in Figure 8.3, which plots predicted probabilities of turnout among those who belong to core cleavage groups versus those who do not. Again, education shows relatively modest differences. In the low education group, turnout is significantly higher among cleavage groups than among the uncleavaged. Accordingly, the slope from low to high is slightly less steep among cleavage groups. By contrast, clear differences are visible with regard to network politicization. Among members of cleavage groups, the slope is either rather flat (discussions) or completely flat (networks size, party signals). In other words, among members of cleavage groups, turnout is high no matter whether their private networks are heavily politicized or void of political content. This is clearly not the case with regard to the uncleavaged. The predicted probability of turnout increases strongly if one moves from apolitical networks to politicized networks.

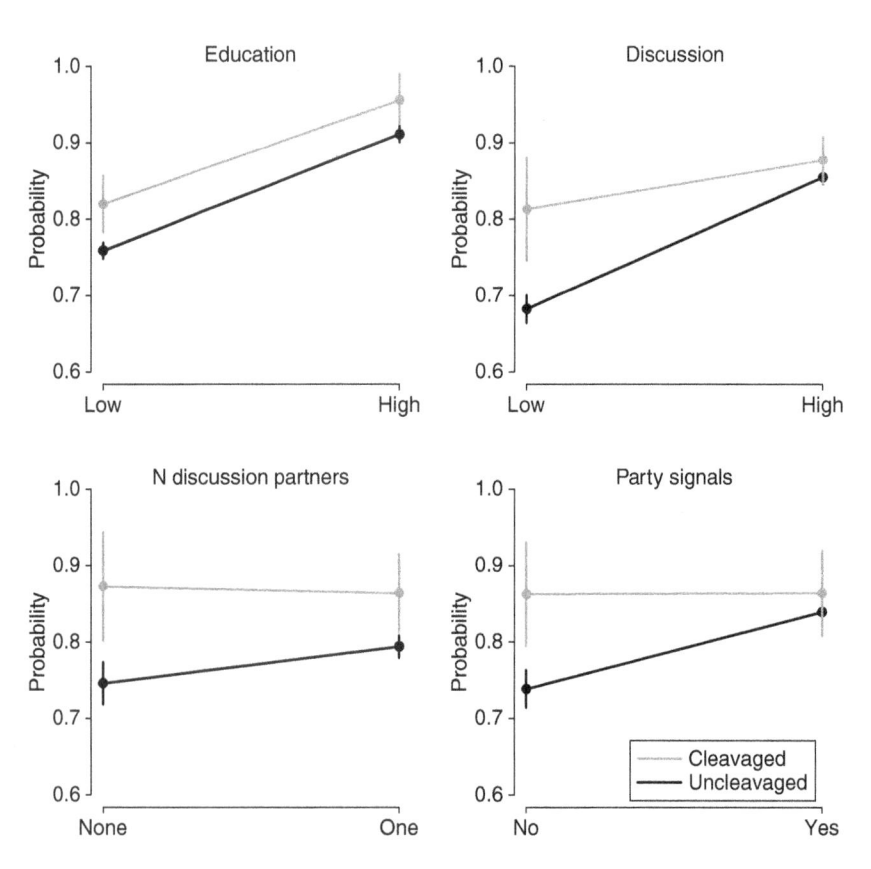

Figure 8.3 Probabilities of turnout depending on sophistication and network politicization

8.6 CONCLUSIONS

"Cleavages are the glue between voters and parties" (Lane and Ersson 1997: 181). However, this glue is drying up. In contemporary Germany, less than 15% of the adult population is linked to the traditional cleavage structure. The most plausible forecast predicts further decline. Similar trends are visible across Europe. Predominantly, the decline of cleavage structures and dealignment processes are discussed in two different frames. The first emphasizes the emancipative power of a highly sophisticated electorate that invents "new" forms of politics and participation beyond the hierarchical and elite-driven modes of "old" cleavage politics. The second focuses on the negative sides of cleavage decline; increasing voter volatility, party switching, late decision-making, and shrinking participation rates. Indeed, turnout decreased in Germany and elsewhere. Moreover, electoral abstention is not evenly distributed among the citizenry; turnout decreases among the low educated and economically deprived but remains high and constant among the higher educated and economically more successful strata of the electorate (see e.g., Schäfer 2011, 2012; Abendschön and Roßteutscher forthcoming).

This chapter has provided evidence for the egalitarian impact of cleavage structures. More precisely, we show that core cleavage groups are characterized by higher levels of political integration (particularly in terms of turnout and party identification) and move in networks with higher levels of politicization compared to marginal cleavage groups and individuals who are not associated with the traditional cleavage structure (thus confirming H1 and H2). With regard to H3, which predicted a varying impact of education on network politicization depending on cleavage membership, the hypothesis is refuted except for one instance. Although we found that among core cleavage groups the effect of (high) education is smaller, with larger standard errors attached to it, only one aspect, i.e., party signals from network partners, survived the strict statistical test. With regard to H4 and looking at the most fundamental indicator of political integration, turnout, the evidence is very clear and highly consistent. Among noncleavage groups, turnout increases with education and network politicization. In contrast, among core cleavage groups, turnout is independent of both the individuals' educational level and the politicization degree of their private networks. Regarding party identification the egalitarian impact of cleavages is visible for education but not for networks. Core cleavage groups, and in particular core Catholics, report having a party identification no matter whether they come from a low or high educational background. Among individuals not attached to the cleavage structure, party identification is clearly associated with higher education. In the case of our third indicator of political integration, cleavage voting, i.e., voting for the CDU/CSU or the SPD, none of the strict tests of differences in marginal effects turned out to be statistically significant.

To sum up, it was one of the cleavage structure's major historical achievements to link citizens of all strata to the political system: those of a higher educational background; those for whom political affairs were high on the personal agenda; and those who were more resource poor, or lacked political curiosity. The decades after the Second World War, when cleavage politics had its zenith, were thus not only characterized by a high level of political stability, but also by high and equal participation. This chapter shows that declined cleavage structures are related to increasing political inequality because education or cognitive mobilization emerges as a new dividing line in the postcleavage constellation of contemporary politics. Moreover, cleavage politics was, and still is, characterized by high levels of network politicization. Members of cleavages received political cues from more sources than just their private networks, in particular from social milieus and linkage organizations. Those who do not belong to cleavage structures, by contrast, are fully dependent on their own participatory resources and the politicizing impact of their private networks. As this chapter demonstrates, network politicization is a powerful predictor of political integration and electoral participation only among those who live outside of cleavage structures. In the postcleavage constellation, therefore, political integration hinges upon education and private networks in a way that was unknown during the heyday of cleavage politics.

9

Political Information Flows and Consistent Voting
Personal Conversations, Mass Media, Party Campaigns, and the Quality of Voting Decisions at the 2009 German Federal election[*]

Rüdiger Schmitt-Beck and Patrick Kraft

9.1 INTRODUCTION

Over more than six decades empirical research has time and again shown that voters are often neither particularly interested in, nor well informed about political matters. Rather, many citizens reveal significant knowledge gaps concerning basic institutions and procedures of democratic decision-making as well as the politics of the day (Converse 1990, 2000, 2006; Neuman 1986; Delli Carpini and Keeter 1996; Lupia and McCubbins 1998; for Germany: Westle 2005; Maier, Glantz, and Barthels 2009). Often, such diagnoses have given rise to worries about the quality of the democratic political process, since voters who don't particularly care about politics appear bound to make mistakes. Like persons playing a game without inner involvement and solid understanding of its rules they run the risk of taking wrong decisions, which in their case means to cast votes for candidates or parties whose policies are "not in accordance with their own values and priorities" (Lau, Andersen, and Redlawsk 2008: 395; Lau and Redlawsk 1997, 2006: 202–28; Delli Carpini and Keeter

---

[*] We are indebted to Richard Lau, the participants of this volume's authors' conference at the WZB Berlin, our colleagues at the Chair of Political Science I of the University of Mannheim and an anonymous reviewer for helpful comments when revising this chapter.

1996: 238–54). This may impair the link of representation between citizens and decision-makers, and undermine the accountability of elites.

According to Downs (1965) that many citizens show little cognitive and motivational involvement in politics should not come as a surprise. Information is costly, and since voters, as individuals, cannot expect their choices to be decisive for the outcome of elections, it seems rational for them to remain in a state of political ignorance. On the other hand, nonetheless aiming to cast choices that are sensible, rational voters, again according to Downs (1965), can resort to relying on external advice when they make up their minds about whom to support at the ballot box. They thus can delegate the costs of obtaining, analysing, and evaluating information to sources that are available within their social environments (Downs 1965: 207–37). In addition to voters' personal attributes, most notably their political understanding and motivation, the quality of electoral choices should thus also depend on how voters are connected to social flows of political information.

While numerous studies have analysed the implications of variations in electors' cognitive and motivational resources for their voting decisions (Converse 1990, 2000, 2006; Delli Carpini and Keeter 1996; Sniderman, Brody, and Tetlock 1991; Zaller 1992; Bartels 1996; Lupia and McCubbins 1998; Lau and Redlawsk 2006), the role of political communications for the quality of electoral choices has to date only rarely been explored. Does voters' exposure to the various sources of political information that are available during election campaigns affect their likelihood of making the right choices at the ballot box? If so, in which ways? These are the questions to be answered by the present chapter. Mainly guided by Downs' (1965) ideas, it seeks to shed light on how voters gather electoral information from external sources and how this affects the quality of their voting decisions.

To determine whether voting decisions are in accordance with citizens' values and interests, we rely on Lau and Redlawsk's (2006) survey-based method of identifying what they label "correct votes." At elections, three sources of political information appear particularly relevant, and we aim for a simultaneous analysis of them all: voters' everyday political conversations, the political coverage of mass media, and the parties' campaign communications (Beck et al. 2002; Gunther, Montero, and Puhle 2007). We first elaborate in theoretical terms what it means if voters choose consistently with their values and interests, and develop general hypotheses about how attending to external sources of electoral information may improve the odds of such decisions. We then describe our data, the construction of our measure of consistent voting, and the strategy of analysis. Our study will be based on the preelection cross-sectional face-to-face survey that was conducted as part of the German Longitudinal Election Study GLES at the 2009 German Federal election. The ensuing section presents the results of stepwise analyses that move from inspecting separately how each of the three information sources contributes to consistent voting to an integrated overall model that estimates effects of engaging in political conversations, media usage, and exposure to parties' campaign communications simultaneously.

9.2 POLITICAL INFORMATION FLOWS AND CONSISTENT VOTING

A "correct" (Lau and Redlawsk 1997, 2006: 202–27) or "consistent" (Baum and Jamison 2006) voting decision can be defined as one that is in accordance with a voters' own values and priorities (Lau, Andersen, and Redlawsk 2008: 395). What does that mean? At parliamentary elections like those in Germany, voters are facing the task of choosing one alternative from a given set of parties. From the perspective of each voter, these parties can be ranked in terms of how well they correspond to his or her basic ideological leaning, policy preferences, performance assessments, group-related identifications, and leader evaluations. In order to vote consistently an elector should decide in favor of that party which is placed on top of this personal rank order. In other words, he or she should vote for that party which overall corresponds best to his or her orientations on these dimensions. This presupposes that voters' electorally relevant stances, assessments, and evaluations must be integrated—by summing up or averaging—into overall scores for each of the parties. In line with the heterogeneity model of voting (Rivers 1988; cf. Blumenstiel in this volume) it is not assumed that when deriving these overall scores all relevant dimensions must carry the same weights across voters. Rather, the notion of consistent voting implies that voters possibly attach different importance to the various facets of electoral politics that in principle can serve as points of reference for vote choices (Lau et al. 2013). In that individualized sense, consistent voting means "voting for the candidate who really *does* best match one's self-defined preferences" (Baum and Jamison 2006: 947).

On the other hand, picking a party that does not rank first with regard to the summary score that can be generated on the basis of its closeness to a voter's ideological and policy stands, performance assessments for the party, and its leadership, as well as party- and group-related identities, qualifies as an "incorrect" choice, because another party would have corresponded better to this individual's political stances—something which obviously escaped this person when deciding how to vote. With full information, such erroneous choices should never occur. Perfectly informed voters should unfailingly cast consistent votes, since they can match all their relevant preferences and priorities exactly with the supply offered by the electoral market. Accordingly, a consistent choice can also be defined as "one that is the same as the choice that would have been made under conditions of full information" (Lau and

Redlawsk 2006: 75). Correspondingly, research has indeed shown that voters' political knowledge and interest are foremost among the factors that explain why some voters vote consistently while others fail to do so (Lau and Redlawsk 2006: 202–28; Lau, Andersen, and Redlawsk 2008; Lau et al. 2013).

According to Downs (1965: 207–37), voters can compensate their deficiencies with regard to political motivation and knowledge by turning to external sources of information for electoral advice. These can include various agencies, such as the persons with whom individuals interact in their private lives, but also organizations that continuously generate and disseminate political messages to the public, most notably the mass media and political parties (Downs 1965: 222; Beck et al. 2002; Gunther, Montero, and Puhle 2007). Attending to information sources such as these should "contribute[s] to making citizens' political choices more faithfully reflect their underlying preferences—i.e., to make individual citizens more of a sovereign master of their own political fate" (Tóka 2010: 129). To obtain a complete understanding of how information flowing from these three sources affects the quality of voting, all of them need to be taken into account simultaneously. While we expect all of them to be relevant for consistent voting, we consider an open question how they relate to one another in terms of their importance. In comparative studies of candidate and party choices personal communication usually emerges as the most powerful source of electoral influence, followed by parties' organizational communications (Katz and Lazarsfeld 1955; Beck et al. 2002; Schmitt-Beck 2004; Magalhães 2007). Our study will reveal whether the ordering is the same with regard to the quality of voting.

While it seems plausible to expect the *intensity of exposure* to each of these information sources to make a difference for the likelihood of consistent voting, more specific attributes of these sources may also be important. Turning to Downs again, two such attributes appear especially consequential: their *quality as information providers*, and their *political congeniality*. Information should be especially helpful to voters when it originates from expert sources and from sources with a political orientation similar to their own (Downs 1965: 230–4; Lupia and McCubbins 1998). In addition, Downs emphasizes that political information from these sources may reach citizens in two ways— either sought-for or by accident, as a byproduct of other activities (Downs 1965: 223). Byproduct learning appears attractive to Downs because of its cost-efficiency. However, that must not guarantee its utility with regard to the quality of electoral choices. Considering that effectively processing information presupposes some minimum level of motivation (Eveland, Shah, and Kwak 2003), it appears rather likely that *actively sought-for* information is more conducive to consistent voting. In the empirical section of this chapter we spell out these general hypotheses in more detail for each of the three relevant sources of electoral information and test how they fare when confronted with data collected at the 2009 German Federal election.

9.3 DATA, DEPENDENT VARIABLE, AND STRATEGY OF ANALYSIS

Data

The following analyses are based on data collected in a face-to-face preelection cross-sectional survey on the occasion of the German Federal election of September 27, 2009, as part of the German Longitudinal Election Study GLES[1]. The survey included 2,173 respondents sampled at random from the population of all persons aged sixteen years or older with German nationality. Since we exclude respondents below voting age (eighteen years) from our analyses, our active sample consists of 2,144 respondents. They were interviewed between August 10 and September 26, 2009.

The Dependent Variable: Consistency of Voting Decisions

To construct the dependent variable of our study we adopt the so-called "normative-naïve" procedure developed by Lau and Redlawsk (1997: 589–90, 596–7; 2006: 77–8). This approach is "naïve" insofar as it starts from voters' own attitudes and beliefs as expressed in surveys, weighing them by the relevance assigned to them by these voters themselves, either implicitly by giving valid answers to the respective questions or not, thus indicating whether they concern them or not, or explicitly by rating their personal importance or saliency. It is "normative" insofar as those orientations whose valence is not self-evident are related to expert judgments. In particular this concerns the closeness of voters' stances regarding ideology and policies to those of the parties, as the latter are located by experts, whereas performance assessments or leader evaluations, for instance, speak for themselves. Our analysis includes the five political parties represented in the German Federal Parliament (CDU/CSU, SPD, FDP, the Greens, and the Left). To emulate Lau and Redlawsk's approach for determining consistent votes to the German multiparty system some adjustments are necessary. Owing to lack of space, we can only describe in rather general terms how we proceeded to create the dependent variable in this chapter; an exhaustive documentation and discussion is provided elsewhere (Kraft 2012).

---

[1] Principal investigators: Hans Rattinger, Sigrid Roßteutscher, Rüdiger Schmitt-Beck, Bernhard Weßels. GESIS Data Archive, Cologne. ZA5300 Data file Version 5.0.0 (GLES 2011c). The data set is freely accessible via the GESIS data archive. All analyses were carried out using the transformation weight and a regional weight that compensates for oversampling in the new states of East Germany.

In accordance with the conceptual foundation outlined above, the *first step* of determining whether survey respondents voted consistently or not is to integrate their party-related stances with regard to a broad set of beliefs and attitudes into summary scores for each of the competing parties. The GLES survey included more attitude dimensions for the two large parties, CDU/CSU and SPD, which prior to the 2009 election had also been governing together in a Grand Coalition, than for the three smaller parties, FDP, the Greens, and the Left. Accordingly, the overall scores for the large parties are based on more ingredients than those for the small parties. The following dimensions are taken into account for all parties: partisanship, distances between self and party Left–Right placements, as well as issue positions (taxation and welfare state, immigration, nuclear energy), parties' perceived performance in government or opposition, and assessments of party competence with regard to each voter's most important valence issue. For the Christian Democrats and Social Democrats their chancellor candidates' Left–Right distances and perceived character traits (leadership, trustworthiness, sympathy, policy competence concerning the economic crisis) as well as retrospective evaluations of the general and personal economic situation are additionally included. To obtain expert appraisals of the true party and candidate positions on Left–Right and position issue scales we refer to the most knowledgeable respondents' judgments.[2] Since the number of attitude and belief dimensions is not constant across parties we resort to averaging for totaling them into party-specific overall scores.

The *second step* consists in determining for each respondent which party obtains the highest overall score, indicating that it conforms best to this person's preferences and priorities. This is the party this individual should choose in order to cast a consistent vote. In the *third step* it is thus determined whether this is the case or not. For that purpose we compare each respondent's first-ranking party to his or her vote intention (or postal vote), as registered in the preelection survey (second votes only). Based on this final operation we construct our dependent variable—a dummy variable that is coded 1, indicating a consistent vote, if the vote intention corresponds to the party scoring best, or coded 0 for an inconsistent vote if a respondent intends to choose another party than the one with the highest score. Complicating things somewhat, under certain circumstances this strict rule is modified in order to take into account the possibility of strategic coalition voting (Blais et al. 2006; Gschwend 2007) in the German multiparty system. German voters' choices

---

[2] For that purpose respondents were selected which provided correct answers to two knowledge questions concerning specifics of the German electoral system, were able to provide assessments of all party leaders, and could place all parties on the Left–Right scale. We use the distance approach instead of the directional approach favored by Lau and Redlawsk (2006) to determine the closeness of voters and parties.

are sometimes guided by a "coalition insurance strategy" which leads to votes for potential junior partners in a desired coalition to prevent them from falling below the 5% threshold of parliamentary representation (Gschwend 2007). For the 2009 Federal election Bytzek and Huber (2011) have shown that preferences for coalitions between CDU/CSU and FDP or SPD and Greens respectively increased the probability of votes for the junior instead of the senior partner of the respective coalition. It seems misleading to classify such choices as inconsistent. We therefore interpret votes also as consistent in cases when a two-party coalition is evaluated most favorably and the prospective senior partner within that coalition is ranked best, but the actual vote is in favor of the junior partner within the same coalition.

Except for our routine to accommodate the possibility of strategic coalition voting our procedure to determine consistent voting at the 2009 German Federal election closely corresponds to well-established practice. Nonetheless, for the sake of transparency, two caveats should not go unmentioned that render this approach somewhat problematic, even if it is difficult to conceive of methodologically feasible alternatives. One concerns the deterministic nature of the indicator of correct voting. The decision rule to classify vote choices as inconsistent does not take into account "how wrong" these decisions are, that is, whether these voters choose parties that score only slightly less well than those identified as the ones they should vote for, or whether they score much worse. The second caveat has to do with the instrument-dependency of this measure. While it is clear in theory which dimensions of beliefs and attitudes should be included to calculate the party scores that are used to determine which party a respondent should vote for (see above), in practice researchers depend on the availability of appropriate measures in surveys. The more dimensions are used, the better, of course, but nonetheless it is clear that reported levels of consistent voting should not simply be taken at face value, since they are to some degree sensitive to what went into their calculation (Lau et al. 2013).

Mindful of these caveats, we can—with the necessary reservation—report that according to our measure the proportion of consistent voting at the 2009 German Federal election amounted to about 80%, which means that according to our measure one out of five voters did not choose the party identified by our procedure as the one he or she should have voted for. Importantly, inconsistent votes were not distributed evenly across political camps. Rather, our data suggest that some parties profited while others were disadvantaged by this phenomenon, although the differences between parties' actual vote shares and those they would have gained if all voters had voted consistently are not large. Specifically, due to inconsistent voting, Social Democrats and Greens together gained two percentage points of votes and the Left one percentage point, whereas CDU/CSU and FDP correspondingly lost three percentage points (cf. Kraft 2012).

Strategy of Analysis

In the following section we present a succession of models that step-by-step carve out how consistent voting, thus measured, is affected by electors' exposure to various sources of political information. We begin this analysis with a baseline model that only includes a set of control variables. Since we aim at assessing the importance of external information sources for consistent voting in comparison to voters' own resources, this baseline model needs to include measures of respondents' motivation and knowledge about politics. We use their statements about how important the election outcome was for them personally as an indicator of political motivation (0 = totally unimportant, to 4 = very important), and an additive index based on two questions pertaining to factual knowledge about aspects of the electoral system used at German Federal elections (relevance of first and second vote, level of electoral threshold) as a measure of political understanding (0 = no correct answers, to 2 = both answers correct). As a general cognitive resource formal education (1 = completed secondary education, 0 = less) should also be relevant for consistent voting. Like these three attributes, age should be related positively to consistent voting, since it can be seen as a measure of voters' political experience (Lau et al. 2013). In addition, we include two demographic controls in our baseline model: region of residence (1 = West Germany, 0 = East Germany), and sex (1 = male, 0 = female).

The fit of this baseline model provides us with a yardstick against which model improvements can be assessed when including further measures of information exposure. With regard to consistent voting it allows us to compare the overall relevance of information from external sources in direct comparison to the key internal resources identified by extant research, most notably voters' cognitive skills and political motivation. We inspect each of the three information sources—discussants, news media, and party communications—separately in a stepwise fashion, moving from testing generic to more specific, conditional hypotheses. What we consider the optimal models will finally be included into a simultaneous estimation of the joint impact of all three sources of electoral information together.

9.4 ANALYSES

Political Conversations and Consistent Voting

According to Table 9.1 both components of political involvement—motivation and understanding—significantly affect voters' likelihood to vote consistently. As expected, and confirming patterns found for American voters (Lau

Table 9.1 Political conversations and consistent voting (odds ratios)

	(1)	(2)	(3)
Frequency of discussion		0.816	0.806
Expertise discussant	0.873	0.574**	0.612**
Expertise discussant × frequency of discussion		1.256**	1.227**
Agreement/disagreement with discussant	1.096	2.112**	1.947**
Agreement/disagreement with discussant × frequency of discussion		0.799*	0.827*
Partisan congruence discussant	2.277***	2.734**	2.322***
Partisan congruence discussant × frequency of discussion		0.939	
Political knowledge	1.367**	1.388**	1.388**
Political motivation	1.260*	1.283*	1.285*
Education	1.346	1.342	1.351
Age	1.002	1.003	1.003
Gender	0.957	0.992	0.988
Region	1.107	1.094	1.097
N	1311	1311	1311
Δ McKelvey & Zavoina's R^2	0.090	0.111	0.109

# $p < 0.10$, * $p < 0.05$, ** $p < 0.01$, *** $p < 0.001$.
Note: Δ McKelvey & Zavoina's R^2: gain relative to baseline model ($R^2 = 0.044$).

and Redlawsk 1997, 2006: 202–228; Lau, Andersen, and Redlawsk 2008; Lau et al. 2013), voters who care more strongly about the election outcome, and persons who know more about politics have better odds to make the right choices. Closer inspection of the data shows that political motivation is even more important than knowledge, although of course it has to be taken into account that the two orientations are closely related to one another. Education as a more general indicator of cognitive resources does not exert an additional influence on the likelihood of consistent voting, nor does persons' electoral experience as indicated by their age. While the key personal resources show the expected relationships, the explanatory power of the baseline model is not overwhelming.[3] But what about political conversations as an external source of political information?

---

[3] The minor differences between the R^2 values of the baseline model reported in the various tables are due to slightly different active samples.

In the run-up to an election many voters talk about politics with members of their personal environments such as spouses and life partners, relatives, friends or coworkers. Such conversations are typically an integral part of the day-to-day interactions taking place within social networks (Wyatt, Katz, and Kim 2000). They can help voters to tap into other network members' reservoirs of political information, taking advantage from them when they make up their minds about how to vote. Numerous analyses have shown that informal social communication is influential with regard to individuals' electoral choices (Lazarsfeld, Berelson, and Gaudet 1968; Huckfeldt and Sprague 1995; Levine 2005; Johnston and Pattie 2006; Zuckerman, Dasovic, and Fitzgerald 2007; Schmitt-Beck 2000; Schmitt-Beck, Partheymüller, and Faas 2012). However it is much less clear whether and under which circumstances it may also affect the quality of these voting decisions (Richey 2008; Sokhey and McClurg 2012; Ryan 2010, 2011; Tóka 2010). In any case, it appears plausible to expect frequent political talks to contribute to a better quality of electoral choices (Tóka 2010). This general expectation is tested in the first column of Table 9.1. To indicate respondents' exposure to electoral communication originating from their personal environment we rely on a measure which registers on how many days during the week before the interview respondents talked "about politics and the political parties with other people, such as members of your family, friends or acquaintances" (range 0-7). Obviously, no significant relationship emerges. The mere frequency of interpersonal exchange about politics does not appear to count for consistent voting.

However, discussant characteristics might be of relevance. As Ryan notes, "[f]irst, the informant must be politically expert. Second, individuals should choose informants with similar viewpoints in order to avoid being misled" (Ryan 2010: 46). Voters should thus be particularly receptive to the advice of discussants that they consider politically knowledgeable and thus a potential source of high-quality information (Huckfeldt 2001). For American voters Richey (2008; see also Sokhey and McClurg 2012; Ryan 2010) found a sizable positive relationship between the cumulated expertise of voters' associates and the likelihood of consistent voting decisions. It can thus be expected that persons will be more likely to vote consistently when they interact with discussants of high political expertise. Moreover, as rational voters should not delegate the gathering and interpretation of information to discussants whose political outlook differs considerably from their own (Downs 1965: 228), political congeniality should also increase voters' receptivity to the information provided by other persons. Perceiving a discussant as a political soul mate creates the impression that this person is politically trustworthy, and thus should be a reliable source of electoral advice. There is substantial evidence that discussants' influence on candidate or party choices is facilitated by agreement and impeded by disagreement in social networks (Lupia and McCubbins 1998: 184-201; Huckfeldt and Sprague 1995;

Schmitt-Beck 2000: 280–5; Johnston and Pattie 2006: 136–7; Levine 2005; Schmitt-Beck, Partheymüller, and Faas 2012). Some American studies also suggest that political consent with discussants goes along with more consistent voting decisions (Sokhey and McClurg 2012; Ryan 2011). Voters should thus be more likely to vote consistently the more their discussants are politically similar to them.

We use two measures to indicate the political congeniality of voters' political conversations, one that is narrowly partisan, and one with a broader focus (cf. Klofstad, Sokhey, and McClurg 2013). The party-specific instrument refers to the perceived vote intention of the person with whom respondents discussed politics most often. It indicates whether in the perception of respondents these discussants aimed to vote for the party which would have been their own consistent choice. The measure can assume three values, ranging from 1 (discussant's party preference corresponds to party respondent should choose in order to vote consistently), over 0 (no discussant, or discussant is uncertain about how to vote or does not intend to vote, or discussant's party preference is unknown to respondent) to −1 (discussant prefers party not corresponding to respondent's consistent choice). The general measure is based on a question inquiring about the amount of disagreement overall experienced during political conversations with the same most important discussants (0 = no dissent at all/respondent never discusses politics, to 3 = often different opinions). Another question elicited respondents' assessment of the political knowledge of their most important discussants, and we use this instrument to indicate the political expertise residing in respondents' social networks (0 = discussant knows nothing about politics/respondent never discusses politics, to 3 = discussant knows a great deal about politics).

The first model of Table 9.1 shows a mixed picture. Neither discussants' political expertise nor the amount of general agreement or disagreement during political conversations seems to play a role for consistent voting. However, voters are much more likely to vote consistently when their main discussant appears to support the party corresponding to their own consistent choice. The general congeniality hypothesis thus receives at least partial confirmation for political conversations as source of political information. The picture becomes even clearer when moving to more complicated model specifications. Now we see more, although highly conditional discussant effects on consistent voting. Model (2) is based on a specification that includes multiplicative interaction terms for the discussant's political expertise as well as our two indicators of dyadic political similarity with the frequency of political conversations. In contrast to model (1) both the expertise of discussants and the amount of agreement or disagreement during political conversations now also appear relevant for consistent voting, although contingent on a high frequency of such talks. In contrast, the effect of partisan congeniality is not affected by how often political discussions take place.

In the final model (3) the irrelevant interaction effect between partisan congeniality and the frequency of discussion is thus omitted. Compared to the baseline model, which predicts voters' correct choices mainly from their personal political motivation and knowledge, this model's additional explanatory power is more than twice as high. For correct voting, the nature of the information flows to which voters are exposed by their most important political conversation partners appears more consequential than their personal cognitive and motivational resources. However, it is not simply political conversation as such that makes the difference. Frequent exchanges are especially beneficial when they take place with network partners that know a lot about politics. Figure 9.1 visualizes this pattern (based on model [3] and holding all other predictors at their sample means). On the other hand, the amount of general agreement or disagreement also matters, but also only under the condition of frequent political talks. Most striking about Figure 9.2 which shows the substance of this relationship is how vulnerable voters appear with regard to detrimental influence originating from discussants with whom they generally disagree. Talking often to someone with whom one overall rather disagrees considerably decreases the odds of consistent vote choices. However, when defined in narrow partisan terms, politically congenial discussants appear highly influential regardless of the intensity of exposure. When voters'

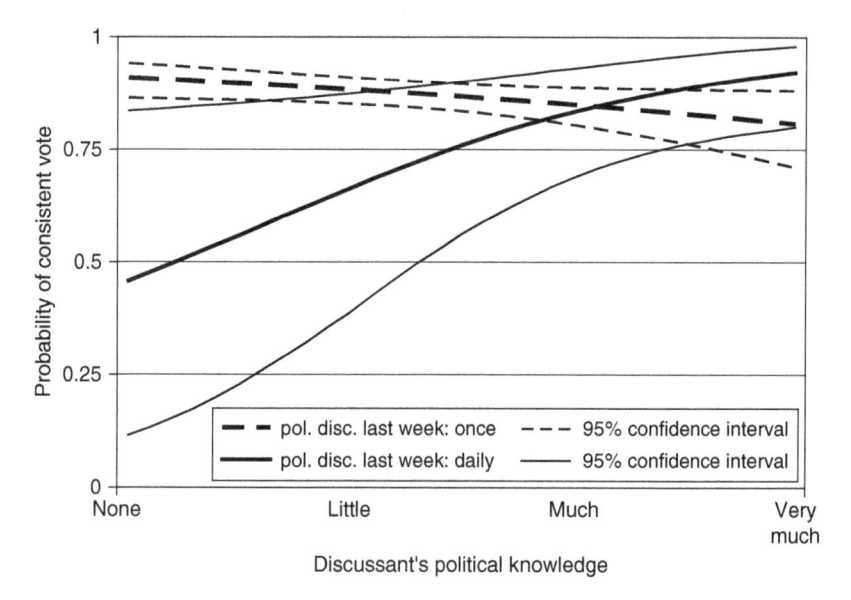

Figure 9.1 Probability of consistent voting by discussant's political expertise and frequency of political discussions

Notes: Predicted probabilities with 95% confidence intervals, based on model (3) in Table 9.1; all other predictors fixed to sample mean.

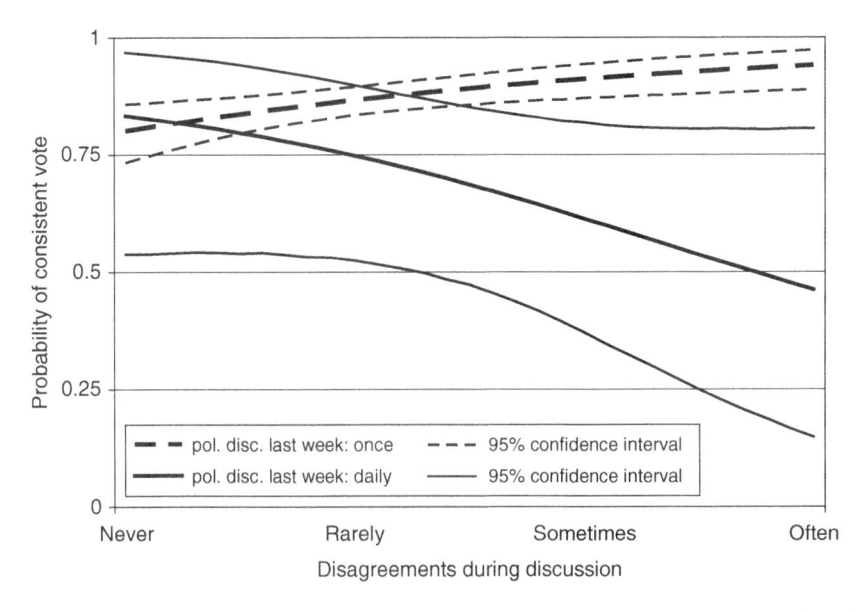

Figure 9.2 Probability of consistent voting by political disagreement during political discussions and frequency of political discussions

Notes: Predicted probabilities with 95% confidence intervals, based on model (3) in Table 9.1; all other predictors fixed to sample mean.

discussants support the parties they themselves should choose to be consistent with their own preferences and priorities, they are likely to vote accordingly. In contrast, interacting with someone who prefers another party considerably decreases one's odds of voting consistently.

News Media Coverage and Consistent Voting

As "professional data-gatherers and publishers" (Downs 1965: 226) journalists provide voters with information that is already preselected, sorted and organized in the news, and interpreted in editorials. Despite the news media's ubiquity as a source of electoral information, their actual importance at elections has for a long time been a matter of dispute. But in recent years several studies have indicated how media messages may indeed affect vote choices (Iyengar and Kinder 1987; Bartels 1993; Druckman 2005). What has always been much clearer, though, is that people learn from the media. Citizens become more knowledgeable by following the news (Barabas and Jerit 2009). To test whether mass media play a similar role with regard to the quality of voting decisions we begin our analysis of media effects by inspecting whether voters are more likely to vote consistently if they attend more frequently to the political coverage of mass media. The measure used is global and simple—an additive index of media exposure incorporating all media included in the GLES study: a broad range of broadsheets (the five outlets of the national quality press—*Die Welt, Frankfurter Allgemeine Zeitung, Süddeutsche Zeitung, Frankfurter Rundschau,* and *die tageszeitung*—and up to two regional daily newspapers) and the dominant tabloid (and by far largest German newspaper) *Bild* as well as the prime time newscasts of the four television channels with the highest ratings, two of which are public (ARD, ZDF) and two commercial (RTL, SAT.1). Like for political discussion, exposure to each medium is measured on a scale ranging from 0 (= no exposure) to 7 (= every day in the last week). In principle, the index has an enormous range (0–84), but respondents are of course very selective in their media habits (mean = 13.7, SD = 7.2).

According to model (1) in Table 9.2 overall media usage is unrelated to consistent voting. Similar to political conversations, the generic intensity hypothesis is refuted for mass media. Media effects are often indeed highly conditional (Schmitt-Beck 2012). In section 2, we have proposed that sought-for information is more beneficial with regard to consistent voting. Newspapers are a type of medium that presupposes some amount of active engagement on the part of its audience, whereas exposure to television news often takes place inadvertently (Baum and Jamison 2006; Prior 2007). Comparative studies of political learning accordingly suggest that the press is overall more conducive to political learning than television news (Druckman 2005). Moreover, extant research suggests that outlets providing information of higher quality are more influential in that regard, which also corresponds to one of our general propositions. According to these studies people learn more from broadsheets—as they provide more and better information—than from tabloids, whereas for television news the type of broadcaster makes a difference. Public affairs programs of commercial broadcasters appear less effective with regard to political learning than those of public broadcasters, which typically offer an information diet that is more voluminous, analytical, and varied (Curran et al. 2009; Aarts and Semetko 2003). Model (2) differentiates media exposure accordingly—with a surprising result: In this more fine-grained estimation a significant relationship emerges for a newspaper, as expected, though this is not for the broadsheet press but the less information-rich tabloid *Bild*, so that the picture is nonetheless somewhat puzzling.

In view of our general propositions, the political congruence between voters and media should also be consequential with regard to consistent voting. While modern news media typically subscribe to norms of balance and neutrality, a certain amount of one-sidedness nonetheless often is present in particular media's reporting and especially commenting (D'Alessio and Allen 2000; Maurer and Reinemann 2006: 107–44), and several studies indicate that such bias or slant may indeed influence audience members' vote choices (Dalton, Beck, and Huckfeldt 1998; Druckman and Parkin 2005; Hopmann et al. 2010;

Table 9.2 Usage of mass media and consistent voting (odds ratios)

	(1)	(2)	(3)	(4)	(5)	(6)	(7)
Usage frequency media overall	1.020			1.020			
Usage frequency public TV news		1.041				1.036	
Usage frequency private TV news		1.006				1.007	
Usage frequency broadsheets		0.972				0.990	
Usage frequency tabloid *Bild*		1.133*				1.129*	1.132*
Partisan congruence media overall			1.311***	1.562#			
Usage freq. media overall × partisan congruence media overall				0.991			
Partisan congruence public TV news					1.120	1.313	
Partisan congruence private TV news					1.183	2.436	
Partisan congruence broadsheets					1.771**	1.533	1.810***
Partisan congruence tabloid *Bild*					1.150	2.882	
Partisan congruence × usage frequency public TV news						0.980	
Partisan congruence × usage frequency private TV news						0.837	
Partisan congruence × usage frequency broadsheets						1.015	
Partisan congruence × usage frequency tabloid *Bild*						0.785	
Political knowledge	1.403**	1.437**	1.453**	1.467**	1.453**	1.489**	1.444**
Political motivation	1.161	1.196#	1.221*	1.177#	1.240*	1.207#	1.240*
Education	1.287	1.476	1.295	1.308	1.308	1.508	1.442
Age	1.004	1.005	1.005	1.003	1.005	1.004	1.007
Gender	0.822	0.768	0.876	0.846	0.876	0.785	0.794
Region	1.230	1.255	1.213	1.186	1.240	1.252	1.269
N	1278	1278	1278	1278	1278	1278	1278
Δ McKelvey & Zavoina's R^2	0.005	0.021	0.018	0.025	0.026	0.053	0.038

# $p < 0.10$, * $p < 0.05$, ** $p < 0.01$, *** $p < 0.001$.
Note: Δ McKelvey & Zavoina's R^2: gain relative to baseline model ($R^2 = 0.041$).

Boomgaarden and Semetko 2012). Hence, we expect that media whose coverage is congruent to voters' own political outlook are especially beneficial with regard to consistent voting. To measure the media's political congeniality we rely on respondents' perceptions of statement bias (Boomgaarden and Semetko 2012; D'Alessio and Allen 2000). Those using a medium were asked whether they could name up to three parties for which, according to their impression, this medium's election coverage was more favorable than for other parties. We match these perceptions with respondents' own party orientations according to a logic roughly corresponding to the one applied for political discussants. For each medium the resulting measure varies between 1 (= medium perceived as favoring only the party the respondent should choose in order to vote consistently) and −1 (= medium perceived as favoring up to three other parties), with 0 indicating that the medium was either not used, or perceived as favoring no party, or as favoring both the consistent party and one or more other parties, on the assumption that message flows in diverse partisan directions, on balance, neutralize one another (Zaller 1996).

The estimates in the third column of Table 9.2 pertain to an additive index created by summing up these medium-specific measures of party-political congruence across all media. They indicate that the overall partisan congeniality of the media perceived by our respondents plays an important role for their consistent voting. The more news media expose citizens to coverage that in their subjective view is favorable for the party identified as their consistent choice, the more they indeed support that party at the polls. The frequency of media use does not moderate this relationship, as can be seen from model (4). However, when splitting up our overall index of media's political congeniality to inspect the moderating role of media type and information quality, only one of the four effects attains statistical significance. Apparently, the substantial overall effect detected by model (3) is only driven by this relationship. According to model (5) the likelihood of choosing correctly increases with the number of broadsheets read that are perceived as supporting the party which would be the consistent choice, and decreases when such newspapers are seen as supporting other parties. As it seems partisan congeniality is beneficial to consistent voting, but only for media that provide an information diet of high quality in terms of amount, breadth, and depth and whose usage presupposes some motivation on the part of its audience. However, the intensity of exposure does not seem to moderate this already highly conditional relationship (model [6]).

Model (7) is thus the most parsimonious representation of how the mass media's coverage of politics affects voters' odds of choosing the parties that best correspond to their own values and priorities. The positive effects for exposure to the tabloid *Bild* and for the perceived partisan congeniality of broadsheets are both sustained in this model. Three of our four general propositions are supported by these data, but only in conjunction with one another. Media effects on consistent voting are thus—like those of personal communication—highly conditional. Compared to the baseline estimation, inclusion of the media as external source of information does not quite double the model's explanatory power. Similar to previous studies of party choice (Schmitt-Beck 2004), with regard to consistent voting the mass media appear thus less influential than people's political conversation partners.

Parties' Campaign Communications and Consistent Voting

The electoral role of the parties' electioneering has only recently begun to attract scholarly interest, but robust evidence has already accumulated which suggests that "campaigns matter" for vote choices (Holbrook 1996; Farrell and Schmitt-Beck 2002; Kaufmann, Petrocik, and Shaw 2008: 163–90). In line with our general intensity hypothesis, according to Lau and Redlawsk's research intense campaigns appear to improve the odds of consistent voting (Lau and Redlawsk 2006: 207–12; Lau, Andersen, and Redlawsk 2008). We therefore generally hypothesize that the likelihood of voting consistently increases with the intensity of voters' campaign contact. Based on measures that in a dichotomous way register respondents' exposure to a range of channels of party communications, we can develop indices of campaign contact. Our most general measure is a count of all forms of campaign contact experienced by a respondent (range 0 = no campaign contact at all, to 8 = exposure to all forms of party communications included in the survey). According to Table 9.3, however, the mere intensity of exposure does not count for correct voting, echoing our findings for political conversations and media use. For all three sources of electoral information the unconditional intensity hypothesis is thus refuted.

While being classified by Downs (1965: 223) as a case for active information search, at least some modern campaign media, such as billboards or television spots, in principle also allow for inadvertent exposure. However, from our general propositions we can derive the expectation that exposure to information from campaign media that need to be sought out actively should be more consequential for consistent voting than accidentally encountered information. Based on a study by Schmitt-Beck and Wolsing (2010) we can distinguish between campaign media that presuppose motivation and activity on the part of voters (approaching street stands of parties, attending campaign rallies, accessing party websites, and subscribing to campaign e-mails or text messages), and campaign media with a high chance of inadvertent exposure (party billboards, television spots, advertisements in the press, party leaflets). We construct additive indices for both inattentive and sought-for campaign exposure by counting the number of contacts across these campaign channels, each ranging from 0 to 4. According to model (2) this distinction is indeed important for campaign effects. Accidentally getting in touch with party communications seems irrelevant for the quality of electoral choices, while actively

Table 9.3 Exposure to parties' campaign communications and consistent voting (odds ratios)

	(1)	(2)	(3)	(4)
Campaign contacts overall	1.030			
Campaign contacts active		1.402*		
Campaign contacts accidental		0.919		
Partisan congruence campaign contacts overall			1.957***	
Partisan congruence campaign contacts active				3.233***
Partisan congruence campaign contacts accidental				1.751***
Political knowledge	1.378**	1.366**	1.369**	1.351*
Political motivation	1.252*	1.241*	1.228*	1.234*
Education	1.239	1.218	1.427	1.436
Age	1.005	1.006	1.005	1.005
Gender	0.836	0.815	0.846	0.843
Region	1.224	1.194	1.127	1.121
N	1306	1306	1306	1306
Δ McKelvey & Zavoina's R^2	0.001	0.021	0.140	0.208

# $p < 0.10$, * $p < 0.05$, ** $p < 0.01$, *** $p < 0.001$.
Note: Δ McKelvey & Zavoina's R^2: gain relative to baseline model ($R^2 = 0.046$).

seeking information from parties matters for the odds of consistent voting. The more intense voters' exposure to sought-for information from political parties' direct communications, the higher their likelihood to vote consistently.

The party from which the campaign information comes should, however, also play a role. We expect voters' exposure to the parties' electioneering to increase the likelihood of consistent voting in particular when it concerns information that correspond to voters' own political outlook. Since it was registered for respondents to which parties' electioneering they were exposed, indices of the partisan content of campaign exposure can be developed. First we construct for each form of electioneering a basic measure that varies between 1 (= via this campaign medium only exposure to messages from the party corresponding to the respondent's consistent vote) and −1 (= via this campaign channel only exposure to messages from other parties). A value of 0 is assigned if a respondent did not get in touch with the respective channel of campaign communications, or came in touch, via this medium, to the consistent party and one or several other parties at the same time. Model (3) is based on an additive index summing up these measures across all eight campaign media. Obviously, the amount to which the party messages that voters receive are one-sided matters a great deal. The more unequivocally the flow of campaign information a voter follows originates from the party identified as the one he or she should choose in order to cast a consistent vote, the stronger the likelihood that this party indeed gains his or her vote. Multisided message flows, in contrast, dissipate that effect, and being predominantly or exclusively exposed to other parties' communications substantially diminishes the odds of consistent voting.

Differentiating our measures further leads to even more specific insights. The fourth column of Table 9.3 combines the two moderating conditions: the partisan congeniality of campaign information and the quality of the channel through which it reaches voters; we see that indeed both interact with regard to consistent voting. The likelihood of voters to choose the party that is consistent with their attitudes increases very substantially when they actively and exclusively expose themselves to that party's—and no other parties'—electioneering by means of talking to its members and volunteers at street stands, attending its rallies, accessing its websites, or subscribing to its electronic messaging services. Slicing the data that way, it becomes clear that accidental, but exclusive exposure to these parties' communications also opens up a path for influence, but to a much lesser degree.

In sum, exposure to the parties' campaign communications is a very important contributor to consistent voting—especially when voters actively seek such information, and as long as this brings them only in touch with the party they should favor in order to vote consistently. Again, none of our general propositions is unequivocally supported by our data; rather, like the other sources of electoral information, parties' electioneering also seems to influence vote choices only in complex conditional ways. While information flows originating from personal discussants or the mass media are also relevant for the likelihood of casting a consistent vote, attending to the parties' electioneering appears more helpful. The additional explanatory power of model (4) is about four times higher than the fit of the baseline model which includes only personal attributes of voters.

Political Information Flows and Consistent Voting: Simultaneous Analysis

According to the well-known "the more the more" rule (Lazarsfeld, Berelson, and Gaudet 1968) we can expect voters' exposure to information flows from personal discussion, news media coverage, and parties' campaign communications to be related phenomena. How, then, do the effects on correct voting found in separate analyses hold up in a simultaneous estimation? Table 9.4 is based on the final models of the previous three steps of our analysis. Most relationships remain unaffected in this more complex model in which each information source's effects are not only controlled for voters' personal characteristics, but also for their exposure to the other information sources. Reading the tabloid

Table 9.4 Exposure to all three information sources and consistent voting (odds ratios)

Frequency of discussion	0.821
Expertise discussant	0.647*
Expertise discussant × frequency of discussion	1.167*
Agreement/disagreement with discussant	1.867**
Agreement/disagreement with discussant × frequency of discussion	0.854#
Partisan congruence discussant	2.032***
Usage frequency tabloid *Bild*	1.052
Partisan congruence broadsheets	1.421#
Partisan congruence campaign contacts active	3.158***
Partisan congruence campaign contacts accidental	1.567***
Political knowledge	1.422**
Political motivation	1.289*
Education	1.530
Age	1.004
Gender	0.905
Region	1.054
N	1282
Δ McKelvey & Zavoina's R^2	0.273

# $p < 0.10$, * $p < 0.05$, ** $p < 0.01$, *** $p < 0.001$.
Note: Δ McKelvey & Zavoina's R^2: gain relative to baseline model ($R^2 = 0.044$).

Bild appears no longer relevant for consistent voting; this relationship which anyway appeared rather puzzling in view of our hypotheses is not sustained in this most complex model specification. Two of the previously found relationships are only marginally significant in our overall model, and thus appear less robust. They concern the partisan character of broadsheets and the interaction between the perceived agreement of discussants' opinions during political conversations and the frequency of these talks. All other relationships are clearly sustained.[4] In terms of model fit this full model is about six times as powerful as the baseline model, which includes voters' personal attributes, most notably their political motivation and knowledge as key resources.

---

[4] We checked for multicollinearity and found it not to impair the estimates of this model. As a robustness test to deal with the problem of the deterministic character of our dependent variable which does not take into account "how wrong" inconsistent votes actually are (cf. Section 9.3, above) we ran the same model including as additional control variable the difference between the overall scores of the first- and second-ranked parties, which we interpret as a measure of the

Remarkably, when inspecting the marginal effects corresponding to the contrasts between the lowest and highest values in the sample, all statistically substantial effects of exposure to external sources of electoral information appear clearly stronger than the effects of the personal attributes of political interest (15%) and knowledge (9%). In particular this pertains to campaign communications. The marginal effects of both sought-for and accidental exposure either exclusively to the correct party's or only to other parties' electioneering amount to more than 60 or 50% respectively, and thus surpass the impact of personal attributes by far. The marginal effect of reading broadsheets that favor the party voters ought to choose to remain consistent with their preferences and priorities is also considerable, amounting to more than 20% for the empirically observed maximum range between reading three newspapers at least once a week whose net favoritism is for the benefit of the correct party, on the one hand, and two papers that on balance favor other parties, on the other. However, it must be borne in mind that this effect is only marginally significant and may thus be insubstantial. The marginal effect of discussing politics with a person in favor of the same as opposed to another party amounts to 17%. Moreover, specifically among voters who discuss politics daily, the odds of voting consistently increases by about 30% when the respective discussant is endowed with very high political expertise instead of being utterly incompetent. On the other hand, when they talk every day to someone with whom they disagree often, their chances of choosing correctly are about 20% lower than when they always agree.

9.5 CONCLUSION

We started this chapter with the observation, over the past decades confirmed by scores of empirical studies, that many voters are neither particularly knowledgeable, nor motivated to improve their knowledge about politics. Time and again, this state of affairs has given rise to worried questioning: If citizens are politically uninterested and unaware, how can they fulfill the role of the sovereign that representative democracy requires them to assume at elections? And

---

difficulty to decide between the two most attractive parties. Including this variable as additional control in the model shows that it is indeed strongly related to consistent voting—inconsistent votes are much more likely when the scores of the first- and second-ranked party are close together. This suggests that most of the "mistakes" made when voters choose inconsistently are rather small. More importantly, most of the relationships between information exposure and consistent voting are sustained when the difficulty to decide is thus taken into account. The only effect that no longer attains even marginal significance in the modified model is the one for the party-political congeniality of the broadsheet press. On the other hand, the interaction effect of agreement and discussion frequency is clearly significant with $p < 0.05$ in that model. Our findings for personal conversations and the parties' electioneering are thus confirmed by this additional analysis, while it appears even more doubtful that the mass media are relevant for consistent voting.

what does it mean for the accountability of political elites if voters do not comprehend what consequences their decisions have for their lives? Incorrect voting decisions (Lau and Redlawsk 1997, 2006), that is, decisions for candidates or parties that are more or less inconsistent with their ideological and policy preferences, performance assessments, group and party identities, as well as candidate evaluations, entail the risk that the chain of responsibility between political elites and citizens created by elections is interrupted and the quality of representative democracy accordingly impaired.

Against this background, the purpose of our analysis was to test some assumptions that have been inspired by Downs' (1965) propositions about the rational ignorance of voters, and in particular the rationality of delegating the task of collecting, analysing, and evaluating information to external agencies. According to this line of thought, citizens are not to be expected to rely only on their own motivational and cognitive resources when deciding how to vote. Rather, they should also take electoral information into account that reaches them from personal sources, such as the individuals with whom they interact in their private lives, as well as from impersonal sources, most prominently the mass media's news coverage and the parties' campaign communications. For the 2009 German Federal election, we indeed found that consistent vote choices were not only more likely among voters who were deeply interested and well versed in political matters, but also among persons who were exposed to social flows of political information that originated from associates with whom they talked about politics, from the mass media, and from political parties.

Our findings suggest that the importance of exposure to external sources of political information overall indeed surpasses the relevance of voters' personal resources to a considerable extent. This can be illustrated using the model shown in Table 9.4. When varying the amount of political interest and knowledge from one standard deviation below to one standard deviation above the respective means while holding all other predictors including information exposure at their mean, the proportion of consistent voters changes by about 10 percentage points. In contrast, even when varying only those attributes of exposure to external information sources which appear clearly robust, i.e., personal conversations and attentiveness to the parties' campaigns, from one standard deviation below to one standard deviation above the mean while holding all other predictors including individuals' internal resources and newspaper readership at their mean, the corresponding change amounts to 35 percentage points. However, the three sources of information do not contribute equally strongly to the quality of voters' decision-making. The parties' electioneering, which by its very nature is biased communication as it aims at influencing vote choices (Downs 1965: 226–7), seems indeed to be more relevant for voters when making up their minds than the two other sources of information. It appears more consequential for the likelihood of consistent voting than even voters' political conversations, which in studies of communication effects on political orientations usually appear as the most powerful source of influence (Schmitt-Beck 2004). In contrast, the effects of exposure to the news media appear not very robust in our analysis, so whether attendance to mass media indeed contributes to consistent voting remains questionable and should be subject to further research. In particular, if and how media effects depend on certain audience attributes is a question not explored here, but certainly meriting further attention (cf. Baum and Jamison 2006).

As starting point of our inquiry we stated four general propositions concerning factors mediating the relevance of external information sources on consistent voting. They emphasized the intensity of exposure, the quality of the information supplied, the political congeniality, and the amount of effort on the part of voters required to get access to the information. Importantly, we found that all three sources of electoral information unfold their influence on the quality of voting in highly contingent ways. In each case we found information effects only to occur under certain conditions, although in partly differing ways. Unequivocally, however, for none of them the mere intensity of exposure counted with regard to consistent voting. According to Downs (1965), for electoral guidance rational information seekers should turn to sources that are politically congenial, in order to avoid being misled. For all three information sources, our findings are in line with this general hypothesis. Regardless of its source, being exposed to information that was one-sided in terms of the party which voters should choose in order to vote consistently, substantially improved the odds of consistent voting. However, for the mass media this only concerned newspapers of higher information quality—and even that finding was not very robust—while with regard to party communications the relationship was particularly pronounced for those forms of electioneering for which exposure presupposed purposive activity on the part of voters. Similarly, the extent of general agreement or disagreement during political discussions appeared only consequential for consistent voting when the frequency of such conversations was high, whereas the effect of interpersonal congruence in narrow partisan terms was not moderated by the intensity of political exchanges. The beneficial role of highly knowledgeable discussants also depended on frequent political talks.

Our observations regarding the role of discussants for consistent voting partly echo findings from US studies (Richey 2008; Sokhey and McClurg 2012; Ryan 2010, 2011), but suggest more complex contingencies than detected there. Concerning campaign communications our analyses also revealed more complex patterns than previous research. In particular, we found the distinction between accidental and sought-for information to be quite consequential. For news media, the type and information quality of the medium makes a difference. Television news does not appear relevant for correct voting, which may be a consequence of its largely neutral or balanced character in partisan terms.

Only print media of higher information quality seem important, although this evidence is not very robust.

Overall, our findings indicate that exposure to external information sources may help voters to make the right choices at the ballot box. Whether voters make sound choices at the polls depends not only on their own motivational and cognitive resources. Although in quite complex ways, turning to external sources of political information may considerably improve their odds of voting consistently. Delegating the costs of obtaining, analysing, and evaluating information to sources available within their social environments pays off for voters—at least as long as they make the right choices when selecting their sources. Yet, further research is necessary to gain deeper insights into these processes. In particular, it is necessary to inquire whether and how voters' own political motivation and sophistication moderate the effects of exposure to external information. Our study concentrated on the complex contingencies emerging from various key attributes of the information sources. But in all likelihood communication effects are not the same for all voters. Rather, it appears plausible to expect those less endowed with these personal resources to profit most from helpful "personal information-acquisition systems" (Downs 1965: 219). Moreover, more suitable data and better instruments would be desirable. These include objective instead of merely perceptional measures of information sources' partisanship, more extensive measures of political discussion networks (e.g., Richey 2008), and measures registering not only exposure to mass media content but the reception of it (Chaffee and Schleuder 1986). Lastly, it would be preferable to rely on panel data, in order to keep problems of endogeneity better under control than it is possible with the cross-sectional data available for our study. Combining preelection measurements of information exposure like those we relied on with postelection measurements of the consistency of actual vote choices appears optimal in that regard.

10

Activation of Fundamentals in German Campaigns

Richard Johnston, Julia Partheymüller, and Rüdiger Schmitt-Beck

Do German election campaigns make history, or merely reveal it? Vote intentions shift during campaigns, but the mere existence of a shift rarely reveals its meaning. Shifts may be induced by the parties' strategic thrust and counterthrust, but they may also be quasi-autonomic. Even shifts that are induced by campaign stimuli may ultimately contribute toward a foreordained result and simply lay bare underlying considerations, including social structure and recent history, enduring aspects of the party battle, and the state of the economy. These factors now carry the term of art, "fundamentals" (Wlezien and Erikson 2002), and some say that the principal role of campaigns is to activate them. For many, this proposition carries a normative charge. Activation seems somehow reassuring. It suggests that campaigns are enlightening events, not—or not just—fields for manipulation. It would be additionally reassuring if campaigns can be shown to narrow gaps in preference and perception between sophisticated and unsophisticated voters.

Although a substantial body of evidence has accumulated in the United States (Kaufmann, Petrocik, and Shaw 2008: 163–90) and some other countries (Johnston et al. 1992; Farrell and Schmitt-Beck 2002), not much is known yet about the German case (but see Schoen 2003a, 2007; Lachat 2007). This chapter focuses on the 2005 and 2009 elections and asks whether and how "fundamentals" are activated during preelection periods—in general but also contingent on the specifics of particular campaigns and on voters' political sophistication. Apart from its intrinsic interest, the case presents a useful contrast with mainly US-based evidence. Five parties commonly achieve representation in Parliament and these parties are relevant to government formation, even if only (as with the Left) in a negative way. The multiplicity of parties makes ideology a potentially important factor in sorting voters within coalitions. And campaigns are short, the 2005 one especially so. Analyses are based on two Rolling Cross-Section (RCS) surveys that covered the final six and eight weeks of the 2005 and 2009 preelection periods, respectively, thus encompassing the entire official campaign.

We begin by stylizing the possible role of fundamental considerations, and asking how applicable a "fundamentalist" view of campaigns is to the German case. Then we consider how we might capture activation in German data. This proves not to be a simple question. We do find evidence for activation, but only for certain considerations and more in some elections than in others. And whether a campaign narrows or widens gaps between high- and low-interest voters depends on who is doing the campaigning.

10.1 GENERAL THEMES

What is a "Fundamental"?

"Fundamentals" comprise two main elements—voters' political predispositions, which remain fixed, and the economy, a target that moves between elections (Gelman and King 1993). *Within* a campaign, critically, a fundamental is a consideration that does not move. To quote Wlezien and Erikson (2002: 971 n. 3), "we define 'fundamentals' not by their specific content, but by the fact that they are long-lasting, either a constant or an accumulation with no decay." They regulate information processing and guide political perception (Zaller 1992; Bartels 2002). All this should lead voters to "join the fold to which they belong" (Lazarsfeld, Berelson, and Gaudet 1968: 73). Whatever else they do, then, election campaigns should activate voters' predispositions (Lazarsfeld, Berelson, and Gaudet 1968; Finkel 1993). For some, this activation indicates that campaigns are normatively beneficial exercises in "enlightenment," in making behaviour conform to citizens' real interests or real opinion (Gelman and King 1993).

Political predispositions are rooted in the historically produced conflict structures of societies, politicized antagonisms that yield stable alliances between groups and parties, typically justified by conflicting ideological narratives. The historical legacy finds expression among individuals in three ways. Structural predispositions include membership in and identification with social groups. Cultural predispositions include ideological identities and worldviews. Organizational predispositions comprise individuals' attachments to political parties (Knutsen and Scarbrough 1995). Although these various types of predisposition are historically related to one another, it is not clear what the motivational ordering is (Knutsen 1997; Levendusky 2009). Moreover, long-term processes of socioeconomic modernization may have decoupled the three orders of predisposition (Knutsen and Scarbrough 1995; Weßels 2000; but see Abramowitz and Saunders 2006), such that a full understanding of the predispositional basis of political behaviour requires taking all elements into account. If activation takes place, we expect that *the narrower the gap between the date of interview and election, the stronger will be the explanatory power of each predisposition.*

The "enlightening" role of campaigns also includes guiding citizens' attention to the state of the economy. This is prominent in Gelman and King (1993), and is a central image in Campbell (2008) and Holbrook (1996). Full substantiation of the claim had to wait for Bartels (2006), which shows in multiple iterations of the American National Election Study that the coefficient on economic perceptions strengthens toward election day. Unlike the considerations in the preceding paragraph, the economy is a moving target. It moves, that is, between elections; within campaigns, as a rule, it is quite fixed.[1]

Cognitive Stratification

As a communications phenomenon, a campaign's impact is likely to be conditional on citizens' cognitive capacity, and electorates are cognitively heterogeneous (Luskin 1987). Normatively, shrinking of cognitive gaps would be a welcome outcome of campaigns—all voters should be similarly "enlightened." Theory yields a surplus of predictions, however. For example, Zaller's (1992) RAS features components with potentially opposed implications: the likelihood of receiving a persuasive message, on one hand, and of yielding to its persuasive content, on the other. If a message is complex, sophistication is a necessary condition for decoding it. If the message is simple, especially if it is charged with evocative emotional content, receiving it is easy. The variance will come from yielding to its content, and in this, sophisticated citizens may be better equipped to call up counterconsiderations from memory. As campaign communication is saturated with symbolic appeals and simplifications, it might be easy to decode (Sarcinelli 1987; Schuessler 2000). Besides, less aware voters may reach sound decisions by using simple heuristics and cognitive shortcuts that campaigns might supply (Sniderman, Brody, and Tetlock 1991). Unsurprisingly, the empirical record is mixed (Andersen 2003; Andersen, Tilley, and Heath 2005; Nadeau et al. 2008; Arceneaux 2006; Lachat 2007).

10.2 DOES THE CONCEPT TRAVEL TO NON-US CONTEXTS?

The argument in Gelman and King rests on more than just voter psychology. It also presupposes a context highly suited to the dynamic reiteration

---

[1] What exactly is being connected to the vote in such estimations is a matter of some controversy, however, as economic judgments may be endogenous to political predispositions (Bowler 1989; Evans and Pickup 2010). Additionally, Matthews and Johnston (2010) suggests that the US pattern is not universal.

of themes. The US party system is simple yet loosely linked to the country's social structure. The parties repeat themes and position themselves in ways that have worked in the past (Adams, Merill III, and Grofman 2005). Election dates are completely predictable. The scale and wealth of the US makes its elections peculiarly consequential, so US voters should be paying attention.

In these respects, Germany is only a partially contrasting case. As in the US, the party system features two ideologically distinct parties that always have provided the heads of government, election dates are quite predictable, and the German economy is the dominant one within Europe. On the other hand, more than two parties are relevant to the choice and thanks to this multiplicity, very different campaigns may proceed side by side. The two main parties sometimes share power. And dates, duration, and intensity of campaigns can vary, as the 2005 and 2009 campaigns attest.

Three issues need clarification, however. First, are group identities, the economy, partisanship, and ideology important to German voters? Second, what factors condition the effect of the processes identified in the American template? Finally, what are the chances that each fundamental is activated?

Fundamentals in the German Case

As in the US, *social cleavages* have long-since been regarded as fundamentals of German voting. Of the four cleavages described by Lipset and Rokkan (1967a), two have been crucial in Germany, the *religious* cleavage and the *class* cleavage (Pappi 1984). Traditionally, Catholics have supported the CDU/CSU, and unionized workers formed the base of the SPD. Although these core groups have shrunk, religion and class remain critical determinants of the vote (Roßteutscher 2012; Arzheimer 2006; Brooks, Nieuwbeerta, and Manza 2006).

It is also highly plausible that German elections process the economy. Although scholarly attention to this topic is sporadic, we know from earlier studies that on election day the economy is important to German voters (Rattinger 1980, 1986). As in the US, economic voting is driven by sociotropic considerations and the direction of voters' gaze is backwards, to retrospective judgments (Rattinger and Faas 2001; Kellermann and Rattinger 2007; Listhaug 2005).

Another "fundamental" of American origin is *partisanship*. The very idea that German voters—indeed European ones more generally—identify with parties has been controversial in the past (Falter, Schoen, and Caballero 2000; Thomassen and Rosema 2009). Today, however, most agree that long-term party attachments are widespread (Norpoth 1978; Falter, Schoen, and Caballero 2000), and a partisan indicator adapted to the multiparty context is now canonical.[2] Identification is especially ubiquitous and strong with the parties that define the system of politicized social cleavages, the SPD and the CDU/CSU (Richardson 1991). Yet some dealignment has occurred: the partisan share in election surveys has declined from some 80% to about 60%, and in the East has hovered around 50% since the mid-1990s. The impact of reported partisanship on the vote has also slightly declined (Arzheimer 2006; Ohr and Quandt 2012). Nonetheless, its influence remains strong, not least because German citizens elect parties, not candidates.

In the Gelman–King account *ideology*, liberal versus conservative in US terms, was one of the clearest fields for activation in their 1988 evidence. So too might we expect this in the German case. As early as 1972, Klingemann confirmed "that the left-right continuum is a meaningful yardstick for German voters" (Klingemann 1972: 102). Most citizens may not be "ideologues" in the sense intended by Converse (1964), but they have repeatedly been shown to attach meaning to the terms "Left" and "Right." Ideology is not just social structure or party by another name, but is an important, increasingly autonomous force (Weßels 2000; van der Eijk, Schmitt, and Binder 2005). Particularly intriguing is the possibility that Left and Right are the ground for manoeuvre in relation to coalition possibilities.

In sum, we think that factors identified as fundamentals in the US also play an important role in Germany. Are there additional factors that should be considered in the German context? Clearly, other factors can be primed in election campaigns, for example, campaign-specific issues or candidate evaluations (Schoen 2004). Such factors do not qualify conceptually as fundamentals, however, to the extent that they are not stable, indeed are objects of persuasion, within election campaigns.

Conditional Moderators

Balance and Intensity. The question of whether the "enlightening" effect of election campaigns is conditional is raised by Gelman and King (1993), but only in a cursory fashion. Part of their argument hinges on resources for communication that are ample and roughly balanced for each side. They conjecture that this is the case for US presidential elections but that it may not for subpresidential races. Indeed, resources are *not* balanced in US House elections and studies of money in those elections (for instance, Jacobson 1980) were in effect the first accounts of campaign effects (Brady, Johnston, and Sides 2006). Even

---

[2] The question reads: Many people in the Federal Republic lean toward a particular party for a long time, although they may occasionally vote for a different party. How about you: do you in general lean toward a particular party? If so, which one? (If yes,) How strongly or weakly do you lean toward this party: very strongly, fairly strongly, moderately, fairly weakly, or very weakly?

presidential elections can get out of balance if one side mistimes its outlays, as happened in 2000 (Johnston, Hagen, and Jamieson 2004). It might be thought that European campaigns are too poorly resourced to have much effect at all. But Andersen, Tilley, and Heath (2005) argue with British evidence that shifts in the fit between opinion and policy between nonelection and election years mimic the pattern outlined by Gelman and King. And Arceneaux (2006) uses the variability of timing in the Eurobarometer survey series to show that economic perceptions improve in predicting vote intention in respondents' own national elections when the temporal distance shrinks. The timescale in each case is coarse, but the findings are consistent with at least the possibility of within-campaign effects.

What of German campaigns? As the CDU/CSU and SPD typically invest around 25 million euros each (Krewel, Schmitt-Beck, and Wolsing 2011: 31; Schmitt-Beck and Faas 2006: 396), the requirement of balance is satisfied, at least for the major parties. But are these sums enough to deliver the requisite intensity? Comparisons are difficult, but a rough calculation suggests that the two big parties have typically commanded between one-third and one-half the financial resources per vote that the US presidential campaigns do. A true comparison must factor in costs, to be sure, but at first blush the German numbers do not seem disabling.[3] The context does suggest a major condition on financial balance, however: Smaller parties—FDP, Greens, and the Left— typically spend less than five million euros. If campaign outlays matter, activation may be mainly a story about big parties.

Moreover, the money is not spent on television advertising. In the mass media, the key factor may be the news stream. Hence, despite roughly balanced financial resources between the major parties, asymmetric patterns of activation (Weßels 1998) can occur given the course of events and changes in the news climate. Since 2002 televised debates of the two large parties' Chancellor candidates have become a staple. These are staged about two weeks before polling day and reach much larger audiences than any other campaign occurrence (Maier and Faas 2011). Otherwise, campaigns are continuous strings of staged events, including opening rallies, party conferences, presentations of election manifestos, and pseudo-events specifically designed to attract media attention. Here too, large parties get considerably more media attention than

---

[3] US data come from the website of the Federal Election Commission (www.fec.gov). We use 2004 as representative of the period on which US generalizations are based. The data for 2008 are unusable as the Obama campaign declined to separate its primary election outlays from its general election ones. The Obama campaign was also the first to decline the lump sum from the Treasury and the limitation on official outlays that comes with it. Although Obama in 2008 is almost certainly the template for the future, the earlier pattern of limited (and equal) official budgets forms the basis for most empirical generalizations. Off-campaign outlays grew in importance all along, and our calculation in the main text includes lower and upper bounds for spending by independent groups.

the small parties (Esser and Hemmer 2008), reinforcing the concentration of debates on the rival candidates for Chancellor. Some scholars have argued, however, that this concentration of coverage on these candidates might rather mute fundamentals, not activate them (Gidengil et al. 2002: 78; Schoen 2004).

Context can also constrain intensity: The two big parties do not always compete with each other. The competitive situation in 2009 was starkly different from that in 2005, for instance, and this gives us some leverage for inspecting how activation effects may depend on campaign attributes. Where 2005 was intensely partisan, 2009 was a prescription for tedium. In a sense, the 2005 campaign was unusual (Schmitt-Beck and Faas 2006). The election was called early (after the SPD lost the state election in its heartland North-Rhine Westphalia) and required the approval from both the Federal president and the Constitutional Court, neither of which came immediately. The opening date of the campaign is ambiguous, but by one reading the campaign was shorter than usual. What followed, however, was characterized by a sharp rhetorical confrontation and clear Left–Right polarization around traditional socioeconomic issues. Although the 2009 campaign took place at the expected time and had a normal duration, the rival candidates for Chancellor were cabinet colleagues in a Grand Coalition and the financial crisis loomed over the event. It was difficult for the parties to attack each other and television news had little to cover (Krewel, Schmitt-Beck, and Wolsing 2011; Bachl and Brettschneider 2011).[4]

Thematic Repertoire and Campaign Strategy. The general observation about intensity shades into the question of a campaign's thematic content. Gelman and King (1993) speculated that a campaign might neglect to activate a strategically favorable consideration. They saw this as a counterfactual, a thought exercise to show that for elections to be predictable a well-executed campaign is—ironically—a logical necessity. They did not expect a presidential candidate actually to fail to run such a campaign, but Johnston, Hagen, and Jamieson (2004) show that just this happened in 2000, a claim confirmed indirectly by Bartels (2006). In a way, the 2000 event could be seen as the exception that proves the rule, an argument generalized by Vavreck (2009). To connect fundamentals to vote choices may, then, require that they be thematized in the campaign.

Although we do not provide an account of specific themes in 2005 or 2009, we can speculate about what the parties' strategies have aimed at and under which contexts certain themes are likely to occur. First, as the core support groups for both major parties have been shrinking, these parties might hesitate

---

[4] Preliminary analysis of news content suggests that on a typical day a viewer might have seen one-half again to twice as many stories about the campaign in 2005 than in 2009. The 2005 TV news content analysis was conducted by Rüdiger Schmitt-Beck, Mona Krewel, and Ansgar Wolsing (2010). The data set is available from the GESIS data archive, Cologne (ZA4997). The 2009 TV news content analysis is part of the German Longitudinal Election Study (GLES). Primary investigators: Hans Rattinger, Sigrid Roßteutscher, Rüdiger Schmitt-Beck, and Bernard Weßels. GESIS Data Archive, Cologne. ZA5306. Data file Version 1.1.0 (GLES 2012c).

to highlight their historical traditions lest they repel the growing number of voters outside the traditional profile. Thus we do not have strong expectations for activation of group membership. Second, the US pattern should hold for the economy: incumbents should prime it when things are fine and challengers should do so when growth is weak or null. Of course, this expectation presupposes that only one of the old parties is the incumbent. Third, partisanship is likely to be a theme in every campaign. Finally, ideological accounts are more likely to occur when the party system is more polarized (Lachat 2008). Finally, the theory of the predictable campaign (Vavreck 2009): strategies should differ according to the party's chances of victory. Frontrunners may adopt a low-intensity strategy while those running behind should campaign more intensely (Campbell 2008).

Length and Surprise Value. According to Stevenson and Vavreck (2000), longer campaigns are more likely than shorter ones to activate fundamentals, in their case, the economy. Critical to this view is that the cumulative intensity of media focus is the key ingredient in activation, with six weeks as the threshold. If mere length of the official period is the key, German campaigns are on the short side. But the Stevenson–Vavreck indicator is as much about the surprise value of the campaign as anything, and simple predictability of the election date allows some form of campaigning regardless of the regulatory context. The seemingly nonstop nature of US presidential campaigns is a case in point. But then, German election dates are quite predictable and most "true" campaigns may be long enough. The 2005–2009 comparison could be an acid test: where the 2009 election took place at the appointed time and the campaign proper spanned more than six weeks, the 2005 election came early and the official campaign barely spanned the Stevenson–Vavreck minimum. (Pulling in the other direction, of course, is that the short 2005 campaign was more intense than the 2009 long one.) If Germany mirrors the larger pattern (Stevenson and Vavreck 2000: 232), intensity should matter more on the Left than on the Right.

Multipartism. German multipartism might complicate matters: perhaps the system processes too many fundamentals for any single activation pattern to dominate. This possibility lurks in the potentially variable role of ideology, for example. But we think that fundamentals as such are mainly about the two large parties. Not only do they dominate campaign communications, but resources are roughly balanced between them. And it is they who are aligned most closely with the cleavage structure and with plausible thematic repertoires (Richardson 1991). This is *not* the same thing as saying that large parties must grow at the expense of others; that we know simply not to be universally true. Nor is this to say that activation of fundamentals is the only thing a German campaign can do. Rather, it is to say that to the extent that fundamentals are activated, they should be so mainly in relation to the big parties. Except, that is, for ideology, which may be implicated more in movement within ideological camps.

Expectations from Previous Research

Schoen (2003a) looked at whether social group members moved towards their "natural" parties during the campaigns of the Federal elections from 1972 to 1998 and found mixed evidence. Panel analyses suggested crystallization effects on the part of indifferent group members but no systematic temporal variation in the strength of structural effects. This finding fits our hunch that, given the declining numbers of traditional cleavage voters, cleavage parties lack the incentive to concentrate mobilization effort on their core. Irrespective of cognitive involvement, activation of traditional social cleavages is unlikely to occur.

Although Weßels (1998) shows that the economy was activated in the 1994 German Bundestag campaign, activation was asymmetric. It was particularly important in bringing sometime CDU/CSU supporters "home." This conforms to our own expectation for asymmetry.

Research on elections between 1980 and 2002 (Schoen 2007) suggests that activation of partisanship is *not* a general feature of German campaigns. This is surprising as partisanship is clearly a recurring campaign theme. One possibility is that partisanship is powerful from the start, such that little room remains for further activation. With partisan dealignment, however, parties may try increasingly to win back former supporters.

In a 1972–1990 comparison between government and opposition parties, Lachat (2007: 187–91) found the trajectories of impact from both Left–Right positioning and partisanship unfolded quite inconsistently during preelection periods. Sometimes impact increased, sometimes it decreased, and sometimes there was no systematic change at all. This irregular pattern might mirror the ebb and flow of party polarization and rapprochement. As the 2005 campaign was overall more polarized, we expect more ideological voting that year than in 2009.

10.3 OPERATIONALIZATION

The Data

Our analyses are based on two Rolling Cross-Section (RCS) surveys (Johnston and Brady 2002) conducted during the run-up to the 2005 and 2009 elections.[5]

---

[5] Sample sizes are: 2005: N = 3,583; panel cases: N = 2,420; 2009: N = 6,008; panel cases: N = 4,027. The 2005 election survey was carried out by Rüdiger Schmitt-Beck and Thorsten Faas (cf. Schmitt-Beck, Faas, and Holst 2006). The data set is available from the GESIS data archive, Cologne (ZA4991). The 2009 survey was conducted as part of GLES. Principal investigators: Hans Rattinger, Sigrid Roßteutscher, Rüdiger Schmitt-Beck, Bernhard Weßels. GESIS Data Archive, Cologne. ZA5303. Data file Version 5.0.0 (GLES 2011d). For technical information see Schmitt-Beck, Faas, and Wolsing (2010).

Both studies were conducted by telephone, with random samples of German citizens aged eighteen and above. Fieldwork spanned six weeks, averaging eighty-six interviews per day, in 2005 and two months, averaging 100 interviews per day, in 2009—such that temporally defined segments of the data (whole days and above) can be analysed as independent draws from the same population, distinguished (random fluctuation aside) only by the passage of time. As outlined below, breaking up our data into small time units to maximally exploit the temporal granularity of our data is a core feature of our analysis.

The Vote

The dependent variable is vote intention, which we cast as a multinomial. The main challenge for modelling activation in a multiparty system lies in a trade-off between model complexity and time granularity. On the one hand, vote choice in a multiparty setting is more complex than in a two-party system. This points to the multinomial. But the limited size of daily samples constrains estimation of complex models, so we must pool across days. On the other hand, pooling reduces temporal granularity. As estimating a single six-category multinomial model risks convergence failure in small samples, even pooled ones, our strategy is to estimate parallel three-category models for the Left and Right sides of the parliamentary spectrum. On the Left, the variable distinguishes the SPD from the combined Greens and Left, leaving all others in the reference category.[6] This coding permits expression of both a general Left propensity and possible heterogeneity within the Left electorate. On the Right, we distinguish the CDU/CSU from the FDP, again with all others in the reference category. This too permits a general Right-leaning propensity to operate, but it also recognizes that neither party is unequivocally more extreme or centrist relative to the other.[7] As it happens, we are still forced to pool consecutive days. We say more about this below.

Social Cleavages

For structural predispositions we use a block of cleavage-related indicators. To capture the religious cleavage we distinguish Catholics and Protestants

---

[6] Collapsing the Greens and the Left might seem odd as their supporters have very different social profiles. For the analysis of social structural activation, however, the small parties are not critical to the overall analysis. For analysis of ideological activation, preliminary analyses (not reported here) indicate that both small parties sit to the Left of the SPD.

[7] To test if our results depend on the breadth of the reference category we reestimated all models with a base category that comprised only supporters of the opposite big cleavage party. Although the overall pattern is the same, activation is somewhat attenuated, unsurprisingly as most activation is likely to occur among undecided citizens and those hesitant to participate.

with dummy variables, leaving areligious respondents and members of other denominations as the reference category. Organizational ties to churches amplify differences (Roßteutscher 2012), so we also include indicators of frequency of church attendance: dummy variables for each of weekly/monthly attenders and less than monthly attenders, with nonattenders and unaffiliated as the reference category. The historic core of the class conflict pits manual workers against the old middle class. We thus single out manual employees, in keeping with convention. But the diversification of occupations requires a more complex setup. We therefore also dummy out the "new middle class" and those who were never gainfully employed. This leaves the "old middle" class as the reference category. For retired respondents previous employment stands in for current employment. Just as church attendance is the amplifier for the religious cleavage, so is union membership for the class one; we therefore include a corresponding dummy variable.

Ideology and Partisanship

For respondents' ideology we use their self-placement on an eleven-point Left–Right scale. For partisanship we take the now-standard German question and construct a dummy variable for each big party, leaving independents and all other partisans as the reference category. To avoid convergence failure, we use one dummy only in each estimation, the SPD for the Left and the CDU/CSU for the Right.

The Economy

As outlined above, year-over-year retrospective sociotropic assessment of the economy is the most important predictor of economic voting in Germany. We dummy out the two categories on each side, leaving "no change" as the reference category.

Cognitive Stratification

For cognitive stratification, we would ideally use an indicator for political sophistication, for which the canonical form is an index of "encyclopaedic" political knowledge (Luskin 1987). As our data sets do not include such knowledge questions, we need a surrogate. General interest in politics suggests itself, in that it denotes motivation—it is hard to imagine anyone becoming knowledgeable about a subject who does not have an interest in it (Neuman 1986). Prior (2010) finds that the indicator is highly reliable in German data.

And in contrast to interest in the campaign, which increases with the approach of election day, general political interest exhibits no trend. This enables us to split all samples at the same point and helps avoid endogeneity. Conveniently, separating the "strongly" and "very strongly" interested from all others splits the sample close to the median.

10.4 LOGIC OF THE ANALYSIS

The basic logic is straightforward. If activation occurs, the statistical relationship between "fundamentals" and the vote should strengthen with time, and this can be tested by running a fixed regression setup through consecutive slices of the RCS and examining its goodness of fit (Gelman and King 1993). Strengthening of fit is *prima facie* evidence for activation.

As our expectations refer to the overall process and not to specific parties within families, we deploy an overall goodness-of-fit measure. Although several measures exist, we use the *expected proportional reduction of error, ePRE*. This measure is based on the expected percentage of correct predictions, *ePCP* (Herron 1999), and quantifies the expected proportional reduction of classification error against the naïve prediction of the percentage classified correctly by chance (Morrison 1969).[8] This measure has an appealingly intuitive

---

[8] For a multinomial model with three categories of the dependent variable *ePCP* is calculated as follows (Herron 1999: 91–2):

$$ePCP = \frac{1}{N}\left(\sum_{y_i=0}\hat{p}_{i,0} + \sum_{y_i=1}\hat{p}_{i,1} + \sum_{y_i=2}\hat{p}_{i,2}\right)$$

with $\hat{p}_{i,c}$ being the ith respondent's predicted probability to belong in category c, N being the number of observations, and given that $\hat{p}_{i,0} + \hat{p}_{i,1} + \hat{p}_{i,2} = 1$.

The *per cent correctly classified by chance*, henceforth PCCC, is not equal to the proportion in the modal category as in the case of the adjusted count R² measure. Instead it can be calculated by the following formula derived by Morrison (1969: 158):

$$PCCC = p_0^2 + p_1^2 + p_2^2$$

with p_c being the proportion of subjects in category c, such that. $p_0 + p_1 + p_2 = 1$.

Values for *ePRE* can then be calculated analogous to the adjusted count R-square measure:

$$ePRE = \frac{ePCP - PCCC}{1 - PCCC}$$

It represents the expected improvement in classification over chance. Computation employs the user-written *Stata* ado-file 'epcp' (Lawrence 2012).

interpretation, similar to the adjusted count R-square measure (Long 1997), yet it is also sensitive to the uncertainty of classification. For example, it distinguishes someone with a 0.51 probability of belonging to a category from someone whose probability is 0.99.[9]

We distinguish among fundamentals by degree of endogeneity and therefore proceed in steps. First, we build a social cleavage model including all variables needed to capture the class and religious cleavages. This model is used as baseline, and the other "fundamentals"—economic perceptions, party identification, and ideological self-perception—are entered later and separately. We thus separate structural predispositions that by their very nature are causally prior to all other fundamentals. These other fundamentals are mental states, so they may be endogenous to structural predispositions as well as to one another. As we have no defensible means to assign priority among the mental states, we enter them separately. We recognize that dynamics we assign to one mental state may actually be attributable to another. For instance, partisan activation may also create the appearance of ideological activation, and vice versa.

The minimum number of consecutive survey days that must be pooled to avoid convergence failures is three days for the overall sample and five days when the sample is split by political sophistication. This framework provides robust estimates on subsamples while yielding enough time points to identify overall trends in the process of activation. Having obtained the *ePRE* values from time slices we plot the linear trend in the relationship between a "fundamental" and vote intention.

10.5 FINDINGS

Activation in General

Activation does not seem to be a universal feature of German campaigns, according to Figure 10.1,[10] but instead is specific to parties and contexts. Although differences are modest, more structure—levels of explanatory power—appears

---

[9] Another useful property of the measure is that it is possible to calculate confidence intervals to quantify postestimation uncertainty (Herron 1999). These confidence intervals do not directly account for sampling error, however, so we refrain from using them. We caution against overstating small changes in classification efficiency that might simply reflect sampling variation.

[10] A bit more formally and for clarity, where Y_t^s is the *ePRE* value estimated for a combination of days, t, for the social structural fundamentals: $\hat{Y}_t^s = \alpha^s + \beta^s \cdot t$ produces the linear plot in the top panel for each side of the parliamentary spectrum.

Where Y_t^m is the *ePRE* for an estimation at t that adds one 'mental fundamental' (perception of the economy, party identification, or Left–Right self-placement) to the baseline structural model: $Y_t^{gain} = Y_t^m - Y_t^s$ is the gain in *ePRE* for the same days; and $\hat{Y}_t^{gain} = \alpha^{gain} + \beta^{gain} \cdot t$ produces the linear plot for the lower panel in Figure 10.1 corresponding to the mental state in question.

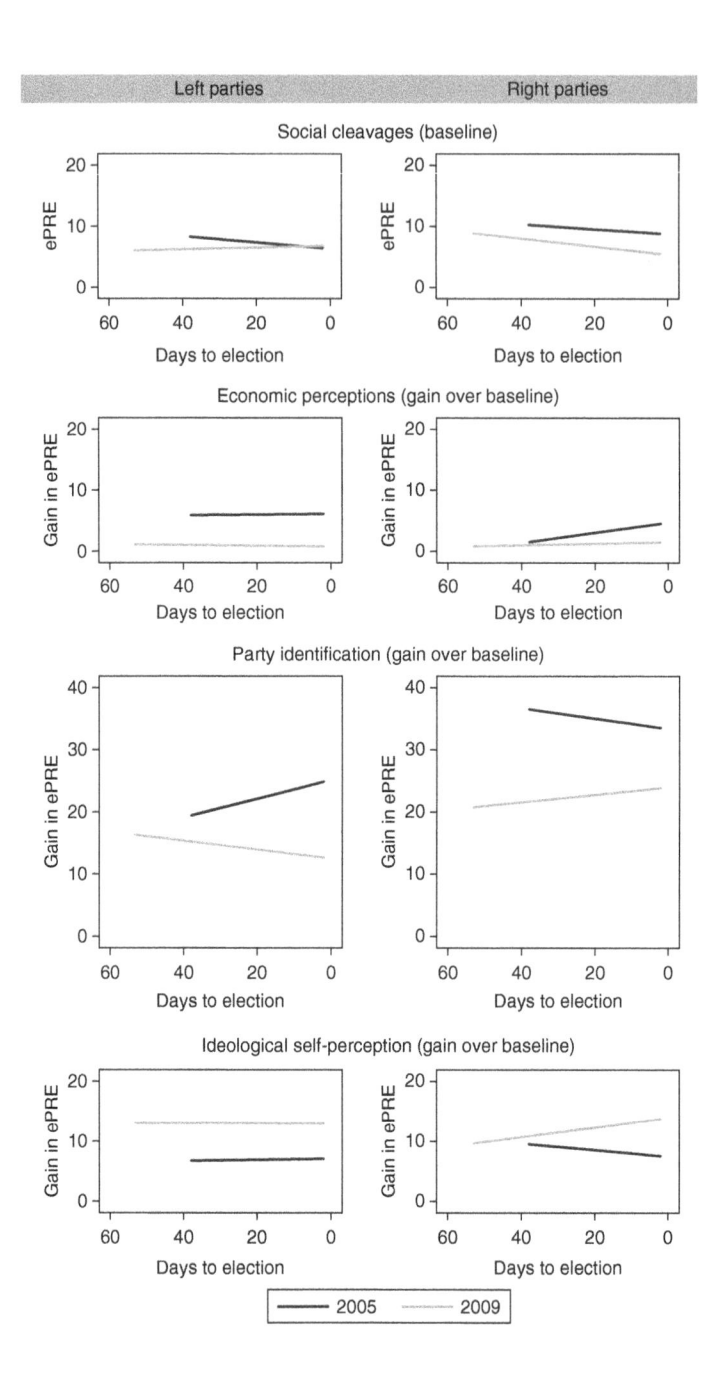

Figure 10.1 Predictive power over the course of the campaign
Note: *ePRE* values smoothed by linear fit.

on the political Right and more dynamics—changes in explanatory power—appear on the Left. More of everything appears in 2005: not only was the vote generally more conditioned by social structure and other "fundamentals" but the campaign also did more to increase that structuring. This nicely corresponds to our observation that 2005 was an intense—and intensely partisan—campaign, where 2009 was not much of a campaign at all. This is consistent with the core logic of the Gelman–King activation model: If a campaign is to activate something, there must first be a campaign. The fact that we see this difference right from the start of the respective observation periods suggests that important message flows must have occurred already well before the campaigns officially began.

Figure 10.1 suggests that German election campaigns do not process much social structure—an observation that extends Schoen's (2003a) findings for the Federal elections between 1972 and 1998. In 2005, knowing where respondents fit in Germany's economic and religious conflict structure improves on naïve prediction by about 10%. In 2009, the improvement is rather smaller. For each year, the overall improvement is about the same across the ideological spectrum. There is little evidence of trend, and to the extent any trend appears, it is *negative*, especially on the Right. This could indicate that campaign communication loosens preexisting ties to the party system. Equally, it could indicate that net mobilization into party preference (from no expressed preference) is less structured by social position than were party preferences at the start of the campaign. Either way, this is not evidence for the activation of sociodemographic fundamentals.

Economic perceptions have a generally greater impact in 2005 than 2009. This might seem surprising, considering the depth of the economic crisis of 2008. But the crisis was not a matter for partisan contestation, not least because the Grand Coalition that governed when it broke out was not blamed for its occurrence and arguably did a good job in handling it (Anderson and Hecht 2012). So prediction improvement from economic judgments is generally meager in that year, as are any discernible gains over the campaign. In 2005, in contrast, economic perceptions mapped onto party preferences strongly. As the campaign unfolded, the SPD-led coalition took credit for the relatively good economic times, all the more so to paper over social-policy fissures within the coalition. All along, economic judgment was a bigger factor in sorting the Left than sorting the Right. But the Left was sorted from the very start: To the extent that there were *gains* in predictive power, all were on the Right.[11]

---

[11] For the graphical representation and interpretation of the results the social cleavage model serves as a baseline. We subtract the *ePRE* value of the social cleavage model from the corresponding value of each of the other three models (economic perceptions, party identification, and ideological self-perception). Thus, the values shown in those graphs should be interpreted as the *gain* in reducing classification error *over the social cleavage baseline model*.

In both overall power and campaign dynamics, the big story is party identification. Knowing whether or not a respondent feels attached to the SPD or the CDU/CSU improves prediction success by 20–30% in 2005 and by 15–20% in 2009. The overall power of the factor is not surprising given the conceptual proximity of the identification to the vote itself. Less banal is the rest of the pattern. The 2005–2009 contrast testifies to the importance of context, as self-described partisanship is less powerful when it is less intensely primed. Nor is partisanship symmetric between Left and Right. The relatively greater consolidation of the Right arguably facilitates a focus on partisanship as such. But in 2005, as the SPD sought to repair the damage wrought by its own neoliberal policy choices, its emphasis on its distinctiveness as a party evidently had the intended effect, as the predictive power of identification increased from a 20% gain over baseline to a 25% one. This is not mirrored on the Right: although prediction efficiency is always stronger, the grip of party identification loosened, not tightened. Dynamic asymmetry persisted in 2009, but reversed its polarity. As in 2005, SPD identification was weaker than its CDU/CSU counterpart, but it also lost grip as the campaign progressed. On the other side, the CDU/CSU vote became more partisan. These findings depart from Schoen's (2007) for earlier elections.

Ideology is a factor of intermediate strength but only modest dynamics. Left–Right self-placement yields prediction gains of about 10%, somewhat bigger than social structure and much bigger than economic perceptions but only one-half to one-third as great as gains from party identification. The impact seems slightly greater on the Left than the Right, possibly as complement to the weaker impact of partisanship; ideological sorting seems a more plausible issue for the more fractionalized Left side of the spectrum. The most striking contrast, however, is between years: In sorting vote intentions ideology is about half again as effective in 2009 as in 2005. This is true on both Left and Right. And on the Right, sorting efficiency grew over the 2009 campaign, where in 2005, the initially weak ideological effect only weakened with time. On the Left, no trend appeared either year. Although the record of within-campaign dynamics is spotty we take the larger pattern to be consistent with the rhetorical content of the campaigns. In 2005, the ideological character of the system was a given (if only to be betrayed by events). By 2009, the patience of the voters on the outer flanks of the electorate with the ideologically amorphous Grand Coalition had worn thin. On the Right, as election day approached this impatience only sharpened.

The Cognitive Gradient

Do campaigns overcome gaps in sophistication? As with the general pattern for campaign dynamics, the answer depends on year and party. Unsurprisingly, high-interest voters exhibit more structure overall than low-interest ones. Gaps

Activation of Fundamentals in German Campaigns 233

are wider in 2005 than in 2009, as are dynamics. But only on the Left does the campaign narrow the gap. On the Right, the gap actually widens. In general, cognitive differentials are greatest in ideological reasoning, as Converse (1964) and Sniderman, Brody, and Tetlock (1991) lead us to expect. Gaps are modest but still clearly discernible for social structure and economic perceptions. The story for party identification is complicated and equivocal.

Figures 10.2 and 10.3 present the evidence. Figure 10.2 gives a complete reading, with explanatory power at each level of political interest. It is visually very demanding, and we present it for completeness. We distil the case in Figure 10.3, which abstracts from key features of Figure 10.2. The left panel of Figure 10.3 works with intercepts in Figure10.2, where the intercept is the smoothed value for the first day of the observation period, roughly the start of the campaign. Entries are the high–low interest gaps between those initial values. For example, at the start of the 2005 campaign cleavage-related information increases the Left correct-prediction rate by about two percentage points more in the high-interest than in the low-interest group. The initial gap in 2009 is closer to five percentage points.[12]

At the start, cognitive gaps are clearer on the Left than on the Right. In 2005 every single contrast on the Left yields a positive value and in 2009 no contrast yields a negative one. The CDU/CSU pattern is more mixed. In 2005, three of the four initial gaps are positive, but one—for party identification—is negative (that is, party identification initially helped prediction more among low-interest than among high-interest voters). In 2009 two CDU/CSU initial gaps are positive (ideology strikingly so) but two are essentially null.

If initial gaps differ between Left and Right, so do shifts in the gaps. This is shown by the panel on the Right of Figure 10.3. Just as the "initial gap" estimation starts with estimated values for the first day of fieldwork, so "expansion/shrinkage" works with the estimated shift over the full period of observation, and compares values for the last day. Values estimated for the last day are then turned into the difference between high- and low-interest voters.[13] On the Left, if gaps in the predictive power for voting are initially large and positive, the basic effect of the campaign is to erase them, at least in the more intense campaign of 2005. The 2009 campaign, in contrast, left the gaps largely intact. *On the Right, however, gaps mostly widen.* (Strictly speaking, they become more

---

[12] Simplifying the terms in note 10, the estimation in Figure 10.3 is as follows. Where: $\hat{Y}_t^h = \alpha^h + \beta^h \cdot t$ is the estimation for the linear plot of values (whether the estimation is for social structural factors or for the gain in impact from a mental state) in the high-interest group in a panel of Figure 10.2; and $\hat{Y}_t^l = \alpha^l + \beta^l \cdot t$ is the corresponding plot for the low-interest group in the same panel; $\alpha^h - \alpha^l$ is the estimate of the initial gap.

[13] Using the same notation as before, such that $\hat{Y}_T^h$ and $\hat{Y}_T^l$ are the estimated high-interest and low-interest values for the last day, T, of the campaign: $(\hat{Y}_T^h - \alpha^h) - (\hat{Y}_T^l - \alpha^l)$ is the estimate for the closing of the gap.

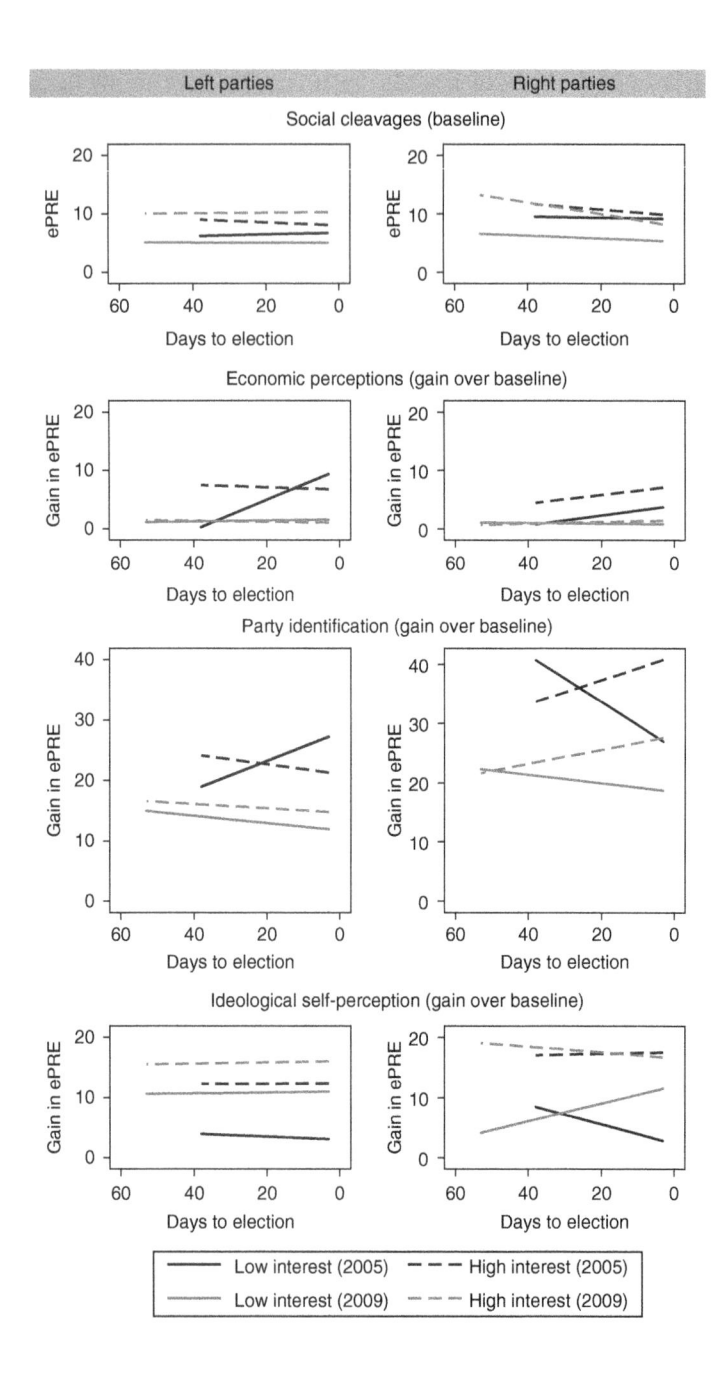

Figure 10.2 Predictive power of fundamentals by political interest

Note: ePRE values smoothed by linear fit.

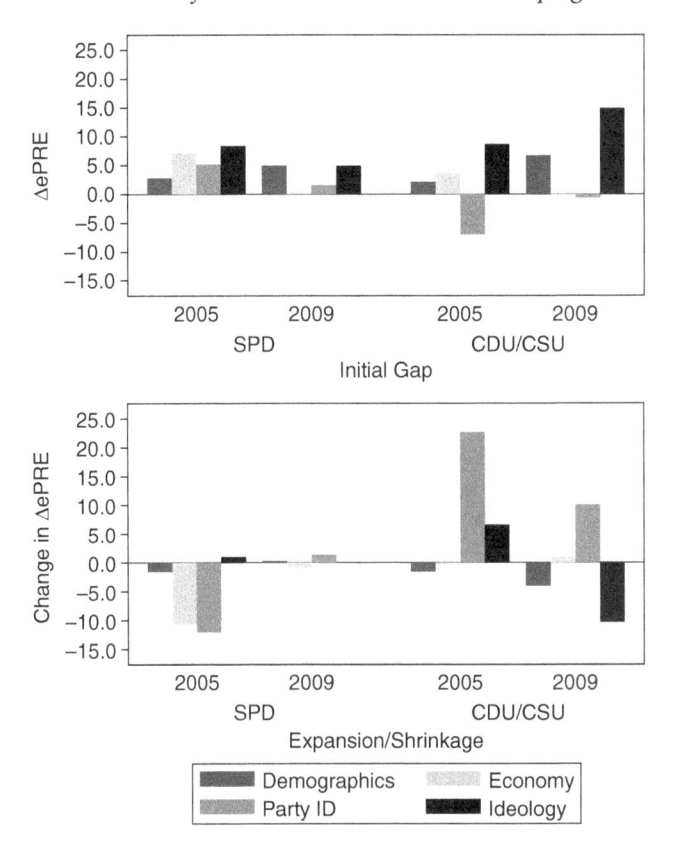

Activation of Fundamentals in German Campaigns 235

Figure 10.3 Gaps in explanatory power between high- and low-interest voters

positive, as initial gaps were sometimes negative.) The basic point for the Right is that for every factor except social structure, the campaign sharpens the cognitive gap; indeed the campaign may itself create the gap.

The asymmetry between Left and Right operates on somewhat different evaluative components:

- It is smallest for the predictive power of structural factors related to the long-standing cleavages of German electoral politics. This complements the fact that social structuring of votes is weak to begin with (if stronger in 2005 than in 2009), and is so for both Left and Right.
- On the Left, gaps close for the economy and for partisanship. Low-interest citizens needed to be taught, as it were, that the economy was relevant to judgment on the SPD-led coalition. Similarly, the campaign may have reminded SPD partisans of why they were so in the first place. At least, the campaign did these things in 2005 (Schmitt-Beck 2009). In 2009, there were few gaps to close.

- On the Right, the outstanding dynamics pertain to party identification. In both years, but especially in 2005, the campaign *widened* the partisanship gap. Figure 10.2 shows that this widening comprised in roughly equal parts an increase in predictive gain among high-interest respondents and a loss in that same quantity among low-interest ones. Overall, as Figure 10.1 reminds us, the partisan component on the Right shrank (although on average it remained at a relatively high level).
- For ideology, the usually wide initial gaps just stayed that way. Except for the Right in 2005: An already wide gap got wider as the campaign advanced. As Figure 10.2 shows, this occurred as the campaign *reduced* the impact of ideology among low-interest voters.

10.6 CONCLUSION

German campaigns activate some electoral considerations some of the time. Not all "fundamentals" are activated: some are active from the very start, while others do not perform impressively at any point. Activation on one side of the ideological spectrum is not mirrored by activation on the other. Most strikingly, however—and substantiating the larger claim by way of counterfactual—some campaigns activate more than others. For electoral factors to be activated by a campaign it does not suffice that an election date is merely stipulated. For the deadline to matter, it must be preceded by a real campaign. If the contestants decline to play the game, citizens risk being as much in the dark at the end as at the beginning.

So at least we infer from 2005 and 2009. Although the 2005 campaign started in an unusual way and was thus somewhat truncated, in many respects it turned into a typical—and real—campaign. Campaigning was intense, certainly by the SPD, and this intensity may have helped the party to recover considerable ground in the last weeks. The economy was engaged, and grew in importance. In keeping with the intensity of the party battle, party identification was strongly implicated and grew in importance as part of the recovery on the Left. The 2009 campaign, in contrast, downplayed the economy and the basic partisan antipathies of German history. Although the Grand Coalition could take credit for steering the country through crisis, the inclusiveness of the governing coalition and the focus of the crisis on international capital markets evidently dulled the edge of electoral reward and punishment. In any case, Chancellor Merkel and her SPD challenger Steinmeier could hardly trade critical comments about how they had jointly managed the shop. This also dulled the edge of partisanship as such.

If the campaigns have an equivocal record in "enlightenment" through activation, so too is the record mixed for differential activation. It is not universally

Activation of Fundamentals in German Campaigns 237

true that the campaigns narrow gaps between high- and low-interest groups in the deployment of fundamentals. But there is a suggestion that they do so on the Left. Again, everything is clearer in the high-intensity year of 2005. In that year, factors in support for (and opposition to) Left parties started the campaign with a wide political-interest differential. This held across a variety of fundamentals. By the end of the campaign, those differentials had essentially been erased. On the Right, no such narrowing of gaps occurred, and some actually widened. We have no explanation for this, but the pattern suggests that we look at the rhetoric of both the Right and Left. Perhaps the Left works off emotional appeals or "easy" issues, while the Right works off "hard" ones (Carmines and Stimson 1980). Then again, the rhetorical roles may be reversed, and rhetoric on the Right may activate fundamentals that bear on the Left. The truth of the matter is that we do not know. But further work on electoral activation, not just in Germany, should look for such contingent patterns. The pattern, especially if it proves to be a recurring one, directs us to consider asymmetry in party appeals or in mobilization strategies.

This last point drives home the fact that this chapter is just a start. Although contingent factors poke through the analyses, the design for this paper is "Olympian," to say the least. The party battle is treated with a very broad brush. For instance, the focus on the overall power of estimations means that we do not look at coefficients of effect, to see who exactly is being moved where and by what. In this we may have been beguiled by the US model. If so, we have revealed its limitations as a modeling strategy. The simple binary choice in the US makes the two sides quite symmetrical, even when non-preference is also being modeled. If one detects activation of partisanship in overall equation statistics, for example, it is not hard to infer what is going on. With five parties and rotating coalitions, in contrast, summary statistics are less specific in their guidance about processes. Indeed, our very setup—parallel estimations for each side and a large reference category for each—may have buried much of the action in a large, undifferentiated residual. This in turn reflected our concern to gaze on the campaigns from a very high altitude and to insist on a rather rigid estimation strategy. In the multiparty case, different independent variables may be best modelled for different dependent variables. The economy, for instance, is a matter for governing parties, and in 2009 the contrast might have been the CDU/CSU and SPD versus all others, rather than versus each other. In both years, activation of partisanship might have been clearer for the old, big parties than for the small ones. And ideology might have been the focus for support for the small parties, especially as they abhor the prospect of a Grand Coalition. Further research is obviously necessary. For now, we take it as a good sign that this initial foray into accounting for campaign activation raised as many questions as it answered.

11

Voters' Motivations
How and Why Short-Term Factors Grow in Importance

Bernhard Weßels

11.1 INTRODUCTION

Over the last decades, a tremendous amount of research and publications have dealt with the question of increasing issue and dealignment patterns. Already in 1975, Schulman and Pomper noted an increase in issue voting in the US (Schulman and Pomper 1975). Dalton and colleagues found that in comparative perspective a decline in class voting took place after the Second World War (Dalton, Flanagan, and Beck 1984). This outcome was confirmed by Franklin and associates (Franklin, Mackie, and Valen 1992). Dalton argued that due to advanced education in Western societies, far more citizens were cognitively able to deal with the complexities of politics and, thus, to act as issue voters in the 1980s than had been in the, then quite recent, 1960s.

It was even suggested that an epoch of free and reasoned vote choice had arrived with the apparent increase of issue voting. Rose and McAllister concluded as early as 1986 that British voters had begun to choose rather than to vote based on long-held allegiances. The relaxation of context-specific norms and social control by embeddedness in social contexts contributed to free choice based on evaluation instead of traditional loyalties and habits. Franklin, for example, argued similarly that the decline in social structural sources of voting had consequently opened the way to a choice between parties based on issue preferences rather than class loyalty (1985: 176). Thus, the voting of enlightened and liberated citizens would more and more imply a truly democratic character of elections.

Why would issues have grown more important for choices? A review of the literature shows that the explanations mainly argue with consequences of social change. Voters are becoming more sophisticated and traditional ties are disappearing, thereby allowing or giving space for considerations of issues in vote choice. Claims about the increasing relevance of issue voting are contested, but, even if they should be true, a simple question has to be raised: Why do voters consider issues, if they are no fools?

This question may sound strange at first glance. Is it not obvious that clever voters should consider issues? The complex answer is "it depends," the simple answer is "no." The reason is quite straightforward: Voters have easier ways to make up their mind like using cues and shortcuts; so why should they bother about rather complicated methods of retrieving information and perform rather complex evaluations in order to come up with a choice? Such a path to vote choice does neither seem reasonable in the rational choice framework nor in frameworks of information processing and decision-making. In other words: Some need or benefit must induce voters to take the extra burden of caring about issues.

This chapter contains an exploration of the conditions of issue voting. The explanations of the increase in issue voting that are provided with the existing hypotheses are not fully convincing. Authors use a resource argument (education) or an argument of emancipation. In their cores, both arguments refer to conditions that might increase opportunities for issue voting. They neglect, however, to give any reason why these opportunities should be grasped by individual voters.

11.2 CONDITIONS AND DEVELOPMENT OF ISSUE VOTING

The debate about issue voting is far from conclusive. This regards the question of increasing relevance as well as the reasons provided for it. The debate and the hypotheses discussed in this context very much resemble trade-off logics: If class voting disappears, issues and other short-term factors will take over. Franklin tentatively concluded for British elections that issue-based voting choice had increased more or less in step with the decline of class voting. Discussion went on since then and the trade-off argument was put forward with more and more confidence. A recent analysis of trends in Germany has shown that the share of voters without party attachment has indeed doubled since 1976. Nonpartisans more often split the ticket, decide late, regard specific issues and candidates as relevant for their choice, or do not vote at all (Dalton 2012; see also Arzheimer 2006). Thus, it seems to be common knowledge that issue voting has gained importance. However, empirical evidence is far from consistent. Aardal and van Wijnen investigated six West European countries for the period from the 1970s to the 1990s and concluded that "contrary to expectations based on modernization theory, we do not find a secular increase in issue voting over time" (2005: 206). They dealt with valence issues. Reviewing the international literature, Schoen and Weins inferred that due to imperfect data—discontinuity in issues taken into account, limited range of issues—robust findings exist neither for the support nor for the rejection of the hypothesis of an increasing relevance of issue voting (2005: 234). Results on position issues are also not necessarily supportive of a rise of issue voting. In Germany, the generic influence of position issues rather declined over the last three general elections from 2002 to 2009 and party-specific issue effects only increased for the Christian Democrats regarding the migration issue and the Social Democrats regarding the issue of nuclear energy. Apart from this, coefficients decreased (Thurner, Mauerer, and Binder 2012: 314-15). Weßels found that the effect of proximity- and performance-oriented issue voting declined between 1976 and 1998 for the core voters of the Christian Democrats and revealed scattered results for the core voters of the Social Democrats (Weßels 2002). Party-specific developments and, thus, party–voter specific developments are not unlikely. Neundorf, for example, showed that the effect of Left–Right positions on Left voting grew constantly stronger from 1990 to 2008 in West Germany, whereas it declined for Right voting (Neundorf 2012).

Whatever the evidence for the rise of issue voting may be, those who support it discuss two general mechanisms related to modernization: the decline of cleavage politics and the increase of cognitive mobilization. What does research say about the relationship between issue voting and long-standing social alliances or between loyalties on the one hand and the cognitive capacities of individuals on the other hand?

Long-standing Loyalties

It is not uncontested that cleavage voting has declined and, seemingly, given way to issue voting. First, it is called into question whether class voting is indeed in decline (Evans 2000; Andersen and Heath 2000; Elff 2009). Second, evidence suggests that there is at least no negative relationship between partisanship and cognitive skills; some evidence even suggests a strong positive relationship. Arzheimer found that cognitive mobilization and change in the composition of society have no effect on partisanship (Arzheimer 2006). Albright measured cognitive skills and access to mass media and consistently predicted an increase in attachment to a party, a relationship stable over time (Albright 2009). Thus, it may be that the most obvious trends in social change are not responsible for a decrease in partisanship. If that is true, the hypothesis that a decline of class voting and loyalties has allowed space for a choice between parties based on issue preferences rather than class loyalty may also not be a viable explanation of issue voting.

To consider the process and mechanism of these developments is not relevant in the first place for understanding the logic of issue voting and the assumed trade-off between issue voting and voting based on social alliances and enduring loyalty. Here, the question is rather to which degree long-standing loyalties condition issue voting. Evans and Andersen (2004) found a strong conditioning of issue voting by partisan attachment (party identification) in a panel study. Their findings suggest that the influence of party identification on issue proximity is much more important than the antagonist influence. This would imply that partisanship provides a kind of "lens" that leads to selective perceptions.

The Role of Cognitive Mobilization and Resources

Concerning the role of education and cognitive mobilization, research results are inconsistent, too. Results of Sniderman et al. support the hypothesis by showing that the better educated and the politically sophisticated attach more weight to issues as a basis of their electoral decision-making; less sophisticated voters rely more on partisanship and social cues (Sniderman, Brody, and Tetlock 1991). However, the better educated also show stronger partisanship than the less educated, as findings of Arzheimer (2006) and Albright (2009) suggest. Dalton et al. see a direct link between the process of cognitive mobilization and the number of citizens willing and able to vote on the basis of policy preferences less and less bound to citizens' social backgrounds. Individualization and modernization processes form the backbone of this development (Dalton, Flanagan, and Beck 1984; Dalton and Wattenberg 2000a).

However, evidence that issues are currently gaining more relevance for vote choice is not consistent. The findings of Arzheimer (2006) and Albright (2009) on the relationship between sophistication and party attachment suggest that it makes sense to ask for the additional benefit of considering issues beyond other criteria for making choices.

The general hypothesis pursued here is that there must be a good reason to take issues into account if voters have an easier way to make up their minds using cues and shortcuts. This simple hypothesis has quite a number of implications. One implication is that any relation to be found to macro conditions, education, or sophistication, describes just a phenomenon and its correlates but does not deliver an explanation. Second, explanations must include reflections about costs and utility of the introduction of issues in voters' decision-making.

Regarding the relationship to education and sophistication, the argument could be that retrieving the respective information is so cheap that additional information costs are rather limited. No one would argue that there are no additional costs at all, minor as they may be. Thus, from here follows only that the likelihood of investing in issues may be higher if information costs are lower (Sniderman, Brody, and Tetlock 1991). However, there must be a benefit on the other side of the equation to make it balanced. Therefore, we are back to the instrumental utility in decision-making.

There is more to the seeming increase in the impact of short-term factors on the vote. Research shows that heterogeneity in voter-decision rules is widespread (Glasgow 1999) and currently employed models of voting behavior ignore the possibility of heterogeneity in the weights attached to issues (Glasgow 1997). This observation is important, but does not lead to an explanation on its own terms. One possible explanation of heterogeneity in the relevance of issues can be derived from the types of cues and shortcuts voters use. An orientation toward incumbency, for example, can serve as an anchor diminishing the influence of short-term factors on voters (Petrocik and Desposato 2004). Furthermore, the structure of political supply has an impact on the importance of issues. The more compact the issue space, the less voters consider issues, the more polarized, the more they do (Alvarez, Nagler, and Niemann 1998). Howell (1986) showed that partisanship and its impact are a combination of standing decisions and political events occurring during the campaign.

These findings show that political supply and the way it is evaluated have an effect on the relevance of short-term factors for voting. They imply that there is also variation in the relationship of endogenous factors in the funnel of causality. There is a wide range of reciprocal effects (Howell 1986) including that partisanship and issue attitudes interact on each other if individuals are aware of party differences on an issue (Carsey and Layman 2006).

The various findings on issue voting suggest a number of hypotheses. One group of arguments refers to the consequences of social change, a second group of arguments to political supply structures. Starting with the consequences of social change, two hypotheses can be derived from the literature. The assumption is that decreasing long-standing loyalties mostly based in social structure have allowed space for real choices based on specific policy considerations (Franklin 1985). This implies that there is a trade-off between party identification and issue voting. Thus, the hypothesis reads as follows:

H1 The stronger individual party attachment is, the less impact issue considerations have on the vote.

A second hypothesis referring to social change as the driving force of issue voting considers the educational revolution and resulting increase in political sophistication of voters (Dalton, Flanagan, and Beck 1984). Thus, the second hypothesis claims:

H2 The higher the educational level and/or the higher the level of political sophistication is/are, the stronger the impact of issue considerations on the vote is.

Regarding political supply, arguments and findings refer to specific situations and cases. They seem not appropriate for a general or generalizable hypothesis. However, one topic that reoccurs in different analyses is polarization. Alvarez and colleagues found that the more polarized the issue space, the more voters consider issues (Alvarez, Nagler, and Niemann 1998). Another finding is that if a party holds a polar position on an issue, this issue is more important for voting for this party (Thurner, Mauerer, and Binder 2012). The respective hypothesis for supply factors is:

> H3 *The more polarized an issue is in the perception of the individual voter, the more important it is for vote choice.*

However, polarization is not the only feature of political supply. One characteristic influencing voting behavior is indifference towards the options on offer (Riker and Ordeshook 1968). In this case, a voter has two possibilities. If the indifference cannot be conquered, choice is meaningless. Thus, it is no surprise that research shows that indifference has a negative impact on turnout (Aarts, Semetko, and Weßels 2005a). The alternative to abstention from voting is to overcome the indifference. If a voter is indifferent towards political choices on given yardsticks or evaluation criteria, she may look for additional criteria in order to check if there is indeed no meaningful difference between the offers. Existing criteria like the generalized evaluation of a party, long-lasting loyalty, or candidate evaluation may then be complemented by issue considerations. Thus, beside the trade-off hypothesis referring to consequences of social change, we formulate a hypothesis on complementing choice criteria. This argument follows the logic of utility as it claims that costly information gathering will only be pursued if necessary. One situation in which additional criteria have a utility that makes it worthwhile to invest is indifference. Therefore, the fourth hypothesis is:

> H4 *The less distinguishable political offers are to a voter, the more likely it is that she will use additional criteria and, in particular, issue considerations.*

There is a second situation that may imply a benefit from investing in additional information in order to arrive at a choice. This is the case when contradictions occur between a relatively persistent loyalty to a party and the general evaluation of the same party. In such a situation, issues may help to decide whether it is worthwhile to defect from the party one identifies with.

> H5 *The less congruence there is between loyalty towards a party and the evaluation of the same party, the more likely it is that a voter considers issues for vote choice.*

The additional dimension of complementing choice criteria is introduced here in order to extend the debate about why voters may (increasingly) use issues in their calculus of voting from characteristics on the demand side to those on the supply side (or to the perception of the supply side). This new dimension has completely different implications than the trade-off mechanism implied by voting and social change. For explaining increasing issue voting, this dimension would imply that changes at the supply side take place in a systematic and continuous way, for example in the form of a programmatic race of political parties to the middle or an increasing contradiction between the "historical identity" of a party and its actual performance. This chapter does not aim at investigating the possibility of a "supply trigger" for seemingly increasing issue voting. We test this frame in order to check whether it provides an individual-level explanation for the consideration of issues by voters. The hypothesis of a trade-off between habitual and real-choice voting due to social change does not provide something similar. It clearly pinpoints the opportunities arising from modernization, but it does not explain why voters should be willing to bear the costs of seizing them. This explanation is exactly the goal of the general hypothesis of this chapter that argues that voters will complement their choice criteria by considering issues, but only if this is necessary.

11.3 ISSUES—CONCEPT AND MEASURES

One major reason why findings on issue voting are heterogeneous not only in comparative perspective but even within countries relates to the fact that truly comparable longitudinal data is rare. A second reason for contradicting research results are different conceptions of issue voting (Schoen and Weins 2005). The term is not used consistently in the literature (Roller 1998; Fiorina 1981). One main differentiation of the character of issues concerns the question whether they relate to positions or goals. In the early 1960s, Stokes introduced the distinction between position issues—for which controversial standpoints exist—and valence issues—where citizens share the related goals (Stokes 1963). Whereas it is in the nature of position issues that they are contested, additional criteria that are creating differences between parties for valence issues are derived from the evaluation of the parties' ability to deal with the respective issues. Roller therefore makes a difference between position-based and performance-based issue orientations (Roller 1998). Additional characteristics refer to the time dimension of evaluations and standards of relevance. Performance evaluation can be retrospective or prospective (Fiorina 1981); relevance can be judged by a sociotropic or egocentric yardstick. Table 11.1 illustrates character and criteria for issue voting.

In our analysis, position and valence issues are considered. Regarding the time dimension, the prospective perspective is chosen for both types of issues. The evaluation criteria are as given in the table: expected performance for valence issues and proximity (technically, distance) for position issues.

Table 11.1 Character of issues and evaluation criteria

Evaluation criteria	Character of an issue	
	Valence	Position
Salience of the issue	egocentric/sociotropic	egocentric
Evaluation criteria	performance	proximity
Time perspective	retrospective/prospective	retrospective/prospective

Table 11.2 Valence issues—mean competence of political parties

Party	Voted for the party		Did not vote for the party	
	Mean (competence)	N	Mean (competence)	N
CDU/CSU	2.00	539	0.28	987
SPD	1.63	341	0.17	1185
FDP	1.21	218	0.07	1308
Greens	1.11	159	0.05	1367
The Left	1.46	226	0.07	1300

Valence issues are measured by the question concerning the most important, second most important, and third most important problem facing Germany, as well as by the follow-up question as to which of the political parties has the best capability to deal with the issue.

Three position issues are available: One refers to the socioeconomic dimension (lower taxes even if this means reduction of welfare spending vs. more welfare spending even if this means higher taxes), the second to the liberal-authoritarian dimension (stricter vs. more relaxed immigration laws). The third issue is placed on the environmental dimension and deals with nuclear power plants (more nuclear power plants should be built vs. nuclear power stations should be closed today). For all three issues, respondents have been asked for their perceptions of parties' positions and their own positions.

The measure for the impact of performance-based issue orientations on the vote is an additive index for each party. It counts for how many valence issues out of the three most important the respondents ascribed the highest competence to the respective party. The variable distribution is documented in Table 11.2.

For parsimony, we refrain from dealing separately with each of the three position issues. We calculated absolute distances between every position of the parties and respondents for each issue. We summed up the three distances, arriving at one measure for all position items for each of the five parties in the German Bundestag. We have tested issue-specific models and the model with the summary-distance measure. There is no significant difference in the patterns we found (see Table 11.4). Table 11.3 shows the distribution of distances for separate issues and the summary distance.

The following analysis uses the mean of the number of valence issues which a party is regarded to have the best capability to deal with and the summary distance across all three issues. In order to demonstrate that the summary measure of distances across the three issues does not hurt the general tendency, we estimated two base models.

The base models include party identification, Left–Right distance as a measure of ideological distance from a party, general party evaluation (like–dislike scales), general candidate evaluation (like–dislike scales), and the two variables that are the most interesting to us: valence-issue competence and position-issue distance.

Table 11.3 Position issues—distances by party

	Voted for the party			
Party	Socioeconomic	Liberal-authoritarian	Environment	N
CDU/CSU	1.48	1.71	2.49	539
SPD	1.64	2.31	1.70	341
FDP	1.40	1.91	2.01	218
Greens	1.74	2.28	1.29	159
The Left	1.90	2.57	1.57	226

	Did not vote for the party			
Party	Socioeconomic	Liberal-authoritarian	Environment	N
CDU/CSU	2.74	2.88	4.46	987
SPD	2.81	3.20	2.60	1,185
FDP	3.00	2.57	3.76	1,308
Greens	2.77	4.09	3.50	1,367
The Left	3.33	3.70	2.69	1,300

	Voted for the party		Did not vote for the party	
Party	Sum of distances	N	Sum of distances	N
CDU/CSU	5.39	539	9.91	987
SPD	5.56	341	8.50	1,185
FDP	5.23	218	9.09	1,308
Greens	5.31	159	10.41	1,367
The Left	5.70	226	9.84	1,300

Voters' Motivations

The model thus includes the classic factors of the funnel of causality except social structure. The logic of the funnel of causality suggests that social structure has no direct effect on voting. Rather, social structure exerts its influence on party attachment, ideology, and general evaluations. The nearer we come to the narrow end of the funnel, the less is the influence of social structure. For this reason, we see no point in including social structure as a determinant of vote choice for our question, namely the role of issues in the vote function. The first model considers the position issues separately, the second the summary measure (Table 11.4).

Table 11.4 Base model of party choice—conditional logistic regression

Model with single position issues

Vote	Coefficient	Standard error	z	P > z	[95% conf. interval]	
Party evaluation	0.520	0.054	9.620	0.000	0.414	0.625
Party identification	0.600	0.128	4.700	0.000	0.349	0.850
Valence issue competence	0.433	0.059	7.390	0.000	0.318	0.548
Distance L-R	−0.033	0.011	−3.010	0.003	−0.054	−0.011
Distance socio-economic	−0.060	0.040	−1.480	0.140	−0.139	0.020
Distance liberal-authoritarian	0.046	0.038	1.190	0.233	−0.029	0.121
Distance environment	−0.149	0.032	−4.670	0.000	−0.212	−0.087
Candidate evaluation	0.107	0.040	2.650	0.008	0.028	0.187

Model with summed distance

Vote	Coefficient	Standard error	Z	P > z	[95% conf. interval]	
Party evaluation	0.517	0.054	9.580	0.000	0.411	0.623
Party identification	0.595	0.126	4.710	0.000	0.348	0.843
Valence issue competence	0.406	0.058	7.050	0.000	0.293	0.520
Distance Left-Right	−0.029	0.011	−2.680	0.007	−0.050	−0.008
Candidate evaluation	0.111	0.040	2.790	0.005	0.033	0.189
Sum of position-issue distances	−0.062	0.020	−3.180	0.001	−0.100	−0.024

Notes: Conditional (fixed-effects) logistic regression; number of observations = 5,224; LR chi^2(8) = 2196.96; Prob > chi^2 = 0; Log likelihood = −609.73676; Pseudo R^2 = 0.643. Conditional (fixed-effects) logistic regression; number of observations = 5,224; LR chi^2(6) = 2180.82; prob > chi^2 = 0; Log likelihood = −617.80503; pseudo R^2 = 0.638.

The models show the same pseudo R-square. Thus, reducing the three position issues to one measure does not hurt. The model with the summary distance is even more effective because the effects of all variables are significant. In contrast, in the model with separate issues the socioeconomic and liberal-authoritarian dimensions do not have significant effects. The effects of party identification, Left–Right distance, party evaluation, and candidate evaluation are almost identical in both models. Competence regarding valence issues shows positive and almost identical effects in both models, whereas the effect of the summary measure of distance is negative: The larger the distance, the less likely voting for the respective party is.

11.4 THE MODERATION OF ISSUE EFFECTS ON THE VOTE

The hypotheses formulated above refer to elements of the trade-off process that suggests modernization and the educational revolution have opened an opportunity for free choice. One of the elements is the decline of party identification. The implication of the respective hypothesis is that voters who identify with a party make less use of issue voting whereas those who are "free" of traditional loyalties make more use of it. For testing this hypothesis, an interaction term of issue voting (both, valence-issue competence, and position-issue distance) has been added to the base regression model. With this model it is possible to estimate the marginal effect of issue considerations conditioned by the strength of party identification.

Results do not contradict the hypothesis. When party identification is weak, issue distance shows a bigger effect on party vote, when it is strong, the effect is not significant and weak. The same applies to valence-issue competence as Figure 11.1 shows.

The second element of the general hypothesis is political sophistication. More specifically, the higher political sophistication is, the more a voter makes use of issue considerations. The measure of political sophistication used here builds on three questions aiming at political knowledge. These three questions refer to elements of the German electoral system and represent different levels of difficulty. In order to account for the different levels, we calculated the sum of correctly answered questions weighted by difficulty. Difficulty is here the inverse of the percentage of correct answers. We standardized the scale range to 0 to 100.

For testing the moderating effect of political sophistication, we introduced an interaction of political sophistication with position-issue distance and valence-issue competence respectively. Figure 11.2 shows the results.

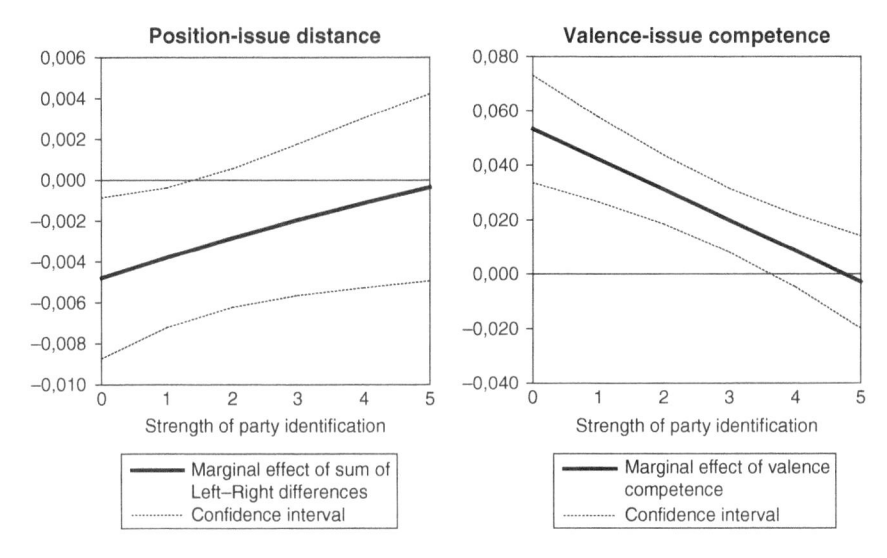

Figure 11.1 The impact of position-issue distance and valence-issue competence on party choice conditioned by strength of party identification

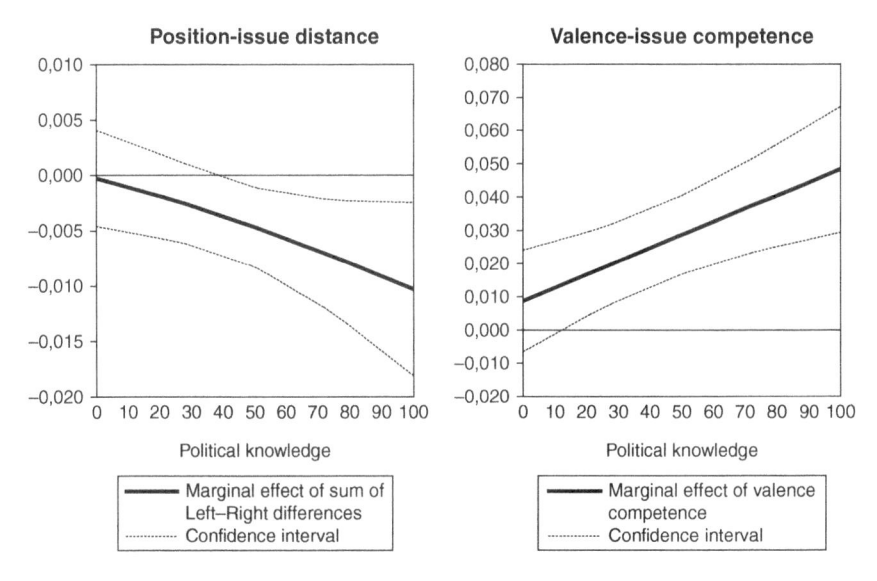

Figure 11.2 The impact of position-issue distance and valence-issue competence on party choice conditioned by political sophistication

Again, results do not contradict the general claim of the modernization thesis. Indeed, the more sophisticated voters are, the larger the negative influence of issue distance and the positive impact of valence-issue competence. When a voter has no political knowledge, issues do not exert an influence on vote choice.

The second set of hypotheses relates to supply conditions. The most prominent hypothesis refers to the degree of polarization of issues. In a strict sense, this condition applies to position issues only. However, if one takes polarization of issue positions as a feature of a party system it may also have an impact on the relevance of valence issues for vote choice. Issue polarization is measured at the individual level. It captures the distance between the closest and the most distant party. The polarization hypothesis is issue-specific. A test should thus look at the concrete issue. Here, we generalize the hypothesis assuming that there is an incentive for voters to consider issues in general when the political space as such is polarized. Therefore, we expect an effect for position issues as well as for valence issues. As for the analyses above, we also have issue-specific results. If the general hypothesis regarding the polarization of the competition structure does not find support, we will check for the specific issues. Figure 11.3 shows the results for the claim that the degree of polarization of the general supply structure matters for voters regarding the consideration of issues.

The findings concerning summed issue distances and valence issues do not support the polarization hypothesis. For valence issues, changes in effect by different degrees of polarization are not significant. Regarding position issues, only a medium polarization shows a slightly significant effect—lower

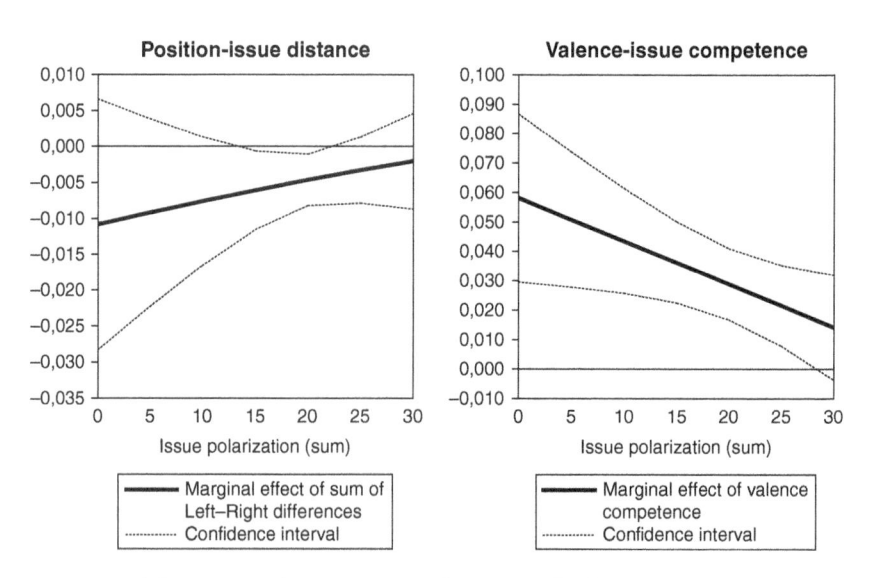

Figure 11.3 The impact of position-issue distance and valence-issue competence on party choice conditioned by issue polarization

and higher degrees of polarization don't. Reviewing results of the effects of the three specific issues and their polarization does not provide support for the specific polarization hypothesis either. Neither the socioeconomic nor the liberal-authoritarian issue shows significant marginal effects. For environment (nuclear energy), the constant marginal effect is not significant when polarization is below seven and otherwise significant. Thus, polarization as such and issue polarization do not necessarily lead to a higher attentiveness regarding issues. The connection for the nuclear-energy item is rather weak when it exists at all. The characteristics of an issue like the degree to which it is contested or polarizes parties do not seem to trigger consideration of issues. This does not contradict the general claim. Together with the following finding, the results suggest that polarization will only matter if issues are considered in vote choice and that this is dependent on other aspects than issue positions.

We see two more aspects relating to supply as relevant. One of those is indifference regarding choices. The argument is here that indifference leads to a search for possibilities to differentiate between political choices and that one way to do this is by extending the criteria to issues. Indifference concerns the degree to which respondents see a difference between parties in their general evaluations (like–dislike scales). If two parties draw level for the best rating there is indifference. The larger the perceived difference becomes, the lower becomes the indifference. Figure 11.4 shows the results. They support the hypothesis for the effect of position as well as for valence issues. In case of indifference, there is a quite strong effect of issues. Issue effects on the vote become insignificant as soon as voters make a difference in terms of the

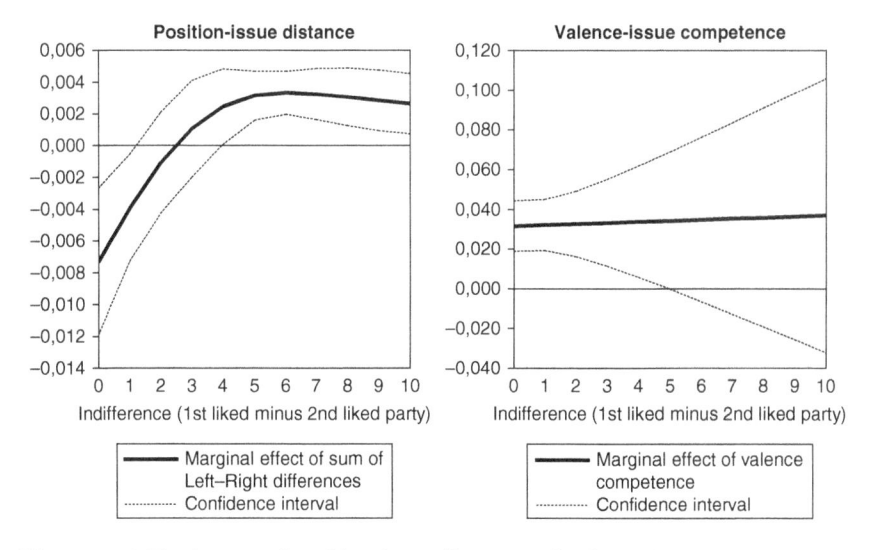

Figure 11.4 The impact of position-issue distance and valence-issue competence on party choice conditioned by indifference (party differentials like–dislike)

Position-issue distance | Valence-issue competence

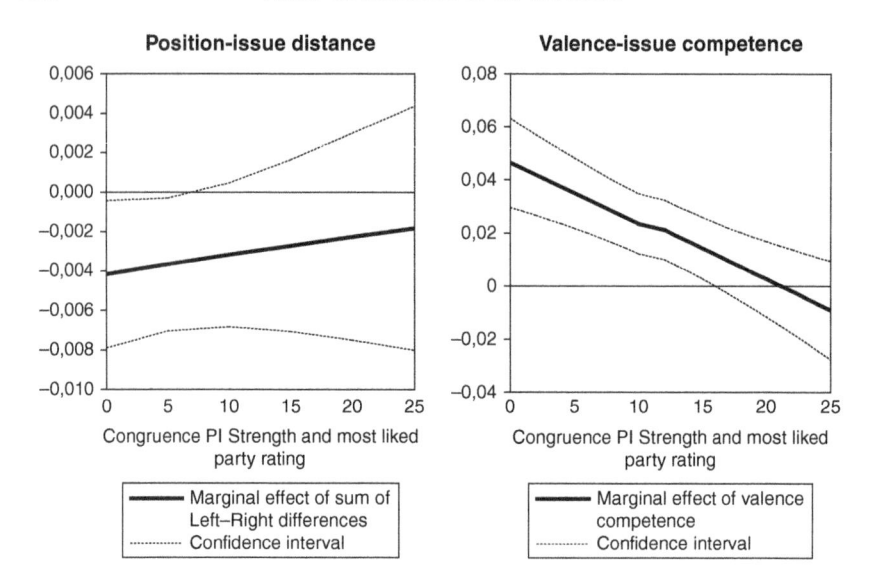

(Two line charts side by side. Left: Position-issue distance, y-axis from −0.010 to 0.006, x-axis "Congruence PI Strength and most liked party rating" 0 to 25, showing marginal effect of sum of Left–Right differences with confidence interval. Right: Valence-issue competence, y-axis from −0.04 to 0.08, x-axis same 0 to 25, showing marginal effect of valence competence with confidence interval.)

Figure 11.5 The impact of position-issue distance and valence-issue competence on party choice conditioned by congruence of party identification and evaluation

general evaluation between choices. Issues are then not needed for making a choice and, thus, they are not applied.

The last aspect concerning evaluation of political supply regards a situation of contradictory orientations toward a choice. More specifically, the question is whether it makes a difference if party identification and the general evaluation of a party on the like–dislike scale are congruent. As strength of party identification ranges from 0 (low) to 5 (high) and like–dislike scales from 0 to 11, we have recoded the latter to 0 to 5. The product of the strength of party identification and the recoded party evaluation is the measure of congruence. Full congruence is reached when both are highest (equal to 25; 0 being the lowest value).

As expected, issues play a role for vote choice when congruence is (or both, party identification and evaluations are) low. When party identification and party evaluation are congruent, the impact of issues on vote choice is not significant at all or to a very small degree (Figure 11.5).

11.5 THE MODERNIZATION HYPOTHESIS AND INDIVIDUAL-LEVEL FINDINGS

Findings are supportive of four out of the five hypotheses formulated above. This concerns the two hypotheses that are compatible with the assumption of modernization as a mechanism producing a trade-off between persistent loyalties to parties and issue voting. One finding is that issue voting is more likely when there is no party identification, a second that more sophisticated voters do consider issues more than less sophisticated ones. The aggregate argument assumes a decrease of party loyalties, an increase in political sophistication, and, as a result, an increase in issue voting. The individual-level relationship does not speak against the micro foundation of the aggregate argument. Of the three hypotheses related to supply characteristics, the polarization hypothesis failed, the indifference and congruence hypotheses found support. How do the outcomes on the trade-off and the supply hypotheses relate to each other and what are the consequences for the assumption of modernization as a trigger for issue voting?

Some findings suggest that an increase in education does not imply a decrease in party loyalties. Therefore, we doubt that modernization triggers issue voting. We rather assume that supply structures are responsible when voters consider issues in their choice making. Our last hypothesis is, thus, the following:

> H6 *If political supply does not offer a clear choice for a voter by simple criteria, that is, in case of indifference, she will consider issues—the more, the better educated she is. If choice is possible by simple criteria, even the most sophisticated voter will not invest in issue considerations for vote choice.*

This hypothesis sets two conditions for the consideration of issues. The major one is the political supply structure, i.e., indifference against choices or not. This condition is expected to moderate the impact of sophistication on the vote. Thus, we tested for marginal effects with a three-way interaction. Figure 11.6 shows the results.

For position issues, the finding is straightforward and in line with the hypothesis: Only in case of indifference, political knowledge shows a systematic and increasing effect on the strength of issue considerations for the vote. Interestingly and in contrast with our expectation, the same is not true for valence issues. Regardless of supply structures, political knowledge here has a positive and significant effect on the strength of issue considerations.

However, with regard to position-based issue voting, the results suggest the following: Education only exerts a positive influence on issue voting when voters feel indifferent about a choice. The assumption that social change automatically increases issue voting cannot be upheld. A trend of increasing influence of issues on voting would require two developments: an increase in education and political knowledge as well as an increase in depolarization and convergence in the performance of political parties.

For valence issues, however, there is no moderation of the effect of political knowledge on issue voting by the perception of political supply structures. We can only speculate why this is the case. One possible answer is that valence issues

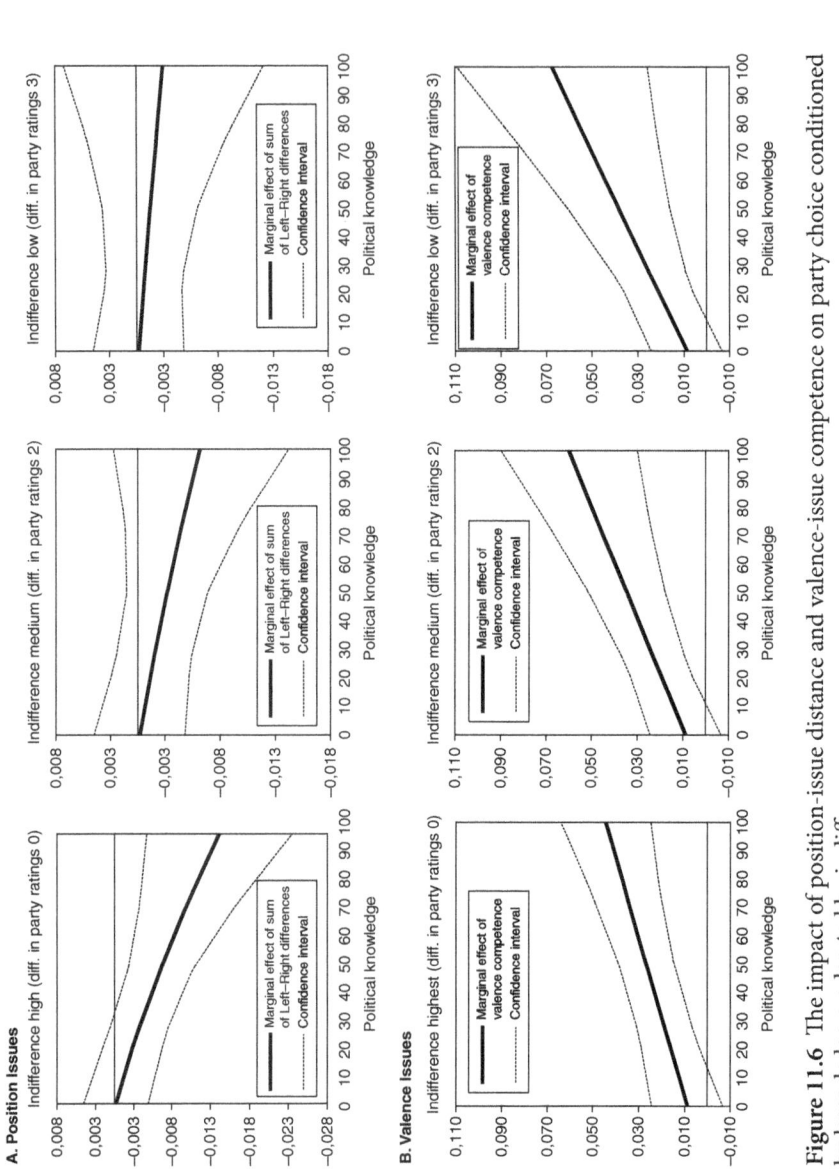

Figure 11.6 The impact of position-issue distance and valence-issue competence on party choice conditioned by knowledge moderated by indifference

require an evaluation of prospective performance in order to make them useful for a choice. This may be more demanding than normally suggested by the literature that assumes that valence and competence are the most common evaluations voters undertake. A second explanation could be that valence competence is only high if voters can differentiate between offers. This would suggest that there is a positive relationship between the difference in the general evaluation of the preferred and the second-best liked party on the one hand and competence in valence issues on the other hand. Indeed, the difference in the general evaluation of the best and second-best party is below 1 when the valence performance is 2 or lower and higher than 1 when valence competence rises to 3. In order to understand the logic of valence-issue considerations on the vote, these relationships have to be explored more thoroughly by future research.

11.6 LEFT–RIGHT AND VALENCE ISSUE VOTING IN COMPARATIVE PERSPECTIVE

Before we can draw general conclusions from the German findings, a check of the claims using international comparative data is necessary. Data from the Comparative Study of Electoral Systems (CSES), module 3, allows us to test the hypotheses put forward here. The CSES 3 advance release includes thirty-seven election studies of which eight had to be excluded because not all variables needed for the analysis were available. The hypotheses can thus be checked in twenty-nine election studies from twenty-five countries—Germany, Iceland, Mexico, and Poland are represented with two elections each. The CSES data does not include specific position issues but Left–Right scales for parties and self that can be used for proximity. Regarding valence issue competence, CSES only asks for the two instead of the three most important problems.

As in the German case, results show that proximity to a party and the evaluation of a party as being competent to solve the most important problems clearly relate to vote choice. In all but one of the twenty-nine studies, Left–Right distance to the party voted for is much smaller than to parties not voted for. In addition, it is true that the valence-issue competence of the chosen party is regarded as being considerably higher than the competence of the parties that were not chosen (Table 11.5). Thus, issues and voting are related in all countries, implying that it makes sense to investigate differences in the impact of issue voting.

For checking the hypotheses on the moderating factors of issue voting, conditional (fixed-effects) logistic regressions have again been estimated, this time adjusted for clusters (election studies). For making the comparison to the German results more convenient, the results are presented in terms of probability changes for voting under moderating conditions.

Table 11.5 Left–Right distance, valence issue competence, and voting

	Left–Right distance to party/parties, means			Valence-issue competence, means		
	Did not vote for	Voted for	Diff. voted-not voted for	Did not vote for	Voted for	Diff. voted-not voted for
AUS 2007	15.3	3.8	−11.5	0.19	1.21	1.03
BRA 2006	20.5	16.6	−3.9	0.16	0.26	0.10
CHE 2007	16.2	4.8	−11.3	0.03	0.44	0.41
CZE 2006	17.9	32.2	14.3	0.01	0.78	0.77
DEU 2005	14.3	4.3	−10.0	0.09	0.75	0.65
DEU 2009	11.5	2.1	−9.5	0.07	1.08	1.01
DNK 2007	17.0	1.9	−15.0	0.09	0.87	0.79
ESP 2008	17.4	2.5	−15.0	0.05	1.48	1.43
EST 2011	15.1	4.7	−10.5	0.07	0.82	0.75
FIN 2007	13.8	4.0	−9.8	0.09	0.86	0.77
FRA 2007	20.4	4.4	−16.0	0.11	1.05	0.95
GRC 2009	18.0	3.9	−14.1	0.04	0.95	0.91
HRV 2007	19.9	5.2	−14.7	0.04	0.81	0.77
IRL 2007	12.0	4.2	−7.8	0.13	0.91	0.77
ISL 2007	13.4	3.3	−10.1	0.06	0.80	0.74
ISL 2009	12.9	3.2	−9.7	0.06	0.85	0.79
ISR 2006	22.5	4.7	−17.8	0.08	0.75	0.67
KOR 2008	15.2	5.8	−9.4	0.07	0.77	0.70
MEX 2006	34.2	4.7	−29.5	0.23	1.45	1.21
MEX 2009	23.1	6.2	−16.9	0.04	1.01	0.97
NLD 2006	14.8	2.6	−12.2	0.11	0.82	0.70
NOR 2005	14.0	2.8	−11.1	0.12	0.87	0.75
NZL 2008	18.1	3.3	−14.8	0.07	0.98	0.91
POL 2005	20.4	5.5	−14.9	0.06	0.89	0.83
POL 2007	20.3	6.9	−13.4	0.21	0.38	0.17
PRT 2009	19.7	4.9	−14.8	0.06	0.82	0.76
SVK 2010	16.8	5.0	−11.9	0.03	0.94	0.91
SWE 2006	15.6	2.9	−12.7	0.04	0.59	0.55
THA 2007	7.7	4.3	−3.4	0.07	0.99	0.92

Source: CSES, module 3, advance release (cses.org).

Voters' Motivations 257

As in the German case, the moderating effects of the strength of party identification, indifference, and the congruence of the strength of party identification and general party evaluation (like–dislike scale) on Left–Right issue voting are all in line with our expectations and statistically significant. Contrary to the German case, the moderating effect of knowledge on the impact of Left–Right

Table 11.6 Moderating effects on Left–Right proximity voting and valence voting

	Germany 2009		CSES 3: pooled cross-section data	
	Distance (lowest to highest)	Valence issue (competence no/yes)	Distance (lowest to highest)	Valence issue (competence no/yes)
PI strength low	−5.28	5.33	−1.62	8.69
PI strength high	−0.39	−0.29	−0.05	4.18
Difference	*−4.88*	*−5.62*	*−1.57*	*−4.50*
Hypothesis	*Supported*	*Supported*	*Supported*	*Supported*
Knowledge 100	−11.33	4.84	−1.08	7.18
Knowledge 0	−0.31	0.88	−1.15	7.28
Difference	*−11.02*	*−3.96*	*0.08*	*0.09*
Hypothesis	*Supported*	*Supported*	*Not significant*	*Wrong direction*
LR polarization low	−11.93	5.81	−1.62	7.90
LR polarization high	−2.25	1.40	−0.61	4.32
Difference	*−9.68*	*−4.40*	*−1.02*	*−3.58*
Hypothesis	*Not supported*	*Not supported*	*Not significant*	*Not supported*
Indifference high	−8.01	3.16	−1.69	6.29
Indifference low	2.89	3.70	1.68	10.14
Difference	*−10.90*	*0.54*	*−3.37*	*3.85*
Hypothesis	*Supported*	*Not supported*	*Supported*	*Wrong direction*
Congruence low	−4.58	4.63	−1.80	8.44
Congruence high	−2.00	−1.16	0.43	4.07
Difference	*−2.57*	*−5.79*	*−2.23*	*−4.37*
Hypothesis	*Supported*	*Supported*	*Supported*	*Supported*

Notes: Own calculation using estimates from conditional (fixed-effects) logistic regression; robust standard errors; CSES 3 models adjusted for 28 clusters (election studies).

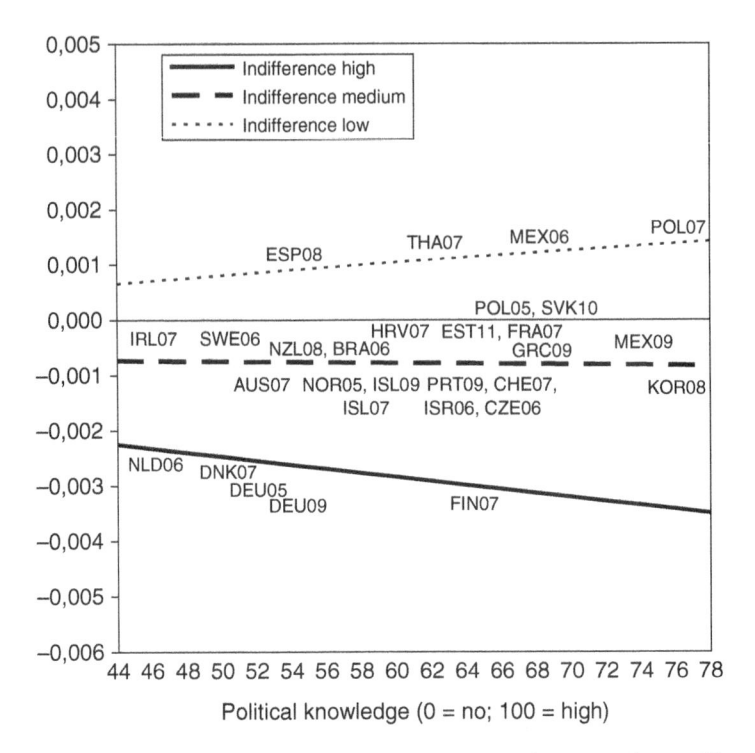

Figure 11.7 The impact of Left–Right distance on party choice conditioned by political knowledge, moderated by political indifference (marginal effects in probability)

Dotted and dashed lines: marginal effects are not significant.

distance on the vote is not significant. The issue polarization hypothesis does not hold up in keeping with the results for the German case (Table 11.6).

Regarding the moderation of the effect of valence-issue competence on the vote, the hypotheses on the strength of party identification and on congruence of party identification and party evaluation are supported. This does not apply to the polarization and indifference hypotheses as well as to the hypothesis on the moderating effect of political knowledge.

Thus, regarding the moderation of proximity voting, the comparative analysis confirms the German results except for political knowledge. The same applies to valence-issue competence voting. Concerning social change characteristics, i.e., the role of party attachment and political sophistication for a rise in issue voting, comparative results do not support the influence of political knowledge. With respect to political supply conditions as a trigger for considering issues if simpler criteria fail to provide a meaningful choice, comparative results are fully confirming our expectations for proximity voting and partly for valence-competence voting.

The last step of the comparative analysis is to check whether Hypothesis 6 is supported. This hypothesis claims that issues will be considered in case of political indifference between possible choices and to a higher degree by the more politically informed. However, whenever a choice can be made by simple criteria, even the most sophisticated voter will not invest in issue considerations for vote choice.

A three-way interaction term has been introduced to capture the moderating effect of indifference on the moderation of issue voting by political knowledge. Two models have been tested. The first is a pooled cross-section model including only microlevel variables. The second model includes country means for indifference instead of microlevel indifference. We introduce the second model in order to show that general supply structures can explain country differences in issue voting. As the microlevel model behaves very similar to the second model, its results are not reported here. The model which included country-level indifference shows the following (Figure 11.7).

In countries with high indifference, Left–Right distance has a clear and statistically significant impact on vote choice (the Netherlands, Denmark, Germany, and Finland). In addition, the marginal effect of Left–Right distance on the vote increases with political knowledge. In countries with medium or low indifference, there is no significant effect of Left–Right distance on the

Table 11.7 Moderating effects of political indifference and political sophistication on Left–Right proximity voting and valence voting

	Germany 2009, indifference at individual level (probability change in percentage points)			CSES 3, indifference at country level (means) (probability change in percentage points)		
	Indifference high	Indifference medium	Indifference low	Indifference high	Indifference medium	Indifference low
Knowledge	Distance (probability change lowest to highest)					
—at 44	−4.63	−2.91	−1.36	−2.48	−0.80	0.72
—at 78	−7.97	−4.86	−2.12	−3.84	−0.91	1.57
Difference	3.33	1.95	0.77	1.36	0.10	−0.85
Hypotheses	Knowledge supported			Knowledge supported		
	Moderation supported			Moderation supported		
Knowledge	Valence issue (probability change competence no to yes)					
—at 44	3.02	3.40	3.78	7.02	6.77	6.52
—at 78	4.31	4.92	5.53	6.88	6.43	5.98
Difference	1.30	1.53	1.76	−0.14	−0.34	−0.53
Hypotheses	Knowledge supported			Knowledge not supported		
	Moderation not supported			Moderation supported		

Notes: Own calculation from estimates from conditional (fixed-effects) logistic regression, robust standard errors, for CSES 3 models adjusted for 28 clusters (election studies).

vote and, even more important, there is no impact of political knowledge on issue voting.

These results are almost identical with the ones found for Germany. For valence-issue competence, the hypothesis is not supported as in the German case, but for different reasons. Knowledge increases the impact of competence voting, although it is not moderated by indifference in the German case. In comparative perspective, increasing knowledge does not contribute to an increasing effect of valence competence on the vote and the levels of its impact differ in line with the hypothesis according to levels of indifference. Table 11.7 summarizes the effects in terms of probability changes. In the first row, the probability of proximity voting decreases from left to right, i.e., with the decrease of indifference, and it increases with knowledge levels (first to second row). In the German case, the latter is also true for competence voting while the moderation by indifference does not work (lower left panel); in comparative perspective, political knowledge does not show a moderating effect (lower right panel).

11.7 CONCLUSIONS

For the past two decades almost, there has been a debate about the rise of issue voting. Theoretical claims about the reasons for the apparently increasing relevance of issues in vote decisions are well developed and rather plausible. Claims have been made to suggest that the educational revolution, social change, and the trends of secularization and individualization accompanying social changes are responsible for the increase. This macroscopic perspective assumes that increasing cognitive skills on the one hand and the liberation from social control in dense social milieus on the other hand create the resources and freedom to choose more carefully. The basic line of these arguments seems to follow a trade-off logic. If, for example, social embeddedness vanishes and, thus, does not produce long-standing loyalties any more, former criteria for vote choice lose their impact and are automatically replaced by short-term considerations like issues.

In this chapter, the question of the relevance of issues for vote choice has been addressed from a different and, to our opinion, more basic angle. Any observation relying on context as an explanatory factor has to be based on individual-level theory. Therefore, we have to ask for the utility of issue considerations for voters in making a choice. Our analysis is inspired by the theoretical assumption that voting is costly in terms of time, resources, and information. Voters are rational enough to invest only as much as they have to. The argument following from here is that because issue voting is more complex than relying on cues, shortcuts, and generalizations it is conditioned by the outcome of simpler criteria like party identification or more easily accessible evaluations like party like–dislike scales. There must be a good reason to consider issues if voters have an easier way to make up their mind using cues and shortcuts. This expectation has at least two implications. The first is that any relation of issue voting to macro conditions, education, or sophistication, describes just a phenomenon and its correlates but does not deliver an explanation. The second implication is that explanations must include reflections about costs and the utility of the introduction of issues in voters' decision-making. The hypothesis following from this is that if political supply does not offer voters a clear choice by simple criteria, voters will consider issues—but only in this case. Otherwise, even the most sophisticated voter will not invest in issue considerations for vote choice. This is the most far-reaching hypothesis in this chapter. Our analysis checks whether it finds support in the German case and in international comparison for twenty-nine election studies from twenty-five countries. The hypothesis has been checked for position issues in the German case and the Left–Right super issue in comparative perspective, and for valence issues both for Germany and internationally.

Results demonstrate that a micro model assuming the consideration of issues in vote choice to be conditional and moderated by the utility of simpler and more easily accessible criteria for choice receives quite some empirical support. Only if simpler and more easily accessible criteria fail to disentangle political offers, issue considerations come into play. This result came out in the German and comparative analysis for position issues regarding the conditioning role of party identification, indifference between the two best-liked political alternatives, and the congruence or incongruence between party identification and the general evaluation of the same party. The interplay of political indifference and political knowledge shows that even the most sophisticated and politically knowledgeable voters refrain from taking issues into account if simpler and more easily accessible criteria are sufficient.

These results complement the findings on issue voting in two ways. First, results show that a micro model that theoretically takes into account the utility of issue voting above other ways of making a choice makes sense. Second, results show that education and political sophistication are not necessarily triggering more issue voting. Whether they do depends a lot on political supply structures. If the difference between political offers is already obvious at a general level without considering special issues, these are not considered. In terms of costs of information processing, this is quite an enlightened way of making decisions.

A point remains open for further exploration. This concerns the way in which issue-competence voting, i.e., valence-issue voting, works. It shows quite some similarity to the conditionality of position-issue voting (role of party identification and congruence of identification and evaluation) but also important differences. The influence of education and political indifference seems shaky and is not confirmed by the international comparison.

The demonstrated conditionality of issue voting clearly indicates that analyses based on macro developments and not considering a model of the utility of vote choice criteria fall short. In order to understand issue voting and its motivations at all, political supply by parties and candidates has to be considered at least as a complementary factor to the increasing resources and abilities of voters.

12

Are Alienation and Indifference the New Features of Elections?

Markus Steinbrecher

12.1 INTRODUCTION

Turnout is at the heart of democracy. It is the decisive mode of political participation in order to transfer power from citizens to political actors, and it is the only kind of political participation used by a majority of the population. However, recent developments show a clear decline of turnout rates in most Western democracies and at all electoral levels. In the case of Germany this development culminated in the lowest turnout rate since the foundation of the Federal Republic in the most recent Federal election in 2009. Only 70.8% of the eligible citizens cast a ballot in this election.

Electoral research has used a multitude of predictors to explain abstention at the individual level, turnout levels at the aggregate level, and the decline in turnout rates over time (e.g., Caballero 2005; Geys 2006a; Rosenstone and Hansen 1993; Steinbrecher, Huber, and Rattinger 2007). Among the strongest individual-level predictors of turnout are sociodemographic characteristics and political attitudes that can be more or less linked to sociological (Lazarsfeld, Berelson, and Gaudet 1944; Berelson, Lazarsfeld, and McPhee 1954; Lipset and Rokkan 1967b) and social-psychological approaches (Campbell, Gurin, and Miller 1954; Campbell et al. 1960b) to electoral research. In contrast to these approaches, rational choice theory does not perform very well in the explanation of abstention (Caballero 2005: 336ff.). As all rational choice approaches regard the decision to show up at the polls or not as dependent on the costs and benefits associated with the act of voting, a major problem for these approaches arises from the difficulty of measuring benefits and costs adequately. An additional problem is that many voters do not act in accordance with the assumptions of the model, well known as the "paradox of voting" (Downs 1957a): Many citizens vote although the associated costs are higher than the benefits.

The calculus of voting (Downs 1957a; Riker and Ordeshook 1968) is the general model to study effects of rational evaluations on turnout. There has been a multitude of attempts to improve the calculus of voting and to operationalize costs and benefits adequately (e.g., Blais 2000; Caballero 2005; Geys 2006b). I will just concentrate on two key aspects that are part of many empirical approaches applying rational choice theory to turnout. The first is alienation, meaning that voters do not feel represented by political actors. The second is indifference, resulting from voters being equally close to or far from two or more political actors. Both alienation and indifference have a negative impact on turnout. Citizens who show a higher level of alienation or indifference or both of them are less likely to participate in elections.

Unfortunately, there is no clear-cut and fully developed framework to analyse the impact of alienation and indifference on abstention. A look at the relevant literature shows very different approaches, despite the common theoretical background. The vast majority of researchers use cross-sectional data and thus are able to gauge the importance of indifference and alienation only in single elections under specific circumstances (Aarts, Semetko, and Weßels 2005b; Adams, Dow, and Merrill III 2006; Adams and Merrill III 2003; Brody and Page 1973; Johnston, Matthews, and Bittner 2007; Katz 2009; Melton 2009; Plane and Gershtenson 2004; Thurner and Eymann 2000; Weisberg and Grofman 1981). In addition, these studies differ with respect to the elections and the electoral levels analysed, the methods applied, the operationalization of alienation and indifference, the control variables included, and the consideration of interaction terms.

From a normative point of view this chapter concentrates on issues that are highly relevant for the stability of a political system. If citizens become more and more alienated or indifferent, politics and political actors seem to lack sufficient appeal, in the case of alienation, or alternatives in the structure of supply, in the case of indifference, to attract political participation and involvement. It might be that rising levels of alienation and indifference among voters in Germany are one of the reasons for declining turnout. It is also possible that alienation and indifference become stronger predictors of turnout by either replacing former explanatory variables of electoral participation or moderating their effects. In this respect this chapter is linked to a branch of electoral and attitudinal research in Germany which has put a significant emphasis on the phenomenon of "*Politikverdrossenheit*," i.e., disenchantment with politics (e.g., Arzheimer 2002; Maier 1999) since the beginning of the 1990s.

Related to these considerations, the main goal of this chapter is to focus on the role of alienation and indifference for explaining turnout and its decline in German Federal elections from 1994 to 2009. Research questions to be answered are, first, whether indifference and alienation have increased among the German electorate since 1994. If there was an increase, rising levels of alienation and indifference would likely show growing dissatisfaction of

Are Alienation and Indifference the New Features of Elections? 265

German citizens with their polity that might be a threat for the political system of Germany and its long-term stability. The second, much more important, question is whether indifference and alienation are stronger predictors of turnout in recent than in earlier elections. If their impact were higher in recent elections that would imply a stronger reaction by citizens to the party system and the supply side of politics in general. The third question is whether the effects of alienation and indifference vary among different groups of the electorate. I will therefore focus on interaction effects between strength of party identification and the perceived duty to vote on the one hand, and alienation as well as indifference on the other. By investigating the extent of these interactions over time I will be able to examine whether perceptions of the supply side of politics are able to diminish the impact of some of the political attitudes which have been traditionally among the most important predictors of electoral participation.

The structure of this chapter will be as follows. The second section (12.2) will provide the theoretical rationale for effects of alienation and indifference on turnout. It will also summarize previous findings and present the hypotheses to be tested in the empirical analyses. The third section (12.3) will describe the data sets used and the operationalization of the most relevant variables. The results of the empirical analyses will be covered in the fourth section (12.4), while the fifth and final section (12.5) will summarize and discuss the findings.

12.2 ALIENATION AND INDIFFERENCE AS PREDICTORS OF TURNOUT

This section will provide the theoretical rationale for effects of alienation and indifference on turnout and will present results of previous analyses employing these two concepts. Connected to the presentation of previous research results I will also focus on challenges related to parties and party systems of the countries studied, the operationalization of alienation and indifference, the control variables included, and the issue of interaction effects.

As already mentioned in the introduction, alienation and indifference are related to the rational choice approach of electoral research. According to this approach, voters' decisions to take part in an election are dependent on the costs and benefits associated with the voting act (Downs 1957a; Riker and Ordeshook 1968). How are alienation and indifference connected to the calculation of the perceived costs and benefits of voting? Both concepts are related to the supply side of politics like comparisons between political parties or politicians by the voters, depending on the respective electoral system. In particular, it is the political or ideological position of parties that matters. An individual is in general more likely to vote if her ideological position is close to one of the parties or if she clearly prefers one of the parties to others—an assumption found in all spatial models of electoral behavior. If two or even more parties do not differ in their programs and agendas an individual would receive the same utility by voting for either one. In the most extreme case, all parties appear to be identical. Then it does not matter which party to vote for at all. Consequently indifference, or higher levels of indifference, lead to a lower probability of showing up at the voting booth.

The logic behind alienation is a bit different, but finally leads to the same result, i.e., lower willingness to participate in an election. In the case of alienation, an individual does not feel represented by parties or political actors in general anymore.[1] This lack of perceived representation occurs when individual issue or ideological positions are far away from those of the parties. An increase of this gap leads to smaller benefits from casting a ballot, and the incentive to participate in an election goes down. Thus, both alienation and indifference have a negative impact on turnout. Although both concepts are based on cost–benefit calculations of voters they also provide information on the quality of the democratic process and the ability of political parties to represent the interests of the voters.

A considerable number of studies have analysed the impact of alienation and indifference on turnout (Aarts, Semetko, and Weßels 2005b; Adams, Dow, and Merrill III 2006; Adams and Merrill III 2003; Behnke 2000; Brody and Page 1973; Johnston, Matthews, and Bittner 2007; Katz 2009; Klein 2002; Melton 2009; Plane and Gershtenson 2004; Thurner and Eymann 2000; Weisberg and Grofman 1981). Most of these studies find the expected negative relationship, but these effects appear to be rather small in comparison to those of other predictors of turnout. In some cases empirical results even show no effects, meaning that alienated and/or indifferent citizens participate like others do.

A large majority of articles on the impact of alienation and indifference concentrates on the United States, a country with a presidential electoral system. Most of the articles focus on turnout in presidential elections (Adams, Dow, and Merrill III 2006; Adams and Merrill III 2003; Brody and Page 1973; Peress 2011; Weisberg and Grofman 1981; Zipp 1985); only one on senate elections (Plane and Gershtenson 2004). However, with only two relevant candidates or parties at hand, American voters are confronted with different choices when compared to parliamentary multiparty systems like Germany. In the case of a multiparty system with a proportional electoral system, a voter is much more likely to find a party that represents his interests better than others and that is also likely to pass the 5% threshold. Thus, different party systems might cause different levels of alienation and indifference in different polities on the one hand, because the number of available candidates or parties has a strong

---

[1] The lack of representation is obviously the most relevant reason of alienation for my purpose; however, alienation might also result from social anomie.

impact on considerations of the voters. On the other hand, the number of available candidates or parties might also have an impact on the operationalization of indifference and alienation by different researchers. Obviously it is much easier to find an adequate measurement of the two concepts in a presidential system with just two relevant candidates.

Many researchers use feeling thermometers towards parties or candidates to gauge alienation and indifference (Aarts, Semetko, and Weßels 2005b; Brody and Page 1973; Johnston, Matthews, and Bittner 2007; Melton 2009; Weisberg and Grofman 1981), while some use positions of candidates or parties and voters on political issues (Adams and Merrill III 2003; Behnke 2000; Klein 2002; Thurner and Eymann 2000). There is also a larger group of researchers that includes ideological distances on the left–right dimension between a voter's and the parties' positions (Adams, Dow, and Merrill III 2006; Katz 2009; Peress 2011; Plane and Gershtenson 2004; Zipp 1985). Some researchers use dichotomous measures for indifference and alienation (Aarts, Semetko, and Weßels 2005b; Melton 2009; Thurner and Eymann 2000; Weisberg and Grofman 1981), although this strategy seems to be arbitrary (Aarts, Semetko, and Weßels 2005b: 610) and implies a homogeneous mechanism linking alienation and indifference with political behavior, namely that all voters in an electorate have the same threshold to become alienated or indifferent, which is very unlikely. In the case of my analysis the problem related to dichotomous measurement of these concepts would be even more severe since an identical dichotomous measure for all Federal elections between 1994 and 2009 would imply that voters have an identical threshold in several elections that have been conducted against a different background (e.g., with respect to party programs, government coalitions, or relevant issues and events).

The majority of articles applies metric or graded measures for the two concepts. If one ignores the minimum and maximum values of these variables, graded measures imply that there is not a single and identical threshold that all voters have to pass to be regarded as alienated or indifferent. Instead, these measures provide information on the extent of a voter's alienation and indifference (Adams, Dow, and Merrill III 2006; Behnke 2000; Brody and Page 1973; Johnston, Matthews, and Bittner 2007; Katz 2009; Klein 2002; Peress 2011; Plane and Gershtenson 2004; Zipp 1985). I think that this is a much more adequate approach to measure individual levels of alienation and indifference, despite the reliability and validity analyses by Melton (2009: 44ff.), who tries to show that dichotomous measures are at least as good as graded measures.

Another major issue is the lack of comparability with respect to control variables. Some just have a look at the bivariate effects of alienation and indifference on turnout (Brody and Page 1973; Weisberg and Grofman 1981), some others use just a limited number of sociodemographics and political attitudes as controls (Aarts, Semetko, and Weßels 2005b; Adams and Merrill III 2003; Adams, Dow, and Merrill III 2006; Behnke 2000; Johnston, Matthews, and

Bittner 2007; Katz 2009; Klein 2002; Melton 2009; Thurner and Eymann 2000). Even the paper with the most extensive list of controls (Plane and Gershtenson 2004) does not include some of the classic and most influential predictors of turnout, like strength of party identification, interest in politics, or the perceived duty to vote (Caballero 2005; Steinbrecher, Huber, and Rattinger 2007). The consequence is a potential overestimation of the effects of alienation and indifference. Thus, even the usually small or nonsignificant effects presented in those articles are subject to bias.

Up to now there have been four contributions on the impact of alienation and indifference on turnout in German elections, by Aarts, Semetko, and Weßels (2005), Behnke (2000), Klein (2002), and Thurner and Eymann (2000). Despite different operationalizations of the two central concepts, the results of these contributions can be summarized very quickly. Alienation and indifference usually have the expected negative impact, but only in bivariate analyses or in models with a very limited set of attitudinal and sociodemographic controls. These results for elections until the 1990s reveal that German voters more or less tend to ignore differences between the parties when coming to their decision whether to vote or not. The analyses in section 12.4 will test whether this conclusion holds for the Federal elections between 1994 and 2009 or not. In contrast to previous contributions my analysis will include a full set of attitudinal variables, in particular the so-called civic attitudes (Campbell, Gurin, and Miller 1954; Campbell et al. 1960b). I hence will be able to run the most robust tests of alienation and indifference effects for turnout in Germany until now.

One of the major themes of this chapter is interaction effects between alienation and indifference on the one hand, and sociodemographic characteristics and political attitudes on the other hand. I already mentioned before that it is very unlikely that all citizens have the same threshold for becoming alienated or indifferent. The same argument can be applied to the impact of both concepts on turnout. Not every citizen with a similar level of alienation or indifference will react identically or with the same likelihood by abstaining from an election. In fact, the impact of both concepts might be dependent on certain attitudes a citizen holds or not, e.g., if he accepts the duty to vote or has a strong party identification. As for most of the other issues addressed before, there has been previous research, but the attempts to identify interaction effects have been far from complete or consistent (Melton 2009: 2): The effect of alienation and indifference might differ among people with different levels of party identification (Adams, Dow, and Merrill III 2006), education (Brody and Page 1973), predispositions related to turnout or habitual voting (Melton 2009; Weisberg and Grofman 1981), and attitudinal cross-pressures (Weisberg and Grofman 1981). In Section 12.4 I will calculate interactions between alienation and indifference on the one hand and the perceived duty to vote and strength of party identification on the other hand, because these attitudes are usually among the strongest predictors of turnout. However, the share of eligible citizens with a party identification or who accept the duty to vote is declining (e.g., Curtice and Park 2010; Dalton 2000; Schoen and Weins 2005: 220ff.). Calculating interaction effects of alienation and indifference with party identification and the acceptance of the duty to vote, I hypothesize that high levels on these attitudes will lead to a reduction or even to a full compensation of the negative effects of alienation and indifference on turnout. In contrast, this means that people with no party attachment or no acceptance of the perceived duty to vote should be much less prone to show up at the polls if they are strongly alienated or indifferent. In addition, by comparing the extent of these interaction effects between different Federal elections, I will be able to examine whether indifference or alienation are able to diminish the impact of long-term party attachments and support for norms or not.

There also has been no previous research on the impact of alienation and indifference on intra-individual changes in turnout behavior. The available long-term panels which span over three consecutive elections would be a natural source for these analyses. However, due to panel attrition and panel mortality it is impossible to run analyses with these data sets: The number of nonvoters is just too small. Instead I will use the available cross-sectional data sets and will combine turnout in the current and the previous election. A typology of four different types of voters results from these two dichotomous variables. This measure of turnout allows at least partly for an analysis of intra-individual changes in turnout and its connection to indifference and alienation. As I will not be able to present all possible comparisons between the types, I will concentrate on voters in both elections and how they differ from the three other types of (non)voters. My hypothesis is that nonvoters in both elections and those citizens that voted in the previous, but not in the current election should display higher levels of alienation and indifference than the regular voters. Those who did not vote in the previous election, but did so in the current election, should not differ from regular voters with respect to the two key predictors.

12.3 DATA, MEASUREMENT, AND OPERATIONALIZATION

To answer the three questions presented in the introduction I will concentrate on the pre- and postelection cross-sectional components of the German election studies for the Federal elections between 1994 and 2009 (ZA3065, ZA3066, ZA3861, ZA4332, ZA5302). The surveys provide a comprehensive database that allows for the analysis of longitudinal developments and inter-individual as well as (at least to a limited extent) intra-individual changes over several elections. With the exception of the 2005 election study when respondents were just asked after the election, and the acceptance of the duty to vote was not part of the questionnaire, these surveys provide an identical design and set of variables.

The subsequent analyses will use two different dependent variables. The first is a dichotomous variable, measuring whether an individual is willing to participate (if asked before the election) or has participated (if asked in the postelection survey) in the respective Federal election. The second dependent variable will be a fourfold typology resulting from the combination of this turnout variable and recalled turnout in the previous Federal election. The four turnout types are: (1) voters in both elections; (2) voters in the previous, but not in the current election; (3) nonvoters in the previous, but in the current election; and (4) nonvoters in both elections.

The core independent variables are indifference and alienation. As pointed out earlier there is no consensus on the adequate measurement of these concepts. However, there is at least some sort of agreement over which variables to use for their calculation. A majority of researchers uses the survey respondents' feelings towards the parties, "because they allow for a multi-dimensional policy space and implicitly incorporate the importance respondents place on the various issues" (Melton 2009: 56f.).

In a multiparty system, it is the most valid strategy to include as much information as possible and thus employ evaluations of all parties available, in order to come close to a realistic model of the selection problem a voter faces (Melton 2009: 43, 53). This means for my analysis that evaluations of CDU (in all states except Bavaria), CSU (in Bavaria), SPD, FDP, the Greens, and the Left will be included. Right-wing parties like the Republicans and NPD are ignored, since evaluations of these parties are available for selected elections only.

It was already mentioned in the previous section that I will use graded measurements of alienation and indifference. This means that these two indicators do not tell categorically whether a voter is indifferent, alienated, or neither. Instead, values of these indices can be interpreted as higher or lower levels of alienation and indifference, respectively. Alienation is measured by calculating the mean over the feeling thermometers of the mentioned set of parties. This average evaluation of the parties is then rescaled to a range from 0 to 1, where 0 means that an individual is not alienated at all (all parties get the best evaluation) and 1 means that an individual is fully alienated (all parties get the worst evaluation). Indifference is gauged by calculating the difference of the feeling thermometers of the two most-preferred parties. The resulting variable is rescaled to a range from 0 to 1, where 0 means a respondent is not indifferent at all (maximum difference between the two most-preferred parties) and 1 means she is fully indifferent (both most-preferred parties get the same evaluation). All other variables in the analysis have been rescaled to a range from 0 to 1 with the exception of age and age squared. Table 12.1 provides an overview of core descriptive characteristics of the most relevant variables in the analysis, i.e., turnout, the voter types, alienation, and indifference.

Table 12.1 Descriptive statistics for turnout, voter types, alienation, and indifference

Variable	Min	Max	Mean (sd)				
			1994	1998	2002	2005	2009
Turnout	0	1	0.904	0.946	0.931	0.882	0.841
Nonvoter currently + previously	0	1	0.049	0.022	0.033	–	0.097
Nonvoter currently, but voter previously	0	1	0.037	0.024	0.026	–	0.051
Voter currently, but nonvoter previously	0	1	0.048	0.043	0.048	–	0.065
Voter currently + previously	0	1	0.867	0.911	0.893	–	0.787
Alienation	0	1	0.552 (0.137)	0.532 (0.140)	0.525 (0.137)	0.517 (0.141)	0.542 (0.146)
Indifference	0	1	0.818 (0.166)	0.813 (0.168)	0.822 (0.174)	0.853 (0.160)	0.837 (0.157)

12.4 THE IMPORTANCE OF ALIENATION AND INDIFFERENCE AS PREDICTORS OF TURNOUT

This section will present the results of the empirical analyses. First, I will have a look at the development of indifference and alienation between 1994 and 2009 and I will present bivariate correlations between both concepts and other sociodemographic, as well as attitudinal variables. Second, I will run binary logistic regression analyses with turnout as the dependent variable. Third, I will introduce interaction effects between the two main variables of interest and party identification, as well as the perceived duty to vote. The final analysis in this section will consist of multinomial logistic regressions for four voter types based on their participatory behavior in two consecutive Federal elections.

Development of Alienation and Indifference and their Correlations with Other Variables between 1994 and 2009

Looking at the development of the levels of alienation and indifference between 1994 and 2009, general trends are presented in Table 12.1, while Tables 12.2 and 12.3 show correlations between sociodemographics and political attitudes on

Table 12.2 Bivariate correlations of alienation and selected variables between 1994 and 2009

Variable	1994	1998	2002	2005	2009
Male	0.198[c]	0.233[c]	0.188	0.243[c]	0.166[a]
Age	0.046[b]	0.056[b]	0.097[c]	0.076[c]	0.118[c]
Education	−0.034[a]	−0.102[c]	−0.114[c]	−0.109[c]	−0.150[c]
East	0.201[c]	0.191[a]	0.192[a]	0.228[b]	0.164[a]
Strength party identification	−0.071[c]	−0.036[a]	−0.034[a]	−0.008	−0.214[c]
Interest in politics	−0.020	−0.030	−0.039[a]	−0.030	−0.138[c]
Satisfaction with democracy	−0.089[c]	−0.104[c]	−0.166[c]	−0.120[c]	−0.196[c]
External efficacy	−0.129[c]	−0.138[c]	−0.178[c]	−0.106[c]	−0.246[c]
Internal efficacy	0.013	−0.016	0.001	−0.018	−0.048[c]
Duty to vote	−0.070[c]	−0.050[b]	−0.086[c]	–	−0.146[c]

Notes: Correlation measures are Cramer's V for gender and East, Pearson's r for age, and Goodman/Kruskal's gamma for the other variables. Levels of significance: [a]$p < 0.05$, [b]$p < 0.01$, [c]$p < 0.001$.

the one hand and indifference and alienation on the other. The overall level of alienation does not change very much over the course of the five Federal elections and is always close to the midpoint of the scale (Table 12.1). Regarding the minor fluctuations of alienation between the five elections (0.517–0.552), the election-specific context obviously does not play a major role for the overall level of alienation. The level of indifference among the German electorate is also very stable between 1994 and 2009 (0.813–0.853). With the Grand Coalition running as incumbent government and the quite boring campaign in 2009 (Rattinger et al. 2011), I would have expected an increase from 2005 to 2009. However, the average level of indifference is higher than the average level of alienation. Thus, the perception of no differences between the two most-preferred parties is clearly more widespread than the feeling of not being represented by any of the parties. All in all, these figures do not provide evidence for a linear growth in indifference and alienation that might have contributed to the decrease of turnout in the period analysed here.

Next, I will turn to the bivariate correlations between alienation on the one hand and sociodemographics as well as political attitudes on the other (Table 12.2). Overall, there is at least one significant correlation for each and every variable and alienation. Younger and lower educated people are more alienated, as are East Germans. With the exception of internal efficacy all attitudinal variables have a constant negative impact on alienation. General patterns are that those respondents being low on these attitudes are more

Are Alienation and Indifference the New Features of Elections? 273

alienated than those with medium or high levels. The extent of this relationship varies between elections and variables, but seems to be strongest and most pronounced in the most recent Federal election of 2009. In total, satisfaction with democracy and external efficacy seem to have the strongest (negative) average correlation with alienation, while the relationship is quite weak (with the exception of 2009) for interest in politics, strength of party identification, and perceived duty to vote. The strong correlation of satisfaction with democracy is not very surprising, as alienation also measures some kind of disenchantment with political parties in particular.

Table 12.3 displays bivariate correlations between indifference and the selected variables. In contrast to the results presented in Table 12.2 there is a much higher number of insignificant correlations. However, as for alienation, I find that those high on the included attitudes usually are feeling less indifferent than those low on them. The most pronounced correlations occur for strength of party identification and age. This means that those with a strong party identification as well as older people feel much less indifferent than their counterparts at the other end of the respective scales. The negative relationship also holds for the other attitudinal variables except internal efficacy in 1998, but these correlations are either insignificant or rather weak. Regarding education, it is interesting to report that those with high educational attainments usually reveal higher levels of indifference.

Summing up these results, the levels of alienation and indifference have not changed very much over these five Federal elections. Among the electorate

Table 12.3 Bivariate correlations of indifference and selected variables between 1994 and 2009

Variable	1994	1998	2002	2005	2009
Male	0.070	0.077	0.079	0.109[b]	0.062
Age	−0.081[c]	−0.128[c]	−0.147[c]	−0.039	−0.113[c]
Education	0.053[c]	0.144[c]	0.135[c]	0.012	0.039[a]
East	0.077[a]	0.094[b]	0.071	0.083	0.050
Strength party identification	−0.300[c]	−0.238[c]	−0.280[c]	−0.200[c]	−0.218[c]
Interest in politics	−0.074[c]	−0.015	−0.043[a]	−0.048[a]	−0.138[c]
Satisfaction with democracy	−0.052[b]	−0.032	−0.030	0.058[b]	−0.097[c]
External efficacy	−0.043	−0.024	−0.014	−0.024	−0.052[b]
Internal efficacy	−0.054[c]	0.012	−0.012	−0.016	−0.040[a]
Duty to vote	−0.106[c]	−0.034	−0.120[c]	–	−0.103[c]

Notes: Correlation measures are Cramer's V for gender and East, Pearson's r for age, and Goodman/Kruskal's gamma for the other variables. Levels of significance: [a]$p < 0.05$, [b]$p < 0.01$, [c]$p < 0.001$.

in general, there have been neither clear-cut, nor linear, nor strong developments. Indifference is always higher than alienation. However, the gap between certain subgroups of the electorate is severe, as indicated by the bivariate correlations, and has increased in some cases, particularly with respect to alienation. It obviously matters for the individual level of alienation or indifference whether somebody is highly educated, is not interested in politics, or does not have a strong identification with a party.

The Impact of Alienation and Indifference on Turnout between 1994 and 2009

After the univariate and the bivariate analyses in the previous subsection, I will now present multivariate results. Table 12.4 includes a comprehensive model for the explanation of turnout including sociodemographics and political attitudes. The analyses are a statistically conservative test of the possible effects of alienation and indifference on turnout in German Federal elections

Table 12.4 Binary logistic regressions for turnout in German Federal elections between 1994 and 2009

Variable	1994	1998	2002	2005	2009
Alienation	−0.083[a]	−0.047	−0.045	−0.233[c]	−0.147[c]
Indifference	−0.067	−0.071	−0.055	−0.110[a]	−0.060[a]
Male	−0.011	−0.017	0.002	−0.011	−0.017
Age	0.003[a]	0.004[b]	0.005[a]	0.007[c]	0.005[c]
Age squared	−0.00003	−0.00004[b]	−0.00003[a]	−0.00006[b]	−0.00004[b]
Education	−0.007	−0.011	0.042[a]	0.086[c]	0.006
East	−0.016	0.024[a]	0.002	−0.023	0.022[a]
Strength party identification	0.093[c]	0.063[c]	0.076[c]	0.127[c]	0.086[c]
Interest in politics	0.100[c]	0.066[a]	0.062	0.165[c]	0.225[c]
Satisfaction with democracy	0.058[b]	0.028	0.030	0.044	0.069[b]
External efficacy	−0.007	0.055[a]	0.038	0.105[b]	0.117[c]
Internal efficacy	0.025	0.011	0.004	0.020	0.051[b]
Duty to vote	0.124[c]	0.146[c]	0.138[c]	–	0.203[c]
Nagelkerke's R^2	0.375	0.363	0.373	0.298	0.550
N	2974	2813	2620	2300	3652

Notes: Coefficients are average marginal effects; unstandardized logistic regression coefficients and robust standard errors can be found in Table 12.8 in the Appendix. Levels of significance: [a] $p < 0.05$, [b] $p < 0.01$, [c] $p < 0.001$.

between 1994 and 2009 because of the inclusion of a multitude of controls. The results show that indifference is not among the significant predictors of electoral participation until 2005, while alienation has a significant negative effect on turnout in the election of 1994, too. Citizens who do not feel represented by political parties are thus less likely to cast a ballot in the Federal elections of 1994, 2005, and 2009.

Among the five elections, 2005 and 2009 stick out because both central variables affect the individual probability of turnout. Note, however, that the perceived duty to vote is not part of the model for 2005 and that this survey just consists of postelection interviews. The absence of the perceived duty results in stronger effects for almost all other variables in the model and might partly explain the strong increase of the average marginal effect of alienation and indifference in comparison to the previous elections. However, even when considering this likely overestimation, there is no doubt about an increasing importance of alienation as predictor of turnout between 1998 and 2009.

In contrast, there is no clear pattern for indifference. While the effect always points in the right direction, with those seeing smaller or no differences between their two most-preferred parties, it is a significant predictor in 2005 and 2009 only. In 1998 and 2002, the nonexistent impact of the two indicators might reflect the clear polarization between the center-Right and the center-Left party camp, accompanied by increased political mobilization in those elections. Both elections provided a considerably polarized campaign that led to a very clear set of alternatives: 1998 saw a race between the long-term CDU/CSU-FDP government under Helmut Kohl and its contenders SPD and Greens under Gerhard Schröder, whose coming to power ended Helmut Kohl's sixteen years in office. The 2002 election campaign was also a polarized one, with Edmund Stoiber running for the possible CDU/CSU-FDP government against Schröder. The 2002 election led to one of the narrowest electoral results ever in Germany, with the incumbent SPD–Greens government on the winning side. For 2009, the severe influence of both alienation and indifference might be attributed to the Grand Coalition formed in 2005: The levels of indifference and alienation did not change much from 2002 to 2009, as shown above, but their impact on the individual turnout decision changed significantly. This indicates that citizens are more sensitive to the supply side of politics in more recent German elections.

Compared to the other explanatory factors in the model, indifference and alienation, if statistically significant, play an important role in predicting the probability of turnout. In 2005, alienation has the strongest (average marginal) effect of all variables in the model, while it is among the best three explanatory factors in 2009 (behind interest in politics and the perceived duty to vote). Overall, the results show that indifference and alienation matter for turnout. Alienation in particular seems to become a more important predictor of turnout over time, so that the question raised in the title can be partly answered in the affirmative. Indifference is an important feature of the elections in 2005 and 2009, indicating that it might have become more difficult for German voters to choose between their two most-preferred alternatives.[2]

Interaction Effects between Alienation and Indifference and Political Attitudes on Turnout between 1994 and 2009

The analysis that begins Section 12.4 showed that the level of alienation and indifference is dependent on certain political attitudes and sociodemographic characteristics. This subsection will illuminate whether the effects of alienation and indifference vary among different groups of the electorate. I will concentrate on just two variables and suggest interaction effects related to strength of party identification and the perceived duty to vote. These two variables were chosen because, first, as seen in the previous subsection as well as in a large set of other analyses, they are usually among the strongest predictors of turnout (e.g., Steinbrecher, Huber, and Rattinger 2007). Second, long-term developments in the level of the perceived duty to vote and party identification show a decline of these attitudes (e.g., Curtice and Park 2010; Dalton 2000; Schoen and Weins 2005: 220ff.). This means that there is a bigger group in the electorate that is no longer driven to the polls by long-term party attachments or perceived norms. Citizens who do not place high values on these two attitudes should be more likely to react to their perception of differences between political parties when considering whether to turn out or not. In contrast, for citizens with strong party attachments and strong support for the perceived duty to vote, alienation and indifference should only have a limited effect or even no impact at all on turnout. By investigating the extent of these interactions over several elections I will be able to examine whether perceptions of the supply side of politics are able to diminish the impact of both predictors. The interaction variables combining the two political attitudes with alienation and indifference result from simple multiplication of the respective variables.

Tables 12.5 and 12.6 show parts of the results of binary logistic regressions that include all variables from the model in the previous subsection and additional interaction terms between alienation (Table 12.5), indifference (Table 12.6), and only one of the two attitudes. Thus, the model is calculated separately for the respective interaction terms related to party identification

---

[2] A reason for the rise in importance of indifference may be that a higher share of voters is indifferent between parties from different ideological camps in more recent elections. While a voter who is indifferent between two parties of the same camp, e.g., CDU/CSU and FDP, might easily solve his indifference by splitting his two votes among both parties, a voter who is indifferent between CDU/CSU and SPD might be more likely to abstain. As indifference with respect to specific parties is not covered in this chapter, this might be a task for future research on the effects of indifference (and alienation) on turnout.

Are Alienation and Indifference the New Features of Elections? 277

Table 12.5 Binary logistic regressions for turnout in German Federal elections between 1994 and 2009, full model including interaction terms for alienation

Variable	1994	1998	2002	2005	2009
Strength party identification					
Alienation	−0.088[a]	−0.039	−0.053	−0.316[c]	−0.161[c]
Strength party identification	0.076[a]	0.083	0.048	−0.063	0.049
Alienation × strength party identification	0.027	−0.035	0.053	0.349[a]	0.066
Duty to vote					
Alienation	−0.154[a]	−0.055	−0.077	–	−0.284[c]
Duty to vote	0.041	0.136[a]	0.099[a]	–	0.039
Alienation × duty to vote	0.141	0.016	0.065	–	0.282[b]

Notes: Coefficients are average marginal effects, based on binary logistic regression analysis. The presented coefficients for each attitude result from separate models for the interaction between alienation and the respective attitude. Levels of significance: [a]$p < 0.05$, [b]$p < 0.01$, [c]$p < 0.001$.

and acceptance of the duty to vote. Note that I do not present the entire results, but limit the tables to the average marginal effects of alienation, indifference, the respective attitude, and the interaction terms. As coefficients in both tables do only provide a limited amount of information on extent and significance of interaction effects, I also present a number of graphs to visualize the effect of alienation and indifference at different levels of strength of party identification and the perceived duty to vote.

The average marginal effect coefficients in Table 12.5 show that, with the exception of 1998 for party identification, a strong party identification or strong support for the perceived duty to vote clearly can compensate for the negative effects of alienation on turnout. This means that at least for a limited number of voters who show a specific combination of alienation and political attitudes, alienation does not have a strong negative effect or no effect at all on electoral participation. Figure 12.1 provides further evidence for this finding by displaying predicted probabilities for turnout at different levels of alienation and strength of party identification.[3] The graphs clearly show that people without an attachment to a party are much more likely to stay at home on election day if they are highly alienated. This effect is particularly pronounced in 2005 and 2009 and might indicate the simultaneous consequences of partisan

---

[3] The other variables in the model are set to their respective mode, median, or mean.

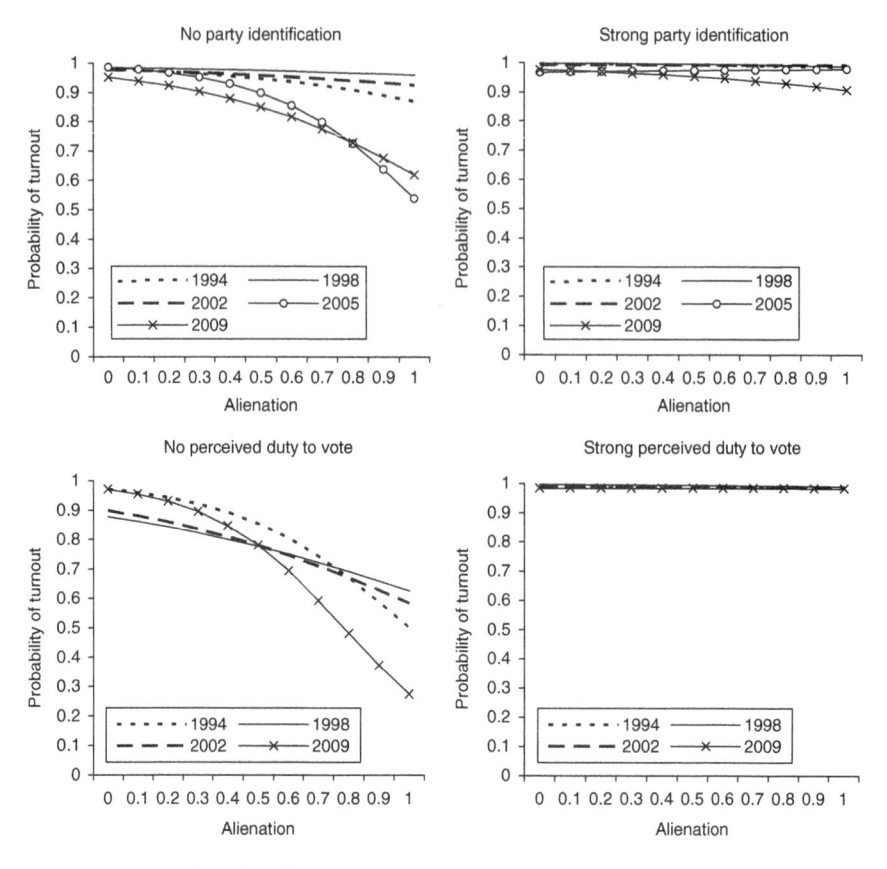

Figure 12.1 Predicted probabilities of turnout for the effect of alienation at different levels of strength of party identification and perceived duty to vote

dealignment and disenchantment with political parties in Germany. Very similar results can be reported for the interaction between duty to vote and alienation: The lack of a perceived duty to vote among some voters clearly offers more room for alienation to keep citizens away from the voting booth, particularly in 2009.

The results for indifference in Table 12.6 are less coherent than those for alienation and thus do not provide consistent evidence for the hypotheses on compensational effects. In general, this means that the interaction between the two attitudes and indifference is dependent to a much higher level on the context of every election. This is also reflected by the graphs in Figure 12.2. For those with a strong party identification and strong support for the duty to vote it does not make a difference at all whether they are indifferent or not on the probability of their showing up at the polls. Among those voters with low values of the respective attitudes, the effects are much less pronounced for indifference compared to those for alienation, if they point in the right direction at all.

Are Alienation and Indifference the New Features of Elections? 279

Table 12.6 Binary logistic regressions for turnout in German Federal elections between 1994 and 2009, full model including interaction terms for indifference

Variable	1994	1998	2002	2005	2009
Strength party identification					
Indifference	−0.120[b]	−0.075	−0.048	−0.040	−0.088[b]
Strength party identification	−0.053	0.052	0.101	0.303[b]	0.005
Indifference × strength party id	0.179[a]	0.013	−0.030	−0.205	0.097
Duty to vote					
Indifference	−0.019	−0.083	0.003	–	−0.037
Duty to vote	0.212[b]	0.126	0.227	–	0.241[c]
Indifference × duty to vote	−0.102	0.023	−0.102	–	−0.045

Notes: Coefficients are average marginal effects, based on binary logistic regression analysis. The presented coefficients for each attitude result from separate models for the interaction between indifference and the respective attitude. Levels of significance: [a]$p < 0.05$, [b]$p < 0.01$, [c]$p < 0.001$.

All in all, these results lead to the conclusion that indifference does not systematically interact with the two selected political attitudes in models for turnout. The lack of consistency clearly shows that indifference as well as this perception of the party system, in combination with party identification or the perceived duty to vote, work differently in every election. Compared to indifference, the results with respect to alienation are much more consistent. High levels of alienation can have a strong impact on turnout if a citizen does not identify with a party or does not accept the citizen duty. As this effect seems to be stronger in the most recent elections of 2005 and 2009 further dealignment or erosion of support for civic norms might lead to even lower levels of turnout in future Federal elections in Germany.

The Impact of Alienation and Indifference on Individual Changes in Turnout between 1994 and 2009

Until now, this chapter has only looked at single elections from a cross-sectional perspective. This subsection will focus on individual changes in turnout from one election to the next by using the fourfold typology introduced previously. These analyses will compare selected types of voters from this typology and have a look at the role that alienation and indifference play in differentiating these types. Table 12.7 presents average marginal effects for alienation and indifference. These

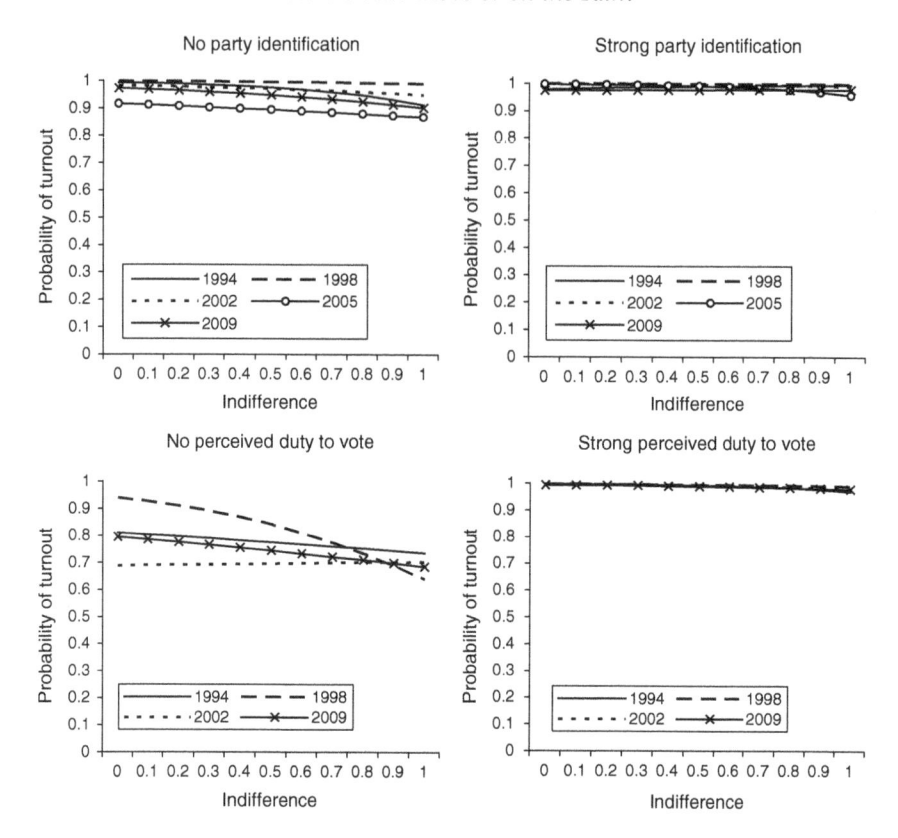

Figure 12.2 Predicted probabilities of turnout for the effect of indifference at different levels of strength of party identification and perceived duty to vote

results are based on multinomial logistic regressions whose entire results can be found in the Appendix (Table 12.9). The baseline category is those respondents who participated both in the current and the previous Federal election. The average marginal effects thus show whether and, if yes, how strongly nonvoters in one of the two or in both elections differ from voters in both elections.

By and large the results in Table 12.7 indicate that alienation and indifference are not very good in explaining changes in participatory behavior from one election to the next. With two significant coefficients for indifference compared to three significant effects for alienation, alienation once again seems to be the slightly more important predictor of turnout. Nonvoters in both elections show both a higher level of alienation and indifference than those respondents who have reported electoral participation in both consecutive elections. Comparisons between other voter types and voters in both elections reveal partly consistent, but mainly insignificant effects: Higher levels of alienation and indifference increase the likelihood of being a voter in the

Are Alienation and Indifference the New Features of Elections?   281

Table 12.7 Multinomial logistic regressions for turnout behavior in two consecutive German Federal elections between 1990 and 2009

	Nonvoter currently + previously	Nonvoter currently, but voter previously	Voter currently, but nonvoter previously
Alienation			
1990/1994	0.109[c]	0.011	−0.034
1994/1998	0.006	0.031	0.017
1998/2002	0.031	0.012	−0.024
2005/2009	0.056[b]	0.086[b]	−0.074
Indifference			
1990/1994	0.064[b]	0.012	0.031
1994/1998	0.022	0.035	0.033
1998/2002	0.046	0.042	0.022
2005/2009	0.057[a]	0.021	−0.057

Notes: Coefficients are average marginal effects; unstandardized multinomial logistic regression coefficients and robust standard errors can be found in Table 12.9 in the Appendix. Baseline category: Voters in previous and current election. Levels of significance: [a]$p < 0.05$, [b]$p < 0.01$, [c]$p < 0.001$.

previous and a nonvoter in the current election, in contrast to being a voter in both elections, confirming my expectations. Those who did not vote in the previous election but voted in the current election seem to be less alienated than the citizens in the reference group. However, interestingly, respondents in this group tend to be more indifferent than voters in both elections at hand. This is only a limited confirmation of my hypotheses and overall does not help to answer the question in the title of this chapter.[4]

12.5 CONCLUSION AND DISCUSSION

The goal of this chapter was to answer the question whether alienation and indifference are the new features of elections and play an important role in the

---

[4] As the models try to explain a dependent variable reflecting changing behavior from one election to the next with cross-sectional information, it does not come as a big surprise that the results deliver only limited evidence in support of the hypotheses.

explanation of electoral abstention in Germany in more recent elections. I first had a look at the development of alienation and indifference in the whole electorate and correlations of both indicators with political attitudes and sociodemographic characteristics. The general level of alienation and indifference does not vary much over the five elections. Thus, there is no trend towards more alienation or indifference in general and there is obviously no strong impact of the context and the events around a particular election on both indicators. However, certain political attitudes do influence the level of alienation and indifference. Citizens with high interest in politics, high levels of efficacy, high acceptance of the perceived duty to vote, high satisfaction with democracy, and a strong party identification either show much lower levels of alienation or indifference or are both less alienated and indifferent.

The multivariate analyses revealed the expected results. Citizens who feel more alienated and indifferent have a lower likelihood to participate in one of the German Federal elections between 1994 and 2009. Overall, the results show that indifference and alienation matter for the explanation of turnout even when powerful predictors of turnout are part of the analysis. This is a finding that clearly differs from the results of previous analyses of elections in Germany (Aarts, Semetko, and Weßels 2005b; Behnke 2000; Klein 2002; Thurner and Eymann 2000). As these contributions mainly focus on earlier Federal elections than this chapter, this finding might indicate that alienation and indifference indeed are becoming more important features of elections in Germany. Alienation in particular has become a more important predictor of turnout over time, so that the question raised in the title can be partly answered with a yes. Indifference is an important feature of the elections in 2005 and 2009. Hence, indifference and alienation matter for turnout, especially in the more recent elections. Electoral research on Germany (and beyond) has to include both concepts in analyses of turnout in order to provide a full picture of the influences that lead to a decision for or against electoral participation in (Federal) elections.

The subsequent analysis on interaction effects between indifference and alienation on the one hand and strength of party identification and the perceived duty to vote on the other did not provide coherent results with respect to indifference. Different combinations of attitudes and indifference matter differently, if at all, in the five elections analysed here. The lack of consistency clearly shows that indifference itself, as well as its combination with political attitudes, works differently in every election. Having in mind the contextual variations of all Federal elections between 1994 and 2009 with respect to party positions, government coalitions, coalition options, campaigning, and events, it is rather convincing not to find consistent interaction effects. This result just reflects the heterogeneity of the five elections. Future analyses hence have to take into account contextual variations and probably should conduct

Are Alienation and Indifference the New Features of Elections? 283

multilevel analyses that combine individual survey data and macrolevel information. The story for interaction effects related to alienation is different. The analyses revealed that the level of alienation clearly matters among those voters who do not identify with a party and who do not support the citizen duty. This result is most pronounced in the elections of 2005 and 2009 and thus might have contributed to the low participation rates in both elections to a limited extent. With respect to future elections, further dealignment and erosion of societal norms, in combination with a higher share of alienated citizens or higher levels of alienation among a larger number of citizens, might lead to even lower levels of turnout in Germany.

Unfortunately, it was not possible to analyse changes in individual turnout behavior over several elections with panel data. To get an idea of the possible impact of alienation and indifference on changes in turnout behavior I combined turnout in two consecutive elections in a fourfold typology. These analyses showed that alienation and indifference are not very good in explaining changes in participatory behavior from one election to the next. Only voters and nonvoters in both elections do almost always differ significantly with respect to alienation and indifference. Nonvoters in both elections are more alienated and indifferent than voters in both elections.

All in all, I am not able to provide a distinct answer to the question in the title of this chapter. However, the analyses made clear that alienation and indifference matter, and alienation in particular seems to have become a more important feature of turnout in recent Federal elections in Germany. The impossibility of presenting a clear answer might be related to some of the shortcomings of my analysis: Only five Federal elections have been analysed in this chapter. A comprehensive approach would require an addition of more Federal elections and an inclusion of other electoral levels. The presented analysis also could not provide information on intra-individual changes of alienation, indifference, turnout, and their interrelation due to the lack of a sufficient number of nonvoters in the available long-term panel surveys. Another critical point may be my operationalization of alienation and indifference. Obviously there is a host of alternative measures for both concepts. However, exploratory analyses with dichotomous or other graded measures not presented in this chapter showed very similar results with respect to the development of the level of alienation and indifference, as well as their impact on turnout in the multivariate models for the Federal elections between 1994 and 2009. Future analyses of turnout should include alienation and indifference as standard predictors. In addition, electoral researchers should also try to gain deeper insights into the causal mechanisms behind alienation and indifference, e.g., by focusing on context factors like "objective" party positions based on party programs to see whether parties become more similar and voters react accordingly with respect to their perceptions and their political behavior.

Appendix

Table 12.8 Binary logistic regressions for turnout in German Federal elections between 1994 and 2009, full model

Variable	1994	1998	2002	2005	2009
Alienation	−1.889[a]	−1.233	−1.077	−2.956[c]	−2.280[c]
	(0.784)	(1.011)	(0.987)	(0.643)	(0.550)
Indifference	−1.524	−1.876	−1.317	−1.393[a]	−0.927[a]
	(0.806)	(1.148)	(0.766)	(0.547)	(0.431)
Male	−0.232	−0.394	0.050	−0.142	−0.264
	(0.219)	(0.263)	(0.264)	(0.185)	(0.148)
Age	0.071[a]	0.113[b]	0.111[a]	0.093[c]	0.079[c]
	(0.034)	(0.037)	(0.045)	(0.026)	(0.022)
Age squared	−0.0007	−0.001[b]	−0.0009[a]	−0.0008[b]	−0.0007[b]
	(0.0003)	(0.0004)	(0.0004)	(0.0002)	(0.0002)
Education	0.152	−0.299	1.011[a]	1.092[c]	0.087
	(0.311)	(0.465)	(0.464)	(0.300)	(0.242)
East	−0.348	0.725[a]	0.057	−0.273	0.356[a]
	(0.218)	(0.285)	(0.255)	(0.199)	(0.147)
Strength party identification	2.126[c]	1.664[c]	1.817[c]	1.606[c]	1.339[c]
	(0.369)	(0.459)	(0.474)	(0.275)	(0.242)
Interest in politics	2.271[c]	1.746[a]	1.484	2.097[c]	3.491[c]
	(0.489)	(0.703)	(0.758)	(0.472)	(0.393)
Satisfaction with democracy	1.312[b]	0.754	0.726	0.554	1.070[b]
	(0.490)	(0.585)	(0.547)	(0.344)	(0.324)
External efficacy	−0.159	1.449[a]	0.909	1.327[b]	1.809[c]
	(0.485)	(0.633)	(0.595)	(0.416)	(0.377)
Internal efficacy	0.573	0.292	0.100	0.257	0.784[b]
	(0.465)	(0.479)	(0.741)	(0.387)	(0.239)
Duty to vote	2.830[c]	3.849[c]	3.291[c]	–	3.145[c]
	(0.302)	(0.355)	(0.446)		(0.228)
Constant	−0.919	−2.034	−2.991	−0.368	−2.891[c]
	(1.289)	(1.612)	(1.553)	(0.935)	(0.771)
Nagelkerke's R^2	0.375	0.363	0.373	0.298	0.550
N	2974	2813	2620	2300	3652

Notes: Unstandardized logistic regression coefficients, robust standard errors in parentheses. Levels of significance: [a] $p < 0.05$, [b] $p < 0.01$, [c] $p < 0.001$.

Table 12.9 Multinomial logistic regressions for turnout behavior in two consecutive German Federal elections between 1990 and 2009

Variable	1990/1994 −/−	1990/1994 +/−	1990/1994 −/+	1994/1998 −/−	1994/1998 +/−	1994/1998 −/+	1998/2002 −/−	1998/2002 +/−	1998/2002 −/+	2005/2009 −/−	2005/2009 +/−	2005/2009 −/+
Alienation	4.465[c] (1.105)	1.061 (1.188)	−0.439 (1.273)	0.848 (1.730)	1.759 (1.089)	0.582 (1.026)	1.949 (1.330)	0.789 (1.392)	−0.389 (1.158)	1.954[b] (0.688)	2.430[b] (0.737)	−0.940 (0.587)
Indifference	2.830[b] (0.976)	0.966 (1.140)	1.058 (0.833)	2.179 (2.198)	2.210 (1.354)	1.092 (0.812)	3.278 (1.989)	1.581 (1.021)	0.894 (0.814)	1.415[a] (0.624)	0.363 (0.531)	−0.857 (0.498)
Male	−0.088 (0.330)	0.214 (0.320)	−0.316 (0.293)	0.669 (0.502)	0.613 (0.319)	0.084 (0.251)	−0.048 (0.402)	0.050 (0.385)	−0.061 (0.273)	0.446[a] (0.195)	0.429[a] (0.207)	0.586[b] (0.170)
Age	−0.070 (0.060)	0.001 (0.052)	−0.143[b] (0.052)	−0.258[c] (0.066)	−0.126[a] (0.056)	−0.113[a] (0.052)	−0.269[c] (0.067)	−0.108 (0.070)	−0.103 (0.054)	−0.112[b] (0.038)	−0.086[a] (0.037)	−0.130[c] (0.030)
Age squared	0.0005 (0.001)	0.00004 (0.001)	0.001 (0.001)	0.002[c] (0.001)	0.001[a] (0.001)	0.0005 (0.001)	0.002[c] (0.001)	0.0007 (0.001)	0.0007 (0.001)	0.0008[a] (0.000)	0.0008[a] (0.000)	0.0009[b] (0.000)
Education	−0.070 (0.469)	0.134 (0.366)	0.130 (0.413)	0.733 (1.083)	0.137 (0.519)	−0.124 (0.339)	−0.578 (0.626)	−1.202 (0.739)	0.064 (0.396)	0.251 (0.320)	−0.377 (0.366)	−0.588[a] (0.247)
East	−0.375 (0.323)	0.949[a] (0.369)	−0.224 (0.244)	−0.923[a] (0.469)	−0.823[a] (0.373)	−0.321[a] (0.256)	−0.504 (0.437)	0.291 (0.369)	−0.270 (0.267)	−0.226 (0.201)	−0.665[b] (0.209)	0.150 (0.172)
Strength party identification	−3.418[c] (0.681)	−1.902[c] (0.541)	−1.776[c] (0.479)	−2.610[b] (0.993)	−1.699[b] (0.507)	−1.972[c] (0.419)	−3.347[c] (0.874)	−1.251 (0.687)	−1.890[c] (0.461)	−2.435[c] (0.396)	−1.069[b] (0.317)	−1.188[c] (0.247)
Interest in politics	−2.152[b] (0.796)	−1.733[b] (0.577)	0.038 (0.596)	−1.654 (1.669)	−1.587[a] (0.682)	−0.937 (0.642)	−3.187[b] (1.216)	−0.936 (1.124)	−1.206 (0.634)	−5.064[c] (0.506)	−3.065[c] (0.553)	−1.330[b] (0.411)
Satisfaction with democracy	−0.130 (0.695)	−2.137[b] (0.685)	−0.229 (0.622)	−2.199[a] (1.063)	−1.115 (0.691)	−1.231[a] (0.563)	−1.637 (0.937)	−1.032 (0.767)	−1.055 (0.586)	−1.594[c] (0.427)	−1.316[b] (0.443)	−0.297 (0.344)

(Continued)

Table 12.9 Continued

Variable	1990/1994 −/−	1990/1994 +/−	1990/1994 −/+	1994/1998 −/−	1994/1998 +/−	1994/1998 −/+	1998/2002 −/−	1998/2002 +/−	1998/2002 −/+	2005/2009 −/−	2005/2009 +/−	2005/2009 −/+
External efficacy	0.248 (0.565)	−0.092 (0.757)	−0.259 (0.559)	−2.919[a] (1.062)	−0.504 (0.885)	−0.022 (0.565)	−1.222 (0.897)	−0.759 (0.941)	−0.615 (0.665)	−2.743[c] (0.583)	−1.275[a] (0.532)	−0.855[a] (0.363)
Internal efficacy	−1.196 (0.676)	−1.027 (0.599)	−1.087 (0.596)	−1.620 (0.922)	0.462 (0.705)	−0.120 (0.505)	−0.203 (1.028)	0.461 (1.036)	−0.266 (0.712)	−1.351[c] (0.325)	−0.473 (0.322)	−0.409 (0.291)
Duty to vote	−3.486[c] (0.437)	−2.454[c] (0.404)	−1.325[b] (0.390)	−4.740[c] (0.507)	−4.260[c] (0.540)	−1.178[a] (0.484)	−4.077[c] (0.579)	−3.776[c] (0.642)	−2.208[c] (0.459)	−4.294[c] (0.317)	−3.220[c] (0.311)	−2.242[c] (0.273)
Constant	−1.498 (2.104)	−0.642 (1.678)	3.002 (1.732)	7.053[a] (2.799)	1.044 (2.282)	2.466 (1.477)	5.450[a] (2.521)	2.292 (2.396)	3.450[a] (1.754)	5.171[c] (1.274)	2.578[a] (1.186)	5.739[c] (0.970)
Nagelkerke's R^2	0.361			0.337			0.339			0.498		
N	2695			2524			2328			3372		

Notes: Unstandardized multinomial logistic regression coefficients, robust standard errors in parentheses. Baseline category: Voters currently + previously (+/+). −/−: Nonvoter currently + previously, +/−: Voter currently, but nonvoter previously, −/+: Voter currently, but voter previously. Levels of significance: [a] $p < 0.05$, [b] $p < 0.01$, [c] $p < 0.001$.

13

Volatility on the Rise? Attitudinal Stability, Attitudinal Change, and Voter Volatility

Hans Rattinger and Elena Wiegand

13.1 INTRODUCTION

Reviewing the classic literature of voting behavior, one finds that early studies have shown that vote choice is quite stable over the course of an election campaign (Lazarsfeld, Berelson, and Gaudet 1944; Berelson, Lazarsfeld, and McPhee 1955). Moreover, some of these studies have reported a considerable stability of vote preference and partisan attitudes between elections (Campbell et al. 1960a; Converse 1962). However, besides the growing complexity and heterogeneity of vote decisions (see Part II of this book), an increase of electoral volatility can be observed in many democracies over the past decades (e.g., Dalton, McAllister, and Wattenberg 2000: 41; Mair 2002). Against this background this chapter is designed to shed light on the volatility of voting behavior using panel data.

On the basis of official aggregate election results one can describe the long-term trends of electoral volatility and stability in Germany, respectively. Figure 13.1 presents the patterns of aggregate volatility in Federal elections since the Second World War. Using the index of volatility V, proposed by Pedersen (1979), the highest levels of volatility can be observed during the formative phase of the postwar German party system. Similar developments appear during the transformation in East Germany after 1989 as well. After the establishment of new parties and a phase of shakedown, volatility decreased to a very low level until 1980. Because of the emergence of the Green Party in the 1980s there was a small rise in volatility, and from then onward one can observe a slow upward trend. If one includes abstention from voting in the definition of electoral instability, one can naturally detect a somewhat higher degree of

288   *Voters on the Move or on the Run?*

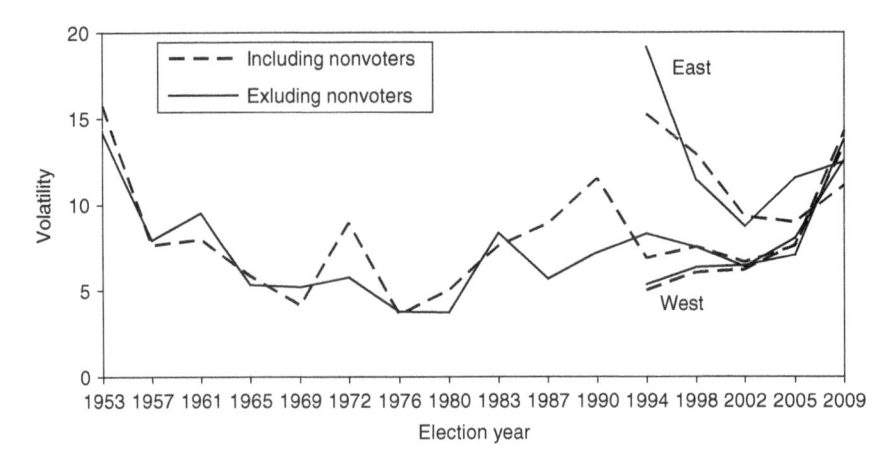

Figure 13.1 Pattern of aggregate volatility in Federal elections in Germany, 1953–2009

volatility. Then, with the last Federal election of 2009, volatility has taken a remarkable upward turn. This can be observed both in East and West Germany.

The amount of electoral volatility may change over time due to differences in the electoral supply as well as due to shifts of voters' preferences on the demand side. Increasing fragmentation of the party system, i.e., a higher number of political parties competing in each election, can be one reason for an increase of electoral volatility (e.g., Pedersen 1983: 47; Bartolini and Mair 1990: 130). Because of party splits and the emergence of new political parties, more suppliers compete for vote shares. On the voters' side, changes in the presence and stability of party attachments and in political preferences as a consequence of modernization processes, i.e. decreasing politicization of the social structure and educational expansion, may lead to higher volatility of voting behavior. This chapter does *not* address the supply side, but concentrates on demand-driven individual volatility over the longer and shorter run and seeks to clarify which properties of voters are associated with vote switching.

In aggregate analyses dealignment is often quoted as one of the prime causes for a rise in electoral volatility (Dalton, McAllister, and Wattenberg 2000: 38ff.; Dalton and Rohrschneider 1990). The process of social modernization according to this argument leads to the erosion of partisan attachments which, in turn, makes it more likely that voters will defect from their partisan affiliation in their voting and makes it less likely that a person will possess such a partisan affiliation that would stabilize voting behavior in the first place. As aggregate data[1] tell us very little about stability or instability at the individual

---

[1] Aggregate data can only give us an impression of the *minimum* change that had to occur at the individual level in order to produce the observed outcome. The overall shifts of voters between parties can be much greater than the minimum net change of party votes reported in Figure 13.1.

level, it is necessary to complement the existing aggregate studies of electoral volatility by analyses at the individual level. The logic behind the dealignment argument is applicable to individual voters only to a limited degree. It would predict, e.g., that people with higher education will have a lower probability of being partisans and, if they are, that the strength of their attachment will be lower, thus making them more prone to vote switching. Recent research, however, does not support the social modernization hypothesis in Germany. High education does not consistently lead to weaker partisan attachments (Berglund et al. 2005: 112f.). Furthermore, individuals with higher cognitive skills are not more likely to be independents than less educated individuals (Zelle 1995b: 327). Whatever the mechanisms underlying the process of a decrease in partisanship are, the proportion of partisans within the electorate has indeed declined slowly (Falter and Schoen 1999: 465–7). This implies the possibility of an increase in volatility. If fewer people within the electorate have long-standing partisan attachments, their vote choice might become more flexible between elections and throughout election campaigns.

This chapter describes and analyses the German electorate in terms of long-term and short-term individual stability and change. What proportion of voters has changed their minds once or more during an election campaign, as well as between subsequent Federal elections and why? As the title of this chapter suggests, we want to investigate how attitudinal stability and change do affect voter volatility and answer the question, to what extent vote switches in the shorter and in the longer run are brought about by political predispositions and attitudes. This program will be pursued as follows: First, classical explanations of voting behavior and potential determinants of stability and change will be discussed. Following this theoretical introduction, a short section will describe the data used here and the measurement of theoretical constructs. The next part of the chapter is devoted to assessing the amount of individual instability in a long-term perspective, i.e., over the course of full legislative terms. This section will describe stability and volatility over the longer run and evaluate its determinants. We will then in a parallel way turn to individual volatility over the course of an election campaign. The chapter concludes with a summary of our main findings and some suggestions for further research.

13.2 EXPLAINING INDIVIDUAL-LEVEL VOLATILITY

Besides changes in the electorate through demographic turnover, it is swing voters who can bring about a shift of power from one election to the next. To revise a previous vote decision means a loss for one party and a gain for another one. Swing voters thus are key actors for changing political power, and political parties try to attract them during election campaigns. While some studies equate swing voting only with party switching and disregard that people can also (occasionally) stay away from elections (Kaase 1967: 71–84; Zelle 1995a: 97–9; Schoen and Falter 2001: 59), our analyses include *all* possible forms of switching. As a simple distinction between stable and swing voters is not sufficient, we will furthermore distinguish here between different types of vote switching. As Germany now has a multiparty system which largely can be grouped into two ideologically opposed camps, voters can switch between parties belonging to one ideological camp, but also between parties of different such camps. The latter change might have to cross a higher psychological barrier than the first one, the question still is: Why do some voters change their mind, while others do not? In this section we will now briefly discuss how some early studies of electoral behavior have attempted to explain swing voting.

As mentioned in the introduction, the decline of voters with party affiliations might affect the stability of voting behavior. The Michigan model (Campbell et al. 1960a) combines party identification with short-term factors in a theoretical framework and thus is adequate to try to explain volatility at the individual level. This model does not primarily focus on swing voting, but one can use it to deduce assumptions about potential causes for vote switching. In its simplest form, this model traces vote decisions back to an interaction between stable long-term party loyalties and short-term variables, such as attitudes towards candidates and political issues, in the idea of a "funnel of causality" (Campbell et al. 1960a: 24). Party identification is assumed to be acquired in early life through parental socialization and should remain stable throughout voters' lifetime (e.g., Campbell et al. 1960a; Converse 1964). Because party identification is viewed as a central organizing force for political attitudes and information, an absence of it could lead to instability of political views and to volatility of party choice. In contrast, partisans, and especially strong partisans, are more likely to exhibit stable voting behavior than politically independent individuals. Thus, we assume that the stronger the party identification is, the lower is the likelihood of vote switching (H1).

But the assumption about stability of partisanship, as suggested in the Michigan model, is not necessarily correct for all citizens. Fiorina (1981) was among the first to propose that party identification might be open to change as voters receive new information, update their evaluations, and reconsider their attachment. So there is an ongoing discussion about its stability and change, with two competing views of stable against moveable partisans. As recent research suggests, both types of partisans, movers and stayers, might exist in Germany as well (Neuendorf, Stegmueller, and Scotto 2011). Some voters can move from one party to another or to independence (or back) because they are dissatisfied or have been influenced by events to update their beliefs about "their" party and its performance. However, we are not concerned here with investigating which mechanisms might lead to volatility of partisanship.

Instead, we will examine the effects of changing partisan affiliations on vote switching.[2] As argued earlier, just like a lack of partisan attachment, a change of party loyalty should contribute to higher instability of the vote decision. Switching party identification between parties might not occur frequently, but if partisan feelings have altered, the vote choice should adapt to this new situation. Swing voting should therefore occur more often among those who have changed or abandoned their partisan attachment (H2).

In addition, party affiliation also is generally supposed to influence the short-term factors contributing to the vote decision. Citizens with partisan attachments tend to receive and accept political information from trusted sources and to reject countervailing messages (Zaller 2004). But it is still possible that short-term preferences are not in line with one's party identification. If attitudes on issues or considerations about the candidates are not consistent with partisan attachments, this should create psychological dissonance within the individual (Campbell et al. 1960a: 80; Lazarsfeld, Bereslon, and Gaudet 1944: 60f.). Persons who have such conflicting considerations should be more likely to switch their vote decision than those with entirely consistent partisan attitudes (H3). If an individual feels attached to the Social Democrats, e.g., but considers the Christian Democrats as the party currently most qualified to solve the nation's important problems, he or she may diverge temporarily from his/her usual vote decision.

The same is true for conflicts regarding attitudes about performance. Besides the effect of long-term partisan attachments on vote decisions, considerations about issue competence are assumed to have a strong influence on voting behavior (cf. Schoen und Falter 2001: 65). The likelihood of swing voting should thus be higher if an individual has conflicting judgments about the parties' qualification for solving the most important societal problems. We expect, therfore, that swing voting should occur more frequently among those who have inconsistent attitudes about political issues (H4).

Vote switching is a dynamic process. Even if partisan attitudes are consistent at a particular point in time they can change over time and therefore cause switching of vote decisions. Individuals may, e.g., vote for different parties in two subsequent elections because they have altered their candidate preference. One can propose a parallel hypothesis for attitudes about the ability of parties to solve the most important issues (as stressed by Schoen and Falter 2001). Such performance-based considerations can also be changed over the entire course of a legislative term or during the few weeks or months prior to an election. Regarding different types of vote switching, changes in attitudes on issues

---

[2] The authors are aware of the problem of endogeneity. Despite disputes about the directional link between party identification and the vote in some European countries and the capability of being differentiated (see Thomassen and Rosema 2009) we expect to observe that vote switching goes hand in hand with changes in party identification.

can help to explain all possible switches between parties because individuals can consider each party as qualified for solving the most important problems for the country. Changing attitudes towards Chancellor candidates, on the other hand, can only explain changes between party camps because usually just the two major mass parties, the Christian and the Social Democrats, present candidates for Chancellor. Taking all of this together we expect that individuals who have changed their attitudes toward candidates (H5) or issues (H6) are more likely to switch their vote than individuals who did not do so, and that there should be systematic differences in these effects on within versus between party camp volatility.

We will assess the impact of these hypothesized effects on stability and change of the vote within two analytical perspectives. As mentioned in the introduction, we are interested both in longitudinal vote switching between successive elections and in individual short-term preference volatility during electoral campaigns. Due to the new kind of data available from a recent short-term campaign panel, stability and change of voting over the course of an election campaign can now also be monitored. The explanation of preference changes during the campaign should not differ systematically from the arguments just presented. Strong partisans should also remain more constant in their vote intentions over the course of an election campaign, and attitude inconsistencies as well as changes due to new information delivered during the campaign should make short-term vote switches more likely. But because every election is characterized by specific circumstances, such as political scandals, specific issues, international events etc., the importance of short-term factors on vote switching can differ from election to election and from week to week during an election campaign (Kellermann 2008: 292). It is well conceivable that some effects might weaken, whereas others increase over the course of electoral campaigning. Since there is no general theoretical rationale why some predictors should change in their explanatory power we cannot make assumptions about the over-time development of their effects. In the next section we will now, prior to entering into the analyses, present the data used for testing our hypotheses and the operational definitions for the theoretical concepts.

13.3 DATA AND MEASUREMENT

Below we will report two sets of analyses that explore, first, long-term volatility between the three Federal elections of 2002 through 2009 and, second, short-term volatility over the election campaign of 2009. Therefore, this research is based on two different data sets, i.e., on the one hand, the GLES face-to-face long-term panel from 2002 to 2009 and, on the other hand, the seven-wave web-based GLES campaign panel 2009. The latter consists of six preelection waves and one postelection wave. A total of 1,462 individuals took part in all these seven waves. In the long-term panel, 829 respondents participated both in 2002 and 2005; 436 respondents were interviewed in all three waves. Both data sets are weighted according to social structural variables and panel attrition in all subsequent analyses. While Section 13.4 relies on the data of the GLES long-term panel, the analyses presented in Section 13.5 draw on the short-term campaign panel.

Due to the panel design, the measurement of swing voting is not based on (inherently unreliable) recall questions. The strength of the data at hand is that we can identify swing voters by their self-reported voting behavior in every Federal election year, and not by asking them to remember their previous vote choice. We have constructed four different types of swing voting as dependent (dummy) variables, as indicated in the previous section. First, there is a variable which includes all possible change, whether it is party switching or to/from nonvoting. In order to determine the motivation for party switches, a second dependent variable captures vote switching which occurred only between parties. Because switches between certain parties have different political consequences and Germany now has a multiparty system, which largely can be divided into two ideologically opposed camps, we have, thirdly, constructed a variable which identifies changes only *within* a camp, i.e., if a voter changes between the Social Democratic Party to the Left or the Greens or between the Liberals and the Christian Democrats.[3] The fourth indicator gauges switching *between* these Left and Right camps, e.g., from the Liberals to the Greens. As these four dependent variables all are dichotomous, we are going to estimate binary logistic regression models to identify determinants of these various types of individual swing voting.

Before starting with our analyses, we still have to clarify how the explanatory variables were operationalized. As argued in the theoretical part of this chapter, the strength of party identification and its volatility should affect the stability of the vote decision. We have therefore constructed an indicator for respondents' strength of party identification by rescaling responses into a five-point scale, ranging from zero to one, where zero means no party identification at all and one a very strong party identification (for question wording and coding details see the Appendix). In order to gauge the impact of partisan instability, inconsistence between party identification and attitudes on issues as well as of attitudinal inconsistency and change, we generated variables ranging from −1 via 0 to +1 (cf., Schoen and Falter 2001: 75). While minus one stands for consistency or stability of these concepts, plus one is assigned to respondents who

---

[3] Because the Pirate Party is quite new, their ideological position is not yet very clear and they cannot be easily grouped into one of these camps. We therefore exclude vote switches from or to this party.

exhibit inconsistent attitudes or have changed their minds compared to the previous measurement. Located in the middle of this continuum, at zero, are those individuals who are indifferent or have switched between substantially relevant answers and indifference or refusal and vice versa.

13.4 LONG-TERM VOLATILITY 2002–2009

This section will now present the results of the empirical analyses about longitudinal volatility between two subsequent elections. The second step of the analysis will concentrate on individual volatility in the shorter run and its determinants (Section 13.5).

Starting with a classification of overall vote switches from 2002 to 2009, Table 13.1 shows how often different votes were cast. To take a look at the development of voters' volatility, this table also presents stability and change between previous Federal elections as captured by earlier three-wave panel surveys from 1994 to 2002 and 1998 to 2005. We here distinguish between six voter types (cf. Rattinger 2007: 45). The first type is very rare and comprises people who have not voted at all in three subsequent Federal elections or have not given an answer as to their vote in every panel wave.[4] Only 1% of all respondents in the panels starting in 1994 and 2002 and around 2% of the participants in the panel beginning 1998 belong to that group. The second voter type accounts for about one-third in all these long-term panels and consists of individuals who remain perfectly stable over all three waves. Type three is also loyal to only one party, but these people refuse to respond or have abstained in one election. Taking voter types two and three together, these people are the core voters for only one party (even if some of them do not always turn out) and comprise almost one-half of the samples. Types four to six are swing voters. While swing voters belonging to the fourth type switch between two parties in three successive elections, types five and six contain voters who swing between two parties and refusal or nonvoting, or even between three parties, respectively. Taken together, approximately one half of each sample has changed their party choice at least once over those two legislative terms. We cannot say that there is a tremendous rise of individual volatility over these fifteen years, but longitudinal swing voting is obviously by no means a rare phenomenon, and that is why we now have a look at the properties of stable and swing voters. As outlined in the theoretical section, we want to investigate whether strong and stable party attachments reduce the likelihood of swing

---

[4] The authors are aware that nonvoting might be different from refusal, but these subcategories are very small in absolute size and that is why it is not meaningful to treat them separately.

Volatility on the Rise? 295

Table 13.1 Classification of voter stability and change across German long-term panels 1994 to 2009

Types	1994–1998–2002 %	N	1998–2002–2005 %	N	2002–2005–2009 %	N
1 Always VA/DK/NA	1.7	24	2.2	15	1.2	5
2 Always one party	32.5	462	37.1	256	34.5	150
3 Switching between one party and VA/DK/NA	20.8	296	17.8	123	13.9	61
4 Switching between only two parties	27.0	383	28.8	199	35.2	153
5 Switching between two parties and VA/DK/NA	11.3	161	9.7	67	7.7	33
6 Switching between three parties	6.7	95	4.3	30	7.6	33

Notes: Entries are column percentages. VA: vote abstention; DK: don't know; NA: no answer.
Sources: ZA4301, ZA4662, ZA5320.

voting, and whether inconsistent and changed attitudes towards candidates and issues help to explain vote switching.

To analyse the determinants of swing voting we calculate binary logistic regressions for the four different types of vote switching defined as our dependent variables in the third section of this chapter. First comes a model for all conceivable changes, no matter whether they involve only parties or refusals or nonvoting as well. We then present one model for the probability of changes only between parties and two more models for party switching only within and only between ideological party camps. The reference category for all dependent variables consists of stable voters. In order to avoid any bias resulting from unique circumstances in one election year we perform these analyses separately for both election pairs of 2002 and 2005, and 2005 and 2009, respectively.[5] The estimation results are presented in Tables 13.2 and 13.3.[6]

The data support only some of our hypotheses. The results indicate that strength and stability of party affiliation indeed are strong predictors for the stability of the vote. Strength of partisanship significantly reduces the likelihood of swing voting across each of the four models (H1). As shown in Tables 13.2 and 13.3 all of these coefficients have the expected negative sign

---

[5] The same substantial results were found by means of pooled logistic regression models, where we disregarded whether changes occurred between the first two or the last two elections.
[6] We have also examined the determinants in a stepwise fashion and have controlled for socio-structural variables like age, education, and gender, but due to no substantial effects and space constraints we only present the full models at hand.

Table 13.2 Binary logistic regressions for different types of vote switching, 2002–2005

	All switches	Switches only between parties	Switches only within party camp	Switches only between party camps
Strength of party identification 2005	−0.12	−0.29	−0.54	−0.95*
Instability of party identification 2002/2005	0.84***	0.92***	0.97***	0.88***
Inconsistence between party identification and issue competence 2005	−0.04	0.14	0.18	0.07
Inconsistent issue competence 2005	0.05	0.09	0.08	−0.02
Changed attitudes on issues 2002/2005	0.27	0.23	0.08	0.53*
Changed attitudes towards candidates 2002/2005	0.5***	0.65***	0.01	1.14***
Constant	0.58**	0.46*	−0.25	−0.37
Mc Fadden's R^2	0.09	0.14	0.09	0.26
N	827	680	577	513

Notes: Entries are logit coefficients. Significance: * $p < 0.05$; ** $p < 0.01$; *** $p < 0.00$.

and are statistically significant for changes between party camps between the Federal elections of 2002 and 2005 as well as in the first three models for 2005 and 2009. People without any party identification are much more likely to switch their vote than individuals with a strong party identification. This result is congruent with earlier findings (e.g., Zelle 1995b; Schoen and Falter 2001: 75ff.). But the strength of party identification loses some of its explanatory power if we also introduce the stability of party identification. Of course, due to multicollinearity modeling the stability of party identification together with its strength somewhat reduces the robustness of the estimates. Unstable party attachments make a parallel vote switch significantly more likely in all models for 2002–2005 and 2005–2009 (H2).

Respondents' party loyalty and its strength are predictors not of change but of stability of voting. On the other hand, consistent with previous research we find evidence that changing attitudes towards candidates for Chancellor are associated with a greater likelihood of swing voting. Our findings imply that individuals who have changed their mind about the Chancellor candidates are more likely to become swing voters (H5). With the exception of the regression model for vote switching within a party camp, all coefficients of changed attitudes towards the candidates exhibit a positive sign and are statistically

Table 13.3 Binary logistic regressions for different types of vote switching, 2005–2009

	All switches	Switches only between parties	Switches only within party camp	Switches only between party camps
Strength of party identification 2009	−1.19*	−1.53*	−1.35*	−1.49
Instability of party identification 2005/2009	1.01***	1.2***	0.73***	0.68*
Inconsistence between party identification and issue competence 2009	0.43	0.35	0.18	0.54
Inconsistent issue competence 2009	−0.21	−0.03	0.24	−0.51
Changed attitudes on issues 2005/2009	0.18	0.04	0.30	0.17
Changed attitudes towards candidates 2005/2009	0.35	0.42*	0.08	0.96***
Constant	1.06**	1.03**	0.18	−0.55
Mc Fadden's R^2	0.18	0.22	0.13	0.24
N	367	328	286	251

Notes: Entries are logit coefficients. Significance: * $p < 0.05$; ** $p < 0.01$; *** $p < 0.00$.

significant in the models for the changes from 2002 to 2005. For changes *within* a party camp we find no effects of attitudes towards candidates, which is not really surprising. Usually just the major parties of the two party camps, the Christian and the Social Democrats, present candidates for Chancellor, so voting changes within a party camp cannot be well explained by altered attitudes towards candidates. Election-specific constellations seem to play some role in explaining vote switching as well. In 2005, changed attitudes about issues had an impact on vote switches between party camps (H6). Comparing this to the other regression models, the effects of attitudes on issues are all in the expected direction, but they are not statistically significant. In 2009, changes in attitudes towards candidates make vote switching significantly more likely just in the two models for switches between individual parties and between party camps.[7] Our results generally do not support our hypotheses H3 and H4 that attitudinal inconsistencies enhance the likelihood of vote switching. The effects of inconsistent attitudes about issues and inconsistence between

---

[7] It must be noted that Angela Merkel as the CDU/CSU candidate for Chancellor has competed against the former Chancellor Gerhard Schröder (SPD) in 2005, whereas in 2009 Frank-Walter Steinmeier was her opponent as the SPD candidate for Chancellor.

party identification and issue competence are not statistically significant in any of the models for 2005 and 2009. Individuals with inconsistent attitudes do not tend to cast their vote for another party more often than individuals with consistent or indifferent attitudes on issues. Overall, the strength and stability of party identifications and attitudes towards Chancellor candidates seem to have had the strongest effects on voting stability and volatility in 2005 as well as in 2009.[8]

A final word is in order regarding model-fit. For logistic regression models there is no simple equivalent to R^2 in OLS-regression. However, several Pseudo R^2s have been developed which cannot be directly interpreted as the explained share of the variance, but higher values still suggest a better model-fit. By considering McFadden's R^2, all models have an acceptable fit. It can therefore be concluded that some reasonable explanatory variables have been identified here to better understand interelection vote stability and switching.

13.5 VOLATILITY DURING THE 2009 CAMPAIGN

Let us now turn our attention to short-term volatility. Table 13.4 presents the distribution of voters' volatility across the short-term campaign panel of 2009. As can be seen, the percentage of the total sample that in every panel wave refused to give a vote intention or mentioned not to vote is substantially higher than in the long-term panel. Over 7% of the respondents fall into that category. In contrast, however, more than 60% of the respondents have a loyal vote intention for just one party. While almost 40% mention the same party over again in all seven panel waves, over 20% combine one party with vote abstention or refusal at least once. On the other hand, we observe a lower incidence of short-term preference changes among voters. Somewhat less than one-third of the panelists switch their party preference among two or more parties over the course of the election campaign. Campaign volatility in Germany thus is markedly lower than volatility over the longer haul. This finding is not really surprising because an election campaign covers a much shorter period of time with far less opportunity for both modifications in the parties' positions and their programs as well as personnel changes than over three subsequent Federal elections. Only those voters who have not yet finally made up their minds at the beginning of the election campaign may switch

---

[8] Concerning the discussion about political sophistication and vote switching, additional regression results do not support the hypothesis of differences (Sniderman, Brody, and Tetlock 1991) by showing that better educated people or those with higher political interest do not differ in the mechanisms of swing voting than less educated people or those with lower political interest.

Table 13.4 Classification of voter stability and change across campaign panel 2009

Types	%	N
1 Always VA/DK/NA	7.6	119
2 Always one party	38.4	608
3 Switching between one party and VA/DK/NA	22.2	352
4 Switching between only two parties	14.8	234
5 Switching between two parties and VA/DK/NA	10.8	170
6 Switching between three or more parties	3.6	58
7 Switching between three or more parties and VA/DK/NA	2.6	42

Notes: Entries are column percentages. VA/DK/NA: as in Table 13.1.

Table 13.5 Number of overall switches, switches between parties and party camps

Number of Switches	All switches (incl. VA/DK/NA)	Switches only between parties	Switches only within party camp	Switches only between party camps
0	46.0	71.8	85.8	90.7
1	22.2	14.1	9.3	4.5
2	14.5	8.8	3.8	3.6
3	10.2	3.7	0.7	1.3
4	4.5	1.2	0.2	0.2
5	2.1	0.5	0.2	0.1
6	0.5	0	0	0

Notes: Entries are column percentages. VA/DK/NA: as in Table 13.1.

their vote intention in the shorter run, whereas every voter can in principle be susceptible to change in the longer run.

Due to the newly available data of the GLES 2009 campaign panel, we can take a closer look at vote switching over the course of the election campaign and investigate how often voters have changed their vote intention between parties of the same camp as well as between parties of different camps. In order to address this issue Table 13.5 contains the number of switches and their frequency. Combining all possible forms of switching, including party switches as well as shifts to and from vote abstention and refusals to reveal any preference, 46% of the respondents have never changed their mind (38.4% voted

Table 13.6 Mean number of different parties voted for by number of vote switches

Number of Switches	All switches (incl. VA/DK/NA)	Switches only between parties	Switches only within party camp	Switches only between party camps
1	1.4	2.1	2.3	1.2
2	1.8	2.3	2.2	2.5
3	2.0	2.6	2.1	2.4
4	2.3	3.0	2.2	2.9
5	2.5	2.7	2.2	2.2
6	2.2	–	–	–

Notes: Entries are mean numbers of different parties voted for. VA/DK/NA: as in Table 13.1.

always for one party and 7.6% reported always VA/DK/NA). On the other hand, over 22% of the respondents switch their vote preference once, and 32% twice or more. This frequency of vote switches may be an expression that some voters are just undecided. All in all, six preference switches would be possible between seven panel waves, but this occurs extremely rarely (only 0.5%). Taking only switches between parties into account, over 70% of the respondents never do this at all over the course of the election campaign. Most of the few respondents who have changed their vote intention across parties between or within a party camp switch their vote preference just once or, less often, twice. Not a single respondent has switched his vote intention only between parties at the maximum of six possible occasions.

To illustrate short-term electoral volatility a little further, we have calculated the average number of different parties mentioned by number of switches (see Table 13.6). Even those voters who have altered their electoral choice four times or more report only a little over two different parties on average. This implies that voters do not sway around freely during the campaign. Instead, most swing voters alternate between just two parties, irrespective of their number of switches. This can be seen in switches only within or only between party camps as well. Even those few voters who have changed their party preference five times within or between party camps have almost all only mentioned two different parties. But such high numbers of switches are extremely seldom. Considering only switches between parties, even those who have changed their mind three or more times over the course of the election campaign have, on average, named well below three parties. Most voters appear to have a limited party choice set and do not oscillate between all possible parties even if they switch their vote intention more frequently.

In addition to the overall number of vote shifts during the election campaign, one might also be interested in their timing. To assess if voters are more likely to change their vote intention at the outset of the election campaign or rather toward the end, Table 13.7 lists the various percentages of vote switching by each subsequent pair of panel waves. Vote switching from one wave to the next varies between 16% and 24%. From the first panel wave to the second, 20% of all respondents switched their vote intention. Whereas 43.5% of these shifts have occurred across parties, the remaining 56.5% involved inconclusive responses or non-voting. Looking just at the first group of switches only between parties, 43.7% did occur within a party camp, and 40.2% between party camps. The remaining 16% involved other parties or the Pirate Party that cannot yet be readily assigned to one ideological camp. All in all, the total amount of party switches as well as their distribution only within or only between party camps remains relatively constant over the course of the campaign panel. The incidence of shifts in vote intentions decreases somewhat from wave two to wave four, and the few switches that occur are more or less equally divided between parties as well as nonvoting. The data show that almost one-quarter of the respondents again change their vote decision from one party to another over the final one to two weeks of the election campaign, i.e., from (preelection) panel wave six to (postelection) wave seven. Moreover, we see that this last-minute volatility emerges most frequently as switches between a party and nonvoting (63.5%). Considering only switches between parties, these are not restricted to vote switches within party camps, as changes between party camps make up about 37% of all such changes between these last two panel waves.

As the next step in our analysis we now look at the explanatory power of the predictors presented earlier for short-term vote switching. For this purpose we have run the identical regression models for the different types of vote

Table 13.7 Share of different types of vote switching by panel waves

Waves	% total switches	% of total switches only between parties	% of total switches between party and VA/DK/NA	% of party switches only within party camp	% of party switches only between party camps
1/2	20.0	43.5	56.5	43.7	40.2
2/3	16.6	41.6	58.4	49.3	33.3
3/4	16.1	47.2	52.8	44.7	38.2
4/5	19.5	52.0	48.0	45.1	41.2
5/6	20.2	44.6	55.4	44.4	36.7
6/7	24.4	36.5	63.5	40.4	37.1

Notes: Entries are percentages. VA/DK/NA: as in Table 13.1.

change from wave to wave as for the long-term panel. In order to save space, Table 13.8 only summarizes the direction and significance of the effects of the independent variables on the probability of changing vote intentions. Zeros indicate insignificant coefficients, whereas minus signs represent significant negative effects and plus signs significant positive effects. The results presented in that table yield a mixed picture. They show that the strength of party identification (H1) and its stability (H2) indeed again have an effect in the expected direction, but are not statistically significant for every pair of panel waves. As assumed, people without a strong party identification are more likely to switch their vote intention than individuals with a strong party identification. An unstable party attachment makes a parallel vote switch significantly more likely, but it should be noted that the party attachments of voters remain—as expected—extremely stable over the course of the campaign.

Changed attitudes towards candidates (H5) and altered attitudes about issue competence (H6) have an influence on the volatility of vote intentions. The significance of these effects varies between the panel waves. The results indicate that the effect of attitudes towards the candidates loses its explanatory power for switches between parties and between party camps over the course of the election campaign. Contrarily, the impact of changed attitudes about issue competence on overall vote switches varies over time, and there is more of an effect at the beginning and at the end of the election campaign. We can further see that in the third panel, wave inconsistent attitudes on issue

Table 13.8 Summary of binary logistic regression results for different types of vote switching, short-term campaign panel 2009

	All switches (incl. VA/DK/NA)	Switches only between parties	Switches only within party camp	Switches only between party camps
Strength of PID	− − − − − −	− 0 0 − − 0	0 − 0 − − 0	− 0 0 0 − 0
Instability of PID	. + + + 0 0	. + + 0 0 +	. 0 0 0 0 +	. 0 + + 0 +
Inconsistence between PID and issue competence	0 0 0 0 0 0	0 0 0 0 0 0	0 0 0 0 0 0	0 0 0 0 0 0
Inconsistent issue competence	0 0 + 0 0 0	0 0 + 0 0 0	0 0 + 0 + 0	0 0 0 0 0 0
Changed attitudes on issues	+ + 0 + 0 +	0 0 0 0 0 0	0 0 0 0 0 0	0 0 0 0 0 0
Changed attitudes towards candidates	0 + + + + 0	+ + + 0 0 0	0 0 0 0 0 0	+ + + 0 0 0

Notes: Entries represent direction and significance of coefficients, with 0 = insignificant, − = significant negative effect, + = significant positive effect, . = not applicable. The six symbols per cell stand for the six subsequent wave comparisons wave-2/wave-1 through wave-7/wave-6 (from left to right). VA/DK/NA: as in Table 13.1.

competence also help to explain vote switching (H4). Inconsistency between party identification and attitudes on issue competence has no impact on individual volatility, neither in the shorter nor in the longer run (H3). Overall, these regression models for switching vote intentions in the shorter run produce a somewhat deviating but not totally different set of findings from the models for vote changes between subsequent elections.

Judging from McFadden's R^2 all models have a satisfactory but not really excellent fit. One might therefore argue that not all relevant variables have been included in our models that would be required to fully account for the switching of vote intentions in the shorter run. However, we should not necessarily assume that each and every act of switching one's voting preference has to be explained by the predictors included here—or some other variables for that matter. There also must be room for the notion that a well-reflected change of mind is not always required if a voter switches from one party to another. We have to allow for the possibility that an (unknown) proportion of moving from one party to another (or even staying with the same party) cannot be explained by any systematic factors but occurs almost accidentally or randomly, so that a vote is cast without recollection of the past vote and without any calculations about the pros and cons of voting this way or another. Not all behavior is the outcome of reasoned choice. Switches between parties during the election campaign might simply be due to hesitation and dithering of voters who actually do not (yet) know which party they should vote for. Therefore these switches cannot be interpreted as actual conversions. It is more likely that such voters are undecided and might hold sympathies for more than one party simultaneously and name the one which is on top just at the moment that they are doing the interview (Zaller 1992: 36).

To take this point of indecision versus meaningful vote switches during an election campaign a little further, we finally make use here of the voter types introduced by Lazarsfeld, Berelson, and Gaudet (1944: 52, 65ff.). In their famous book *The People's Choice* they have distinguished four voter types, namely partisans, crystallizers, waverers, and party changers. Partisans are loyal party voters who have a vote intention already at the beginning of the election campaign, maintain this vote choice over its course, and, finally, vote for that party. This group of voters has made their vote choice well before or at the beginning of the election campaign and express a stable vote intention throughout. In contrast, crystallizers are a group of people who have no vote intention at the outset of the campaign, but later acquire one. They proceed from initial "don't know" or refusal to a clearly stated vote decision. Waverers are the first type with actual changes of vote intentions during the election campaign. People belonging to this type start out with a party choice, but then abandon it—and later return to their initial vote intention. Those people could sway back and forth from their initial party to another party or detour to response insecurity or refusal—and then

Table 13.9 Modified Lazarsfeld types in 2009 campaign panels

Modified Lazarsfeld types	Voters in 2009 campaign panel
Partisans	38.4
Crystallizers	19.0
Waverers within camp	6.4
Waverers between camps	2.6
Party changers within camp	9.1
Party changers between camps	10.1
VA/DK/NA in final wave	14.4
N	1583

Notes: Entries are column percentages among voter types. VA/DK/NA: as in Table 13.1.

come back to their originally preferred party. And, finally, party changers are those voters who start out with a vote intention and then change to another party during the election campaign—and finally vote for that second party (see Lazarsfeld, Berelson, and Gaudet 1944: 65f.). In a multiparty system like Germany these voter types can be modified by splitting up waverers and party changers according to swings within and between party camps. Table 13.9 presents the distribution of these six voter types and nonvoters in the 2009 election panel.

Just as in the 1940 US study, most German voters were partisans in 2009. Those voters had made their vote decision well before the beginning of the campaign and mention the same party in all seven panel waves. In contrast, 19% of respondents are crystallizers and acquire a vote intention over the course of the campaign. Those voters switch their vote intention from indecision to a party choice just once during the campaign. Waverers and party changers can change their party preference more often. But, as we have seen in Table 13.5, only few voters do change their mind more than twice. Moreover, the occurrence of waverers is relatively rare. While 6% swayed back and forth between parties of one camp, only 3% fluctuate between parties of different camps and then come back to their initial vote choice. On the other hand, 19% of all respondents do really convert to a different party than they intended to vote for at the outset of the election campaign. These conversions do equally occur between parties of different camps and within one camp. Finally, 14% of the panelists do not vote at all at the end of the election campaign, no matter whether they have switched during the campaign or not.

13.6 CONCLUSIONS

The aim of this chapter was to compare and investigate long-term as well as short-term voter volatility. We have therefore built on the (small number of) studies analysing long-term stability and change, and have provided new insights into individual campaign volatility. Our results show—not surprisingly—that there is considerably more long-term than short-term volatility. Over three subsequent elections nearly half of the respondents have changed their vote decision at least once, while almost two-thirds exhibit stable voting behavior over the course of the 2009 election campaign. As we have seen, well below 20% change their vote intention more than twice during the campaign. But even more frequent switching does not automatically lead to a higher number of different parties that people want to vote for. Our findings clarify that most swing voters do not oscillate wildly between all possible parties or indecision or abstention every time they are interviewed during the election campaign, but rather have a limited choice set of usually two parties, even if they switch their vote intention among these more often.

Besides the assessment of both temporal aspects of electoral volatility we were likewise interested in explaining individual-level volatility. According to our results, the stability and strength of party identification serve as massive stabilizing factors of the vote decision. The stronger and more stable partisan attachments are, the less likely individuals are to change their party preference over the shorter as well as the longer run. Conversely, changed attitudes towards candidates and issues do contribute to the explanation of individual volatility. It must, however, be borne in mind that election-specific constellations play a role in explaining vote switching. Thus, election-specific issues or events can cause more or less swing voting, and that is why attitudes towards candidates or issues may have a greater importance in one election than they do in other election years. All in all, our model fits indicate that the search for determinants of vote switching is not yet over.

Stability and change of individual long-term as well as short-term party choice might also be a function of randomness and heterogeneity. Inter- as well as intrapersonal heterogeneity could contribute to the explanation of volatility of the vote decision. There might be several groups of voters distinguishable by the process of arriving at their vote decision. Those voters with a stable and strong party identification will not be very volatile. Another group of voters may switch their vote due to changed attitudes towards candidates or issues. Finally, a third group of voters might be highly volatile without their switches being susceptible to explanations by changed attitudes—and thus have to be regarded as random. To find out which individual belongs to which group, more research will be required. In the same vein, differences between the individual weights of the determinants of the vote decision or changes of the (self-reported) reasons for the vote decision may further clarify the issue of individual volatility. Separate groups of individuals may have quite different rationales for their vote decision. For some, the candidates might be most important for their party choice, and for others, party performance might be more relevant than their party attachment.

Further research might also experiment with slightly different measures of the explanatory variables. Instead of just gauging the lack of consistence and stability, as we did here, one might obtain higher explanatory power by also modeling the direction of these inconsistencies and changes. Also, we have not taken into account how and why attitudes towards candidates or issues do change over time. Information obtained from the media as well as through interpersonal communication may well be a cause of such attitudinal changes. This angle should thus also be addressed in much more comprehensive studies of electoral volatility.

Finally, our findings suggest that individual volatility during the course of the campaign is not very strong in Germany. However, it could be that this particular election represents an exception due to a very quiet campaign in 2009 that by many has been described as "boring," since after four years in a Grand Coalition the major two parties could not really go after each other in full confrontation. Because the intensity of an election campaign might affect voters' decisions and increase the probability of vote switching, the parallel analysis of further election campaigns is indispensable.

Appendix: Question Wording and Construction of Variables

Strength of party identification: Five-point scale ranging from 0 (no party identification) to 1 (very strong party identification). Question: "All in all, how strongly or weakly attached are you to this party?" The original categories of "very weak" and "weak" were collapsed into one because of the very low number of cases in each.

Instability of party identification: Dynamic variable indicating stability or change of party identification from t–1 to t, with values of –1 (if individual identifies with the same party in t and t–1), 0 (if change occurs half of the way, i.e., to or from answers such as "no, I am not attached to a particular party" or "don't know"), +1 (if individual is attached to different parties in t and t–1). Question: "Many people in Germany feel close to a particular political party for a longer period of time even if they occasionally vote for another party. What about you? In general terms, do you feel attached to a particular political party? And if so, which one?"

Inconsistent issue competence: Static variable indicating inconsistence between allocations of issue competence for the most and second most important problem at time t, ranging from –1 (competence for both issues is attributed to one party), via 0 (indifferent, i.e., answers such as "all parties are equally good," "no party," or "don't know") to +1 (issue competence is ascribed to two different parties). Question: "You consider...to be the most/second most important issue. Which party do you think is best able to solve this problem?"

Inconsistence between party identification and issue competence: Static variable indicating inconsistence between party identification and issue competence at time t, ranging from –1 (consistency between party identification and attribution of issue competence), via 0 (if no party identification or indifferent on issue competence) to +1 (if issue competence is ascribed to a different party than one identifies with). Questions: As above.

Changed attitudes on issue competence: Dynamic variable indicating stability or change of evaluations of issue competence from t–1 to t, ranging from –1 (if issue competence is ascribed to the same party in t and t–1), via 0 (if indifferent, i.e., answers such as "all parties are equally good," "no party," or "don't know") to +1 (if issue competence is ascribed to different parties in t and t–1). Question: As above.

Changed attitudes towards candidates: Dynamic variable indicating stability or change of Chancellor preference from t–1 to t, ranging from –1 (if same candidate for Chancellor is preferred in t and t–1), via 0 (if indifferent, including answers such as "neither of them" or "don't know") to +1 (if different candidates for Chancellor are preferred in t and t–1). Question: "Angela Merkel and Gerhard Schröder (Frank-Walter Steinmeier) are the candidates of the two major parties for the position of Chancellor. Whom would you prefer to see as Chancellor after the Federal election?"

Part IV

Conclusion

14

Voters on the Move or on the Run?

Bernhard Weßels, Hans Rattinger, Sigrid Roßteutscher, and Rüdiger Schmitt-Beck

The one or two last decades of electoral research have left no doubt. There is no longer an easy way to explain voting behavior and understand election outcomes. Voting behavior is in flux. The question is which direction electoral change will take. There are two principal alternatives. Unfortunately, to make things more complex, they may be related. One option is a process of changing voting behavior, i.e., a change in the calculus of voting. Voters would indeed, then, be on the move. The alternative is that the relationship to politics is changing in general; citizens are becoming disaffected, in other words, they are on the run. Even if there is an answer to the question concerning which of the two alternatives predominates over electoral change, a second question would follow: What do we learn from this answer? Does a differentiated integrative analysis provide a more detailed understanding of electoral behavior and does this help us to grasp the course of public policy and the working of the governmental system, a hope Bartels (2010) articulated? The chapters in this volume try to shed light on the flux in voting behavior, conceptually integrated by the two dimensions heterogeneity and complexity that the framework of this volume regards as the core of electoral change. We will discuss the findings of the book along the lines of the introductory chapter.

Heterogeneity in the calculus of voting has certainly increased. Our analyses clearly show that it can hardly be justified to use one universal model for explaining behavior of all individuals. This homogeneity assumption in general voting models does not hold up with respect to individual characteristics of voters, political objects, institutional settings, or campaign features. Chapter 2 demonstrates that social as well as attitudinal characteristics and cognitive abilities make a difference for the calculus of voting. Consideration weights for variables traditionally used to explain vote choice differ socially, attitudinally, and cognitively to a high degree. Social characteristics, rather, make a difference for long-term factors of vote choice like party identification; attitudinal and cognitive characteristics impact both the consideration weights for long- and short-term factors like candidate evaluations or issues. The link between political orientations and evaluations and voting behavior is strongest among those with high cognitive abilities. They can better adapt to increasing complexity, whereas less sophisticated voters have become less predictable over the last decade. Despite this widening gap, there is quite some intrapersonal stability—at least in the more sophisticated part of the electorate. Long-term panel analysis reveals a high probability that voters who consider issues in one election will also do so in the next.

Individual characteristics are not the only factor contributing to heterogeneity of voting behavior. Supply characteristics matter, too. That party-specific vote functions exist does not come as a surprise when we consider issue-ownership of parties. There are, however, more general aspects of supply producing differences in the amount to which voters take factors into account. One is party size. The importance of leadership evaluation depends on the size of the party. For bigger parties that are most likely to bring personnel into government leadership, evaluations matter more. Parties' extremity or ambiguity regarding issues and ideological position makes a difference for the role proximity plays for vote choice. These two findings do not only apply to the German voter. An analysis of voting behavior in nineteen countries and twenty-two elections confirmed that these findings can be generalized and are not specific for Germany. Supply characteristics and changes have still more implications. Many parliamentary party systems have become bigger and with the number of parties the number of potential government coalitions has increased. This would not have to be of any relevance, but it has been observed that coalitions have gained more and more attention as objects of choice. In Germany, the continuous increase in ticket splitting of nominal and list vote is a clear indication of the increasing relevance of coalitions for voters. As Chapter 4 demonstrates, coalition evaluations are not just derivates of party evaluations. For the heterogeneity of the individual vote function, this adds a new, too often neglected element to strategic as well as expressive voting that is—to make voting even more complex—moderated by coalition expectations.

The fourth aspect that increases heterogeneity is of an institutional nature. All citizens of member countries of the European Union and of any federal country are confronted with voting at different levels—regional, national, European—which makes a difference. Multilevel voting challenges party identification as a relatively fluid and adaptive attitude, at least if individuals are not strong or very strong partisans. Electoral participation, which is multiplied in multilevel electoral systems, is the core mechanism of reactivation or of volatility, instability, and the decline of party identification (Chapter 5). The second-order election approach claims that the dynamic would rather not speak for a reactivation. This seems to be too far-reaching a conclusion, because our findings suggest that, in contrast to theoretical expectations, individual turnout differentials between elections at different levels are not significantly related to cost–benefit calculations of voters. The analysis with panel data also suggests that the criteria for making a vote choice are not very different between elections at different levels. If at all, second-orderness of elections must be seen as a continuous rather than a binary concept (Chapter 6). The increase in the opportunity of electoral participation that paves the way to higher dynamics, fluidity, and heterogeneity in voting and vote-choice mechanisms seems to be more relevant.

A further aspect increasing heterogeneity is the influence of campaign features. Although campaigns should principally foster homogeneity, for example activation for participation and for comparative assessment of political offers, they produce heterogeneity because campaign actors attempt to make a difference to competitors. One factor contributing to heterogeneity of voting behavior is the amount of money spent in a campaign. Our results confirm what has been found in other countries: The more money is spent, the better will the candidates fare in terms of votes gained. In addition, research on election campaigns suggests that personalized local campaigning has become a common feature even in nonplurality systems. The German case, with its two-tier system—nominal and list vote—offers candidates a direct opportunity of personalized campaigning and voters a particular opportunity of responding to this. Voters with a unitary preference, i.e., straight-ticket voters for nominal and list, react rather negatively on personalized campaigning. Voters who split ticket are rather positively drawn to the candidate if she runs a personalized campaign. Thus, the sources of heterogeneity springing from the institutional setup and from the way political supply presents itself are intertwined.

These findings lead directly to the second dimension explaining voters' flux, namely increasing complexity. One of its aspects is the diversification of social structures. Whereas in the "golden age" of parties, whenever that was, social cleavages were the glue between voters and parties, leading to rather stable partisanships, social changes in recent years have dissolved this relationship. Only 15% of the adult population today are still linked to traditional cleavages. But how do the other 85% find orientation? While turnout, for example, does not vary for cleavage-bound voters with different levels of education and social networks, education, and private networks matter a lot for the turnout of voters not bound to cleavages. As Chapter 8 highlights, in postcleavage constellation, political mobilization depends upon education and private networks to an extent unknown some decades ago. There are means to cope with complexity beside traditional cues, milieus, and loyalties, but these are strongly individualized and depend on resources and communication. Political communication seems to become crucial for the instruction of a preference-consistent vote as well. Beyond individual resources, i.e., education and political knowledge, mass-media communication, talking about politics with associates, and political information from political parties contribute to voting "correctly." In fact, parties' campaigning strategies and propaganda is the most relevant among the three different ways of political communication. One way out of complexity for voters is to delegate costs of obtaining and weighting information to external sources. Chapter 9 suggests that effects of campaigning may be strongest among those voters with weak personal resources. However, Chapter 10 shows that campaigns have a mixed record in "activation" by agendas and issues. Enlightenment through activation seems to work best on the political Left. Approaching "activation of fundamentals" with a model applied in the US shows its limitations when it comes to choice situations that are more complex than in the binary case of viable political offers. However, Chapters 8 to 10 tell in unison the story that political communication either in personal networks or by political parties may provide personal information-acquisition systems that help to deal with complexity.

That complexity does not arise more or less automatically just because habitual voting or voting based on loyalties decreases and issue voting increases, is the outcome of Chapter 11. Theories and hypotheses which claim that macro-social changes implying reduced reliance on traditional cues and loyalties automatically lead to a higher consideration weight of issues when making a choice, neglect the necessary individual-level foundation of such a process. In particular, if voters become more sophisticated, it seems plausible that they question the utility of additional criteria for vote choice. Consequently, Chapter 12 demonstrates that better education and higher political sophistication do not necessarily trigger more issue voting. Whether issues are considered or not rather depends on supply structures. If the difference between political offers is already obvious by more general and less costly evaluations, even highly educated and politically sophisticated voters refrain from entering the complexity of issue voting. The enlightened way of making decisions is not to bear more information costs than necessary for coping with complexity. This result came out in the German and the comparative analysis of twenty-nine election studies from twenty-five countries for position issues regarding the conditioning role of party identification, indifference between the two best-liked political alternatives, and the congruence or incongruence between party identification and the general evaluation of the same party. As in the previous chapters dealing with information and campaigning, a rather sophisticated individual information-acquisition system sorting out the necessary from the unnecessary seems to be the voters' answer to complexity.

The crucial role of loyalties as stabilizing factors, even in case of unsatisfactory political supply, clearly emerges from the last two chapters of the book. Increasing disaffection of citizens toward politics may result either from supply changes not fitting preferences or from preference change not fitting supply. Behavioral consequences do not systematically follow from indifference towards political parties but certainly from alienation from parties. Citizens turn their back on elections. Most important is that alienation has become more and more a strong predictor of turnout over time. Longitudinal analysis of German data suggests, however, that neither indifference against nor alienation from political supply has increased over the last decades. But, although it is not increasing, alienation produces more and more abstention. The effect of the level of alienation on the decision to vote is stronger among those not identifying with a party or regarding voting as a citizen duty. How powerful loyalties like party identification are in preventing voters from running away from parties in general is shown by the analysis and explanation of volatility patterns in Chapter 13. The number of voters turning away from their party preference and to no other party between one election and the next is about one-third of German voters. Among this group, the effect of instability of party identification on voting behavior is highest. This does not imply that voters who identify with a party do not switch. But it seems that they rather switch to other parties and most likely to parties within the same camp. Switching does not happen without reason. Most swing voters do not oscillate wildly. They switch as a result of changed attitudes towards candidates or issues. Thus, the belief that party identification has to go along with stable and rather habitual voting patterns does not hold true any more, if it did ever. Switching may be a temporary answer to inconsistency between loyalty and evaluation of political supply. Nonetheless, partisanship remains a powerful buffer against voters' flux and in particular against turning away from parties.

How do these findings help us to understand electoral change? If we regard the changing electoral behavior as a reaction to complexity and put the question in the title of this book into this context, "voters being on the move" implies their adaptation to complexity. Seeing "voters on the run" would mean that they are increasingly turning away from politics, separating themselves from it, and becoming disaffected. Thus, moving implies coping with complexity in a structured way; running implies random reaction or exit. Regardless whether voters are on the move or on the run, both situations would increase heterogeneity.

The findings in this book suggest that voters are rather on the move than on the run. Increasing heterogeneity is mainly a result of increasing complexity—though increase in complexity is of course partly a result of increasing heterogeneity. Heterogeneity is the voters' reaction to the increasing complexity of their social context, which no longer provides simple clues for political orientations and choices (due to the dissolution of milieus and the process of individualization), as well as changes in political supply, including larger electoral party systems with more options to choose between, the revolution of political communication, and changing campaign strategies.

The variety of reactions implies heterogeneity. This heterogeneity, however, is not unstructured. One common pattern is a split in the electorate regarding voters' ability to adapt to new supply features along the dimension of cognitive ability. This holds true for Germany and in comparative perspective. Less sophisticated voters have become less predictable over the last decade. Thus, the dominant view that cognitive mobilization and modernization processes are responsible for ever increasing heterogeneity and fragmentation in voting behavior certainly does not tell the full story. It rather seems that with cognitive mobilization, a restructuring of voting patterns has emerged that electoral research has only partly deciphered up to now. The results of this book suggest that *structured heterogeneity* seems to be an appropriate term for this phenomenon.

Avoiding or reducing the burden of gathering information about parties, issues, candidates, and everything else that may be important in conjunction with an upcoming election seems to be a standing feature of voting behavior. The traditional way of reducing information costs was to rely on loyalties and the group context. With the withering away of social milieus and the process of individualization, this is not a choice anymore, or only for very few voters.

Two general mechanisms structuring heterogeneity are identified in this book: The first mechanism is the creation of individual information-acquisition systems; the second is a particular way of information selection.

Individual information-acquisition systems are the voters' answer to the problem of information becoming constantly more complex, requires processing, and is no more just "inherited" as may have been the case in dense and homogeneous social milieus. Our findings suggest that the way acquisition and processing of information are done seems to be anything but random. The individual strategies to acquire information have to compensate for what was delivered by cleavage-embededdness in earlier decades. Weaker social context obviously does not imply a weakening of the role of social context. Today, the prior function of group and cleavage-based political communication is replaced by smaller networks of personal political communication. Costs of obtaining and weighting information are delegated or shared and, thus, minimized.

The second mechanism is information selection. If personal political networks provide the relevant information, the selection mechanism identifies the necessary information, i.e., sorts out the necessary from the unnecessary in a very rational way. Selection is based on utility for making a choice. Only if further criteria are needed to identify differences between political offers or political actors, is additional information taken into account. Otherwise, the search for information stops as soon as information is sufficient to make a difference.

Mechanisms of processing information are the one element structuring heterogeneity. A second dimension is the differentiation of voters into four major groups with different trajectories to voting behavior and choice. Two axes divide the electorate: the degree of political sophistication and the degree of partisanship. Cleavage-boundedness does not play a major role anymore.

Not much more than 10 to 15% of voters belong to the core cleavage groups. Voting behavior of citizens with a lower degree of political knowledge and a party affiliation still works the traditional, habitual way. If not partisan, electoral behavior of politically not very sophisticated citizens is hard to predict. Sophisticated voters with party identification rather show loyalty. This does not necessarily imply stable voting. Voice is possible, but exit unlikely. The fourth group, i.e., sophisticated voters who are not partisan, seem to have developed structured information-acquisition systems allowing them to cope with the complexity of information and political supply.

A third dimension structuring heterogeneity is the characteristics of political supply. If individual information-acquisition systems are the key for understanding electoral behaviour, it is evident that the content of information about political supply must matter. Regarding the utility of information for choice, it is obvious that political supply can contribute significantly to make choices easier. The more clarity there is between alternatives, be it party profiles, issues, or candidates, the less complex and less conditional vote choice will be.

The overall conclusion to be drawn from the generalized findings is clearly the following: Social and cognitive structures make heterogeneity not arbitrary. The key to heterogeneity is political sophistication and knowledge on the one hand, communication networks and information processing systems on the other hand. Heterogeneity is an answer to complexity, mainly to complexity of political supply. The more structured political supply is, the more structured heterogeneity will be. Understanding the interplay needs the analysis of long- and short-term dynamics and a comparative perspective.

In terms of the working of the democratic process as a whole, structured heterogeneity has to be put into the context of complexity of political supply. The implication for the understanding of the working of democracy is that just looking at the voters can only contribute a little to the understanding of election outcomes. An integrated approach of electoral research needs to take into account the contingencies of voting behavior on political supply.

APPENDIX

Study Description and Data Sources

GLES German Longitudinal Election Study

The GLES project is long-term funded by the German Science Foundation (DFG). The complex study design allows the in-depth analysis of electoral behavior, its short- and long-term dynamics, and cross-level analysis to mass-media content and candidates at national elections. At the core are extensive face-to-face pre- and postelection cross-section surveys of a random sample of voters. For the analysis of long-term dynamics, the cross-sections are complemented by long-term cross-election panels interviewing the same respondents as interviewed in the cross-sections. Short-term dynamics are taken care of by a rolling cross-section survey and an online campaign panel. Measures of short-term dynamics at the voters' level are complemented by quantitative content analysis of major newspapers and television news. A candidate campaign survey allows the analysis of activities and political orientations of those running for the national parliament. The period between elections is analysed by an online tracking survey program, including long-term media agenda analysis. In addition, a module on TV debates is included in the study design. The study of multilevel electoral behavior at times when state elections or European elections occur is possible by the long-term online tracking survey or, when concurrent elections occur at times of Federal elections, with the cross-sections (see Figure A1 for the modules). All parts of the study are well integrated for combining analysis across data sources. Two modules are embedded in international comparative projects, the module for the Comparative Study of Electoral Systems running in the postelection cross-section and the candidate campaign survey being part of the Comparative Candidate Survey (CCS).

The GLES is a public data project. All data are available to the (scientific) public as soon as technically ready. Data are provided by GESIS, Leibniz Institute for the Social Sciences. Data and documentation including English versions of the questionnaires can be downloaded at http://www.gesis.org/en/elections-home/gles/.

Data from other German Election Studies

This volume also draws on other election studies, prominently among them the study "Politische Einstellungen, politische Partizipation und Wählerverhalten im vereinigten Deutschland" (Political attitudes, political participation, and voters' behavior in united Germany), a panel running pre and post across three elections (1994, 1998, 2002). This data, as well as other data used in the book are available at the GESIS data archive (see http://www.gesis.org/en/elections-home/german-federal-elections/).

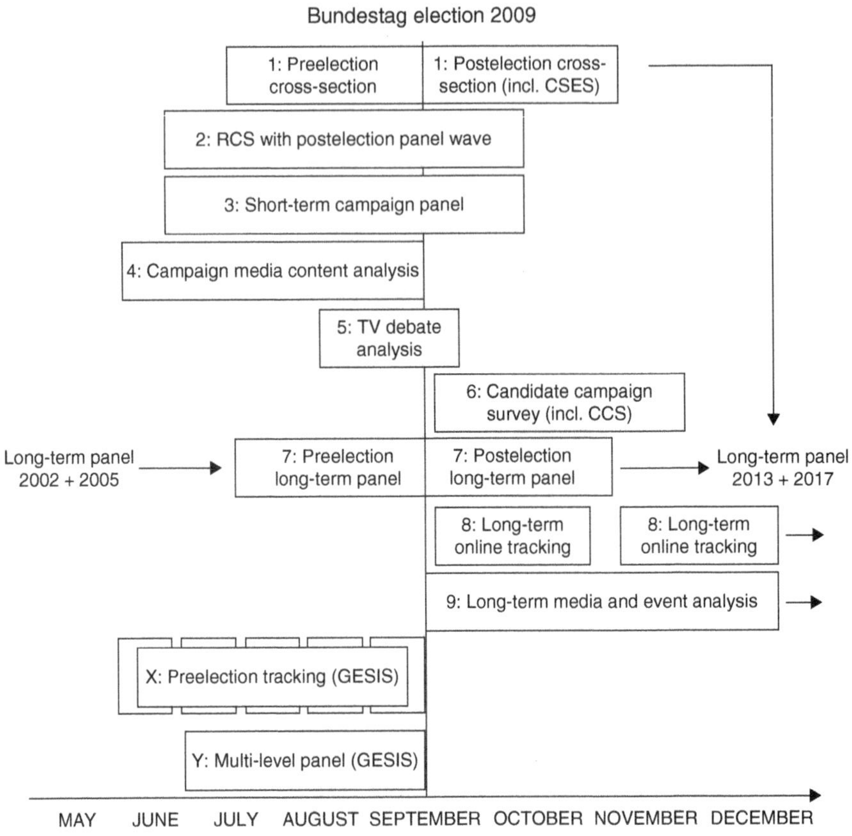

320   *Appendix*

Figure A1 Overview of the GLES design at the Bundestag election 2009

CSES, the Comparative Study of Electoral Systems

This book uses comparative data on electoral behavior, too. Germany has been partner of CSES from its very beginning, and at each election from 1998 onwards, the CSES module was conducted in Germany. Since 2009, the CSES module is part of the post-election cross-section of the German Longitudinal Election Study (GLES). CSES is a public data project, too. The book uses CSES module III data. Data and documentation are available at http://cses.org/.

References

Aardal, Bernt, and Pieter van Wijnen (2005). "Issue Voting," in Jacques Thomassen (ed.), *The European Voter. A Comparative Study of Modern Democracies*. Oxford: Oxford University Press, pp. 192–212.

Aarts, Kees, and Holli A. Semetko (2003). "The Divided Electorate. Media Use and Political Involvement," *Journal of Politics*, 65/3, 759–84.

Aarts, Kees, Holli A. Semetko, and Bernhard Weßels (2005a). "Electoral Turnout," in Jacques Thomassen (ed.), *The European Voter. A Comparative Study of Modern Democracies*. Oxford: Oxford University Press, pp. 64–83.

Aarts, Kees, Holli A. Semetko, and Bernhard Weßels (2005b). "Wahlbeteiligung in Deutschland und bei europäischen Nachbarn," in Jürgen W. Falter, Oscar W. Gabriel, and Bernhard Wessels (eds.), *Wahlen und Wähler. Analysen aus Anlass der Bundestagswahl 2002*. Wiesbaden: VS Verlag für Sozialwissenschaften, pp. 595–617.

Abendschön, Simone, and Sigrid Roßteutscher (forthcoming). "Partizipation junger Erwachsener—Steigt die soziale und politische Ungleichheit?," in Sigrid Roßteutscher, Thorsten Faas, and Ulrich Rosar (eds.), *Bürger und Wähler im Wandel der Zeit. 25 Jahre Wahl- und Einstellungsforschung in Deutschland*. Wiesbaden: Springer VS.

Abramowitz, Alan I., and Kyle L. Saunders (2006). "Exploring the Bases of Partisanship in the American Electorate. Social Identity vs. Ideology," *Political Research Quarterly*, 59/2, 175–87.

Achen, Christopher H. (1992). "Social Psychology, Demographic Variables, and Linear Regression. Breaking the Iron Triangle in Voting Research," *Political Behavior*, 14/3, 195–211.

Achen, Christopher H. (2005). "Two-Step Hierarchical Estimation. Beyond Regression Analysis," *Political Analysis*, 13/4, 447–56.

Adams, James (2001). "A Theory of Spatial Competition with Biased Voters," *British Journal of Political Science*, 31/1, 121–58.

Adams, James, Jay Dow, and Samuel Merrill III (2006). "The Political Consequences of Alienation-Based and Indifference-Based Voter Abstention. Applications to Presidential Elections," *Political Behavior*, 28/1, 65–86.

Adams, James, and Samuel Merrill III (2003). "Voter Turnout and Candidate Strategies in American Elections," *The Journal of Politics*, 65/1, 161–89.

Adams, James, Samuel Merill III, and Bernhard Grofman (2005). *A Unified Theory of Party Competition. A Cross-National Analysis Integrating Spatial and Behavioral Factors*. Cambridge: Cambridge University Press.

Adams, James, et al. (2006). "Are Niche Parties Fundamentally Different from Mainstream Parties? The Causes and the Electoral Consequences of Western European Parties' Policy Shifts, 1976–1998," *American Journal of Political Science*, 50/3, 513–29.

Albright, Jeremy J. (2009). "Does Political Knowledge Erode Party Attachments? A Review of the Cognitive Mobilization Thesis," *Electoral Studies*, 28/2, 248–60.

Aldrich, John H. (1993). "Rational Choice and Turnout," *American Journal of Political Science*, 37/1, 246–78.
Alesina, Alberto F., and Eliana La Ferrara (2002). "Who Trusts Others?," *Journal of Public Economics*, 85/2, 207–34.
Alesina, Alberto F., and Howard Rosenthal (1995). *Partisan Politics, Divided Government, and the Economy.* Cambridge: Cambridge University Press.
Allardt, Erik (1968). "Past and Emerging Political Cleavages," in Otto Stammer (ed.), *Party Systems, Party Organisations, and the Politics of the New Masses.* Berlin: Freie Universität, Institute of Political Science, pp. 66–74.
Allison, Paul D. (2002). *Missing Data.* Thousand Oaks: Sage.
Alvarez, R. Michael, Jonathan Nagler, and Jennifer R. Niemann (1998). *Parties, Issue Spaces, and Voting. A Comparative Perspective.* Paper prepared for presentation at the 56th Annual Meeting of the Midwest Political Science Association, Chicago, IL, April 25–28, 1998.
Andersen, Robert (2003). "Do Newspapers Enlighten Preferences? Personal Ideology, Party Choice and the Electoral Cycle. The United Kingdom, 1992–1997," *Canadian Journal of Political Science/Revue Canadienne De Science Politique*, 36/3, 601–19.
Andersen, Robert, and Anthony Heath (2000). *Social Class and Voting. A Multi-Level Analysis of Individual and Constituency Differences,* CREST Working Paper, Number 83, September 2000. London/Oxford: Centre for Research into Elections and Social Trends.
Andersen, Robert, Anthony Heath, and Richard Sinnott (2002). "Political Knowledge and Electoral Choice," *Journal of Elections, Public Opinion & Parties*, 12/1, 11–27.
Andersen, Robert, James Tilley, and Anthony F. Heath (2005). "Political Knowledge and Enlightened Preferences. Party Choice through the Electoral Cycle," *British Journal of Political Science*, 35/2, 285–303.
Andersen, Robert, Min Yang, and Anthony F. Heath (2006). "Class Politics and Political Context in Britain, 1964–1997. Have Voters Become More Individualized?," *European Sociological Review*, 22/2, 215–28.
Anderson, Christopher (1995). *Blaming the Government. Citizens and the Economy in Five European Democracies.* Armonk, NY: M.E. Sharpe.
Anderson, Christopher (1995). *Blaming the Government. Citizens and the Economy in Five European Democracies.* London: Sharpe.
Anderson, Christopher, and Jason D. Hecht (2012). "Voting When the Economy Goes Bad, Everyone Is in Charge, and No One Is to Blame. The Case of the 2009 German Election," *Electoral Studies*, 31/1, 5–19.
Anderson, Christopher, and Daniel S. Wood (1996). "Barometer Elections in Comparative Perspective," *Electoral Studies*, 15/4, 447–60.
Apter, David E. (1964). *Ideology and Discontent.* New York: Free Press.
Arcenaux, Kevin (2006). "Do Campaigns Help Voters Learn? A Cross-National Analysis," *British Journal of Political Science*, 36/1, 159–73.
Armitage, Christopher J., and Mark Conner (2000). "Attitudinal Ambivalence. A Test of Three Key Hypotheses," *Personality and Social Psychology Bulletin*, 26/11, 1421–32.
Arzheimer, Kai (2002). *Politikverdrossenheit. Bedeutung, Verwendung und empirische Relevanz eines politikwissenschaftlichen Begriffs.* Wiesbaden: Westdeutscher Verlag.

Arzheimer, Kai (2006). "'Dead Men Walking?' Party Identification in Germany, 1977–2002," *Electoral Studies*, 25/4, 791–807.

Arzheimer, Kai, and Harald Schoen (2005). "Erste Schritte auf kaum erschlossenen Terrain. Zur Stabilität der Parteiidentifikation in Deutschland," *Politische Vierteljahresschrift*, 46/4, 629–54.

Asher, Herbert (1983). "Voting Behavior Research in the 1980s. An Examination of Some Old and New Problem Areas," in Finifter Ada W. (ed.), *Political Science. The State of the Discipline*. Washington: ASPA, pp. 339–88.

Auspurg, Katrin, and Thomas Hinz (2011). "Group Comparisons for Regression Models with Binary Dependent Variables—Problems and Pitfalls Illustrated by Differences in Educational Opportunities between Cohorts," *Zeitschrift für Soziologie*, 40/1, 62–73.

Austen-Smith, David, and Jeffrey Banks (1988). "Elections, Coalitions, and Legislative Outcomes," *American Political Science Review*, 82/2, 405–22.

Bachl, Marko, and Frank Brettschneider (2011). "The German National Election Campaign and the Mass Media," *German Politics*, 20/1, 51–74.

Banaszak, Lee Ann, and Peter Doerschler (2012). "Coalition Type and Voter Support for Parties. Grand Coalitions in German Elections," *Electoral Studies*, 31/1, 46–59.

Barabas, Jason, and Jennifer Jerit (2009). "Estimating the Causal Effects of Media Coverage on Policy-Specific Knowledge," *American Journal of Political Science*, 53/1, 73–89.

Bargsted, Matias A., and Orit Kedar (2009). "Coalition-Targeted Duvergerian Voting. How Expectations Affect Voter Choice under Proportional Representation," *American Journal of Political Science*, 53/2, 307–23.

Barisione, Mauro (2009). "So, What Difference Do Leaders Make? Candidates' Images and the 'Conditionality' of Leader Effects on Voting," *Journal of Elections, Public Opinion and Parties*, 19/4, 473–500.

Bartels, Larry M. (1993). "Messages Received. The Political Impact of Media Exposure," *American Political Science Review*, 87/2, 267–85.

Bartels, Larry M. (1996). "Uninformed Votes. Information Effects in Presidential Elections," *American Journal of Political Science*, 40/1, 194–230.

Bartels, Larry M. (2002). "Beyond the Running Tally. Partisan Bias in Political Perceptions," *Political Behavior*, 24/2, 117–50.

Bartels, Larry M. (2006). "Priming and Persuasion in Presidential Campaigns," in Henry E. Brady and Richard Johnston (eds.), *Capturing Campaign Effects*. Ann Arbor: University of Michigan Press, pp. 78–112.

Bartels, Larry M. (2010). "The Study of Electoral Behavior," in Jan E. Leighley (ed.), *The Oxford Handbook of American Elections and Political Behavior*. Oxford: Oxford University Press, pp. 239–61.

Bartle, John (1997). "Political Awareness and Heterogeneity in Models of Voting. Some Evidence from the British Election Studies," *Journal of Elections, Public Opinion & Parties*, 7/1, 1–22.

Bartle, John (2000). "Political Awareness, Opinion Constraint and the Stability of Ideological Positions," *Political Studies*, 48/3, 467–84.

Bartle, John (2003). "Partisanship, Performance and Personality. Competing and Complementary Characterizations of the 2001 British General Election," *Party Politics*, 9/3, 317–45.

Bartle, John (2005). "Homogeneous Models and Heterogeneous Voters," *Political Studies*, 53/4, 653–75.

Bartle, John, and Paolo Bellucci (2009). "Introduction. Partisanship, Social Identity and Individual Attitudes," in John Bartle and Paolo Bellucci (eds.), *Political Parties and Partisanship. Social Identity and Individual Attitudes*. London: Routledge, pp. 1–25.

Bartolini, Stefano, and Peter Mair (1990). *Identity, Competition and Electoral Availability. The Stabilisation of European Electorates 1885–1985*. Cambridge: Cambridge University Press.

Basinger, Scott J., and Howard Lavine (2005). "Ambivalence, Information, and Electoral Choice," *American Political Science Review*, 99/2, 169–84.

Baum, Matthew A., and Angela S. Jamison (2006). "The Oprah Effect. How Soft News Helps Inattentive Citizens Vote Consistently," *The Journal of Politics*, 68/4, 946–59.

Bawn, Kathleen, and Zeynep Somer-Topcu (2012). "Government versus Opposition at the Polls. How Governing Status Affects the Impact of Policy Positions," *American Journal of Political Science*, 56/2, 433–46.

Beck, Paul Allen, et al. (2002). "The Social Calculus of Voting. Interpersonal, Media, and Organizational Influences on Presidential Choices," *American Political Science Review*, 96/1, 57–73.

Beck, Ulrich (1992). *Risk Society. Towards a New Modernity*. London: Sage.

Beck, Ulrich (2007). *Weltrisikogesellschaft*. Frankfurt am Main: Suhrkamp.

Beck, Ulrich, and Elisabeth Beck-Gernsheim (2002). *Individualization. Institutionalized Individualism and its Social and Political Consequences*. London: Sage.

Beckmann, Ruth, Philipp Trein, and Stefanie Walter (2011). "Dominanz der Ökonomie. Entscheidet die Wirtschaftslage Wahlen?," in Evelyn Bytzek and Sigrid Roßteutscher (eds.), *Der unbekannte Wähler? Mythen und Fakten über das Wahlverhalten der Deutschen*. Frankfurt am Main/New York: Campus, pp. 231–52.

Behnke, Joachim (2000). "Die Erklärung von Wahlenthaltung mit Hilfe von räumlichen Modellen," in Jan van Deth, Hans Rattinger, and Edeltraud Roller (eds.), *Die Republik auf dem Weg zur Normalität. Wahlverhalten und politische Einstellungen nach acht Jahren Einheit*. Opladen: Leske + Budrich, pp. 281–96.

Behnke, Joachim (2001). "Parteineigung als Fakt oder Parteineigung durch Fakten. Der Einfluss von Issues auf das Wahlverhalten," *Kölner Zeitschrift für Soziologie und Sozialpsychologie*, 53/3, 521–46.

Bélanger, Éric, and Bonnie M. Meguid (2008). "Issue Salience, Issue Ownership, and Issue-based Vote Choice," *Electoral Studies*, 27/3, 477–91.

Benoit, William L. (2007). *Communication in Political Campaigns*. New York: Peter Lang.

Berelson, Bernard R., Paul F. Lazarsfeld, and William N. McPhee (1954). *Voting. A Study of Opinion Formation in a Presidential Campaign*. Chicago: University of Chicago Press.

Berelson, Bernard R., Paul F. Lazarsfeld, and William N. McPhee (1955). *Voting. A Study of Opinion Formation in a Presidential Campaign* (1st edn., 2nd impr.). Chicago: University of Chicago Press.

Berglund, Frode, et al. (2005). "Party Identification and Party Choice," in Jacques Thomassen (ed.), *The European Voter. A Comparative Study of Modern Democracies.* New York: Oxford University Press, pp. 106–24.
Bergmann, Michael (2011). *IPFWEIGHT: Stata Module to Create Adjustment Weights for Surveys* <http://ideas.repec.org/c/boc/bocode/s457353.html> accessed February 14, 2013.
Bieber, Ina, and Sigrid Roßteutscher (2011). "Große Koalition und Wirtschaftskrise. Zur Ausgangslage der Bundestagswahl 2009," in Hans Rattinger et al. (eds.), *Zwischen Langeweile und Extremen. Die Bundestagswahl 2009.* Baden-Baden: Nomos, pp. 17–31.
Blais, André (2000). *To Vote or Not to Vote. The Merits and Limits of Rational Choice Theory.* Pittsburgh, PA: University of Pittsburgh Press.
Blais, André (2006). "What Affects Voter Turnout?," *Annual Review of Political Science*, 9, 111–25.
Blais, André, John H. Aldrich, Indridi H. Indridason, and Renan Levine (2006). "Do Voters Vote for Government Coalitions? Testing Downs' Pessimistic Conclusion," *Party Politics*, 12/6, 691–705.
Blaschke, Olaf (2002). *Konfession im Konflikt. Deutschland zwischen 1800 und 1970: ein zweites konfessionelles Zeitalter.* Göttingen: Vandenhoek & Ruprecht.
Blau, Peter M. (1974). "Parameters of Social Structures," *American Sociological Review*, 39/5, 615–35.
Blau, Peter M. (1977a). *Inequality and Heterogeneity.* New York: Free Press.
Blau, Peter M. (1977b). "A Macrosociological Theory of Social Structure," *American Journal of Sociology*, 83/1, 26–54.
Blumenstiel, Jan Eric, and Thomas Plischke (2012). *Analyzing Intra-Personal Heterogeneity of Voter Decision-Making over Time.* Paper prepared for presentation at the IPSA XXVII World Congress of Political Science, Madrid, Spain, July 8–12, 2012.
Blumenstiel, Jan Eric, and Hans Rattinger (2012). "Warum haben Sie das getan? Subjektive Gründe der Wahlentscheidung bei der Bundestagswahl 2009," in Rüdiger Schmitt-Beck (ed.), *Wählen in Deutschland. Special issue 45 of Politische Vierteljahresschrift.* Baden-Baden: Nomos, pp. 251–75.
Boomgaarden, Hajo, and Holli A. Semetko (2012). "Nachrichten-Bias. Medieninhalte, Bevölkerungswahrnehmungen und Wahlentscheidungen bei der Bundestagswahl 2009," in Rüdiger Schmitt-Beck (ed.), *Wählen in Deutschland. Special issue 45 of Politische Vierteljahresschrift.* Baden-Baden: Nomos, pp. 345–70.
Bowler, Shaun (1989). "Comparative Economic Assessments and the Endogeneity of Left/Right Self Placement," *European Journal of Political Research*, 17/1, 35–49.
Bowler, Shaun, and David M. Farrell (2011). "Electoral Institutions and Campaigning in Comparative Perspective. Electioneering in European Parliament Elections," *European Journal for Political Research*, 50/5, 668–88.
Bowler, Shaun, Jeffrey A. Karp, and Todd Donovan (2010). "Strategic Coalition Voting. Evidence from New Zealand," *Electoral Studies*, 29/3, 350–7.
Box-Steffensmeier, Janet M., and Renee M. Smith (1998). "Investigating Political Dynamics Using Fractional Integration Methods," *American Journal of Political Science*, 42/2, 661–89.

Boyd, Richard W. (1986). "Election Calendars and Voter Turnout," *American Politics Quarterly*, 14/1-2, 98–104.
Boyd, Richard W. (1989). "The Effects of Primaries and Statewide Races on Voter Turnout," *Journal of Politics*, 51/3, 730–9.
Brady, Henry E., Richard Johnston, and John Sides (2006). "The Study of Political Campaigns," in Henry E. Brady and Richard Johnston (eds.), *Capturing Campaign Effects*. Ann Arbor: University of Michigan Press, pp. 1–26.
Brennan, Geoffrey, and Loren E. Lomasky (1993). *Democracy and Decision. The Pure Theory of Electoral Preference*. Cambridge: Cambridge University Press.
Brody, Richard A., and Benjamin I. Page (1973). "Indifference, Alienation and Rational Decisions. The Effects of Candidate Evaluations on Turnout and the Vote," *Public Choice*, 15/Summer, 1–17.
Brooks, Clem, Paul Nieuwbeerta, and Jeff Manza (2006). "Cleavage-based Voting Behavior in Cross-national Perspective. Evidence from Six Postwar Democracies," *Social Science Research*, 35/1, 88–128.
Budge, Ian, Ivor Crewe, and Dennis Farlie (1976). *Party Identification and Beyond*. London: John Wiley & Sons.
Budge, Ian, and David Farlie (1983). *Explaining and Predicting Elections. Issue Effects and Party Strategies in Twenty-Three Democracies*. London: Allen & Unwin.
Burden, Barry C., and David C. Kimball (2002). *Why Americans Split Their Ticket. Campaigns, Competition, and Divided Government*. Ann Arbor: University of Michigan Press.
Burnham, Kenneth P., and David R. Anderson (2004). "Multimodel Inference. Understanding AIC and BIC in Model Selection," *Sociological Methods & Research*, 33/2, 261–304.
Butler, David, and Donald Stokes (1969). *Political Change in Britain. Forces Shaping Electoral Choice*. New York: St. Martin's Press.
Bytzek, Evelyn, and Sascha Huber (2011). "Koalitionen und strategisches Wählen," in Hans Rattinger et al. (eds.), *Zwischen Langeweile und Extremen. Die Bundestagswahl 2009*. Baden-Baden: Nomos, pp. 247–63.
Caballero, Claudio (2005). "Nichtwahl," in Jürgen W. Falter and Harald Schoen (eds.), *Handbuch Wahlforschung*. Wiesbaden: VS Verlag für Sozialwissenschaften, pp. 329–65.
Campbell, Angus (1960). "Surge and Decline. A Study of Electoral Change," *Public Opinion Quarterly*, 24/3, 397–418.
Campbell, Angus, Gerald Gurin, and Warren E. Miller (1954). *The Voter Decides*. Evanston, IL: Row, Peterson and Company.
Campbell, Angus, et al. (1960a). *The American Voter*. Chicago: University of Chicago Press.
Campbell, Angus, et al. (1960b). *The American Voter*. New York: Wiley.
Campbell, James E. (1997). *The Presidential Pulse of Congressional Elections* (2nd edn.). Lexington: Unversity Press of Kentucky.
Campbell, James E. (2008). *The American Campaign. U.S. Presidential Campaigns and the National Vote*. College Station, TX: Texas A&M University Press.
Carey, John M., and Matthew Soberg Shugart (1995). "Incentives to Cultivate a Personal Vote. A Rank Ordering of Electoral Formulas," *Electoral Studies*, 14/4, 417–39.

Carman, Christopher, and Robert Johns (2007). *Attitudes to Coalitions and Split-ticket Voting. The Scottish Parliament Election of 2007*. Paper prepared for presentation at the workshop on Voters, Coalitions and Democratic Accountability, University of Exeter, Exeter, October 5–6, 2007.
Carmines, Edward G., John P. McIver, and James A. Stimson (1987). "Unrealized Partisanship. A Theory of Dealignment," *The Journal of Politics*, 49/2, 376–400.
Carmines, Edward G., and James A. Stimson (1980). "The Two Faces of Issue Voting," *The American Political Science Review*, 74/1, 78–91.
Carrubba, Cliff, and Richard J. Timpone (2005). "Explaining Vote Switching Across First- and Second-Order Elections," *Comparative Political Studies*, 38/3, 260–81.
Carsey, Thomas M., and Geoffrey C. Layman (2006). "Changing Sides or Changing Minds? Party Identification and Policy Preferences in the American Electorate," *American Journal of Political Science*, 50/2, 464–77.
Carty, R. Kenneth, and Munroe Eagles (1999). "Do Local Campaigns Matter? Campaign Spending, the Local Canvass and Party Support in Canada," *Electoral Studies*, 18/1, 69–87.
Cayrol, Roland (1991). "European Elections and the Pre-electoral Period. Media Use and Campaign Evaluations," *European Journal of Political Research*, 19/1, 17–29.
Chaffee, Steven H., and Joan Schleuder (1986). "Measurement and Effects of Attention to Media News," *Human Communication Research*, 13/1, 76–107.
Chernev, Alexander (2003). "When More is Less and Less is More. The Role of Ideal Point Availability and Assortment in Consumer Choice," *Journal of Consumer Research*, 30/2, 170–83.
Clark, Terry Nichols, and Seymour M. Lipset (2001). *The Breakdown of Class Politics. A Debate on Post-Industrial Stratification*. Washington/Baltimore: Woodrow Wilson Center Press/Johns Hopkins University Press.
Clarke, Harold D., et al. (2009a). *Performance Politics and the British Voter*. Cambridge: Cambridge University Press.
Clarke, Harold D., et al. (2009b). "Travel Tips for Students of Electoral Choice. The Dynamic of Partisanship in Britain and Elsewhere," in John Bartle and Paolo Bellucci (eds.), *Political Parties and Partisanship. Social Identity and Individual Attitudes*. London: Routledge, pp. 88–106.
Coleman, James S. (1990). *Foundations in Social Theory*. Cambridge, MA/London: Belknap Press.
Converse, Philip E. (1962). "Information Flow and Stability of Partisan Attitudes," *Public Opinion Quaterly*, 26/4, 578–99.
Converse, Philip E. (1964). "The Nature of Belief Systems in Mass Publics," in David E. Apter (ed.), *Ideology and Discontent*. New York: Free Press, pp. 206–61.
Converse, Philip E. (1966). "The Concept of a Normal Vote," in Angus Campbell et al. (eds.), *Elections and Political Order*. New York: Wiley, pp. 9–39.
Converse, Philip E. (1969). "Of Time and Partisan Stability," *Comparative Political Studies*, 2/2, 139–71.
Converse, Philip E. (1976). *The Dynamics of Party Support. Cohort-Analyzing Party Identification*. Beverly Hills, CA: Sage.
Converse, Philip E. (1990). "Popular Representation and the Distribution of Information," in John A. Ferejohn and James H. Kuklinski (eds.), *Information and Democratic Processes*, Urbana/Chicago: University of Illinois Press, pp. 369–88.

Converse, Philip E. (2000). "Assessing the Capacity of Mass Electorates," *Annual Review of Political Science*, 3/1, 331–53.

Converse, Philip E. (2006). "Democratic Theory and Electoral Reality," *Critical Review*, 18/1–3, 297–329.

Costa, Dora L., and Matthew E. Kahn (2003). "Civic Engagement and Community Heterogeneity. An Economist's Perspective," *Perspectives on Politics*, 1/1, 103–11.

Cox, Gary W. (1997). *Making Votes Count. Strategic Coordination in the World's Electoral Systems*. Cambridge: Cambridge University Press.

Cox, Karen E., and Leonard J. Schoppa (2002). "Interaction Effects in Mixed-Member Electoral Systems. Theory and Evidence from Germany, Japan, and Italy," *Comparative Political Studies*, 35/9, 1027–53.

Craig, Stephen C., Michael D. Martinez, and James G. Kane (2005). "Ambivalence and Response Instability. A Panel Study," in Stephen C. Craig and Michael D. Martinez (eds.), *Ambivalence and the Structure of Political Opinion*. New York: Palgrave Macmillan, pp. 55–71.

Curran, James, et al. (2009). "Media System, Public Knowledge and Democracy. A Comparative Study," *European Journal of Communication*, 24/1, 5–26.

Curtice, John (1989). "The 1989 European Elections. Protest or Green Tide?," *Electoral Studies*, 8/3, 217–30.

Curtice, John, and Alison Park (2010). *Will Anyone Vote? Prospects for Turnout in the General Election*. London: National Centre for Social Research.

D'Alessio, Dave, and Mike Allen (2000). "Media Bias in Presidential Elections. A Meta-Analysis," *Journal of Communication*, 50/4, 133–56.

Dalton, Russell J. (1984). "Cognitive Mobilization and Partisan Dealignment in Advanced Industrial Democracies," *The Journal of Politics*, 46/1, 264–84.

Dalton, Russell J. (2000). "The Decline of Party Identifications," in Russell J. Dalton and Martin P. Wattenberg (eds.), *Parties without Partisans. Political Change in Advanced Industrial Democracies*. Oxford: Oxford University Press, pp. 19–36.

Dalton, Russell J. (2002). *Citizen Politics. Public Opinion and Political Parties in Advanced Industrial Democracies* (3rd edn). Chatham, NJ: Chatham House.

Dalton, Russell J. (2008). *Citizen Politics. Public Opinion and Political Parties in Advanced Industrial Democracies* (5th edn). Washington, DC: CQ Press.

Dalton, Russell J. (2011). "Left-Right Orientations, Context, and Voting Choices," in Russell J. Dalton and Christopher J. Anderson (eds.), *Citizens, Context, and Choice*. New York: Oxford University Press, pp. 103–25.

Dalton, Russell J. (2012). "Apartisans and the Changing German Electorate," *Electoral Studies*, 31/1, 35–45.

Dalton, Russell J., Paul A. Beck, and Robert Huckfeldt (1998). "Partisan Cues and the Media. Information Flows in the 1992 Presidential Election," *American Political Science Review*, 92/1, 111–26.

Dalton, Russell J., Scott C. Flanagan, and Paul Allen Beck (1984). *Electoral Change in Advanced Industrial Democracies. Realignment or Dealignment?* Princeton, NJ: Princeton University Press.

Dalton, Russell J., Ian McAllister, and Martin P. Wattenberg (2000). "The Consequences of Partisan Dealignment," in Russell J. Dalton and Martin P. Wattenberg (eds.), *Parties without Partisans. Political Change in Advanced Industrial Democracies*. Oxford: Oxford University Press, pp. 38–63.

Dalton, Russell J., Ian McAllister, and Martin P. Wattenberg (2002a). "The Consequences of Partisan Dealignment," in Russell J. Dalton and Martin P. Wattenberg (eds.), *Parties Without Partisans. Political Change in Advanced Industrial Democracies* (1st publ. in paperback). Oxford: Oxford University Press, pp. 37–63.

Dalton, Russell J., Ian McAllister, and Martin P. Wattenberg (2002b). "Political Parties and their Publics," in Richard K. Luther and Ferdinand Müller-Rommel (eds.), *Political Parties in the New Europe*. Oxford: Oxford University Press, pp. 19–42.

Dalton, Russell J., and Robert Rohrschneider (1990). "Wählerwandel und Abschwächung der Parteineigung von 1972 bis 1987," in Max Kaase and Hans-Dieter Klingemann (eds.), *Wahlen und Wähler. Analysen aus Anlaß der Bundestagswahl 1987*. Opladen: Westdeutscher Verlag, pp. 297–324.

Dalton, Russell J., and Martin P. Wattenberg (2000a). *Parties without Partisans. Political Change in Advanced Industrial Democracies*. Oxford: Oxford University Press.

Dalton, Russell J., and Martin P. Wattenberg (2000b). "Partisan Change and the Democratic Process," in Russell J. Dalton and Martin P. Wattenberg (eds.), *Parties without Partisans. Political Change in Advanced Industrial Democracies*. Oxford: Oxford University Press, pp. 261–84.

Dalton, Russell J., and Martin P. Wattenberg (2000c). "Unthinkable Democracy. Political Change in Advanced Industrial Democracies," in Russell J. Dalton and Martin P. Wattenberg (eds.), *Parties without Partisans. Political Change in Advanced Industrial Democracies*. Oxford: Oxford University Press, pp. 2–18.

Dalton, Russell J., and Martin P. Wattenberg (2002). "Unthinkable Democracy. Political Change in Advanced Industrial Democracies," in Russell J. Dalton and Martin P. Wattenberg (eds.), *Parties Without Partisans. Political Change in Advanced Industrial Democracies* (1st publ. in paperback). Oxford: Oxford University Press, pp. 3–16.

Dassonneville, Ruth, Marc Hooghe, and Bram Vanhoutte (2012). "Age, Period and Cohort Effects in the Decline of Party Identification in Germany. An Analysis of a Two Decade Panel Study in Germany (1992–2009)," *German Politics*, 21/2, 209–27.

de Vreese, Claes H., Edmund Lauf, and Jochen Peter (2007). "The Media and European Parliament Elections. Second-rate Coverage of a Second-order Event?," in Wouter van der Brug and Cees van der Eijk (eds.), *European Elections & Domestic Politics. Lessons from the Past and Scenarios for the Future*. Notre Dame: University of Notre Dame Press, pp. 116–30.

de Vries, Catherine E. (2010). "EU Issue Voting. Asset or Liability? How European Integration Affects Parties' Electoral Fortunes," *European Union Politics*, 11/1, 89–117.

de Vries, Catherine E., and Sara B. Hobolt (2012). "When Dimensions Collide. The Electoral Success of Issue Entrepreneurs," *European Union Politics*, 13/2, 246–68.

de Vries, Catherine E., et al. (2011). "Individual and Contextual Variation in EU Issue Voting. The Role of Political Information," *Electoral Studies*, 30/1, 16–28.

Debus, Marc (2012). "Sozialstrukturelle und einstellungsbasierte Determinanten des Wahlverhaltens und ihr Einfluss bei Bundestagswahlen im Zeitverlauf. Westdeutschland 1976 bis 2009," in Rüdiger Schmitt-Beck (ed.), *Wählen in Deutschland. Special issue 45 of Politische Vierteljahresschrift (PVS)*. Baden-Baden: Nomos, pp. 40–62.

Delli Carpini, Michael X., and Scott Keeter (1996). *What Americans Know about Politics and Why It Matters*. New Haven: Yale University Press.

Denver, David, et al. (2003). "Constitutional Campaigning in Britain 1992-2001. Centralization and Modernization," *Party Politics*, 9/5, 541-59.

Denver, David, and Gordon Hands (1993). "Measuring the Intensity and Effectiveness of Constituency Campaigning in the 1992 General Election," *British Elections and Parties Yearbook*, 3/1, 229-42.

Denver, David, and Gordon Hands (1997). "Challengers, Incumbents and the Impact of Constituency Campaigning in Britain," *Electoral Studies*, 16, 175-93.

Denver, David, Gordon Hands, and Ian MacAllister (2004). "The Electoral Impact of Constituency Campaigning in Britain, 1992-2001," *Political Studies*, 52/2, 289-306.

Downs, Anthony (1957a). *An Economic Theory of Democracy*. New York: Harper & Row.

Downs, Anthony (1957b). "An Economic Theory of Political Action in a Democracy," *Journal of Political Economy*, 65/2, 135-50.

Downs, Anthony (1965). *An Economic Theory of Democracy* (paperback edn.). Boston: Addison Wesley.

Druckman, James N. (2005). "Media Matter. How Newspapers and Television News Cover Campaigns and Influence Voters," *Political Communication*, 22/4, 463-81.

Druckman, James N., and Michael Parkin (2005). "The Impact of Media Bias. How Editorial Slant Affects Voters," *Journal of Politics*, 67/4, 1030-49.

Duch, Raymond M., Jeff May, and David A. Armstrong (2010). "Coalition-directed Voting in Multiparty Democracies," *American Political Science Review*, 104/4, 698-719.

Duverger, Maurice (1963). *Political Parties. Their Organization and Activity in the Modern State*. New York: Wiley.

Eatwell, Roger (2003). "Ten Theories of the Extreme Right," in Peter H. Merkl and Leonard Weinberg (eds.), *Right-Wing Extremism in the Twenty-first Century*. London: Frank Cass, pp. 45-70.

EES (2009). *European Parliament Election Study 2009, Voter Study, Advance Release* [Database]. <http://www.piredeu.eu> accessed 11 November 2013.

Elff, Martin (2009). "Social Divisions, Party Positions, and Electoral Behaviour," *Electoral Studies*, 28/2, 297-308.

Elff, Martin, and Sigrid Roßteutscher (forthcoming). *Church Affiliation, Church Attendance and the Support for Christian Democrats*. Unpublished manuscript.

Elff, Martin, and Sigrid Roßteutscher (2011). "Stability or Decline? Class, Religion and the Vote in Germany," *German Poltics*, 20/1, 107-27.

Enelow, James M., and Melvin J. Hinich (1984a). "Probabilistic Voting and the Importance of Centrist Ideologies in Democratic Elections," *Journal of Politics*, 46/2, 459-78.

Enelow, James M., and Melvin J. Hinich (1984b). *The Spatial Theory of Voting. An Introduction*. Cambridge: Cambridge University Press.

Erikson, Robert S., Michael B. MacKuen, and James A. Stimson (2002). *The Macro-Polity*. New York: Cambridge University Press.

Esser, Frank, and Katharina Hemmer (2008). "Characteristics and Dynamics of Election News Coverage in Germany," in Jesper Strömbäck and Lynda Lee Kaid (eds.), *Handbook of Election News Coverage around the World*. London: Routledge, pp. 289-307.

Evans, Geoffrey (2000). "The Continued Significance of Class Voting," *Annual Review of Political Science*, 3, 401-17.

Evans, Geoffrey, and Robert Andersen (2004). "Do Issues Decide? Partisan Conditioning and Perceptions of Party Issue Positions across the Electoral Cycle," *British Elections & Parties Review*, 14/1, 18–39.

Evans, Geoffrey, and Mark Pickup (2010). "Reversing the Causal Arrow. The Political Conditioning of Economic Perceptions in the 2000–2004 U.S. Presidential Election Cycle," *Journal of Politics*, 72/4, 1236–51.

Eveland, William P., and Myiah Hutchens Hiveley (2009). "Political Discussion Frequency, Network Size and 'Heterogeneity' of Discussion as Predictors of Political Knowledge and Participation," *Journal of Communication*, 59/2, 205–24.

Eveland, William P., Dhavan V. Shah, and Nojin Kwak (2003). "Assessing Causality in the Cognitive Mediation Model. A Panel Study of Motivations, Information Processing, and Learning during Campaign 2000," *Communication Research*, 30/4, 359–86.

Ezrow, Lawrence, et al. (2011). "Mean Voter Representation and Partisan Constituency Representation. Do Parties Respond to the Mean Voter Position or to Their Supporters?," *Party Politics*, 17/3, 275–301.

Falter, Jürgen W. (1991). *Hitlers Wähler*. München: C.H. Beck.

Falter, Jürgen W., and Harald Schoen (1999). "Wahlen und Wählerverhalten," in Thomas Ellwein and Everhard Holtmann (eds.), *50 Jahre Bundesrepublik Deutschland: Rahmenbedingungen—Entwicklungen—Perspektiven. Special issue 30 of Politische Vierteljahresschrift (PVS)*. Opladen: Westdeutscher Verlag, pp. 454–70.

Falter, Jürgen W., Harald Schoen, and Claudio Caballero (2000). "Dreißig Jahre danach. Zur Validierung des Konzepts „Parteiidentifikation" in der Bundesrepublik," in Markus Klein et al. (eds.), *50 Jahre empirische Wahlforschung in Deutschland. Entwicklung, Befunde, Perspektiven, Daten*. Wiesbaden: Westdeutscher Verlag, pp. 235–71.

Farah, Barbara G. (1980). *Political Representation in West Germany. The Institution and Maintenance of Mass Elite Linkages*. Michigan: University of Michigan.

Farrell, David M., and Rüdiger Schmitt-Beck (eds.) (2002). *Do Political Campaigns Matter? Campaign Effects in Elections and Referendums*. London: Routledge.

Ferrara, Federico, Erik S. Herron, and Misa Nishikawa (2005). *Mixed Electoral Systems. Contamination and Its Consequences*. Basingstoke: Palgrave Macmillan.

Festinger, Leon (1957). *A Theory of Cognitive Dissonance*. Stanford: Stanford University Press.

Fine, Gary Alan, and Brooke Harrington (2004). "Tiny Publics. Small Groups and Civil Society," *Sociological Theory*, 22/3, 341–56.

Finkel, Steven E. (1993). "Reexamining the 'Minimal Effects' Model in Recent Presidential Campaigns," *Journal of Politics*, 55/1, 1–21.

Fiorina, Morris P. (1981). *Retrospective Voting in American National Elections*. New Haven, CT: Yale University Press.

Fiorina, Morris P. (1996). *Divided Government*. Needham Heights: Simon & Schuster.

Fishbein, Martin, and Icek Ajzen (1975). *Belief, Attitude, Intention, and Behavior. An Introduction to Theory and Research*. Reading: Addison-Wesley.

Fisher, Justin, and David Denver (2009). "Evaluating the Electoral Effects of Traditional and Modern Modes of Constituency Campaigning in Britain 1992–2005," *Parliamentary Affairs*, 62/2, 196–210.

Fournier, Patrick, et al. (2003). "Issue Importance and Performance Voting," *Political Behavior,* 25/1, 51–67.
Franklin, Charles H., and John E. Jackson (1983). "The Dynamics of Party Identification," *American Political Science Review,* 77/4, 957–73.
Franklin, Mark (1985). *The Decline of Class Voting in Britain. Changes in the Basis of Electoral Choice* 1964–1983. Oxford: Oxford University Press.
Franklin, Mark (1996). "Electoral Participation," in Laurence LeDuc, Richard G. Niemi, and Pippa Norris (eds.), *Comparing Democracies. Elections and Voting in Global Perspective.* Thousand Oaks, CA: Sage, pp. 216–35.
Franklin, Mark (2001). "How Structural Factors Cause Turnout Variations at European Parliament Elections," *European Union Politics,* 2/3, 309–28.
Franklin, Mark (2004). *Voter Turnout and the Dynamics of Electoral Competition in Established Democracies since 1945.* Cambridge: Cambridge University Press.
Franklin, Mark, and Sara B. Hobolt (2011). "The Legacy of Lethargy. How Elections to the European Parliament Depress Turnout," *Electoral Studies,* 30/1, 67–76.
Franklin, Mark, Thomas T. Mackie, and Henry Valen (eds.) (1992). *Electoral Change. Responses to Evolving Social and Attitudinal Structures in Western Countries.* Cambridge: Cambridge University Press.
Franklin, Mark, Cees van der Eijk, and Erik Oppenhuis (1996). "The Institutional Context. Turnout," in Cees van der Eijk and Mark N. Franklin (eds.), *Choosing Europe? The European Electorate and National Politics in the Face of Union.* Ann Arbor: The University of Michigan Press, pp. 3–10.
Franklin, Mark, and Till Weber (2010). "American Electoral Practices in Comparative Perspective," in Jan E. Leighley (ed.), *Oxford Handbook of American Elections and Electoral Behaviour.* Oxford: Oxford University Press, pp. 667–84.
Franzese, Robert J., Jr. (2005). "Empirical Strategies for Various Manifestations of Multilevel Data," *Political Analysis,* 13/4, 430–46.
Fuchs, Dieter, and Hans-Dieter Klingemann (1990). "The Left-Right Schema," in M. Kent Jennings and Jan W. van Deth (eds.), *Continuities in Political Action.* Berlin/New York: de Gruyter, pp. 203–34.
Gabriel, Oscar W. (2011). "Der rote Osten. Ist Ostdeutschland politisch ganz anders?," in Evelyn Bytzek and Sigrid Rossteutscher (eds.), *Der unbekannte Wähler. Mythen und Fakten über das Wahlverhalten der Deutschen.* Frankfurt am Main/New York: Campus, pp. 157–76.
Gelman, Andrew, and Gary King (1993). "Why Are American Presidential Election Campaign Polls So Variable When Voters Are So Predictable?," *British Journal of Political Science,* 23/4, 409–51.
Gelman, Andrew, and Hal Stern (2006). "The Difference between 'Significant' and 'Not Significant' Is Not Itself Statistically Significant," *The American Statistician,* 60/4, 328–31.
Gelman, Andrew, et al. (2008). "A Weakly Informative Default Prior Distribution for Logistic and Other Regression Models," *The Annals of Applied Statistics,* 2/4, 1360–83.
Gerber, Alan S., Gregory A. Huber, and Ebony A. Washington (2010). "Party Affiliation, Partisanship, and Political Beliefs. A Field Experiment," *American Political Science Review,* 104/4, 720–44.

Gerber, Alan S., and Todd Rogers (2009). "Descriptive Social Norms and Motivation to Vote. Everybody's Voting and So Should You," *The Journal of Politics*, 71/1, 178–91.
Geys, Benny (2006a). "Explaining Voter Turnout. A Review of Aggregate-level Research," *Electoral Studies*, 25/4, 637–63.
Geys, Benny (2006b). "'Rational' Theories of Voter Turnout. A Review," *Political Studies Review*, 4/1, 16–35.
Gidengil, Elisabeth, et al. (2002). "Priming and Campaign Context. Evidence from Recent Canadian Elections," in David M. Farrell and Rüdiger Schmitt-Beck (eds.), *Do Political Campaigns Matter? Campaign Effects in Elections and Referendums*. London: Routledge, pp. 76–91.
Giebler, Heiko, and Aiko Wagner (2011). *Contrasting First and Second Order Electoral Behaviour. Determinants of Individual Party Choice in European and National Elections (under review)*. Unpublished manuscript.
Giebler, Heiko, and Andreas M. Wüst (2010). "Campaigning on an Upper Level? Individual Campaigning in the 2009 European Parliament Elections in its Determinants," *Electoral Studies*, 30/1 (Special Symposia of Electoral Studies "Electoral Democracy in the European Union" edited by Sara B. Hobolt and Mark Franklin), 53–66.
Giebler, Heiko, and Andreas M. Wüst (2011a). "Campaigning on an Upper Level? Individual Campaigning in the 2009 European Parliament Elections in its Determinants," *Electoral Studies*, 30/1, 53–66.
Giebler, Heiko, and Andreas M. Wüst (2011b). "Individuelle Wahlkämpfe bei der Europawahl 2009. Länderübergreifende und ebenenspezifische Befunde," in Jens Tenscher (ed.), *Kampagnen nach Wahl*. Wiesbaden: VS Verlag für Sozialwissenschaften, pp. 121–52.
Glantz, Alexander (2011). *Wahlentscheidungen auf der Spur. Der Einfluss individueller und situativer Faktoren auf Entscheidungsstrategien*. Wiesbaden: VS Verlag für Sozialwissenschaften.
Glantz, Alexander, Severin Bathelt, and Jürgen Maier (forthcoming). "Politische Kenntnisse in Deutschland. Entwicklung und Determinanten, 1949–2009," in Sigrid Roßteutscher, Thorsten Faas, and Ulrich Rosar (eds.), *Bürger und Wähler im Wandel der Zeit. 25 Jahre Wahl- und Einstellungsforschung in Deutschland*. Wiesbaden: Springer VS.
Glasgow, Garrett (1997). *Heterogeneity, Salience, and Voter Decision Rules for Candidate Preference*, Political Methodology Working Paper. Pasadena, CA: California Institute of Technology.
Glasgow, Garrett (1999). *Heterogeneity in the Impact of Issues on Vote Choice*, Political Methodology Working Paper. Pasadena, CA: California Institute of Technology.
Glasgow, Garrett (2001). "Mixed Logit Models for Multiparty Elections," *Political Analysis*, 9/2, 116–36.
Glasgow, Garrett (2005). "Evidence of Group-Based Economic Voting. NAFTA and Union Households in the 1992 U.S. Presidential Election," *Political Research Quarterly*, 58/3, 427–34.
GLES (2011a). *Candidate Campaign Survey, Survey and Structural Data (GLES 2009). Principal investigators: Hans Rattinger, Sigrid Roßteutscher, Rüdiger Schmitt-Beck, Bernhard Weßels, Thomas Gschwend, Hermann Schmitt, Andreas Wüst, Thomas*

Zittel. *GESIS Data Archive, Cologne. ZA5318 Data file, Pre-Release1.0* [online dataset]. <doi:10.4232/1.10377>.

GLES (2011b). *Pre-election Cross Section (GLES 2009)*. Principal investigators: Hans Rattinger, Hans, Sigrid Roßteutscher, Rüdiger Schmitt-Beck, Bernhard Weßels. *GESIS Data Archive, Cologne. ZA5300 Data file Version 5.0.0* [online dataset]. <doi:10.4232/1.10997>.

GLES (2011c). *Multi Level Panel (GLES 2009)*. Principal investigators: Hans Rattinger, Sigrid Roßteutscher, Rüdiger Schmitt-Beck, Bernhard Weßels. *GESIS Data Archive, Cologne. ZA5304 Data file Version 2.1.0* [online dataset]. <doi:10.4232/1.10363>.

GLES (2011d). *Rolling Cross-Section Campaign Survey with Post-election Panel Wave (GLES 2009)*. Principal investigators: Hans Rattinger, Sigrid Roßteutscher, Rüdiger Schmitt-Beck, Bernhard Weßels. *GESIS Data Archive, Cologne. ZA5303 Data file Version 5.0.0* [online dataset]. <doi:10.4232/1.10996>.

GLES (2012a). *Long-term Panel 2005-2009-2013 (GLES 2009)*. Principal investigators: Hans Rattinger, Sigrid Roßteutscher, Rüdiger Schmitt-Beck, Bernhard Weßels, Steffen Kühnel, Oskar Niedermayer, Bettina Westle. *GESIS Data Archive, Cologne. ZA5321 Data file Version 1.0.0* [online dataset]. <doi:10.4232/1.11145>.

GLES (2012b). *Long-term Online Tracking, Cumulation 2009–2011 (GLES)*. Principal investigators: Hans Rattinger, Sigrid Roßteutscher, Rüdiger Schmitt-Beck, Bernhard Weßels. *GESIS Data Archive, Cologne. ZA5357 Data file Version 1.0.0* [online dataset]. <doi:10.4232/1.11389>.

GLES (2012c). *Campaign Media Content Analysis, TV (GLES 2009)*. Principal investigators: Hans Rattinger, Sigrid Roßteutscher, Rüdiger Schmitt-Beck, Bernhard Weßels. *GESIS Data Archive, Cologne. ZA5306 Data file Version 1.1.0* [online dataset]. <doi: 10.4232/1.11401>.

Gluchowski, Peter (1983). "Wahlerfahrung und Parteiidentifikation. Zur Einbindung von Wählern in das Parteiensystem der Bundesrepublik," in Max Kaase and Hans-Dieter Klingemann (eds.), *Wahlen und politisches System. Analysen aus Anlaß der Bundestagswahl 1980*. Opladen: Westdeutscher Verlag, pp. 442–77.

Gomez, Brad T., and Matthew J. Wilson (2001). "Political Sophistication and Economic Voting in the American Electorate. A Theory of Heterogeneous Attribution," *American Journal of Political Science*, 45/4, 899–914.

Granovetter, Mark S. (1973). "The Strength of Weak Ties," *American Journal of Sociology*, 78/6, 1360–80.

Granovetter, Mark S. (1983). "The Strength of Weak Ties. A Network Theory Revisited," *Sociological Theory*, 1/1, 201–33.

Green, Donald P., and Bradley Palmquist (1990). "Of Artifacts and Partisan Instability," *American Journal of Political Science*, 34/3, 872–902.

Green, Donald P., and Bradley Palmquist (1994). "How Stable is Party Identification?," *Political Behavior*, 16/4, 437–66.

Green, Donald P., and Eric Schickler (2009). "A Spirited Defence of Party Identification against its Critics," in John Bartle and Paolo Bellucci (eds.), *Political Parties and Partisanship. Social Identity and Individual Attitudes*. London: Routledge, pp. 180–99.

Green, Donald P., and David H. Yoon (2002). "Reconciling Individual and Aggregate Evidence Concerning Partisan Stability. Applying Time-Series Models to Panel Survey Data," *Political Analysis*, 10/1, 1–23.

Green, Jane, and Sara B. Hobolt (2008). "Owning the Issue Agenda. Party Strategies and Vote Choices in British Elections," *Electoral Studies*, 27/3, 460–76.
Green, Jane, and Will Jennings (2012). "The Dynamics of Issue Competence and Vote for Parties in and out of Power. An Analysis of Valence in Britain, 1979–1997," *European Journal of Political Research*, 51/4, 469–503.
Greifeneder, Rainer, Benjamin Scheibehenne, and Nina Kleber (2010). "Less May Be More When Choosing is Difficult. Choice Complexity and Too Much Choice," *Acta Psychologica*, 133/1, 45–50.
Grofman, Bernhard, Frank Wayman, and Matthew Barreto (2009). "Rethinking Partisanship. Some Thoughts on a Unified Theory," in John Bartle and Paolo Bellucci (eds.), *Political Parties and Partisanship. Social Identity and Individual Attitudes*. London: Routledge, pp. 60–74.
Gschwend, Thomas (2007). "Ticket-splitting and Strategic Voting under Mixed Electoral Rules. Evidence from Germany," *European Journal of Political Research*, 46/1, 1–23.
Gschwend, Thomas, Ron Johnston, and Charles Pattie (2003). "Split-Ticket Patterns in Mixed-Member Proportional Election Systems. Estimates and Analyses of their Spatial Variation at the German Federal Election, 1998," *British Journal of Political Science*, 33/1, 109–27.
Gschwend, Thomas, and Henk van der Kolk (2006). "Split Ticket Voting in Mixed Member Proportional Systems. The Hypothetical Case of The Netherlands," *Acta Politica*, 41/2, 163–79.
Gschwend, Thomas, and Thomas Zittel (2012). "Machen Wahlkreiskandidaten einen Unterschied? Die Persönlichkeitswahl als interaktiver Prozess," in Rüdiger Schmitt-Beck (ed.), *Wählen in Deutschland. Special issue 45 of Politische Vierteljahresschrift (PVS)*. Baden-Baden: Nomos, pp. 371–92.
Gunther, Richard, and Larry Diamond (2001). "Types and Functions of Parties," in Larry Diamond and Richard Gunther (eds.), *Political Parties and Democracy*. Baltimore/London: The John Hopkins University Press, pp. 3–39.
Gunther, Richard, and Larry Diamond (2003). "Species of Political Parties," *Party Politics*, 9/2, 167–99.
Gunther, Richard, Jose Ramón Montero, and Hans-Jürgen Puhle (eds.) (2007). *Democracy, Intermediation, and Voting on Four Continents*. Oxford: Oxford University Press.
Hainmueller, Jens, and Holger L. Kern (2008). "Incumbency as a Source of Spillover Effects in Mixed Electoral Systems. Evidence from a Regression-Discontinuity Design," *Electoral Studies*, 27/2, 213–27.
Hayes, Danny (2009). "Has Television Personalized Voting Behavior?," *Political Behavior*, 31/2, 231.
Heath, Anthony, et al. (1999). "Between First and Second Order. A Comparison of Voting Behaviour in European and Local Elections in Britain," *European Journal of Political Research*, 35/3, 389–414.
Herron, Erik S., and Misa Nishikawa (2001). "Contamination Effects and the Number of Parties in Mixed-superposition Electoral Systems," *Electoral Studies*, 20/1, 63–86.
Herron, Michael C. (1999). "Postestimation Uncertainty in Limited Dependent Variable Models," *Political Analysis*, 8/1, 83–98.

Hix, Simon, and Michael Marsh (2011). "Second-Order Effects plus Pan-European Political Swings. An Analysis of European Parliament Elections across Time," *Electoral Studies*, 30/1, 4–15.

Hobolt, Sara B. (2005). "When Europe Matters. The Impact of Political Information on Voting Behaviour in EU Referendums," *Journal of Elections, Public Opinion and Parties*, 15/1, 85–109.

Hobolt, Sara B., and Jeffrey A. Karp (2010). "Voters and Coalition Governments," *Electoral Studies*, 29/3, 299–307.

Hobolt, Sara B., Jae-Jae Spoon, and James R. Tilley (2008). "A Vote Against Europe? Explaining Defection at the 1999 and 2004 European Parliament Elections," *British Journal of Political Science*, 39, 93–115.

Hobolt, Sara B., and Jill Wittrock (2011). "The Second-order Election Model Revisited. An Experimental Test of Vote Choices in European Parliament Elections," *Electoral Studies*, 30/1, 29–40.

Holbrook, Thomas M. (1996). *Do Campaigns Matter?* Thousand Oaks: Sage.

Hopmann, David Nicolas, et al. (2010). "Effects of Election News Coverage. How Visibility and Tone Influence Party Choice," *Political Communication*, 27/4, 389–405.

Howell, Susan E. (1986). "Candidates and Attitudes. Revisiting the Question of Causality," *The Journal of Politics*, 48/2, 450–64.

Huber, John D., and G. Bingham Powell, Jr. (1994). "Congruence between Citizens and Policymakers in Two Visions of Liberal Democracy," *World Politics*, 46/3, 291–326.

Huber, Sascha, et al. (2009). "Erwartungsbildung über den Wahlausgang und ihr Einfluss auf die Wahlentscheidung," in Oscar W Gabriel, Jürgen W. Falter, and Bernhard Weßels (eds.), *Wahlen und Wähler. Analysen aus Anlass der Bundestagswahl 2005*. Wiesbaden: VS Verlag für Sozialwissenschaften, pp. 562–84.

Huckfeldt, Robert (2001). "The Social Communication of Political Expertise," *American Journal of Political Science*, 45/2, 425–38.

Huckfeldt, Robert, Paul E. Johnson, and John Sprague (2005). "Individuals, Dyads, and Networks. Autoregressive Pattern of Political Influence," in Alan S. Zuckerman (ed.), *The Social Logic of Politics. Personal Networks as Contexts for Political Behavior*. Philadelphia: Temple University Press, pp. 21–50.

Huckfeldt, Robert, and John Sprague (1995). *Citizens, Politics, and Social Communication. Information and Influence in an Election Campaign*. Cambridge: Cambridge University Press.

Inglehart, Ronald (1990). *Culture Shift in Advanced Industrial Society*. Princeton, NJ: Princeton University Press.

Inglehart, Ronald, and Christian Welzel (2005). *Modernization, Cultural Change and Democracy. The Human Development Sequence*. Cambridge: Cambridge University Press.

Irwin, Galen A., and Joop J. van Holsteyn (2003). *They Say It Can't Be Done? Strategic Voting in Multi-party Proportional Systems. The Case of the Netherlands*. Paper prepared for presentation at the Annual Meeting of the American Political Science Association, Philadelphia, August 28–31, 2003.

Iyengar, Shanto, and Donald R. Kinder (1987). *News That Matters. Television and American Opinion*. Chicago: University of Chicago Press.

Iyengar, Sheena S., and Mark R. Lepper (2000). "When Choice Is Demotivating. Can One Desire Too Much of a Good Thing?," *Journal of Personality and Social Psychology,* 79/6, 995–1006.
Jackman, Robert W. (1987). "Political Institutions and Voter Turnout in the Industrial Democracies," *American Political Science Review,* 81/2, 405–23.
Jackman, Robert W., and Ross A. Miller (1995). "Voter Turnout in the Industrial Democracies During the 1980s," *Comparative Political Studies,* 27/4, 467–92.
Jacobson, Gary C. (1980). *Money in Congressional Elections.* New Haven: Yale University Press.
Jennings, M. Kent (1990). "The Crystallization of Orientations," in M. Kent Jennings and Jan W. van Deth (eds.), *Continuities in Political Action.* Berlin/New York: De Gruyter, pp. 313–48.
Johnston, Richard, and Henry E. Brady (2002). "The Rolling Cross-Section Design," *Electoral Studies,* 21/2, 283–95.
Johnston, Richard, Michael G. Hagen, and Kathleen Hall Jamieson (2004). *The 2000 Presidential Election and the Foundations of Party Politics.* Cambridge: Cambridge University Press.
Johnston, Richard, J. Scott Matthews, and Amanda Bittner (2007). "Turnout and the Party System in Canada, 1988–2004," *Electoral Studies,* 26/4, 735–45.
Johnston, Richard, et al. (1992). *Letting the People Decide. Dynamics of a Canadian Election.* Stanford: Stanford University Press.
Johnston, Ron, and Charles Pattie (2006). *Putting Voters in their Place. Geography and Elections in Great Britain.* Oxford: Oxford University Press.
Johnston, Ronald J., and Charles J. Pattie (1995). "The Impact of Spending on Party Constituency Campaigns at Recent British General Elections," *Party Politics,* 1/2, 261–73.
Johnston, Ronald J., and Charles J. Pattie (1999). "Aspects of the Interrelationships of Attitudes and Behavior as Illustrated by a Longitudinal Study of British Adults. 2. Predicting Vote Intentions, Strength of Party Identification, Change in Both," *Environment and Planning,* 31/7, 1279–94.
Jones, Bryan D. (1999). "Bounded Rationality," *Annual Review of Political Science,* 2, 297–321.
Jusko, Karen Long, and W. Phillips Shively (2005). "Applying a Two-Step Strategy to the Analysis of Cross-National Public Opinion Data," *Political Analysis,* 13/4, 327–44.
Kaase, Max (1967). *Wechsel von Parteipräferenzen.* Meisenheim am Glan: Anton Hain.
Kaase, Max (1984). "Personalized Proportional Representation. The Model of the West German Electoral System," in Arend Lijphart and Bernard Grofman (eds.), *Choosing an Electoral System.* New York: Praeger, pp. 155–64.
Karp, Jeffrey A. (2009). "Candidate Effects and Spill-over in Mixed Systems. Evidence from New Zealand," *Electoral Studies,* 28/1, 41–50.
Karp, Jeffrey A., Susan A. Banducci, and Shaun Bowler (2007). "Getting Out the Vote. Party Mobilization in a Comparative Perspective," *British Journal for Political Science,* 38/1, 91–112.
Katz, Elihu, and Paul F. Lazarsfeld (1955). *Personal Influence. The Part Played by People in the Flow of Mass Communication.* Glencoe, IL: The Free Press.

Katz, Gabriel (2009). *Policy-based Abstention in Brazil's 2002 Presidential Election*, VTP Working Paper No. 80, March 2009. Pasadena: California Institute of Technology, Division of the Humanities and Social Sciences.

Katz, Richard S. (2006). "Party in Democratic Theory," in Richard S. Katz and William Crotty (eds.), *Handbook of Party Politics*. London: Sage, pp. 34–46.

Katz, Richard S., and Peter Mair (1995). "Changing Models of Party Organization and Party Democracy. The Emergence of the Cartel Party," *Party Politics*, 1/1, 5–28.

Kaufmann, Karen M., John R. Petrocik, and Daron R. Shaw (2008). *Unconventional Wisdom. Facts and Myths about American Voters*. New York: Oxford University Press.

Kellermann, Charlotte (2008). *Trends and Constellations. Klassische Bestimmungsfaktoren des Wahlverhaltens bei den Bundestagswahlen 1990–2005*. Baden-Baden: Nomos.

Kellermann, Charlotte, and Hans Rattinger (2005). "'Round up the usual suspects'. Die Bedeutung klassischer Bestimmungsfaktoren der Wahlentscheidung bei den Bundestagswahlen 1994 bis 2002," in Jürgen W. Falter, Oscar W. Gabriel, and Bernhard Weßels (eds.), *Wahlen und Wähler. Analysen aus Anlass der Bundestagswahl 2002*. Wiesbaden: VS Verlag für Sozialwissenschaften, pp. 189–212.

Kellermann, Charlotte, and Hans Rattinger (2007). "Wahrnehmungen der Wirtschaftslage und Wahlverhalten," in Hans Rattinger, Oscar W. Gabriel, and Jürgen W. Falter (eds.), *Der gesamtdeutsche Wähler. Stabilität und Wandel des Wählerverhaltens im wiedervereinigten Deutschland*. Baden-Baden: Nomos, pp. 329–256.

Kelley, Stanley Jr. (1983). *Interpreting Elections*. Princeton: Princeton University Press.

Kernell, Samuel (1977). "Presidential Popularity and Negative Voting. An Alternative Explanation of the Midterm Congressional Decline of the President's Party," *American Political Science Review*, 71/1, 44–66.

Key, Jr., Vladimir Orlando (1961). *Public Opinion and American Democracy*. New York: Alfred A. Knopf.

Kinder, Donald R., and D. Roderick Kieweit (1981). "Sociotropic Politics: the American Case," *British Journal for Political Science*, 11, 129–61.

King, Gary (1997). *A Solution to the Ecological Inference Problem. Reconstructing Individual Behaviour from Aggregate Data*. Princeton: Princeton University Press.

Klein, Markus (2002). "Instrumentelles oder expressives Wählen? Eine empirische Untersuchung am Beispiel der Hamburger Bürgerschaftswahl vom 21. September 1997," *Zeitschrift für Soziologie*, 31/5, 411–34.

Klingemann, Hans-Dieter (1972). "Testing the Left-Right Continuum on a Sample of German Voters," *Comparative Political Studies*, 5/1, 93–106.

Klingemann, Hans-Dieter (1973). "Issue-Kompetenz und Wahlentscheidung," *Politische Vierteljahresschrift*, 14/2, 227–56.

Klingemann, Hans-Dieter, and Max Kaase (2001). *Wahlen und Wähler. Analysen aus Anlaß der Bundestagswahl 1998*. Wiesbaden: Westdeutscher Verlag.

Klingemann, Hans-Dieter, and Bernhard Weßels (2001). "Political Consequences of Germany's Mixed-Member System. Personalization at the Grass-Roots?," in Matthew Soberg Shugart and Martin P. Wattenberg (eds.), *Mixed Member Electoral Systems. The Best of Both Worlds?* Oxford: Oxford University Press, pp. 279–96.

Klingemann, Hans-Dieter, and Bernhard Weßels (2009). "How Voters Cope with the Complexity of Their Political Environment. Differentiation of Political Supply,

Effectiveness of Electoral Institutions, and the Calculus of Voting," in Hans-Dieter Klingemann (ed.), *The Comparative Study of Electoral Systems*. New York: Oxford University Press, pp. 237–65.

Klofstad, Casey A. (2007). "Talk Leads to Recruitment. How Discussions about Politics and Current Events Increase Civic Participation," *Political Research Quarterly*, 60/2, 180–91.

Klofstad, Casey A., Anand Sokhey, and Scott D. McClurg (2013). "Disagreeing about Disagreement. How Conflict in Social Networks Affects Political Behavior," *American Journal of Political Science* 57/1, 120–134.

Knoke, David (1990). *Political Networks. The Structural Perspective*. Cambridge: Cambridge University Press.

Knutsen, Oddbjørn (1997). "The Partisan and Value based Component of Left-Right Self-placement. A Comparative Study," *International Political Science Review*, 18/2, 191–225.

Knutsen, Oddbjørn, and Elinor Scarbrough (1995). "Cleavage Politics', in Jan W. van Deth and Elinor Scarbrough (eds.), *The Impact of Values*. Oxford: Oxford University Press, pp. 492–523.

Kohler, Ulrich (2011). "Estimating the Potential Impact of Nonvoters on Outcomes of Parliamentary Elections in Proportional Systems with an Application to German National Elections from 1949 to 2009," *Electoral Studies*, 30/3, 497–509.

Kossinets, Gueorgi, and Duncan J. Watts (2009). "Origins of Homophily in an Evolving Social Network," *American Journal of Sociology*, 115/2, 405–50.

Kraft, Patrick (2012). *Correct Voting in Deutschland. Eine Analyse der Qualität individueller Wahlentscheidungen bei der Bundestagswahl 2009*, MZES Working Paper 148. Mannheim: Mannheimer Zentrum für Europäische Sozialforschung (MZES).

Krassa, Michael A. (1988). "Context and the Canvass. The Mechanisms of Interaction," *Political Behavior*, 10/3, 233–46.

Krewel, Mona, Rüdiger Schmitt-Beck, and Ansgar Wolsing (2011). "The Campaign and Its Dynamics at the 2009 German General Election," *German Politics*, 20/1, 28–50.

Kriesi, Hanspeter, and Pascal Sciarini (2004). "The Impact of Issue Preferences on Voting Choices in the Swiss Federal Elections, 1999," *British Journal of Political Science*, 34/4, 725–59.

Kroh, Martin (2003). *Parties, Politicians, and Policies. Orientations of Vote Choice Across Voters and Contexts*. Berlin: Self-publishing.

Kroh, Martin (2012). "Die abnehmende Bedeutung des Elternhauses. Intergenerationale Übertragung von Parteibindungen in Deutschland 1984 bis 2010," in Rüdiger Schmitt-Beck (ed.), *Wählen in Deutschland. Special issue 45 of Politische Vierteljahresschrift (PVS)*. Baden-Baden: Nomos, pp. 203–26.

Kroh, Martin, and Peter Selb (2009). "Individual and Contextual Origins of Durable Partisanship," in John Bartle and Paolo Bellucci (eds.), *Political Parties and Partisanship. Social Identity and Individual Attitudes*. London: Routledge, pp. 107–20.

Krosnick, Jon A. (1988). "The Role of Attitude Importance in Social Evaluation. A Study of Policy Preferences, Presidential Candidate Evaluations, and Voting Behavior," *Journal of Personality and Social Psychology*, 55/2, 196–210.

Krosnick, Jon A., et al. (1993). "Attitude Strength. One Construct or Many Related Constructs?," *Journal of Personality and Social Psychology*, 65/6, 1132–51.

Kwak, Nojin, et al. (2005). "Talking Politics and Engaging Politics. An Examination of the Interactive Relationship between Structural Features of Political Talk and Discussion Engagement," *Communication Research*, 32/1, 87–111.

Lachat, Romain (2007). *A Heterogeneous Electorate. Political Sophistication, Predisposition Strength, and the Voting Decision Process*. Baden-Baden: Nomos.

Lachat, Romain (2008). "The Impact of Party Polarization on Ideological Voting," *Electoral Studies*, 27/4, 687–98.

Lachat, Romain (2009). *Issue Ownership and Issue Salience Effects. A Two-stage Model of the Voting Decision Process*, CIS Working Paper, No. 50, 2009. Zurich: Center for Comparative and International Studies (ETH Zurich and University of Zurich).

Lane, Jan-Erik, and Svante Ersson (1997). "Parties and Voters: What Creates the Ties?," *Scandinavian Political Studies*, 20/2, 179–96.

Lau, Richard R., David J. Andersen, and David P. Redlawsk (2008). "An Exploration of Correct Voting in Recent U.S. Presidential Elections," *American Journal of Political Science*, 52/2, 395–411.

Lau, Richard R., and David P. Redlawsk (1997). "Voting Correctly," *The American Political Science Review*, 91/3, 585–98.

Lau, Richard R., and David P. Redlawsk (2006). *How Voters Decide. Information Processing during Election Campaigns*. Cambridge: Cambridge University Press.

Lau, Richard R., Parina Patel, Dalia F. Fahmy, and Robert R. Kaufman (2013). "Correct Voting Across Thirty-Three Democracies. A Preliminary Analysis," *British Journal of Political Science*. Available on CJO 2013. <doi: 10.1017/S0007123412000610>.

Lavine, Howard (2001). "The Electoral Consequences of Ambivalence toward Presidential Candidates," *American Journal of Political Science*, 45/4, 915–29.

Lawrence, Christopher N. (2012). *epcp.ado* [stata routine]. <http://www.cnlawrence.com/research/data> accessed September 14, 2012.

Lazarsfeld, Paul F., Bernard Berelson, and Hazel Gaudet (1944). *The People's Choice. How the Voter Makes up his Mind in a Presidential Campaign*. New York: Columbia University Press.

Lazarsfeld, Paul F., Bernard Berelson, and Hazel Gaudet (1968). *The People's Choice. How the Voter Makes Up his Mind in a Presidential Campaign* (3rd edn). New York: Columbia University Press.

Levendusky, Matthew S. (2009). *The Partisan Sort. How Liberals Became Democrats and Conservatives Became Republicans*. Chicago: University of Chicago Press.

Levine, Jeffrey (2005). "Choosing Alone? The Social Network Basis of Modern Political Choice," in Alan Zuckerman (ed.), *The Social Logic of Politics. Personal Networks as Contexts for Political Behavior*. Philadelphia: Temple University Press, pp. 132–51.

Lewis-Beck, Michael S., and Martin Paldam (2000). "Economic Voting. An Introduction," *Electoral Studies*, 19, 113–21.

Lewis-Beck, Michael S., and Mary Stegmaier (2007). "Economic Models of Voting," in Russell J. Dalton and Hans-Dieter Klingemann (eds.), *The Oxford Handbook of Political Behavior*. Oxford: Oxford University Press, pp. 518–37.

Lijphart, Arend (1997). "Unequal Participation. Democracy's Unresolved Dilemma," *American Political Science Review*, 91/1, 1–14.

Linhart, Eric, and Sascha Huber (2009). "Der rationale Wähler in Mehrparteiensystemen. Theorie und experimentelle Befunde," in Christian H. Henning, Eric Linhart, and

Susumu Shikano (eds.), *Parteienwettbewerb, Wählerverhalten und Koalitionsbildung. Festschrift zum 70. Geburtstag von Franz Urban Pappi*. Baden-Baden: Nomos, pp. 133–60.

Lipset, Seymour M., and Stein Rokkan (1967a). "Cleavage Structures, Party Systems, and Voter Alignments. An Introduction," in Seymour M. Lipset and Stein Rokkan (eds.), *Party Systems and Voter Alignments. Cross-National Perspectives*. New York/London: Collier-Macmillan, pp. 1–64.

Lipset, Seymour M., and Stein Rokkan (1967b). *Party Systems and Voter Alignments. Cross-National Perspectives*. New York/London: Collier-Macmillan.

Listhaug, Ola (2005). "Retrospective Voting," in Jacques Thomassen (ed.), *The European Voter. A Comparative Study of Modern Democracies*. Oxford: Oxford University Press, pp. 213–34.

Lobo, Marina Costa (2008). "Parties and Leader Effects. Impact of Leaders in the Vote for Different Types of Parties," *Party Politics*, 14/3, 281–98.

Long, J. Scott (1997). *Regression Models for Categorical and Limited Dependent Variables*. Thousand Oaks: Sage.

Long, J. Scott, and Jeremy Freese (2006). *Regression Models for Categorical Dependent Variables Using Stata* (2nd edn.). College Station: Stata Press Publication.

Luhmann, Niklas (2009). "Zur Komplexität von Entscheidungssituationen," *Soziale Systeme*, 15/1, 3–35.

Lupia, Arthur (1994). "Shortcuts versus Encyclopedias. Information and Voting Behavior in California Insurance Reform Elections," *The American Political Science Review*, 88/1, 63–76.

Lupia, Arthur, and Mathew D. McCubbins (1998). *The Democratic Dilemma. Can Citizens Learn What They Need to Know?* Cambridge/New York: Cambridge University Press.

Luskin, Robert C. (1987). "Measuring Political Sophistication," *American Journal of Political Science*, 31/4, 856–99.

Luskin, Robert C. (1990). "Explaining Political Sophistication," *Political Behavior*, 12/1, 41–58.

Macdonald, Stuart Elaine, Ola Listhaug, and George Rabinowitz (1991). "Issues and Party Support in Multiparty Systems," *The American Political Science Review*, 85/4, 1107–31.

Magalhães, Pedro C. (2007). "Voting and Intermediation. Informational Biases and Electoral Choices in Comparative Perspective," in Richard Gunther, Jose Ramon Montero, and Hans-Jürgen Puhle (eds.), *Democracy, Intermediation, and Voting on Four Continents*. Oxford: Oxford University Press, pp. 208–54.

Maier, Jürgen (1999). *Politikverdrossenheit in der Bundesrepublik Deutschland. Dimensionen—Determinanten—Konsequenzen*. Opladen: Leske + Budrich.

Maier, Jürgen, and Thorsten Faas (2011). " 'Miniature Campaigns' in Comparison. The German Televised Debates, 2002–09," *German Politics*, 20/1, 75–91.

Maier, Jürgen, Alexander Glantz, and Severin Barthels (2009). "Was wissen die Bürger über Politik? Zur Erforschung der politischen Kenntnisse in der Bundesrepublik Deutschland 1949 bis 2008," *Zeitschrift für Parlamentsfragen*, 40/3, 561–79.

Maier, Michaela, and Jens Tenscher (eds.) (2006). *Campaigning in Europe—Campaigning for Europe*. Münster: LIT.

Mair, Peter (2002). "In the Aggregate. Mass Electoral Behaviour in Western Europe," in Hans Keman (ed.), *Comparative Democratic Politics. A Guide to Contemporary Theory and Research*. London: Sage, pp. 122–40.

Markus, Gregory B., and Philip E. Converse (1979). "A Dynamic Simultaneous Equation Model of Electoral Choice," *American Political Science Review*, 73/4, 1055–70.

Marsden, Peter V. (1987). "Core Discussion Networks of Americans," *Annual Sociological Review*, 52/1, 122–313.

Marsden, Peter V. (1988). "Homogeneity in Confiding Relations," *Social Networks*, 10/1, 57–76.

Marsh, Michael (1998). "Testing the Second-Order Model after Four European Elections," *British Journal of Political Science*, 28/4, 591–607.

Marsh, Michael, and Slava Mikhaylov (2010). "European Parliament Elections and EU Governance," *Living Reviews in European Governance*, 5/4, 1–30.

Matthews, John Scott, and Richard Johnston (2010). "The Campaign Dynamics of Economic Voting," *Electoral Studies*, 29/1, 13–24.

Maurer, Marcus, and Carsten Reinemann (2006). *Medieninhalte. Eine Einführung*. Wiesbaden: VS Verlag für Sozialwissenschaften.

McClurg, Scott D. (2003). "Social Networks and Political Participation. The Role of Social Interaction in Explaining Political Participation," *Political Research Quarterly*, 56/4, 449–64.

McClurg, Scott D. (2006). "The Electoral Relevance of Political Talk. Examining Disagreement and Expertise Effect in Social Networks on Political Participation," *American Journal of Political Science*, 50/3, 737–54.

McDonald, Michael P. (2010). "American Voter Turnout in Historical Perspective," in Jan E. Leighley (ed.), *American Elections and American Electoral Behaviour*. Oxford: Oxford University Press, pp. 125–43.

McPherson, Miller, Lynn Smith-Lovin, and James M. Cook (2001). "Birds of a Feather. Homophily in Social Networks," *Annual Review of Sociology*, 27/1, 415–44.

Meffert, Michael F., et al. (2011). "More than Wishful Thinking. Causes and Consequences of Voters' Electoral Expectations about Parties and Coalitions," *Electoral Studies*, 30/4, 804–15.

Meffert, Michael F., and Thomas Gschwend (2010). "Strategic Coalition Voting. Evidence from Austria," *Electoral Studies*, 29/3, 339–49.

Melton, James Douglas (2009). *Do Parties' Ideological Positions Matter? The Effects of Alienation and Indifference on Individuals' Turnout Decisions*. Dissertation thesis. Urbana: University of Illinois at Urbana-Champaign.

Middleton, Russell (1962). "National TV Debates and Presidential Voting Decisions," *The Public Opinion Quarterly*, 26/3, 426–29.

Miller, Arthur H., and Martin P. Wattenberg (1985). "Throwing the Rascals Out. Policy and Performance Evaluations of Presidential Candidates, 1952–1980," *The American Political Science Review*, 79/2, 359–72.

Miller, Arthur H., Martin P. Wattenberg, and Oksana Malanchuk (1986). "Schematic Assessments of Presidential Candidates," *American Political Science Review*, 80/2, 521–40.

Miller, Bernhard, and Thomas Meyer (2011). *To the Core of the Niche Parties. Conceptual Clarity and Valid Measurement for a Much Employed Concept*. Unpublished manuscript. Mannheim: University of Mannheim.

Miller, Warren E., and J. Merrill Shanks (1996). *The New American Voter.* New Haven, CT: Yale University Press.
Mood, Carina (2010). "Logistic Regression. Why We Cannot Do What We Think We Can Do, and What We Can Do About It," *European Sociological Review,* 26/1, 67–82.
Morrison, Donald G. (1969). "On the Interpretation of Discriminant Analysis," *Journal of Marketing Research,* 6/2, 156–63.
Müller-Rommel, Ferdinand (1998). "The New Challengers. Greens and Right-wing Populist Parties in Western Europe," *European Review,* 6/02, 191–202.
Müller, Jochen, and Marc Debus (2012). "'Second order'-Effekte und Determinanten der individuellen Wahlentscheidung bei Landtagswahlen. Eine Analyse des Wahlverhaltens im deutschen Mehrebenensystem," *Zeitschrift für Vergleichende Politikwissenschaft,* 6/1, 17–47.
Müller, Walter, and Markus Klein (2012). "Die Klassenbasis in der Parteipräferenz des deutschen Wählers. Erosion oder Wandel?" in Rüdiger Schmitt-Beck (ed.), *Wählen in Deutschland. Special issue 45 of Politische Vierteljahresschrift (PVS).* Baden-Baden: Nomos, pp. 85–110.
Nadeau, Richard, et al. (2008). "Election Campaigns as Information Campaigns. Who Learns What and Does it Matter?," *Political Communication,* 25/3, 229–48.
Neuendorf, Anja, Daniel Stegmueller, and Thomas J. Scotto (2011). "The Individual-level Dynamics of Bounded Partisanship," *Public Opinion Quarterly,* 75/3, 458–82.
Neuman, W. Russell (1986). *The Paradox of Mass Politics. Knowledge and Opinion in the American Electorate.* Cambridge, MA: Harvard University Press.
Neundorf, Anja (2012). "Die Links-Rechts-Dimension auf dem Prüfstand. Ideologisches Wählen in Ost- und Westdeutschland 1990 bis 2008," in Rüdiger Schmitt-Beck (ed.), *Wählen in Deutschland. Special issue 45 of Politische Vierteljahresschrift (PVS).* Baden-Baden: Nomos, pp. 227–50.
Nickerson, David W. (2008). "Is Voting Contagious? Evidence from Two Field Experiments," *American Political Science Review,* 102/1, 49–57.
Niedermayer, Oskar (2008). "Werteorientierungen in der Parteien- und Wahlforschung," *Politische Studien,* 59/1, 34–40.
Nohlen, Dieter (1978). *Wahlsysteme der Welt. Daten und Analysen.* München: Piper.
Norpoth, Helmut (1978). "Party Identification in West Germany. Tracing an Elusive Concept," *Comparative Political Studies,* 11/1, 36–61.
Norris, Pippa (1999). *Critical Citizens. Global Support for Democratic Government.* Oxford: Oxford University Press.
Norris, Pippa (2000). *A Virtuous Circle. Political Communications in Postindustrial Societies.* Cambridge: Cambridge University Press.
Norris, Pippa, et al. (1999). *On Message. Communicating the Campaign.* London: Sage.
Ohr, Dieter, and Markus Quandt (2012). "Parteiidentifikation in Deutschland. Eine empirische Fundierung des Konzepts auf Basis der Theorie Sozialer Identität," in Rüdiger Schmitt-Beck (ed.), *Wählen in Deutschland. Special issue 45 of Politische Vierteljahresschrift (PVS).* Baden-Baden: Nomos, pp. 179–202.
Oppenhuis, Erik (1995). *Voting Behavior in Europe.* Het Spinhuis: Amsterdam.
Oppenhuis, Erik, Cees van der Eijk, and Mark N. Franklin (1996). "The Party Context. Outcomes," in Cees van der Eijk and Mark N. Franklin (eds.), *Choosing Europe? The European Electorate and National Politics in the Face of Union.* Ann Arbor: The University of Michigan Press, pp. 287–305.

Pappi, Franz Urban (1984). "The West German Party System," *West European Politics,* 7/4, 7–26.
Pappi, Franz Urban (2002). "Die politisierte Sozialstruktur heute. Historische Reminiszenz oder aktuelles Erklärungspotential?," in Frank Brettschneider, Jan van Deth, and Edeltraud Roller (eds.), *Das Ende der politisierten Sozialstruktur.* Opladen: Leske + Budrich, pp. 25–64.
Pappi, Franz Urban, and Jens Brandenburg (2010). "Sozialstrukturelle Interessenlagen und Parteipräferenz in Deutschland. Stabilität und Wandel seit 1980," *Kölner Zeitschrift für Soziologie und Sozialpsychologie,* 62/3, 459–83.
Pappi, Franz Urban, and Paul W. Thurner (2002). "Electoral Behaviour in a Two-vote System. Incentives for Ticket Splitting in German Bundestag Elections," *European Journal of Political Research,* 41/2, 207–32.
Parsons, Talcott (1977). *The Evolution of Societies.* Englewood Cliffs, NJ: Prentice Hall.
Partheymüller, Julia, and Rüdiger Schmitt-Beck (2012). "The "Social Logic" of Demobilization. The Influence of Political Discussants on Electoral Participation at the 2009 German Federal Election," *Journal of Elections, Public Opinion and Parties,* 22/4, 457–78.
Pattie, Charles, Ron J. Johnston, and Eric A. Fieldhouse (1995). "Winning the Local Vote. The Effectiveness of Constituency Campaign Spending in Great-Britain, 1983–1992," *American Political Science Review,* 89/4, 969–83.
Pattie, Charles, et al. (1994). "Measuring Local Campaign Effects. Labour Party Constituency Campaigning at the 1987 General Election," *Political Studies,* 42/3, 469–79.
Pedersen, Mogens N. (1979). "The Dynamics of European Party Systems. Changing Patterns of Electoral Volatility," *European Journal of Political Research,* 7/1, 1.
Pedersen, Mogens N. (1983). "Changing Patterns of Electoral Volatility in European Party Systems 1948–1977. Explorations in Explanation," in Hans Daalder and Peter Mair (eds.), *Western European Party Systems. Continuity and Change.* Beverly Hills: Sage, pp. 29–66.
Peress, Michael (2011). "Securing the Base. Electoral Competition under Variable Turnout," *Public Choice,* 148/1–2, 87–104.
Persson, Torsten, and Guido E. Tabellini (2000). *Political Economics. Explaining Economic Policy.* Cambridge: MIT Press.
Peterson, David A. M. (2005). "Heterogeneity and Certainty in Candidate Evaluations," *Political Behavior,* 27/1, 1–24.
Petrocik, John R. (1996). "Issue Ownership in Presidential Elections, with a 1980 Case Study," *American Journal of Political Science,* 40/3, 825–50.
Petrocik, John R., William L. Benoit, and Glenn J. Hansen (2003). "Issue Ownership and Presidential Campaigning, 1952–2000," *Political Science Quarterly,* 118/4, 599–626.
Petrocik, John R., and Scott W. Desposato (2004). "Incumbency and Short-Term Influences on Voters," *Political Research Quarterly,* 57/3, 363–73.
Plane, Dennis L., and Joseph Gershtenson (2004). "Candidates' Ideological Locations, Abstention, and Turnout in U.S. Midterm Senate Elections," *Political Behavior,* 26/1, 69–93.
Poguntke, Thomas (2011). "Ratlose Zwerge. Sind die Volksparteien am Ende?," in Evelyn Bytzek and Sigrid Roßteutscher (eds.), *Der unbekannte Wähler? Mythen und Fakten*

über das Wahlverhalten der Deutschen. Frankfurt am Main/New York: Campus, pp. 115–32.
Poguntke, Thomas, and Paul Webb (eds.) (2005). *The Presidentialization of Politics*. Oxford: Oxford University Press.
Popkin, Samuel L. (1991). *The Reasoning Voter. Communication and Persuasion in Presidential Campaigns*. Chicago: The University of Chicago Press.
Porter, Stephen Robert (1995). *Political Representation in Germany. The Effects of Candidate Selection Committees*. Rochester/New York: University of Rochester.
Pregibon, Daryl (1981). "Applications of Resistant Fitting to a Class of Non-Linear Regression-Models (Abstract)," *Biometrics*, 37/1, 189.
Prior, Markus (2007). *Post-Broadcast Democracy. How Media Choice Increases Inequality in Political Involvement and Polarizes Elections*. Cambridge: Cambridge University Press.
Prior, Markus (2010). "You've Either Got It or You Don't? The Stability of Political Interest over the Life Cycle," *Journal of Politics*, 72/3, 747–66.
Rabinowitz, George, and Stuart Elaine MacDonald (1989). "A Directional Theory of Issue Voting," *American Political Science Review*, 83/1, 93–121.
Rabinowitz, George, James W. Prothro, and William Jacoby (1982). "Salience as a Factor in the Impact of Issues on Candidate Evaluation," *The Journal of Politics*, 44/1, 41–63.
Rallings, Colin, and Michael Trasher (2005). "Not All 'Second-Order' Contests are the Same. Turnout and Party Choice at the Concurrent 2004 Local and European Parliament Elections in England," *The British Journal of Politics & International Relations*, 7/4, 584–97.
Rattinger, Hans (1980). *Wirtschaftliche Konjunktur und politische Wahlen in der Bundesrepublik Deutschland*. Berlin: Duncker & Humblot.
Rattinger, Hans (1986). "Collective and Individual Economic Judgments and Voting in West Germany, 1961–1984," *European Journal of Political Research*, 14/4, 393–419.
Rattinger, Hans (2000). "Die Bürger und ihre Parteien," in Jürgen W. Falter, Oscar W. Gabriel, and Hans Rattinger (eds.), *Wirklich ein Volk? Die politische Orientierungen von Ost- und Westdeutschland im Vergleich*. Opladen: Leske + Budrich, pp. 309–39.
Rattinger, Hans (2007). "Wechselwähler 1990 bis 2002," in Hans Rattinger, Oscar W. Gabriel, and Jürgen W. Falter (eds.), *Der gesamtdeutsche Wähler. Stabilität und Wandel des Wählerverhaltens im wiedervereinigten Deutschland*. Baden-Baden: Nomos, pp. 37–65.
Rattinger, Hans, and Thorsten Faas (2001). "Wahrnehmungen der Wirtschaftslage und Wahlverhalten 1977 bis 1998," in Hans-Dieter Klingemann and Max Kaase (eds.), *Wahlen und Wähler. Analysen aus Anlaß der Bundestagswahl 1998*. Wiesbaden: Westdeutscher Verlag, pp. 283–307.
Rattinger, Hans, et al. (2011). *Zwischen Langeweile und Extremen. Die Bundestagswahl 2009*. Baden-Baden: Nomos.
Reif, Karlheinz (1997). "European Elections as Member State Second-order Elections Revisited," *European Journal for Political Research*, 31/1-2, 115–24.
Reif, Karlheinz, and Hermann Schmitt (1980). "Nine Second-Order National Elections—A Conceptual Framework for the Analysis of European Election Results," *European Journal of Political Research*, 8/1, 3–44.

Rémond, Réne (2000). *Religion und Gesellschaft in Europa. Von 1789 bis zur Gegenwart.* München: C.H. Beck.
RePass, David E. (1971). "Issue Salience and Party Choice," *The American Political Science Review,* 65/2, 389–400.
Richardson, Bradley M. (1991). "European Party Loyalties Revisited," *American Political Science Review,* 85/3, 751–75.
Richey, Sean (2008). "The Social Basis of Voting Correctly," *Political Communication,* 25/4, 366–76.
Riker, William H., and Peter C. Ordeshook (1968). "A Theory of the Calculus of Voting," *American Political Science Review,* 62/1, 25–42.
Rittberger, Berthold (2012). "Institutionalizing Representative Democracy in the European Union. The Case of the European Parliament," *Journal of Common Market Studies,* 50/Supplement 1, 18–37.
Rivers, Douglas (1988). "Heterogeneity in Models of Electoral Choice," *American Journal of Political Science,* 32/3, 737–57.
Rohrschneider, Robert, and Nick Clark (2008). "Second-Order Elections versus First-Order Thinking. How Voters Perceive the Representation Process in a Multi-Layered System of Governance," in Cees van der Eijk and Hermann Schmitt (eds.), *The Multilevel Electoral System of the EU.* Mannheim: Connex, pp. 137–62.
Rohrschneider, Robert, and Franziska Jung (2012). "SS: Germany's Federal Election in September 2009—Elections in Times of Duress—Introduction," *Electoral Studies,* 31/1, 1–4.
Roller, Edeltraud (1998). "Positions- und performanzbasierte Sachfragenorientierungen und Wahlentscheidung. Eine theoretische und empirische Analyse aus Anlaß der Bundestagswahl 1994," in Max Kaase and Hans-Dieter Klingemann (eds.), *Wahlen und Wähler. Analysen aus Anlaß des Bundestagswahl 1994.* Opladen/Wiesbaden: Westdeutscher Verlag, pp. 173–219.
Rose, Richard, and Ian McAllister (1986). *Voters Begin to Choose. From Closed-Class to Open Elections in Britain.* London: Sage.
Rosenstone, Steven J., and John Mark Hansen (1993). *Mobilization, Participation, and Democracy in America.* New York: Macmillan.
Roßteutscher, Sigrid (2009). *Religion, Zivilgesellschaft, Demokratie.* Baden-Baden: Nomos.
Roßteutscher, Sigrid (2012). "Die konfessionell-religiöse Konfliktlinie zwischen Säkularisierung und Mobilisierung," in Rüdiger Schmitt-Beck (ed.), *Wählen in Deutschland. Special issue 45 of Politische Vierteljahresschrift (PVS).* Baden-Baden: Nomos, pp. 111–33.
Roßteutscher, Sigrid (2013). "Werte und Wertewandel," in Steffen Mau and Nadine Schöneck (eds.), *Handwörterbuch zur Gesellschaft Deutschlands.* Wiesbaden: Springer VS, pp. 936–48.
Roy, Jason (2009). "Voter Heterogeneity. Informational Differences and Voting," *Canadian Journal of Political Science,* 42/1, 117–37.
Roy, Jason (2011). "Information Heterogeneity, Complexity and the Vote Calculus," *Journal of Elections, Public Opinion & Parties,* 21/1, 29–56.
Rudi, Tatjana, and Harald Schoen (2005). "Ein Vergleich von Theorien zur Erklärung des Wählerverhaltens," in Jürgen W. Falter and Harald Schoen (eds.), *Handbuch Wahlforschung.* Wiesbaden: VS Verlag für Sozialwissenschaften, pp. 305–23.

Ryan, John Barry (2010). "The Effects of Network Expertise and Biases on Vote Choice," *Political Communication,* 27/1, 44–58.
Ryan, John Barry (2011). "Social Networks as a Shortcut to Correct Voting," *American Journal of Political Science,* 55/4, 753–66.
Sarcinelli, Ulrich (1987). *Symbolische Politik. Zur Bedeutung symbolischen Handelns in der Wahlkampfkommunikation der Bundesrepublik Deutschland.* Opladen: Westdeutscher Verlag.
Särlvik, Bo, and Ivor Crewe (1983). *Decade of Dealignment. The Conservative Victory of 1979 and Electoral Trends in the 1970s.* Cambridge/New York: Cambridge University Press.
Scarrow, Susan E. (1996). *Parties and their Members. Organizing for Victory in Britain and Germany.* Oxford: Oxford University Press.
Scarrow, Susan E. (2001). "Germany. The Mixed-Member System as a Political Compromise," in Matthew Soberg Shugart and Martin P. Wattenberg (eds.), *Mixed Member Electoral Systems. The Best of Both Worlds?* Oxford: Oxford University Press, pp. 55–69.
Schäfer, Armin (2011). "Der Nichtwähler als Durchschnittsbürger. Ist die sinkende Wahlbeteiligung eine Gefahr für die Demokratie?," in Evelyn Bytzek and Sigrid Roßteutscher (eds.), *Der unbekannte Wähler? Mythen und Fakten über das Wahlverhalten der Deutschen.* Frankfurt am Main/New York: Campus, pp. 133–54.
Schäfer, Armin (2012). "Beeinflusst die sinkende Wahlbeteiligung das Wahlergebnis? Eine Analyse kleinräumiger Wahldaten in deutschen Großstädten," *Politische Vierteljahresschrift,* 53/2, 240–64.
Schattschneider, Elmer Eric (1942). *Party Government.* Westport, CT: Greenwood Press.
Schmitt-Beck, Rüdiger (2000). *Politische Kommunikation und Wählerverhalten. Ein internationaler Vergleich.* Wiesbaden: Westdeutscher Verlag.
Schmitt-Beck, Rüdiger (2004). "Political Communication Effects. The Impact of Mass Media and Personal Conversations on Voting," in Frank Esser (ed.), *Comparing Political Communication. Theories, Cases, and Challenges.* Cambridge: Cambridge University Press, pp. 293–322.
Schmitt-Beck, Rüdiger (2009). "Kampagnendynamik im Bundestagswahlkampf 2005," in Oscar W. Gabriel, Bernhard Weßels, and Jürgen W. Falter (eds.), *Wahlen und Wähler. Analysen aus Anlass der Bundestagswahl 2005.* Wiesbaden: VS Verlag für Sozialwissenschaften, pp. 146–76.
Schmitt-Beck, Rüdiger (2011). "Parteibindung," in Hans Rattinger et al. (eds.), *Zwischen Langeweile und Extremen. Die Bundestagswahl 2009.* Baden-Baden: Nomos, pp. 155–64.
Schmitt-Beck, Rüdiger (2012). "Comparing Effects of Political Communication", in Frank Esser and Thomas Hanitzsch (eds.), *The Comparative Handbook of Communication Research.* New York: Routledge, pp. 400–09.
Schmitt-Beck, Rüdiger, and Thorsten Faas (2006). "The Campaign and its Dynamics at the 2005 German General Election," *German Politics,* 15/4, 393–419.
Schmitt-Beck, Rüdiger, Thorsten Faas, and Christian Holst (2006). "Der Rolling Cross-Section Survey. Ein Instrument zur Analyse dynamischer Prozesse der Einstellungsentwicklung. Bericht zur ersten deutschen RCS-Studie anlässlich der Bundestagswahl 2005," *ZUMA-Nachrichten,* 58/May, 13–49.

Schmitt-Beck, Rüdiger, Thorsten Faas, and Ansgar Wolsing (2010). *Kampagnendynamik bei der Bundestagswahl 2009. Die Rolling-Cross-Section-Studie im Rahmen der 'German Longitudinal Election Study'* 2009, Working paper 134. Mannheim: Mannheimer Zentrum für Europäische Sozialforschung (MZES).

Schmitt-Beck, Rüdiger, and David M. Farrell (2002). "Studying Political Campaigns and Their Effects," in David M. Farrell and Rüdiger Schmitt-Beck (eds.), *Do Political Campaigns Matter? Campaign Effects in Elections and Referendums*. Abingdon: Routledge, pp. 1–21.

Schmitt-Beck, Rüdiger, Mona Krewel, and Ansgar Wolsing (2010). *Kampagnen-Dynamik. Mobilisierungs- und Persuasionseffekte von Fernsehnachrichten auf Wähler während des Bundestagswahlkampfs 2005*, Report to the German Research Foundation (DFG). Mannheim: University of Mannheim.

Schmitt-Beck, Rüdiger, and Christian Mackenroth (2010). "Social Networks and Mass Media as Mobilizers and Demobilizers. A Study of Turnout at a German Local Election," *Electoral Studies*, 29/3, 392–404.

Schmitt-Beck, Rüdiger, and Julia Partheymüller (2012). "Why Voters Decide Late. A Simultaneous Test of Old and New Hypotheses at the 2005 and 2009 German Federal Elections," *German Politics*, 21/3, 299–316.

Schmitt-Beck, Rüdiger, Julia Partheymüller, and Thorsten Faas (2012). "Einflüsse politischer Gesprächspartner auf Parteipräferenzen. Zur 'sozialen Logik' des politischen Verhaltens bei der Bundestagswahl 2009," in Rüdiger Schmitt-Beck (ed.), *Wählen in Deutschland. Special issue 45 of Politische Vierteljahresschrift (PVS)*. Baden-Baden: Nomos, pp. 465–88.

Schmitt-Beck, Rüdiger, and Stefan Weick (2001). "Die dauerhafte Parteiidentifikation—nur noch ein Mythos?," *Informationsdienst Soziale Indikatoren*, 26, 1–5.

Schmitt-Beck, Rüdiger, Stefan Weick, and Bernhard Christoph (2006). "Shaky Attachments. Individual-level Stability and Change of Partisanship among West German Voters, 1984–2001," *European Journal of Political Research*, 45/4, 581–608.

Schmitt-Beck, Rüdiger, and Ansgar Wolsing (2010). "Der Wähler begegnet den Parteien. Direkte Kontakte mit der Wahlkampfkommunikation der Parteien und ihr Einfluss auf das Wählerverhalten bei der Bundestagswahl 2009," in Karl-Rudolf Korte (ed.), *Die Bundestagswahl 2009. Analysen der Wahl-, Parteien-, Kommunikations- und Regierungsforschung*. Wiesbaden: VS Verlag für Sozialwissenschaften, pp. 46–68.

Schmitt, Hermann (2005). "The European Parliament Elections of June 2004. Still Second-Order?," *West European Politics*, 28/3, 650–79.

Schmitt, Hermann (2009). "Partisanship in Nine Western Democracies. Causes and Consequences," in John Bartle and Paolo Bellucci (eds.), *Political Parties and Partisanship. Social Identity and Individual Attitudes*. London: Routledge, pp. 75–87.

Schmitt, Hermann, and Soren Holmberg (1995). "Political Parties in Decline?," in Hans-Dieter Klingemann and Dieter Fuchs (eds.), *Citizens and the State (Beliefs in Government Series, Vol. 1)*. Oxford: Oxford University Press, pp. 95–133.

Schmitt, Hermann, and Dieter Ohr (2000). *Are Party Leaders Becoming More Important in German Elections? Leader Effects on the Vote in Germany, 1961–1998*. Paper prepared for presentation at the Annual Meeting of the American Political Science Association, Washington, DC, August 31 to September 3, 2000.

Schmitt, Hermann, Alberto Sanz, and Daniela Braun (2009). "Motive individuellen Wahlverhaltens in Nebenwahlen. Eine theoretische Rekonstruktion und empirische

Überprüfung," in Oscar W. Gabriel, Bernhard Weßels, and Jürgen W. Falter (eds.), *Wahlen und Wähler. Analysen aus Anlass der Bundestagswahl 2005*. Wiesbaden: VS Verlag für Sozialwissenschaften, pp. 585–605.

Schmitt, Hermann, and Cees van der Eijk (2008). "There is Not Much Eurosceptic Non-Voting in European Parliament Elections," in Aleks Szczerbiak and Paul Taggart (eds.), *Opposing Europe? The Comparative Party Politics of Euroscepticism. Volume 2: Comparative and Theoretical Perspective*. Oxford: Oxford University Press, pp. 208–37.

Schoen, Harald (2003a). "Gleich und gleich gesellt sich gern—auch im Wahlkampf? Zur politischen Prägekraft der Sozialstruktur in Abhängigkeit von der Nähe zum Wahltag," *Kölner Zeitschrift für Soziologie und Sozialpsychologie*, 55/2, 299–320.

Schoen, Harald (2003b). *Wählerwandel und Wechselwahl. Eine vergleichende Untersuchung*. Wiesbaden: Westdeutscher Verlag.

Schoen, Harald (2004). "Der Kanzler, zwei Sommerthemen und ein Foto-Finish. Priming-Effekte bei der Bundestagswahl 2002," in Jan W. van Deth and Edeltraud Roller (eds.), *Die Bundestagswahl 2002. Analysen der Wahlergebnisse und des Wahlkampfs*. Wiesbaden: VS Verlag für Sozialwissenschaften, pp. 23–50.

Schoen, Harald (2007). "Campaigns, Candidate Evaluations, and Vote Choice. Evidence from German Federal Election Campaigns, 1980–2002," *Electoral Studies*, 26/2, 324–37.

Schoen, Harald, and Jürgen W. Falter (2001). "It's time for a change! Wechselwähler bei der Bundestagswahl 1998," in Hans-Dieter Klingemann and Max Kaase (eds.), *Wahlen und Wähler. Analysen aus Anlaß der Bundestagswahl 1998*. Wiesbaden: Westdeutscher Verlag, pp. 57–89.

Schoen, Harald, and Cornelia Weins (2005). "Der sozialpsychologische Ansatz zur Erklärung von Wahlverhalten," in Jürgen W. Falter and Harald Schoen (eds.), *Handbuch Wahlforschung*. Wiesbaden: VS Verlag für Sozialwissenschaften, pp. 187–242.

Schrott, Peter R. (1990). "Electoral Consequences of 'Winning' Televised Campaign Debates," *The Public Opinion Quarterly*, 54/4, 567–85.

Schuck, Andreas R.T., et al. (2011). "Party Contestation and Europe on the News Agenda. The 2009 European Parliament Elections," *Electoral Studies*, 30/1, 41–52.

Schuessler, Alexander A. (2000). *A Logic of Expressive Choice*. Princeton: Princeton University Press.

Schulman, Mark A., and Gerald M. Pomper (1975). "Variability in Electoral Behavior. Longitudinal Perspectives from Causal Modeling," *American Journal of Political Science*, 19/1, 1–18.

Scott, William A. (1966). "Measures of Cognitive Structure," *Multivariate Behavior Research*, 1, 391–5.

Scott, William A. (1968). "Attitude Measurement," in G. Lindsey and E. Aronson (eds.), *The Handbook of Social Psychology*. Reading: Addison-Wesley, pp. 204–73.

Shikano, Susumu, Michael Herrmann, and Paul W. Thurner (2009). "Strategic Voting under Proportional Representation. Threshold Insurance in German Elections," *West European Politics*, 32/3, 634–56.

Shively, W. Phillips (1979). "The Development of Party Identification among Adults. Exploration of a Functional Model," *The American Political Science Review*, 73/4, 1039–54.

Shugart, Matthew S., Melody Ellis Valdini, and Kati Suominen (2005). "Looking for Locals. Voter Information Demands and Personal Vote-Earning Attributes of Legislators under Proportional Representation," *American Journal of Political Science*, 29/2, 437–49.

Shugart, Matthew S., and Martin P. Wattenberg (2001). *Mixed-Member Electoral Systems. The Best of Both Worlds?* Oxford: Oxford University Press.

Simon, Herbert A. (1957). *Models of Man: Social and Rational.* New York: Wiley.

Sniderman, Paul M., Richard A. Brody, and Philip E. Tetlock (1991). *Reasoning and Choice. Explorations in Political Psychology.* Cambridge/New York: Cambridge University Press.

Sokhey, Anand Edward, and Scott D. McClurg (2012). "Social Networks and Correct Voting," *The Journal of Politics*, 74/3, 751–64.

Steinbrecher, Markus, Sandra Huber, and Hans Rattinger (2007). *Turnout in Germany. Citizen Participation in State, Federal, and European Elections since 1979.* Baden-Baden: Nomos.

Stevens, Daniel (2007). "Mobilization, Demobilization and the Economy in American Elections," *British Journal of Political Science*, 37/1, 165–86.

Stevenson, Randolph T., and Lynn Vavreck (2000). "Does Campaign Length Matter? Testing for Cross-National Effects," *British Journal of Political Science*, 30/2, 217–35.

Stokes, Donald E. (1963). "Spatial Models of Party Competition," *American Political Science Review*, 57/2, 368–77.

Tavits, Margit (2008). "Policy Positions, Issue Importance, and Party Competition in New Democracies," *Comparative Political Studies*, 41/1, 48–72.

Thomassen, Jacques (1976). "Party Identification as a Cross-National Concept. Its Meaning in the Netherlands," in Ian Budge, Ivor Crewe, and Dennis Farlie (eds.), *Party Identification and Beyond. Representations of Voting and Party Competition.* London: John Wiley & Sons, pp. 63–79.

Thomassen, Jacques, and Martin Rosema (2009). "Party Identification Revisited", in John Bartle and Paolo Bellucci (eds.), *Political Parties and Partisanship. Social Identity and Individual Attitudes.* London: Routledge, pp. 42–59.

Thompson, Megan M., Mark P. Zana, and Dale W. Griffin (1995). "Let's Not Be Indifferent About (Attitudinal) Ambivalence," in Richard E. Petty and John A. Kosnick (eds.), *Attitude Strength. Antecedents and Consequences.* Mahwah: Lawrence Erlbaum Associate Publishers, pp. 361–86.

Thurner, Paul W., and Angelika Eymann (2000). "Policy-specific Alienation and Indifference in the Calculus of Voting. A Simultaneous Model of Party Choice and Abstention", *Public Choice*, 102/1–2, 51–77.

Thurner, Paul W., Ingrid Mauerer, and Martin Binder (2012). "Parteienspezifisches Issue-Voting bei den Bundestagswahlen 2002 bis 2009," in Rüdiger Schmitt-Beck (ed.), *Wählen in Deutschland. Special issue 45 of Politische Vierteljahresschrift (PVS).* Baden-Baden: Nomos, pp. 302–20.

Thurner, Paul W., Ingrid Mauerer, and Marc Debus (2011). *Conditionality of Party-Specific Issue-Voting in German Elections 1987–2009. A Conditional Logit Approach.* Paper prepared for presentation at the EPSA 2011 Meeting, Dublin, June 16–18, 2011.

Tóka, Gábor (2010). "The Impact of Everyday Political Talk on Involvement, Knowledge and Informed Voting," in Michael R. Wolf, Laura Morales, and Ken'ichi

Ikeda (eds.), *Political Discussion in Modern Democracies. A Comparative Perspective*. London: Routledge, pp. 129–44.

Tufte, Edward R. (1975). "Determinants of the Outcomes of Midterm Congressional Elections," *American Political Science Review*, 69/3, 812–26.

Tufte, Edward R. (1978). *Political Control of the Economy*. Princeton, NJ: Princeton University Press.

van der Brug, Wouter (2004). "Issue Ownership and Party Choice," *Electoral Studies*, 23/2, 209–33.

van der Brug, Wouter, and Anthony Mughan (2007). "Charisma, Leader Effects and Support for Right-Wing Populist Parties," *Party Politics*, 13/1, 29–51.

van der Brug, Wouter, Cees van der Eijk, and Mark Franklin (2007). *The Economy and the Vote. Economic Conditions and Elections in Fifteen Countries*. Cambridge: Cambridge University Press.

van der Eijk, Cees, and Mark Franklin (eds.) (1996). *Choosing Europe? The European Electorate and National Politics in the Face of Union*. Ann Arbor: The University of Michigan Press.

van der Eijk, Cees, and Mark Franklin (2009). *Elections and Voters*. Houndmills: Palgrave Macmillan.

van der Eijk, Cees, Mark Franklin, and Erik Oppenhuis (1996). "The Strategic Context. Party Choice," in Cees van der Eijk and Mark Franklin (eds.), *Choosing Europe? The European Electorate and National Politics in the Face of the Union*. Ann Arbor: The University of Michigan Press, pp. 332–65.

van der Eijk, Cees, and Martin Kroh (2008). *Optimal Choice of Electoral Preference Data*. Paper prepared for presentation at the Annual Meeting of the American Political Science Association, Boston, August 28–31, 2008.

van der Eijk, Cees, Hermann Schmitt, and Tanja Binder (2005). "Left-Right Orientations and Party Choice," in Jacques Thomassen (ed.), *The European Voter. A Comparative Study of Modern Democracies*. Oxford: Oxford University Press, pp. 167–91.

van der Eijk, Cees, et al. (2006). "Rethinking the Dependent Variable in Voting Behavior. On the Measurement and Analysis of Electoral Utilities," *Electoral Studies*, 25/3, 424–47.

van Egmond, Marcel (2007). "European Elections as Counterfactional National Elections," in Wouter van der Brug and Cees van der Eijk (eds.), *European Elections & Domestic Politics. Lessons from the Past and Scenarios for the Future*. Notre Dame: University of Notre Dame Press, pp. 32–50.

van Wijnen, Pieter (2000). "Candidates and Voting Behaviour," *Acta Politica*, 35/Winter, 430–558.

Vavreck, Lynn (2009). *The Message Matters. The Economy and Presidential Campaigns*. Princeton: Princeton University Press.

Verba, Sidney, Kay Schlozman, and Henry Brady (1996). *Voice and Equality. Civic Voluntarism in American Politics*. Cambridge, MA: Harvard University Press.

Vetter, Angelika, and Oscar W. Gabriel (1998). "Candidate Evaluations and Party Choice in Germany, 1972–94. Do Candidates Matter?," in Christopher J. Anderson and Carsten Zelle (eds.), *Stability and Change in German Elections. How Electorates Merge, Converge, or Collide*. Westport: Praeger, pp. 71–98.

Volkens, Andrea, et al. (2011). *Database of the Manifesto Project (MRG/CMP/MARPOR)* [Online database]. <https://manifestoproject.wzb.eu/> accessed February 11, 2013.

Völkl, Kerstin, et al. (eds.) (2008). *Wähler und Landtagswahlen in der Bundesrepublik Deutschland*. Baden-Baden: Nomos.

Wagner, Aiko (2013). *Die Mikrofundierung von Duvergers Gesetz. Strategisches Wahlverhalten als Wirkungsweise politischer Institutionen*. Baden-Baden: Nomos.

Wagner, Aiko, and Bernhard Weßels (2012). "Parties and their Leaders. Does it matter how they match? The German General Elections 2009 in comparison," *Electoral Studies*, 31/1, 72–82.

Wagner, Markus (2011a). "Defining and Measuring Niche Parties," *Party Politics* [published online, May 18, 2011]. <http://ppq.sagepub.com/content/early/2011/05/18/1354068810393267.abstract> accessed February 11, 2013.

Wagner, Markus (2011b). "When Do Parties Emphasise Extreme Positions? How Strategic Incentives for Policy Differentiation Influence Issue Importance," *European Journal of Political Research*, 51/1, 64–88.

Walgrave, Stefaan, Jonas Lefevere, and Anke Tresch (2011). *Associative Issue Ownership. Disentangling the Dimensions of Issue Ownership*. Paper prepared for presentation at the 6th ECPR General Conference, Reykjavik, University of Iceland, August 26, 2011.

Wattenberg, Martin P. (1991). *The Rise of Candidate-Centered Politics*. Cambridge, MA: Harvard University Press.

Weakliem, David L. (1991). "The Two Lefts? Occupation and Party Choice in France, Italy, and the Netherlands," *American Journal of Sociology*, 96/6, 1327–61.

Weber, Till (2007). "Campaign Effects and Second-Order Cycles. A Top-Down Approach to European Parliament Elections," *European Union Politics*, 8/4, 509–36.

Weber, Till (2011). "Exit, Voice, and Cyclicality. A Micrologic of Midterm Effects in European Parliament Elections," *American Journal of Political Science*, 55/4, 907–22.

Weisberg, Herbert F., and Bernard Grofman (1981). "Candidate Evaluations and Turnout," *American Politics Quarterly*, 9/2, 197–219.

Welch, Michael R., David Sikkink, and Matthew T. Loveland (2007). "The Radius of Trust. Religion, Social Embeddedness and Trust in Strangers," *Social Forces*, 86/1, 23–46.

Welzel, Christian (2006). "Democratization as an Emancipative Process. The Neglected Role of Mass Motivations," *European Journal of Political Research*, 45/6, 871–96.

Weßels, Bernhard (1991). "Vielfalt oder strukturierte Komplexität? Zur Institutionalisierung politischer Spannungslinien im Verbände- und Parteiensystem in der Bundesrepublik," *Kölner Zeitschrift für Soziologie und Sozialpsychologie*, 43/3, 454–75.

Weßels, Bernhard (1998). "Wahlpräferenzen in den Regionen. Stabilität und Veränderung im Wahljahr 1994—oder: Die 'Heimkehr' der CDU/CSU-Wähler von 1990," in Max Kaase and Hans-Dieter Klingemann (eds.), *Wahlen und Wähler. Analysen aus Anlass der Bundestagwahl 1994*. Opladen: Westdeutscher Verlag, pp. 259–84.

Weßels, Bernhard (2000). "Gruppenbindung und Wahlverhalten. 50 Jahre Wahlen in der Bundesrepublik," in Markus Klein et al. (eds.), *50 Jahre empirische Wahlforschung in Deutschland: Entwicklung, Befunde, Perspektiven, Daten*. Wiesbaden: Westdeutscher Verlag, pp. 129–58.

Weßels, Bernhard (2002). "Ideologische Atomisierung oder Wählerwandel? Wahlverhalten in Deutschland 1976–1998," in Frank Brettschneider, Jan van Deth, and Edeltraud Roller (eds.), *Politik heute. Das Ende der politisierten Sozialstruktur?* Opladen: Leske + Budrich, pp. 49–80.

Weßels, Bernhard (2007). "Re-Mobilisierung, 'Floating' oder Abwanderung," in Frank Brettschneider, Oskar Niedermayer, and Bernhard Weßels (eds.), *Die Bundestagswahl 2005. Analysen des Wahlkampfs und der Wahlergebnisse.* Wiesbaden: VS Verlag für Sozialwissenschaften, pp. 395–419.

Weßels, Bernhard, and Mark N. Franklin (2009). "Turning Out or Turning Off. Do Mobilization and Attitudes Account for Turnout Differences between New and Established Member States at the 2004 EP Elections?," *Journal of European Integration,* 31/5, 609–26.

Weßels, Bernhard, and Aiko Wagner (2011). "Regionale Differenzierung des Wahlverhaltens," in Hans Rattinger et al. (eds.), *Zwischen Langeweile und Extremen. Die Bundestagswahl 2009.* Baden-Baden: Nomos, pp. 119–29.

Westle, Bettina (2005). "Politisches Wissen und Wahlen," in Jürgen W. Falter, Oscar W. Gabriel, and Bernhard Weßels (eds.), *Wahlen und Wähler. Analysen aus Anlass der Bundestagswahl 2002,* Wiesbaden: VS Verlag für Sozialwissenschaften, pp. 484–512.

Whiteley, Paul, and Patrick Seyd (1992). "Labour's Vote and Local Activism. The Impact of Local Constituency Campaigns," *Parliamentary Affairs,* 45/4, 582–95.

Willmann, Johanna E. (2011). *Cross-Pressured Partisans. How Voters Make up Their Minds when Parties and Issues Diverge.* Paper prepared for presentation at the ECPR General Conference, University of Iceland, Reykjavik, August 25–27, 2011.

Wlezien, Christopher (2005). "On the Salience of Political Issues. The Problem with 'Most Important Problem,'" *Electoral Studies,* 24/4, 555–79.

Wlezien, Christopher, and Robert S. Erikson (2002). "The Timeline of Presidential Election Campaigns," *Journal of Politics,* 64/4, 969–93.

Wüst, Andreas M., and Dieter Roth (2005). "Parteien, Programme, Wahlverhalten," in Jens Tenscher (ed.), *Wahl-Kampf um Europa. Analysen aus Anlass der Wahlen zum Europäischen Parlament 2004.* Wiesbaden: VS Verlag für Sozialwissenschaften, pp. 56–85.

Wüst, Andreas M., et al. (2006). "Candidates in the 2005 Bundestag Election. Mode of Candidacy, Campaigning and Issues," *German Politics,* 15/4, 420–38.

Wyatt, Robert O., Elihu Katz, and Joohan Kim (2000). "Bridging the Spheres. Political and Personal Conversation in Public and Private Spaces," *Journal of Communication,* 50/1, 71–92.

Zaller, John (1992). *The Nature and Origins of Mass Opinion.* Cambridge: Cambridge University Press.

Zaller, John (1996). "The Myth of Massive Media Impact Revived. New Support for a Discredited Idea," in Diana C. Mutz, Paul M. Sniderman, and Richard A. Brody (eds.), *Political Persuasion and Attitude Change.* Ann Arbor: University of Michigan Press, pp. 17–78.

Zaller, John (2004). "Floating Voters in U.S. Presidential Elections, 1948–2000," in Willem E. Saris and Paul M. Sniderman (eds.), *Studies in Public Opinion. Attitudes, Nonattitudes, Measurement Error, and Change.* Princeton: Princeton University Press, pp. 166–211.

Zelle, Carsten (1995a). *Der Wechselwähler. Politische und soziale Erklärungsansätze des Wählerwandels in Deutschland und den USA*. Opladen: Westdeutscher Verlag.

Zelle, Carsten (1995b). "Social Dealignment versus Political Frustration. Contrasting Explanations of the Floating Vote in Germany," *European Journal of Political Research*, 27/3, 319–45.

Zipp, John F. (1985). "Representatives and Voting. An Assessment of the Impact of 'Choices' vs. 'Echoes,'" *American Political Science Review*, 79/1, 50–61.

Zittel, Thomas, and Thomas Gschwend (2007). "Individualisierte Wahlkämpfe im Wahlkreis. Eine Analyse am Beispiel des Bundestagswahlkampfes von 2005," *Politische Vierteljahresschrift*, 48/2, 293–321.

Zittel, Thomas, and Thomas Gschwend (2008). "Individualised Constituency Campaigns in Mixed-Member Systems. Candidates in the 2005 Elections," *West European Politics*, 31/5, 978–1003.

Zuckerman, Alan S. (2005). *The Social Logic of Politics. Personal Networks as Contexts for Political Behavior*. Philadelphia: Temple University Press.

Zuckerman, Alan S., Josip Dasovic, and Jennifer Fitzgerald (2007). *Partisan Families. The Social Logic of Bounded Partisanship in Germany and Britain*. Cambridge: Cambridge University Press.

Index

abstention 243, 287, 295, 298–9, 305; *see also* turnout
activation 218, 229, 236
Adams, James 44, 90, 220, 266
ambiguity 44, 49–53, 59–62
ambivalence 24–5, 30
attitudinal inconsistency 291–8, 302
attitudinal stability 289–90, 306

Bartels, Larry M. 3, 5, 10,26, 219,311
Baum, Matthew A. 195, 206, 215
Budge, Ian 41–2, 90

calculus of voting 9–10, 264, 311
campaign:
   intensity 142–3, 147, 150, 153–5
   style 143–4, 147, 150, 151, 153–5, 156–8
campaigning 88, 91, 105, 110, 114
   effects 91, 104
Campbell, Angus 8–10, 18, 66, 90, 92, 103, 116, 119, 179, 224, 263, 268, 287, 290
candidate:
   nomination 142
   orientation 34
   performance 140–1
   personal vote share 146–50
   recognition 153, 162
Catholicism 169, 171, 172, 174, 176, 179, 181–6, 189, 191
   church affiliation/attendance 171–4, 176, 179, 182
   Christian democracy 169, 172, 174, 179
choice criteria 8, 11, 23, 40–1, 243–4, 262, 313
cleavage 102, 220, 226, 231
   decline 167, 168, 172, 173, 176, 179, 191, 192
   parties 103, 104, 168–70, 172, 174, 179
   politics 169–71, 179, 192
   postcleavage society 169–71, 173–7, 179, 192
   structures 88, 103, 167, 173, 176, 191, 193
   voting 23, 88, 169, 172–4, 175, 179, 182, 183, 186–8
coalition:
   considerations 65–6
   preferences 78–85
cognitive mobilization 167, 179, 173, 174, 180, 192, 240
Coleman's bathtub 144–5, 160

Comparative Study of Electoral Systems (CSES) 41, 58, 255, 320
complexity:
   of choice situation 22, 27, 36, 40, 67, 70, 312–14
   of political supply 7–8, 13, 70–1, 313
conditional logistic regression 31, 47, 247
consideration weights 27
Converse, Philip E. 90, 221
correct voting 193–216
   and representative democracy 193–4, 213–14
   definition 195–6
   measurement 197–9
cross-pressures 18, 25, 31

Dalton, Russell J. 4, 20, 50, 103, 169, 173, 238, 241, 288
dealignment 89, 103, 105, 110, 169–71, 174, 179, 191, 269, 279, 288–9
deviant voting 89, 90, 91, 92, 94, 99, 100, 104, 105, 110, 111, 113, 114
Downs, Anthony 28, 45, 50, 66–7, 86, 194, 196, 202, 205, 209, 214, 215, 216, 263–4, 265–6
duty to vote 265, 268–70, 271, 272–3, 274–80, 282–6

ecological fallacy 119–20, 144–5
economy, role of in campaigns 217, 218, 219, 220, 224, 225, 231
Eijk, Cees van der 42, 44, 91, 122
election:
   first-order/national election/Federal Election 89, 91, 92, 93, 94, 95, 97, 99, 100, 105, 110, 113, 114
   second-order 88, 89, 91, 92, 93, 94, 95, 96, 97, 99, 100, 104, 105, 111, 113, 114, 115–16, 117–19, 135
election campaigns 194, 196, 209–11, 211–13, 214–15
   effects 218, 221–2, 225
   expenditure 222
electoral cycle 118
electoral mobilization 121, 123–4, 130–1, 134
electoral research 3–5, 311
electoral system 22, 68, 100, 139–40, 141–2, 156, 266
electoral volatility 287–9, 300, 305–6
enlightenment 217, 218, 219, 221, 236

Erikson, Robert S. 91, 217, 218
EU-issue voting 122, 136
European Parliament election 89, 96, 97, 99, 100, 105, 110, 111, 113
Evans, Geoffrey 172, 240
expressive voting 68–70, 86–7
extremity 43–5, 49, 56, 59–63

Fiorina, Morris P. 90, 244, 290
Franklin, Mark 42, 44, 91, 122
fundamentals 217, 218, 223, 231, 236–7
funnel of causality 10, 44, 242, 247, 290

Gelman, Andrew 218, 219, 223, 231
German Longitudinal Election Study (GLES) v, 13
government evaluation 121–2, 123, 130–1, 134
government participation 41–3, 61–2
Grofman, Bernhard 90, 102, 220, 264

heterogeneity of voting 7–9, 10, 12, 13, 18–22, 40, 60, 63, 195, 242, 282, 311–13, 317
homogeneity assumption 17, 20

ideology 28, 265–6, 267
　activation 221, 225, 227, 232
　Left-Right 41–5, 47, 50–1, 61–2
incumbency effect 147, 150, 243, 251, 253, 259
indifference 243, 251, 253, 259
individualization 4, 89, 114, 168–9, 241, 315
information acquisition 316
　personal information acquisition 196, 216
information costs 241, 243
integration, political 167, 168, 173–80, 182, 183, 185, 187, 189–92
intra-individual homogeneity 37–8
involvement 103, 104
issue:
　effects 247–9, 255–8
　orientation 245
　ownership 41–2, 54
　salience 24
issue voting 313
　cognitive mobilization 241
　conceptions 244
　modernization theory 240, 250, 260
　partisanship 241
　political sophistication 34, 248
　utility 242–3, 260

Jamison, Angela S. 195, 206, 215

King, Gary 119 n.4, 144, 218, 219, 223, 231

Lau, Richard R. 21, 193, 194, 195, 196, 197, 198 n.2, 199, 200, 201, 209, 214
Lazarsfeld, Paul F. 18, 25, 66, 171, 176, 196, 202, 211, 218, 263, 264, 303–4
Lipset, Seymour M. 23, 168–9, 220
logistic regression 295–8, 302

mass media 194, 196, 205–9, 211–13, 215–16
Merrill III, Samuel 44, 220, 266
Michigan model 8, 10, 28, 89–90, 290
Miller, Warren E. 10, 28–9, 44
mobilization 91, 103
modernization 9, 88, 114, 170, 218, 240, 248, 252–3, 288, 316
multilevel:
　(electoral) system 88, 89, 91, 92, 93, 94, 100, 113
　model 59–63
　voting 89
multiparty systems 66, 224

networks:
　homogeneity, homophily 172–5
　politicization 168, 172–80, 182–5, 188–92
　private, social 168, 170–8, 180, 186, 190–2
　size, number of partners 177, 178, 183, 184, 188–90
nonvoting, see turnout

panel data 116, 124–5, 287, 292–3
paradox of voting 263
parties, effective number of 6–7
partisanship 23, 89–90, 103, 112, 170, 220, 240, 289; see also party identification
party identification 28, 119, 130, 133–4, 169, 179, 182, 183, 186–8, 191, 220–1, 265, 268–9, 271, 272–3, 274–80, 282–6
　activation 232
　changes 88, 89, 90, 94, 96, 97, 99, 100, 102, 105, 110
　concept 89–91
　decline/increase 88, 89, 95, 97, 99, 100, 113, 114, 169, 170, 290–1, 293, 296–8, 302–3, 305–6, 289–90
　effect on vote choice 31
　partisanship 89–114
　stability/instability 88, 89, 94, 102, 103, 104, 105, 112, 113, 114
　strength 91, 92, 94, 96, 97, 99, 100, 104, 105, 110, 111, 112, 113, 114
party leaders 47–9, 59–60
party size 41–2, 48–52, 55, 59–63
party system, differentiation 7, 39, 70–2, 288
performance 42–3, 47, 54–5
personalization 48, 60, 64

Index

political competition 42, 44, 50, 58
political discussion 103, 105, 174, 177, 178, 180, 182, 184–7, 188, 190–2, 194, 196, 200–5, 211–13, 214–16
political equality 168, 173–5, 177, 178, 180, 185–8, 190–2
political interest 119, 121, 130, 194, 196, 200–1, 204, 208, 213, 213–14, 216
political involvement 268, 272–3, 274–6, 282–6
political knowledge 168, 170, 174, 193, 194, 196, 198, 198 n.2, 200–1, 202, 203, 204, 205, 212, 213–15
political motivation, *see* political interest
political participation 168–70, 172, 174, 175, 177–9, 182, 186, 191, 192, 263, 264, 274–86
political sophistication 25–6, 77, 86, 168–70, 174, 178, 180, 185, 189–92
political stability 168, 192
pooled cross-section model 259
position issues 43, 50, 244–5, 253
 impact on vote choice 249, 257
postcleavage society 169–71, 173–7, 179, 192
Pregibon's beta 37
priming 221, 224

rational choice theory 90, 263–4, 265–6
Redlawsk, David P. 21, 193, 194, 195, 196, 197, 198 n.2, 201, 209, 214

Schuessler, Alexander A. 68, 87, 219
second-order approach 117–19, 135
Shanks, J. Merrill 10, 28–9, 44
sincere voting 122–3, 133–4
social milieu 169–72, 175, 176, 192
social structure 167, 168, 170, 171, 185

socialization 102, 103, 105
sophistication 103, 104
 effects 27, 36
 gaps 219, 232–6
spatial models 42–3, 45, 50–3, 60–1
Stein, Rokkan 23, 168–9, 220
Stokes, Donald E. 42, 244
strategic voting 67–70
supply side of politics 4, 6–7, 243, 253, 312, 317

theory of reasoned action (TORA) 29–30
ticketsplitting 74–7, 140, 158–59
turnout 89, 91, 92, 93, 97, 99, 102, 105, 110, 113–15, 172–5, 177–9, 182, 183, 186–91, 192, 263–86
 decline 263, 264, 279
 individual 263, 269, 270, 274–86
 level 263
 nonvoter 179, 183

unions, union membership 168, 171–3, 176, 177, 179, 182

valence issues 42, 45, 54–5, 61–3, 245, 253
volatility 5–6
vote functions, election-specific 128–29, 131–2
vote switching 131, 132, 288–93, 295–9, 301
voter types of Lazarsfeld, Paul F. 303–4

Wlezien, Christopher 217, 218
working-class, worker 169, 171, 172, 174, 176, 177, 179, 181–4, 186–9
 social democracy 169, 172, 174, 179

Zaller, John 208, 219, 291